THE BROTHERS GRIMM AND THE MAKING OF GERMAN NATIONALISM

In the first comprehensive English-language portrait of Jacob and Wilhelm Grimm as political thinkers and actors, Jakob Norberg reveals how history's two most famous folklorists envisioned the role of literary and linguistic scholars in defining national identity. Convinced of the political relevance of their folktale collections and grammatical studies, the brothers Grimm argued that they could help disentangle language groups from one another, redraw the boundaries of states in Europe, and counsel kings and princes on the proper extent and character of their rule. They sought not only to recover and revive a neglected native culture for a contemporary audience but also to facilitate a more harmonious and enduring relationship between the traditional political elite and an emerging national collective. Through close historical analysis, Norberg reconstructs how the Grimms wished to mediate between sovereigns and peoples, politics and culture.

JAKOB NORBERG is Associate Professor of German Studies at Duke University. He is the author of *Sociability and Its Enemies: German Political Thought After 1945* (2014) and numerous articles in journals such as *PMLA*, *Cultural Critique*, *Textual Practice*, *New German Critique*, *Zeitschrift für deutsche Philologie*, and *Sprache und Literatur*.

THE BROTHERS GRIMM AND THE MAKING OF GERMAN NATIONALISM

JAKOB NORBERG
Duke University

Shaftesbury Road, Cambridge CB2 8EA, United Kingdom

One Liberty Plaza, 20th Floor, New York, NY 10006, USA

477 Williamstown Road, Port Melbourne, VIC 3207, Australia

314–321, 3rd Floor, Plot 3, Splendor Forum, Jasola District Centre, New Delhi – 110025, India

103 Penang Road, #05–06/07, Visioncrest Commercial, Singapore 238467

Cambridge University Press is part of Cambridge University Press & Assessment, a department of the University of Cambridge.

We share the University's mission to contribute to society through the pursuit of education, learning and research at the highest international levels of excellence.

www.cambridge.org
Information on this title: www.cambridge.org/9781009073363

DOI: 10.1017/9781009063890

© Cambridge University Press & Assessment 2022

This work is in copyright. It is subject to statutory exceptions and to the provisions of relevant licensing agreements; with the exception of the Creative Commons version the link for which is provided below, no reproduction of any part of this work may take place without the written permission of Cambridge University Press.

An online version of this work is published at http://dx.doi.org/10.1017/9781009063890 under a Creative Commons Open Access license CC-BY-NC-ND 4.0 which permits re-use, distribution and reproduction in any medium for non-commercial purposes providing appropriate credit to the original work is given. You may not distribute derivative works without permission. To view this license, visit https://creativecommons.org/licenses/by-nc-nd/4.0

All versions of this work may contain content reproduced under license from third parties. Permission to reproduce this third-party content must be obtained from these third-parties directly. When citing this work, please include a reference to the DOI: 10.1017/9781009063890

First published 2022
First paperback edition 2025

A catalogue record for this publication is available from the British Library

ISBN 978-1-316-51327-9 Hardback
ISBN 978-1-009-07336-3 Paperback

Cambridge University Press & Assessment has no responsibility for the persistence or accuracy of URLs for external or third-party internet websites referred to in this publication and does not guarantee that any content on such websites is, or will remain, accurate or appropriate.

Till barnen

Contents

Acknowledgments *page* viii

    Introduction   1

1 The Philologist King: Politics and Knowledge in the Nationalist Era   22

2 Folk Hatred and Folktales: The Nationalist Politics of the *Children's and Household Tales*   51

3 The Prince of Germany: Wilhelm Grimm and the Philologist as Redeemer   85

4 Love of the Fatherland and Fatherly Love: Jacob Grimm's Political Thought   114

5 The Mother Tongue at School: Jacob Grimm and the Institutions of Nation Building   142

6 The Names of the Barbarians: The Philologist, the Tribe, and the Empire   159

    Conclusion   181

Notes   186
Bibliography   227
Index   247

Acknowledgments

The Volkswagen Foundation funded the initial research for this book, and it was completed during research leaves from Duke University. Colleagues at Duke were immensely helpful. Stefani Engelstein gave invaluable advice and encouragement. Julianne Werlin provided unceasing intellectual inspiration. Heidi Madden at Perkins Library speedily resolved numerous difficulties. Thomas Pfau, Henry Pickford, and Kata Gellen were models of collegiality and generosity. My work also profited greatly from conversations with several scholars at other universities and research centers, including Gabriel Trop, Eric Downing, Karen Hagemann, and Konrad Jarausch (Chapel Hill); Matthew Birkhold and May Mergenthaler (Ohio); Natalie Binczek and Dorothea Walzer (Bochum); Arnd Wedemeyer (Berlin), Till van Rahden (Montréal), Iwan-Michelangelo d'Aprile and Vinzenz Hoppe (Potsdam); Till Dembeck (Luxembourg); John Noyes (Toronto); Fritz Breithaupt (Indiana); Bill Donahue (Notre Dame); Michael Jennings (Princeton); and Jeffrey Hertel (Hillsdale). For their friendship, I thank Iyman Ahmed, Priscilla Layne, and Chandra Wright.

Introduction

The Philologist, the King, and the Nation

In August 1846, the folktale collector, grammarian, mythographer, and lexicographer Jacob Grimm (1785–1863) wrote a letter to the Prussian king, Frederick William IV (1795–1861), in which he urged the monarch to support the German-speaking population of the duchies of Schleswig and Holstein, the areas between Denmark and the German lands.[1] At the time, the Danish king, Christian VIII, was also the duke of the twin duchies and in the summer of 1846, he had publicly declared that they must allow female succession, a reform that would secure continued Danish rule; the Danish royal family was running out of male heirs.[2] This attempt by the Danish crown to preserve Danish influence over Schleswig and Holstein disturbed German nationalists, among them Jacob Grimm and the five co-signers of his letter, all of them prominent academics in Berlin. A Prussian commitment to protect the German-speaking inhabitants would, Grimm wrote, lift the spirits of the duchies' Germans and help contain the ambitions of the Danish king. Grimm's letter to the king insisted on the principle of nationality: Germans should not be ruled by non-Germans, a "german area [*deutsches gebiet*]" not be chained to a "foreign country [*ein fremdes land*]."[3]

The argument in Grimm's address to the Prussian king drew on his expertise in Germanic languages and ancient history. It should be recognized as law, Grimm asserted, that those who speak the same language are members of the same nation: "[A]ll who speak the German tongue also belong to the German people and should be able to count on the mighty help of Germany in a time of need."[4] He quickly added that ancient German tribes, such as the Cimbri and the Teutons, had historically populated the areas.[5] The primordial communities had not been Danish, he claimed, and hence any Danes in the duchies were latecomers, without a strong historical claim to the territories.[6] To Grimm, all German speakers belonged to the German nation and the German nation was entitled to a specific territory, namely the territory that German speakers had occupied since the time of the first Germanic tribes. Presented as a sincere expression of patriotic concern couched in rhetorical conventions of humility toward royalty, the group of scholars headed by Grimm implied that they possessed politically relevant knowledge: the Prussian king could benefit from philological and historical input on where the true borders ran between peoples.

Grimm's letter indicated a subtle shift between old and new ways to conceive of politics, legitimate rule, and territorial disputes. Grimm lauded the Prussian king's "sense of justice," his "strength," and "wisdom"[7] – traditional virtues ascribed to monarchs. However, he defined the tension over Schleswig and Holstein as a national conflict, one between two distinct peoples who should be disentangled and separately governed. He did not discuss any royal or dynastic rights but instead suggested that knowledge of diachronic linguistic study, ethnic history, and historical occupancy should decide the fate of the duchies. The main purpose of the address may even have been to reconcile monarchy and nationality; it sought to stir the king into action, but with the aim of protecting the linguistic and spatial integrity of the nation. The philologist Jacob Grimm wanted to mediate between the king whom he served and respected and the nation that he had studied and even mapped out.

Against the background of this letter, I would like to introduce a figure: the "philologist king." I use this phrase to mark a departure from the philosopher king, who appeared at the beginning of the history of Western political thought. In the writings of Plato, especially the *Republic*, the philosopher king names a coincidence of authority and knowledge that could come into being if a ruler would begin to philosophize or a philosopher could be prevailed upon to assume the burdens of rule.[8] According to Plato, both are remote possibilities,[9] since the ruler with governing experience has to ascend to the heights of a genuine philosopher, but actual philosophers tend to look at human affairs as a distraction from the supersensible world of forms[10] and deem the "honors of this present world ... mean and worthless."[11] This unlikely coincidence would, however, be the condition for the salvation of the city,[12] because only the ruling philosopher or the philosophizing king would concentrate on "the greatest and most necessary of all things,"[13] namely to ensure that the human community approximate an ideal condition in which everyone would receive what is good and fitting for them.[14] The philosopher king could only begin to establish this condition in the city by virtue of a singular focus on justice, which ultimately rests on knowledge of the ideas, the self-subsisting entities that constitute the only real world.[15] In Plato's view, the phenomenal world available to the human senses merely represents an imperfect derivation of the ideas, knowable for those with access to the ordered structure of the actual universe.[16]

In Plato's conception of the philosopher king, metaphysical knowledge should serve as the proper foundation of governance. Jacob Grimm did not quarrel with Plato, but by seeking to advise the king and nudge him in the right direction on the basis of his historical and linguistic expertise, Grimm implied the need for a different convergence of knowledge and authority than the one envisioned in the venerable Platonic tradition. Grimm stood for the application of methodically retrieved and highly detailed empirical knowledge of languages and the history of groups of speakers to the political project of establishing non-arbitrary units of rule. In so doing, he sought to promote philology, the scrupulous genealogical study of literary and linguistic development on the basis of surviving textual documents,[17] as the discipline best able to uncover the preconditions of legitimate authority. Thorough and systematic knowledge of grammatical change as well as legal and literary history was essential to understanding how culturally distinct peoples had evolved over time in particular locations, each one defined and united by an individualized language. Germans could and should be separated from Danes, and neither people ruled by non-national, alien regimes. Only a new alliance between historically oriented scholarship and political government would ensure a stable and peaceful human order of differentiated nations. In this sense, Grimm's nationalist interventions encapsulated an epochal shift away from a conception of political rule guided by philosophical thought to one guided by the study of multiple cultures and their distinctive traits. Grimm wished for a "philologist king." The historically evolved nation, not eternal metaphysical ideas, should stand as the ultimate reality of the state.[18]

Known today as an iconic collector of folktales, legends, and myths, as a grammarian and dictionary builder, Jacob Grimm was a political figure of his time. Shaped by ideas circulating after the French Revolution, he believed that rule could only obtain legitimacy if it was respectful of an already extant people's identity; that the people could only be adequately defined in linguistic and historical terms; and that the philologist, equipped with a rigorously achieved understanding of the people's cultural and linguistic past, could reliably perform its demarcation, even in a situation of competing claims about its extension and territorial home. Grimm was a nationalist in the sense that he believed in the congruence of the political order with the national community,[19] but the notion of a "philologist king" captures his belief in the vital function of disciplinary knowledge for the establishment or restoration of such congruence. The king, Grimm believed, had to be philologically well informed.

Grimm devoted his life to scholarship, professed his preference for undisturbed quiet, and admitted that he was relieved not to have to make political decisions.[20] In that sense, the philologist shared the Platonic philosopher's supposed reluctance to amass power and govern;[21] Grimm, too, had little care for the honors of this present world. He did, however, declare interest in giving rule a proper, even scientific foundation, by making the philological knowledge of the nation the basis of the territorial order. Throughout his life, he repeatedly spoke with confidence about the proper boundaries of nations and did so in a period during which borders in Central Europe were redrawn many times and tiny states integrated into larger units. At the time of Grimm's birth in 1785, there were several hundred German political entities[22] – kingdoms, electorates, duchies, landgraviates, margraviates, bishoprics, imperial cities – loosely integrated in the patchwork that was the Holy Roman Empire; Germany was a "maze of dwarfish princedoms"[23] or a "confused archipelago of principalities."[24] In the year of Grimm's death, in 1863, that number had been reduced to just below forty units, after the dissolution of the Holy Roman Empire; the Napoleonic conquest and reconfiguration of German lands; and the reorganization of the continent's politics at the Congress of Vienna, which resulted in the construction of a confederation of sovereign German states, the *Deutscher Bund*. The plethora of principalities had been consolidated into a smaller number of sovereign entities, with two dominant states (Prussia, Austria), seven midrange states (Bavaria, Württemberg, Hanover, Sachsen, Baden, Hessen-Darmstadt, and Hesse), and about thirty microstates or statelets.[25]

Grimm's youth in particular coincided with a period of political volatility and apparent malleability. Areas changed hands several times over short time periods and principalities were conquered, reallocated, restored, or absorbed, and boundaries redrawn.[26] The young Jacob and Wilhelm Grimm (1786–1859) would themselves experience regime changes and political reconfigurations in their hometown Kassel in Hesse, where Jacob, the older brother, worked as a civil servant under more than one ruler. During the brothers' lifetime, then, the shape and internal organization of Germany did not seem settled once and for all. Jacob Grimm may have had an ambivalent, flickering interest in day-to-day politics, but he was consistently and sometimes passionately preoccupied with the delineation of units *for* politics in an era during which those units were being redefined.

The notion of a philologically informed ruler thus appeared at a particular juncture, when old borders were being erased or revised, and, equally important, traditional feudal and religious justifications of local princely rule were losing their self-evidence. It was in this context that the philologist arrived as a proponent and guardian of a new focus and foundation of politics: the nation, the linguistically and culturally defined people, with its ultimate origin in a supposedly authentic and natural community, the ancient tribe. As the address to the king indicates, the brothers Grimm and most of their fellow nationalists never fundamentally disputed the wisdom and rightness of a strong monarchical government[27] even in the post-revolutionary age of its destabilization and desacralization. They did, however, repudiate the prerogative of kings and lords to seize, purchase, or abandon areas as if they were private possessions, without regard for the nationality of their inhabitants; this was in fact still the attitude of traditional autocrats and conservative thinkers.[28] Like many of their fellow nationalists in early nineteenth-century Europe, the Grimms believed in a new principle of legitimate rule: rulers and ruled should hail from the same cultural and linguistic group, like reign over like,[29] and the king be one among many of the same ethnic kind.[30] Royal regimes, shorn of religious sanctification or private-patrimonial rights, could secure legitimacy only if they recognized and persuasively represented cohesive national communities.[31] As in the letter to the Prussian king, the philologist Grimm ultimately sought to facilitate the marriage of constitutionalized monarchy and geographically bounded nationality. Decidedly not a radical, he stood, he declared to a newspaper just before the elections to the first German national parliament in 1848, for "a free, united fatherland," but one ruled by "a powerful king," which meant that he repudiated all "republican desires [*republikanische Gelüste*]."[32] By means of such a program, monarchy could lend political unity and capacity to the nation, and the depth and dignity of the nation could help renew and revitalize monarchy – within clearly delineated borders.

Jacob Grimm and his brother Wilhelm believed that modern rulers would benefit from philological counsel, not exactly on how to acquire and maintain power – the philologist could offer no Machiavellian know-how – but on how to identify and respect the particular and naturally evolved linguistic and ethnic character of populations. Grimm would even go further and demand that the king evince an attachment to one and only one people. Legitimate government was, for him, not first and foremost a matter of a just distribution of goods, protected basic rights, or popular consent, but of a close cultural *fit* between rulers and ruled. Even if the philologist could not direct the king or tell him how to rule by offering prescriptions grounded in philological expertise, the best king in Grimm's eyes would be a ruler who was a friend of the vernacular word, emotionally tied to one particular people rather than desiring to rule over many. This king would ideally possess something of the philologist's intimate knowledge of and love for the *Volk*, construed as a national community of familiarity and solidarity. Instead of a philosophizing ruler, a ruler with the soul of a philosopher,[33] there would be a philologizing king, a king with the heart of a philologist.

A New Image of the Brothers Grimm

With its focus on the brothers Grimm as supporters of a new type of ruler, a philologist king, this book seeks to make two contributions. First, it sets out to transform the established image of the brothers Grimm as homey folklorists, lovers of German words and stories, by situating them more systematically and thoroughly in the intellectual and political context of their day. By doing so, however, it also wants to cast light on early nineteenth-century nationalism and its intellectual exponents, the academic entrepreneurs of modern politicized nationhood, with particular attention to the relationship between new methods of knowledge production and established political institutions and forms of authority.

For us today, the fame of the Jacob and Wilhelm Grimm is above all tied to the enduring success of their early book *Children's and Household Tales* [*Kinder- und Hausmärchen*]. This volume, translated again and again into numerous languages, has come to define the fairy-tale genre and turned the brothers Grimm into world-famous storytellers. Many Germans also associate the brothers with the still used multivolume German dictionary that they began late in their careers, the *Deutsches Wörterbuch*. A more productive scholar than his brother, Jacob Grimm published an enormous work of German grammar, *Deutsche Grammatik*, quickly recognized as a pioneering work of linguistic history, which established the so-called Grimm's Law on the basis of observed regularities in sound shifts across time. Many commentators see the link between the scholarly projects of folktale collection, dictionary compilation, and diachronic grammatical analysis and the attempt to cultivate or even generate a national consciousness among a growing nineteenth-century reading public. "Nationalism," a contemporary historian of Germany writes, "was ... a cause of the educated middle class, who defined (even created) the idea of a German nation with their grammars, dictionaries, and collections of folk tales."[34]

This is not an uncommon claim, but the historian neglects to tell us that the authors of the most celebrated and influential German grammar, German dictionary, and German folktale collection were Jacob Grimm and his brother. Behind the phrase "the educated middle class," one finds two actual individuals, a pair of philologists, Jacob Grimm and Wilhelm Grimm, and the two really were immensely prolific. The poet Heinrich Heine jokingly speculated that Jacob Grimm had sold his soul to the devil to complete single-handedly the colossal German grammar, and that tome was only one of his many contributions.[35]

The importance of the brothers Grimm for the rise of German national consciousness has rarely been under dispute, and their wish to "stimulate national sentiment" is well documented.[36] German scholars have also mapped out the political opinions of Jacob Grimm especially,[37] reconstructed his relationship with emerging ideologies of his era,[38] and sometimes also criticized, or even ridiculed, his somewhat dilettantish relationship to the realities of political life.[39] Nor have scholars neglected to consider the value commitments that guided the revision and progressive embellishment of their influential folktale collection. American folklorists and literary scholars, for example, have uncovered the editorial efforts of Wilhelm Grimm in particular to remove references to sexuality and deviant behavior[40] and reinforce the early nineteenth-century bourgeois ideology of honesty, diligence, and industriousness.[41] In this way, studies have rightfully focused on how the Grimms and their fellow collectors explored the world of popular dialects, tales, and tunes to forge a secular, cross-class vernacular culture that could facilitate national integration.[42] Grimms' tales are still one of the most famous examples of how university-educated, broadly "middle-class" enthusiasts contributed to cultural nation building in the nineteenth century.

This book intends to show, however, that the Grimms' energies or at least their hopes and dreams were also directed toward the princes, electors, and kings who governed German lands, and it sets out to capture with greater precision than before how the brothers envisioned the relationship between their own scholarship and national-political projects, and the tie between the authority of philological research and the power of traditional elites. The Grimms, who were lifelong civil servants employed or sponsored by very traditional leaders, saw themselves not just as public educators of the people but as mediators between rulers and ruled. As nationally oriented philologists, the Grimms cared about and sought to give definition to the *Volk*, but they were also attentive to the current regimes they knew so well and believed that kings should receive proper philological advice of the kind exemplified in the 1846 letter to the Prussian ruler. This reconstruction of philology's vocation, as illustrated most prominently by Jacob Grimm, points to the political purpose of a new set of research disciplines devoted to the exploration of national being, such as vernacular literary and historical legal studies. Grimm's voluminous reconstructions of German grammar, German legal antiquities, and the history of German tribes ultimately belonged to a vision of a mutually reinforcing alliance between politics and knowledge production deemed appropriate to an era of politicized national collectives. We can thus locate the philologist's efforts in a constellation composed of three elements, where the scholar appears as a mediator between the king, on the one hand, and the linguistically and culturally defined people, on the other. The philologist could mobilize disciplinary knowledge to broker a new relationship between regimes and peoples on the basis of shared nationality.

This book's focus on the triad king–philologist–people is more appropriate for an era in which the memory of the French Revolution and the notion of popular consent to rule pervaded the political imagination[43] and news of regicides, republics, and new law codes circulated among broad population groups,[44] but which was nonetheless still politically dominated by restored, consolidated, or constrained monarchies. Even after the era of transatlantic revolutions, European kings retained massive possessions, remained heads of state, led armies, conducted diplomacy, managed bureaucracies, cultivated courtly rituals, and even exploited new forms of mass communication;[45] intellectuals responded to the situation by seeking to reconcile a recognition of popular freedom with the persistence of traditional rule.[46] Jacob and Wilhelm Grimm were representatives of their age: they were neither radical democrats set on toppling the king nor staunch monarchists who rejected ideas of popular influence and constitutional checks on government. Instead, they believed in forms of adjustment between a unitary people and an informed, moderate, and loving king, within the frame of a philologically outlined nationhood. Political rule could become less intrusive and coercive, more adaptable and sensitive, if the people could be reminded of their evolved historical and cultural character and disentangled from arbitrary political boundaries indifferent to nationality, and if the princes and kings could gain a deeper understanding and more heartfelt appreciation of the nation's invaluable particularity. By seeking to reawaken the people and gently rein in the ambitions of kings, the philologist wanted to worked toward a more harmonious coincidence of nation and monarchical rule.

The Character of Nationalism

Attention to the figure of the philologist king will facilitate a deeper understanding of the Grimms' vocation in the political world of their era and more broadly illuminate the ambitions of modern, nationally oriented philology. In addition, the focus of this study will cast some light on the peculiar character of nationalism itself, which has often been regarded as politically influential but philosophically feeble, lacking the developed justifications that rival ideologies possess.[47] Liberalism, socialism, and conservatism have all been philosophically articulated by key figures in the history of political thought, such as Thomas Hobbes, Karl Marx, and Edmund Burke. By contrast, defenders of nationalism have been rare and the canon of nationalist philosophical works correspondingly slender;[48] the principle of nationality, one historian claims, was developed by narrow "second-rank thinkers"[49] and its doctrines, the sociologist Ernest Gellner writes, "are hardly worth analyzing."[50] But celebrated political philosophers did not simply decline to work out a defense for the nation; they did not quite appreciate nationalism's force and persistence. While prominent thinkers imagined and prophesized the growth of bureaucracy (Max Weber), the revolutionary upheavals of modern society (Mikhail Bakunin), the spread of conformism in egalitarian societies (Alexis de Tocqueville), or the accelerated rate of technological change and the eruption of class conflict (Marx), the struggle for national self-determination arguably found no prophet or early analyst among the most illustrious minds.[51] Among those who did develop a philosophy of nationalism, German thinkers around 1800 predominate.[52] Johann Gottfried Herder (1744–1803) is known for his enthusiastic celebration of the dynamic plurality of culturally distinct human communities. In his *Addresses to the German Nation* from 1808, Johann Gottlieb Fichte (1762–1814) proclaimed the necessity of a vigorous, organized political defense of such communities as shared sources of meaning and objects of morally valuable attachment. Yet Herder and Fichte are exceptions and hardly count among the most revered and famous political thinkers.

The philosophical and normative deficit in nationalism persists to this day. Few political theorists attempt to justify the special solidarity within a nation or the integrity of national borders, although there are a handful of exceptions.[53] The perpetuation of strong national group loyalty is rarely viewed as an important political goal in itself and is frequently seen as an obstacle to the formation of more inclusive and tolerant societies, although the active dismantling of enduring cultural identities is perhaps not understood as a moral priority either.⁵⁴ In view of the relative paucity of normative arguments for nationalism, the anthropologist Benedict Anderson famously suggested that it is simply not a conceptually articulated ideology to be compared with liberalism or conservatism, but something more akin to a religion in its appeal to finite individuals' hopes for a some kind of afterlife in the form of an indefinitely enduring collective, namely the national community.⁵⁵

This obviously does not mean that nationalism throughout its history has lacked supporters among scholars or intellectuals, although they have not gained much respect in the realm of political thought. This study of the philologist king as an ideal is intended to explore the character and logic of the ambitions and efforts of nationalists, as exemplified by the careers and thought of Jacob Grimm and his brother Wilhelm. The brothers were not philosophers or politicians or activists, but rather librarians, collectors, editors, lexicographers, and grammarians,⁵⁶ who for the most part were employed by German princely states of different sizes. They searched through archives for manuscripts; compiled enormous inventories of poetic, narrative, mythological, historical, and legal materials; and transcribed tales and legends that circulated among people of their time, all to retrieve, organize, and disseminate the traces of an ancient but localizable German collective life as an object of indispensable significance even to the state and its head, the king. In this endeavor, the Grimms were not alone but emerged as two of the most prominent and groundbreaking representatives of a much larger group of professional and amateur scholars in folkloristics, historical linguistics, literary and legal history, and national historiography, fields devoted to the exploration, or the demonstration, of the historical depth, character, and spatial home of the German nation. There were, one can say without much exaggeration, entire academic disciplines or subdisciplines with particular scholarly-technical skills dedicated to the delineation and substantiation of the nation.⁵⁷ Nor were the Grimms internationally isolated; Jacob Grimm's Serbian contemporary, ally, and counterpart Vuk Karadžić (1787–1867), to name just one example, similarly forged links between linguistic study and national demarcation.⁵⁸

Even so, the political purpose in the Grimms' efforts can sometimes be hard to discern, in part because of their peculiar, non-philosophical or even anti-philosophical style of presentation, in which methodical accumulation took precedence over explicit argumentation. Jacob Grimm's late work on the history of the German language was a huge compilation of surviving textual data on ancient German communities, but its slender introduction briefly stated that the whole was political "through and through," and Grimm sent a copy to the Prussian king.⁵⁹ The sheer mass of the evidence itself, the immense accretion of details, should apparently be seen as a consequential political act, meant to establish the undeniable historical reality of shared nationhood in all its antiquity and particularity. The librarian and archivist Grimm gravitated toward a kind of argument by exhaustive inventory, and to some, he embodied an overgrown philology, a love of words inflated to gargantuan proportions. Contemporary Hegelians, schooled in a sophisticated philosophy of the period, could complain that Jacob Grimm's works represented vast heaps of materials barely "penetrated by spirit" – untouched by reflection.⁶⁰

Still, Grimm's assemblages of relics and scraps were meant to quell any doubt about the long historical existence of a uniquely German population in a particular geographic location, a unit understood as a necessary precondition for the claim to contemporary statehood. One of Grimm's chief strategies of nationalist persuasion was indeed the collection, the literary "treasure trove":⁶¹ the collection of German tales, the collection of German legends, the collection of German legal antiquities, the collection of German words. His work sought to assemble compilations that could inspire and concentrate affective attachment, solidify and sacralize the vernacular, and even be advanced as repositories of a genuinely *collective* intellectual or artistic property that could give body to the imagined community. The nationalist Jacob and Wilhelm Grimm never formulated an explicit set of interlocking doctrines but rather put together a series of textual objects, most widely known among them the *Children's – and Household Tales*, that could serve as points of communal identification meant to anchor a new public self-image shared across societal strata and political hierarchies in a particular space. Few have so consistently delivered to the reading public materials devised to promote easy acceptance of a common heritage. To refer again to Benedict Anderson, the Grimms may be two of history's most famous "visionary drudges,"⁶² tireless compilers of plausible-seeming evidence for "nation-ness."⁶³ The philologist scholar assembled, transcribed, edited, and published and by so doing sought to establish a distinct and located nationhood as an obdurate, undeniable fact of political life.

Nationalism and the Value of Particularity

The expression "philologist king" points to an envisaged relation between disciplinary knowledge and the exercise of political rule in the era of modern statehood. Jacob Grimm claimed that philological experts with their patiently gathered wealth of genetic information about history, law, grammar, and religion could ensure that modern rule – more centralized and more territorially consolidated than in previous times – would correspond to discernible geographic boundaries of peoples and protect their documented historical lives. Yet, the reference to the Platonic figure of the philosopher king is also meant to signal the polemical edge of philologically informed politics. The scholar of language and literature really did want to dethrone a version of the philosophizing ruler. Looking at early nineteenth-century central Europe, one could claim that the vision of a philologist king appeared in the wake of the devastation wrought by a philosopher king of sorts, which is to say that he appeared in the German lands occupied by a French, Napoleonic administration intent upon a rational reordering of the polity according to universalist principles. In general terms, the figure of the philologist king was conjured to resist an alliance of enlightened universalism and imperial rule that sought to break with obsolete and obstructive institutions, sweep away the encrustations of the past, and install a more efficient and uniform system of administration.[64] Jacob and Wilhelm Grimm intensified their study of ancient Germanic literary works as a politically relevant domain of objects when they lived and worked in the French vassal kingdom of Westphalia, ruled by Napoleon's younger brother Jérôme Bonaparte (1784–1860), who had been tasked with introducing Germans to a rationalized form of rule.

In short, the philologist presented himself as the loving protector of the particular and the local against the onslaught of modern imperial rule committed to universal principles of societal organization. The groundbreaking studies of comparative linguistics in the nineteenth century, to which Jacob Grimm made absolutely central contributions, were predicated on the rejection of the ideal of one universal language.[65] There were, to Jacob Grimm and his peers among Romanticist linguists, only ever a plurality of empirical languages, affiliated but clearly differentiated and idiosyncratic idioms that had evolved in time and space.[66] The capacity for speech did unite humankind, but this human ability only became manifest in the diversity of irreducibly particular tongues.[67] Languages should be cherished for their individual peculiarities rather than eliminated as failures to realize universal norms or unfortunate barriers to transparent global communication.

This commitment to particularity emerged early in Grimm's writings. "Every individuality," the young Jacob Grimm wrote in an 1811 review of the Danish philologist Rasmus Rask's (1787–1832) introduction to Old Norse, "must be held as sacred, also in the realm of language; we ought to wish that even the smallest and most despised dialect is left to itself and its own nature and does not suffer any brutality [*Gewaltsamkeit*], since it is certain that it secretly possesses virtues even compared to the largest and most honored language."[68] As the reference to brutality signals, the repudiation of one quasi-universal yardstick for judging local phenomena, along with the loving attention to the minute characteristics of those phenomena, possessed a political dimension. The demand that the ruler must know and love the nation, be willing to adapt to its evolved character, and respect its internal dynamism was meant to prevent injuries to local society perpetrated by arrogant and ignorant supra-local, imperial regimes. Grimm represented a politicized cultural nominalism, for which skepticism about universals supported skepticism of empire building and central control.[69] Politically imposed "uniformity [*Uniformität*]"[70] and "uniformization [*Einförmigmachung*],"[71] Jacob Grimm wrote in letters to his brother Wilhelm and his teacher Friedrich Carl von Savigny (1779–1861), was only meant to render territories and subjects legible and pliable by an overbearing center of power. The modernizing French regime in Grimm's own region did not constitute an advance, but a condescending violation of evolved communal life.

Philology was the study of particularity, and the philologist king would be sensitive to the varied texture of communal life. However, Grimm was not an entirely consistent defender of the local and the particular. His loving valorization of the small and neglected, no matter how rare, parochial or obscure, would seem to contradict his advocacy of the unified German nation, which was obviously a much larger unit than a cluster of villages or a small province. In the quotation cited earlier, Grimm first speaks of the value of dialects, not national languages.[72] In the very same review, though, he also pointed out that even Danish, spoken by more than a million people around 1811, would be powerfully influenced by German, the mightier Germanic tongue. He did not seem to mind such a relation of dominance between larger and smaller languages. The German language and German literature, he wrote, would "rule" over smaller idioms but not do so in an "ignoble" way [*die deutsche literatur herrscht auf keine unedle weise*].[73] It looks as though Grimm was ultimately willing to compromise the integrity of the small for the rise of the great, at least if the latter was German.

Grimm did have to grapple with the inevitable tension between local ways of life and an emerging national culture, the subtle charms of the dialect and the standardized language for a much larger, integrated communicative space. He genuinely deplored the erosion of local practices and idioms and yet considered a homogenized written German language an indispensable achievement that could not be bought too dearly.[74] Entangled in this contradiction, Grimm increasingly came to view the nation as an "enlarged particular,"[75] the most extensive unit that could still plausibly be viewed as a form of individuated being. If rule could be made national, it would resist, by means of careful adjustments to the trends of standardization and centralization, the waves of even greater, imperial ambition. To Grimm, the nation-state appears to have emerged, over his career, as the only possible modern vessel of the particular, a political form that would prevent the triumph of a vaster and more coercive, more uniform and homogenizing (French) imperial rule. The fortified, sovereign nation-state was a compromise, a last protective wall for the particular.

Despite the love for locality and tradition, Grimm did not wish to reverse all political changes and territorial consolidations that had been established in post-revolutionary Europe. He was not exactly a conservative figure, did not consistently believe that one could return to intensely local and individualized forms of life, and he certainly did not hope to restore destabilized hierarchies and reintroduce the traditions of dynastic or theological justifications that supported them. His advocacy for the German nation and national unification were, on the contrary, quite disruptive, as was shown in the conflict over territories such as the duchies of Schleswig-Holstein, the topic of Grimm's 1846 letter to the Prussian king. Rather than demand continued adherence to traditional principles of political legitimacy resting on notions of divine sanction and royal patrimony, the philologist Grimm insisted on a new political sensitivity to the historically formed body of the national people, which represented the ultimate object of all his scholarly investigations. Grimm above all spoke for the entirely modern, national principle of legitimizing of political power[76] and sought to represent that principle to the rulers of the day. In his mind, the best king would not be philosopher, a lover of universally valid wisdom and hence fit to govern anyone, but a philologist, a lover of the vernacular language and national character with all their particular traits and hence attached to one, now more unified people.

The Paradoxes of Nationalism

The focus on Jacob Grimm and his brother reveals a figure who stands for a particular conjunction of ruling and knowing or claims to possess a combined epistemic and political authority. The late eighteenth and early nineteenth centuries witnessed the emergence of more than one type who sought to bridge political and intellectual activities. Toward the end of the eighteenth century, so-called enlightened despots gathered philosophers around them to create a court culture of wit and flair, but also to draw on their assistance in the project of augmenting absolutist power through rational reform; Voltaire (1694–1778), an iconic figure of the Enlightenment, was a guest of the Prussian ruler Frederick the Great (1712–1786). In the early nineteenth century, new forms of mass communication such as the regularly appearing newspaper spawned the figure of the political journalist and committed intellectual who operated outside of state institutions and encouraged the members of the reading public to think critically about, resist, or even overthrow traditional regimes; the philosopher and journalist Karl Marx (1818–1883) comes to mind, or the previously mentioned poet, essayist, and correspondent Heinrich Heine. However, this study of Jacob and Wilhelm Grimm, two linguists and folklorists who spent most of their lives as civil servants attached to court libraries, state-funded universities, and academies with royal support, suggests that we must pay attention to another type, who was neither a philosopher close to the enlightened despot nor a radical intellectual in the expanding public sphere. The political philologist presented himself as an expert on nationhood who sought to connect people and ruler, facilitate the adjustment of government to vernacular culture and in this way play a pivotal role in the momentous transformation of modern European political space after the French Revolution, the Napoleonic conquests, and the contested restoration period that followed.

By looking at the Grimms as nationalists, this book pursues a series of goals. It aims to enhance our understanding of the ideological background to the world's most read folktale collection, *The Children's- and Household Tales*, expand and deepen the picture of the brothers Grimm by reconstructing their self-appointed task of mediation between ruler and ruled, sharpen our appreciation for modern vernacular philology as a nation-building enterprise, clarify the inherent need of nationalist ideology for certain kinds of cultural knowledge, and explore the political imagination of a core group of the German nationalist intelligentsia. The first point about the *Children's- and Household Tales* warrants some elaboration, given the popularity and ubiquity of the Grimms' stories. While scholars have often tried to tease out the nationalist message *in* the folktales with sometimes meager results,[77] this study takes a different approach by situating the collection in the context of a *repertoire* of genres deployed by nationalist intellectuals; the political function of the folktales as a medium of a supposed national spirit emerges more clearly when we see how the folktale collection appeared in coordination with the hortatory poem or the militant pamphlet.

In a sense, it was the Grimms' wish that the literary voice of the people *not* be compromised by current politics, since their claim about the need for a nationally oriented state depended on the prior historical existence of the national people and their spontaneous, independent folk culture. Early nationalism spoke with a peculiar double voice: the assertive, militant voice of struggle and sacrifice but also the plain, folksy, apparently nonpolitical voice of the fairy tale, folk song, legend, and joke. Indeed, nationalism will emerge in this book as perhaps the most literary of ideologies, since it absolutely required documentation of an already ongoing, ethnically particular life, which could then serve as the legitimate basis of statehood. As a result of this key nationalist assumption, two scholars of folklore and folk narratives – the brothers Grimm – could view themselves not just as disciplinary experts or guardians of rustic traditions but also as purveyors of knowledge and materials of crucial value to the forming state.

This examination of the brothers Grimm and their preferred areas of study, style of argumentation, ideological assumptions, and explicit interventions will also bring the tensions and paradoxes within nationalism into sharper relief. A sequence of chapters in this book reveals the types of problems that Jacob Grimm encountered while tirelessly assembling and promoting a national cultural heritage for the purpose of achieving congruence between the nation and the state. Even for Grimm himself, nationalism emerged as a program increasingly riddled with inconsistencies and paradoxes. There were cracks and conflicts that he could not paper over, between the idea of royal rule and the notion of a politically active national people, between the preservation of local particularity and the wish for national unity, and between the clearly imperial roots of philology and its present nationalist mission.

To begin with, Grimm had to face the ideological limitations of nationalism as a set of beliefs focused on the nature and integrity of the political unit that nonetheless had no obvious, internally generated response to a series of fundamental political questions, such as the selection of leaders, the distribution of goods, or the ultimate location of sovereignty. Over time, Grimm also did come to see more clearly that institutions and policies that contributed to nation building often enforced the erasure of cherished local cultures, a melancholy development that he regretted and yet had to accept as an inevitable cost. Nationalism, which professed the sacred significance of pluralism in an international setting, entailed regimentation and homogenization within the national unit; it set about to eliminate "all kinds of fragmentation, localism and regionalism."[78] Finally, the political desire to make the state align with the nation was premised on the natural coincidence of language, people, territory, and authority, a bundling that was difficult to uphold once studies of ancient tribal or barbarian life, conducted by Grimm himself, revealed a turbulent history of formative cultural encounters – often recorded in the textual sources of dominant empires. In this way, a close investigation of Grimm as the representative of philologically informed rule will demonstrate how he had to confront the peculiarly thin or incomplete character of nationalism, nation building's tendency to root out local individuality, and historical patterns of migration and mingling within the frame of empire. The philologist set out to facilitate a new kind of national rule but ended up revealing its costs and contradictions.

Chapter Outlines

The Brothers Grimm and the Making of German Nationalism contains six chapters, each of which looks at a key aspect of the Grimms' nationalist political thought; the book is thematically rather than chronologically or biographically structured. It opens with an analysis of Grimm's mature political project, as formulated and presented a couple of years before the 1848 revolutions, and then moves to the nationalist function of the brothers' most famous and enduring literary work, their globally recognized and widely imitated collection of folktales. In this way, the first half of the book presents the central political interventions of the brothers Grimm, namely their vision of the grammarian and lexicographer as an expert arbiter of legitimate state extension, and their portrayal of the collector and editor as a redeemer of national being and the natural poetic voice of the folk. The second half of the book then looks more closely at paradoxes and contradictions in their outlook, such as Jacob Grimm's hesitation and even obfuscation in debates over the ultimate locus of political sovereignty, his ambivalence about the modern institutional tools of top-down nation building, and his muted admission that the discipline of philology may originally have been an imperial project rather than a national one. A summary of each chapter follows and helps clarify the sequence of arguments.

The Philologist King: The first chapter portrays the vision of a philologist king by reconstructing Jacob Grimm's political thought in the 1840s when he emerged as a leader of the new association of Germanist philologists in 1846 and a prominent delegate in the first German national parliament formed in 1848. Speaking in different venues, Grimm declared his commitment to national unity supported by disciplinary knowledge of language, literature, law, and myth. In particular, he claimed that the philologist could demarcate national collectives on the basis of verifiable knowledge of grammatical differentiation and by so doing provide states with a sound, even scientific foundation that would ensure legitimate rule. The chapter analyzes how Grimm put forward research findings about the grammatical and phonetic distinctiveness of different European and especially Germanic languages to suggest epistemically authoritative answers to questions about non-arbitrary, linguistically, and culturally grounded political units in the post-revolutionary era. Grimm did not wish to subvert monarchy even in revolutionary moments, but he insisted on the coincidence of royal rule with a national homeland, the boundaries of which could be traced by the philologist.

Folk Hatred and Folktales: The second chapter moves back in time to the first decades of the nineteenth century to reconstruct the biographical and historical background to the most widely known project of the brothers Grimm, the *Children's- and Household Tales*. Jacob and Wilhelm Grimm began the collection when they were in their twenties and Jacob worked as a civil servant in Kassel, partly under French rule. While previous researchers have sought to identify clear nationalist strands in the collection itself, this chapter offers a different approach. By surveying the larger repertoire of genres preferred by leading nationalists of the time, such as propagandistic pamphlets and war songs, the chapter uncovers the specific ideological function of the folktale collection as a literary proof of a cultural nationhood that arguably predated political structures and, according to the brothers, should impose constraints on the extent of rule. Influenced by the tumultuous geopolitical situation during the Napoleonic wars, the brothers believed that the state should coincide with the German nation and thought that the independent existence of this cultural unit was most authentically corroborated by collections of materials such as their folktales. Nationalism was, to the brothers Grimm, a creed crucially dependent on literary and historical documentation, which they could supply.

The Prince of Germany: The third chapter looks at Wilhelm Grimm's early conception of the philologist as a redeemer of national being, formulated at the time of his early work on the folktale collection. Grimm was decisively shaped by the university teacher and mentor of both brothers, the law professor Friedrich Carl von Savigny, who was known for his belief that the historicist legal scholar served as the primary custodian of the national legal corpus. Following Savigny's example, Wilhelm Grimm argued that the philologist must strive to retrieve, clarify, disseminate, and thereby guard the nation's folk culture. The nation represented a viable basis for rule, but the nation's history was not generally known; rather, it had to be explored, preserved, and transmitted by publicly oriented scholarship. In this sense, there was a vital philological dimension to modern conceptions of political legitimacy, and the philologist had to assume the important, even glorious task of reconstructing and reintroducing politically crucial cultural materials. Inspired by the folktales' own imagery of resurrection and rejuvenation, the young Wilhelm Grimm even pictured the philologist as called upon to reawaken the nation from its slumber: the philologist was a redeemer.

Love of the Fatherland and Fatherly Love: Chapter 4 is the first of three chapters that focus on Jacob Grimm, the more prolific and politically involved of the two brothers. The fourth chapter reconstructs Jacob Grimm's political biography and presents his lifelong government service in German principalities, punctuated by dramatic, public displays of political commitment. Faced with the conflict between rigid, patriarchal rule by monarchs to whom he was often tied as a civil servant and his own vision of the nation as a naturally evolving community of solidarity and even love, Grimm came to hope for the eventual appearance of a loving king, a king with a philologist's heart, genuinely attached to one national people. Jacob Grimm wished to facilitate harmony between the people and the king and in this way help resolve a key political tension of his day, namely the one between princely sovereignty and popular influence. The chapter also reconstructs the curiously thin nature of Grimm's political beliefs: while he was confident, insistent, and at times even strident in debates over the territorial shape of the nation, he was considerably less vocal on other, domestic political issues, including discussions of rights and the distribution of goods in a society increasingly dominated by the so-called social question. In these areas, his nationalism provided no guidance. Grimm concentrated on one particular dimension of political legitimacy – national rule – and had little to say about other aspects of governance.

The Mother Tongue at School: This chapter looks at a persistent problem within nationalist ideology, as it emerged in Jacob Grimm's reflections on the rise of mandatory schooling toward the latter part of his career, in the 1840s and 1850s. School systems can impose a uniform language across a large territory, effectively giving shape to a national people. This became increasingly clear to Grimm himself as he witnessed the emergence of a veritable army of schoolteachers in the mid-nineteenth century. While he approved of greater national unification by means of mass schooling, the rise of public education also forced him to consider that the nation may not grow from below to delimit the proper reach of a state. Instead, an extant state apparatus could forge a more standardized culture by institutional means, at the expense of the more natural-seeming transmission of language and customs in families and localities. Hence the state and its head may not need a philologist to trace extant national boundaries. Indeed, the school system itself, a necessary institution in the developed modern state, threatened local cultures with extinction and hence deprived regional populations of the memory that Grimm had pledged to protect as a philologist.

The Names of the Barbarians: The sixth and final chapter shows how Jacob Grimm's idea of self-enclosed and culturally autonomous peoples was troubled by the international interaction that he uncovered in his historical work on ancient German tribes, completed in the revolutionary year of 1848. Seeking to unify his knowledge of diachronic linguistics and ethnic history in one final grandiose work of summation, Grimm paid special attention to the one thing that had survived myriad tribes – their names – but conceded that names were always generated by outside observers; names, Grimm admitted, were never chosen, always given. When Jacob Grimm dug as deep as he possibly could into prehistory, he found not proud acts of autonomous self-naming by nations but only boundary-defining *encounters* between groups and peoples. Grimm suspected that such cultural encounters, moreover, had first become visible within the domains of imperial civilizations that housed multiple peoples and languages. In the end, the practice of philology with its comparative grasp of distinct but affiliated languages and cultures was an imperial phenomenon. The nationalist figure of the philologist, Jacob Grimm's own writings ironically suggested, was the inheritor not of the self-enclosed tribe but of the trans-regional, polyethnic empire.

As the chapter outlines indicate, each one reconstructs and critically examines a particular facet of the nationalist imagination, or a particular element in its cluster of interconnected ideals and fantasies: the nation's definable territorial home (Chapter 1), the authentic folk narrative (Chapter 2), the ancient collective poetry of the people (Chapter 3), the passionate attachment to the sacred fatherland (Chapter 4), the intimacy and naturalness of the mother tongue (Chapter 5), and the heroic history of the ancient tribe (Chapter 6).

The Philologist at the Court

A final question should close this Introduction: did the Prussian king ever listen to the philologist's advice? Was there, during the careers of the brothers Grimm, ever a figure deserving of the title philologist king, a ruler with an interest in the people as defined and studied by the philologist? The Prussian ruler Frederick William IV certainly knew Jacob and Wilhelm Grimm. After the king of Hanover had removed the brothers from their professorial positions at the university in Göttingen after a conflict over the kingdom's constitution in the late 1830s, the Prussian monarch approved the recruitment of the controversial but increasingly revered scholars to Berlin in 1840 and welcomed them personally during an audience in 1841.[79] Jacob Grimm was quite taken by the king's friendly demeanor and felt personal loyalty to the ruler who had put an end to a precarious period in his life without an official, salaried position.[80] At the time of his recruitment, Grimm was quick to recognize the Prussian king as a man of "noble will" and great promise for all of Germany.[81] The king, a man of "profound though not precise religious conviction,"[82] was also known for being indecisive, and even easily nudged and influenced.[83] Frederick William IV, then, might have been open to advice from a renowned philologist. Yet, while the Grimm brothers returned to the court for social occasions now and then, they never came close to advancing into the role of advisors and never joined an inner circle. In the end, the king was, as one might expect, surrounded by a camarilla composed of noblemen. The one academic who did work closely with the king was the aged but indefatigable naturalist Alexander von Humboldt (1769–1859);[84] in comparison, Jacob and Wilhelm Grimm were entirely peripheral figures. The idea of a philologist king was an animating vision, a fantasy, and very far from an actual courtly reality.

At one point, however, the Prussian king did ask Jacob Grimm to resolve a conflict on the basis of his linguistic expertise. When announcing a new medal of honor to be awarded to Prussian and German men of science and letters, the king encouraged Humboldt to consult with Jacob Grimm after a ministerial dispute about the spelling of a word in the statute.[85] Should the word for "German" be written with a *t*, as in *teutsch*, or a *d*, as in *deutsch*? The answer, provided in the Grimm's dictionary in an entry written by Wilhelm, was *deutsch*.

CHAPTER I

The Philologist King
Politics and Knowledge in the Nationalist Era

The Germanists

In early September 1846, Germanist scholars from almost twenty states in the German Confederation met at an academic congress for the first time, in the city of Frankfurt am Main.[1] The purposes of the assembly, the *Germanisten-Versammlung*, were roughly those of modern-day conferences: to exchange ideas, stimulate further study, promote the discipline, and of course socialize and get to know one another "personally."[2] The representatives of other, more established disciplines of the modern German research university had already begun to meet annually. The Association of German Natural Scientists and Physicians had organized conferences for a little more than two decades, starting in 1822, and the Association of German Philologists and Pedagogues assembled for the first of their conferences in 1838.[3] The Germanist historians, jurists, and philologists knew they were latecomers,[4] even academic upstarts, representatives of an only recently and quite slowly institutionalized discipline with relatively few university chairs.[5]

Opening the protocols of the roughly 200 Germanists,[6] one might expect to find discussions specific to the field, such as reports on methods and findings, debates among exponents of different orientations or schools, celebrations of achievements, and announcements of new projects, all in line with the attempt to consolidate the new discipline. Yet the topics were more political. The entire first day was dedicated to presentations on the dispute over Schleswig and Holstein, the two duchies in between Germany and Scandinavia, a contested area with a mixed Danish-speaking and German-speaking population of about 800,000 inhabitants.[7] A number of scholars, some of them hailing from the area and deeply invested in the debate, made the case against further Danish integration of the duchies, in the form of arcane legal-historical reasoning concerning the limited rights of the Danish crown or through claims about the predominance of

German culture in the areas. The question was explosive; in the decades to come, Danish and German troops would fight wars over the area.[8]

The session was introduced by a general address given by the new association's chairman, Jacob Grimm, probably the only scholar in attendance whose name remains recognizable to a present-day reader. Grimm did not speak directly about any particular scholarly issue but chose to articulate a fundamental concern for all Germanists: "Let me begin," he opened, "by asking the simple question: What is a people? [*Lassen Sie mich mit der einfachen Frage anheben: Was ist ein Volk?*]."[9] *What is a people* – this was the question to which Jacob Grimm believed he had an adequate response, an authoritative answer, with profound political consequences. Along with his peers, Grimm presented himself as an expert on the long history, orderly communal forms, and shared language of the Germans,[10] and he inserted himself into the debates of the day as a legitimate interpreter of the nation as a distinct being. He knew what a people was and believed that this knowledge was of momentous political significance; by delineating a particular people, he could prepare the ground for the reorganization of contemporary politics around the body of the *Volk*. Philological premises, methods, and insights, Grimm held, could help establish the precondition of legitimate politics, namely "congruency" between the institutions of rule and linguistic and cultural nationhood.[11] Grimm's philologist was not a lawgiver, not a sovereign, not a leader or tribune speaking in the name of the people, but he could, he claimed, delimit the people as a nation and hence determine the unit that could be represented, governed, and spoken for.

This chapter has four parts. It will begin with a portrait of Jacob Grimm that highlights his reputation among his peers around the time of the first Germanist convention in 1846; characterizes the direction and significance of his scholarly achievement; and analyzes his way of framing the ensuing debates, partly academic and partly political. In a second step, it will situate Grimm's programmatic statements on the people in the broader context of political ideology in Germany after the French Revolution and argue that the Germanist-nationalist project had absorbed the post-revolutionary premise of popular sovereignty but melded it with a historicist particularism; the existence of a *German* people, nationalists believed, required the construction of a German state.

The third part of the chapter then reconstructs how the vision of the national collective in shared possession of a territory understood as a homeland inevitably led to conflict between competing states, a dynamic manifest in the controversial scholarly discussion of clashing German and Danish territorial claims. In fact, the philologists claimed for themselves the ability to guide and perhaps even adjudicate such disputes on the basis of historical, ethnographic, and linguistic knowledge. In a fourth and final segment, a non-exhaustive set of contrasting figures, such as the philosopher at the court and the critical journalist, will serve to illuminate some features of the political philologist and the particular conception of the relationship between knowledge and rule that this figure represented. Taken as a whole, this chapter reconstructs how Jacob Grimm's nationalist philology responded to the political challenges of his era.

The Philologist Jacob Grimm

The scholars gathered in Frankfurt in the fall of 1846 quickly elected Jacob Grimm as their chairman by acclamation.[12] Few figures, perhaps none, embodied the association more perfectly and commanded a similar respect among the assembled linguists, historians, and jurists.[13] Grimm's reputation rested on a number of scholarly accomplishments, among them the *German Grammar* (1819, 1826, 1831, 1837) but also his *German Legal Antiquities* (1829) and *German Mythology* (1835). Each of these multivolume works had performed a feat of historical recuperation. Grimm's *German Grammar* was not a distilled set of rules meant as prescriptions for speakers.[14] Instead, it contained a reconstruction of the genealogies of several Germanic languages – Gothic, Old High German, Old English, Old Saxon, Old Norse, Old Friesian, and then also Middle High German and New High German along with other modern Germanic languages – as they had branched out from a common source through a series of systematic transformations over time.[15] The study of German legal history, a two-volume work that Grimm had completed with relative ease and joy,[16] moved the focus away from the legacy of Roman law, championed by his teacher Friedrich Carl von Savigny, to piece together evidence of a communal legal tradition native to ancient Germanic life.[17] Grimm's work on German mythology, finally, sought to compile the fragmented evidence of an indigenous German religion, a system of mythology affiliated with the better known Nordic traditions, but one that had been shattered by Christianization and subsequently devalued as primitive.[18]

Viewed as parts of a single project, Grimm's studies of language, law, and religion were intended to dispel the notion of German cultural inferiority compared with classical or French civilization and allow the full range of historical German life to be recognized as ancient, rich, and distinctive. The result was a massive cultural history of the German people that spanned the areas of grammar, lexicography, customs, narratives, law, and even prehistory.[19] Grimm believed that Germanic ancestors had spoken a tongue that was supple and well structured rather than coarse and clumsy; upheld an old and often colorful and poetic law suited to their community rather than living in barbarous anarchy; and maintained a structured and dignified relationship with the transcendent rather than superstitiously submitting to primitive fetishes.[20] When he appeared before his fellow scholars in August 1846, Grimm represented an ambitious and consistent endeavor to restore, in the medium of scholarship, the neglected and scattered substance of Germanic culture and convert it into an object of attachment and respect.[21] His sequence of multivolume works sought to bring about a "relocation of cultural value," which was non-cosmopolitan and non-classicist in character.[22]

Speaking to the relatively new scholarly community of Germanists and expected to confirm its coherence and common subject matter, Jacob Grimm chose to address a fundamental issue: what makes a people – how can one define it? The unity of the Germanist scholars in their different disciplines was based, Grimm implied, not in a shared method or approach but in a common orientation toward a single object, a people. Grimm's answer to the question he had posed was, according to himself, as "simple" as the question itself:[23] a people, a *Volk*, was nothing but the name for a community of human beings who spoke the same language.[24] Those who spoke German were members of the German people, despite any confessional, social, political, or ideological divisions; their shared medium of communication revealed a common identity more fundamental and significant than any apparent disunity: "our ancestors were Germans before they were converted to Christianity [*unsere Vorfahren sind Deutsche gewesen, ehe sie zum Christentum bekehrt wurden*]."[25]

Grimm's answer to his own question was philological in nature. It was philological in the sense that Grimm viewed the question of the people from the vantage point of his own expertise: he believed peoplehood was related to his primary focus of study, the internal structure and evolution of related but distinct languages teased out on the basis of available documentation. However, it was also philological in the sense that the philologist, the expert on comparative and diachronic linguistics, could fix criteria of national belonging and present himself as the legitimate arbiter of membership, the one who could determine the people's contours. In the middle of the nineteenth century, the "people" was undeniably a political concept, emotionally evocative and dense with connotations;[26] after all, revolutions had been staged in the name of the people, countries formed, and constitutions established. To define the people philologically, as Jacob Grimm did, ultimately meant to address or even intervene in politics with philological means, an implication of which Grimm was aware.

Although linguistic difference in most cases would be obvious to any speaker, the philologist, Grimm believed, could reliably discern what was and was not genuinely German – hence the need for his expertise. According to Grimm and his peers in early historical linguistics, language was an organized body of sounds, and individual (Germanic) languages had achieved distinctiveness in comparison with others by moving through series of phonetic shifts over time.[27] For instance, the *Tu* of Latin had become the *Thu* of Gothic and later the *Du* of Old High German, a sequence that displayed a regular, patterned progression from T to TH to D across the vocabulary.[28] Such modifications revealed an internal principle of evolution in language, a veritable law,[29] but they simultaneously indexed, Grimm believed, the gradual differentiation of communities from some earlier group.[30] Among Germanic languages, High German had experienced a so-called second shift, and this change also marked a difference between the German and North-Germanic or Nordic peoples, among them the Danes. (The designation of the peoples was itself a contentious issue, with Grimm consistently and imperiously proposing the name German or *deutsch* for all groups we would today call German*ic* – Grimm fairly transparently used the term to suggest the centrality of German over supposedly subaltern languages.[31]) Degrees of structured "slippages" in phonology[32] indicated the difference among affiliated languages, and hence also among communities – peoples – that had diverged over time. Close scholarly attention to diachronically developed, empirically observable grammatical differences thus allowed the philologist, Grimm thought, to discern distinctions among nations and authorized him to separate them from one another.

When it came to distinguishing Germans from Danes – the most pressing question of the mid-1840s and at the first convention of the Germanists – Grimm went back and forth on how close or distant the languages were. In the edition of his grammar that appeared about half a decade before the Frankfurt conference, he assumed a fundamental split between Nordic languages, spoken in Scandinavia, and other German languages.[33] Grammatical features such as definite articles attached as suffixes to words were typical of Nordic languages and not shared by German (*the* bread is "*das* Brot" in German but "brød*et*" in Danish and "bröd*et*" in Swedish). But in a major publication on linguistic history two years after the meeting, he downplayed this distinction between German and Nordic somewhat and emphasized the genetic unity of all Germanic idioms; their differential traits were fairly late divergences. Regardless of his scholarly position at any given time, however, Grimm believed himself to be in possession of tools of discrimination; distinctions between nations, he held, must ultimately be performed on the basis of observations of grammatical developments, which was the field of expertise of philologists who tracked linguistic changes in surviving textual sources. The philologist best understood the "fixed rules [*feste Regeln*]" that governed the "unfolding of the German tongue [*Entfaltungen deutscher Zunge*]."[34]

When Grimm defined peoples as linguistic communities and suggested grammatical criteria to discern their boundaries, he also presented the comparative scholarship of individuated languages and their distinctive traits as an instrument of political boundary drawing. Rivers and mountain ranges may seem to separate groups, Grimm noted in his opening address to the Germanists, but topography alone did not delimit peoplehood. If groups on both sides of some conspicuous geographical edge were found to speak the same language, they belonged to one and the same people; "language alone," Grimm claimed, could "determine a border [*die Grenze setzen*]" and hence help delineate, in a dependable fashion, the size and shape of a national territory.[35] Political units and their territorial outlines should, Grimm continued more allusively, be made to correspond to the habitats of peoples, that is, to groups of individuals whose common tongue constituted indisputable proof of their cohesiveness. The possibly distant but nonetheless inevitable future would be one in which all arbitrary "barriers [*Schranken*]" had fallen and the imperfect spatial order of the present had been dissolved as a distraction from the histories of actual peoples.[36] Once states had become coextensive with spoken languages and hence with peoples, political borders would shed their current arbitrariness and attain a natural validity.[37]

Grimm assumed that particular patterns of linguistic difference were coterminous with national divisions that in turn had to be politically and territorially honored; insights into the "innermost household"[38] of languages as self-sufficient, rule-governed systems of sound ultimately yielded political imperatives. Grimm himself assumed that there was a continuum between his scholarly work and political engagement, and the terms he used in his writings on grammar could appear in public declarations made with a political intent. An example would be the obviously charged distinction German and "un-German," *deutsch* and *undeutsch*. With an understanding of orderly, lawlike phonetic transformations, Grimm was able to trace the journey of individual words through patterned sound shifts, such as the Latin P*ater* and the German V*ater*, and distinguish cases of actual identity of words across related languages from merely accidental likenesses.[39] He could also recognize the words that had gone through the process of shifts and thus truly belonged to the linguistic organism (such as the German V*ater*), and those that had arrived at some later date and hence had not been modified (such as the German P*atriotismus*), remaining visible as later imports. No linguist before Grimm, the intellectual historian Sarah Pourciau writes, had been able to draw "so definite a distinction between inside and out."[40] Guided by his comprehension of systematic phonetic transformations, Grimm believed he could spot authentically German words in contrast to more recent loanwords; some expressions were, he declared in his 1822 grammar, simply "un-German [*undeutsch*]."[41]

To Grimm, however, this rigorously grounded detection of what did and did not belong to the core German lexicon represented a particularly clear and validating example of a more general sense of what did and did not constitute German national culture, and ultimately also what was and was not fitting and conducive to the German people in the realm of politics. In Grimm's view, his grasp of the nation-grounding German language in its freely developing organic unity and the related wholeness of the German people even permitted him to render judgment on particular rulers and governmental actions, insofar as they respected or neglected, strengthened or weakened, the unity and autonomy of Germany. Grimm could speak dismissively of a king who did not appropriately honor the German language[42] and condemn a state policy that did not further the cause of the unification of German-speaking populations in different areas[43] on the grounds that they were manifestly *undeutsch* – un-German. As a particularly well-informed and dedicated student of the linguistically defined nation and its particular history and culture, Grimm thus thought that the philologist could claim the authority to comment on political rule; he possessed a vantage point and a measuring instrument by which to assess the politics of the day. A king or regime, and most importantly the shape of a territory or unit of governance, had to be in conformity with the character of the nation, and the philologist possessed the competence to determine whether or not this requirement had been satisfied – whether something was German or un-German.

There were examples of Grimm's self-confident assumptions in the 1846 inaugural address. He ended his opening speech to the assembled Germanists by turning to the city chosen for their first convention: Frankfurt am Main. Jacob Grimm reminded his audience that Frankfurt had been the historical center of German imperial rule and hence stood as a reminder of past German interconnection and unity.[44] Charlemagne had once wandered the streets of Frankfurt, Grimm noted, and people had often looked to the city in anxious anticipation of decisions determining the fate of Germany.[45] The Germanists were even gathering in the Kaisersaal or Emperor Hall in the Römer, a Medieval building that had once been the site of coronation banquets during the Holy Roman Empire.[46] As the chairman of the meeting, Grimm was seated directly under a portrait of Maximilian I,[47] the Holy Roman Emperor from 1508 to 1519. In "spaces such as these," Grimm then concluded in the very final line of his address, "only German things should transpire and nothing un-German! [*in solchen räumen darf nur deutsches, und nicht undeutsches geschehen!*]."[48] Invoking a history of imperial German rule at the end of his talk, Grimm restated his belief in the possibility of distinguishing between the inside and outside of the German nation. This was the special competency of the Germanists – they could tell the German apart from the un-German, a skill guaranteed by their linguistic insight.

Grimm's ending exhortation was a fitting introduction to the general business of the congress; the Germanists were focused on determining the proper boundaries of Germany, especially so on the first day. Immediately following Grimm's opening address to his fellow scholars were a series of lectures and debates about Schleswig and Holstein, the focal point of German nationalist efforts around the time of the congress, the perceived test case for German unification in the late 1840s, and possibly the first nationalist cause to generate a wider and more genuine public resonance.[49] The conflict with Denmark over the two duchies would later prove to be the dominant and most difficult foreign policy problem to be dealt with by the new German national parliament two years later, in 1848.[50] During the opening day of the Germanist association, all five featured speakers defended the German claim to the duchies using different legal, cultural, and linguistic arguments for the incorporation of Schleswig and Holstein into a German political structure.[51] Grimm did not give one of these lectures, but he would, over the next four to five years, prove to be an intransigent advocate of the struggle against any attempt by the Danish crown to tie the duchies closer to Denmark, even as this stance caused friction with the monarchical Prussian government from which he received financial support.[52]

Grimm's engagement in the cause of the two duchies, based as it was in his belief that he could discern the boundaries of people and adjudicate claims over lands, was not an isolated campaign in his life. He had, throughout his career, commented on whether or not some population or strip of land was German. When he was working as a secretary of the

Hessian delegation to the Congress of Vienna in 1814 and 1815, the young Jacob Grimm declared himself opposed to Prussian dominance over Poles. It would be fair, just, and right, he wrote to his brother Wilhelm from Vienna in 1814, to grant the Poles freedom and independence rather than wish for their integration under Prussian rule; they had been shamelessly divided and humiliated.[53] He voiced similar positions publicly in the magazine *Rheinischer Merkur*.[54] Poland was not part of Germany, Grimm wrote in a dispatch, and Prussia would not be stronger for housing one million Poles.[55] Concerned with the form and cohesion of culturally and linguistically German principalities, the young Hessian Grimm held distinctly "un-Prussian" views.[56]

However, the question of national delineation was not always so clearcut. In another article published in *Rheinischer Merkur* in the fall of 1814, Grimm tackled the issue of Alsace, a province wedged between German lands and France. While he noted the preference of the Alsatians to be French citizens rather than the subjects of a smaller German principality, he could not accept this as a permanent arrangement, since the Alsatians were, in his mind, indisputably German, linguistically and culturally: "those who speak our language are part of our body and blood and can be called un-German but never become un-German [*unsere sprache redet, ist unseres leibs und bluts und kann undeutsch heiszen, allein nicht undeutsch werden*]."[57] Alsatians were Germans and must at some point join Germany, when the political situations had improved. Linguistic and cultural belonging to a nation ought to trump civic attachment.

Long before the ethnic and linguistic character of Schleswig and Holstein had become a widely discussed topic in German-language media and began to fuel a more broadly based national movement, Grimm had started to develop and publicize his philological approach to European geopolitics. As early as in his twenties, he presented himself as competent to declare who was German, which territories a German king must rule, and which should be respected as non-German. Grimm's attempt to anchor political claims in investigations into linguistic history did not necessarily help him settle borders once and for all. In his 1846 address, Grimm drew on his path-breaking research of linguistic change over time to paint an image of languages as plastic organisms. Languages, Grimm claimed, moved through series of alterations that marked them out as distinct, but they could also expand and contract, rise and fall, and some languages had vanished completely while new ones had emerged. The Gothic language had died out, as had the Frankish tongue, although many Germanic words survived in the French language. By contrast,

English clearly was a Germanic language, although it had absorbed a Romance lexicon so extensive that Grimm viewed the resulting idiom a "wondrous mixture," one that already in his time seemed poised for "world domination."[58] His brief comment seems to suggest that a language that could not quite be contained within his grammatical categories would also not remain within the boundaries of a particular location; the mixed language of English would expand far beyond any national frontiers. German, finally, had itself undergone dramatic transformations, and Grimm related how dialects had retreated over time, in large part due to the hegemony of one standardized written language initially forged by Martin Luther. Grimm thus reported on how languages had evolved, atrophied, or become standardized, appeared and disappeared in history, which also had to mean that linguistically defined peoples were not eternally stable.

For Grimm, the record of linguistic change, including the deaths and births of entire languages, did not mean that rulers, administrators, or scholars ever had the right or even the opportunity to shape peoples. The languages that defined peoplehood could not be successfully created, constructed, or purified from above; the evident long-term plasticity of languages did not authorize the present generation to try to roll back past foreign influence, regrettable as this influence might have been. To Grimm, it would be both rash and futile to seek to redeem the English language by ripping out the Romance vocabulary.[59] Analogously, the introduction of Roman law in Germanic lands may once have done damage to a native tradition, but the development could hardly be reversed; uncompromising legal purism struck Grimm as impossible, even "unbearable."[60] When dealing with complex, historically shaped systems such as languages or bodies of law, Grimm indicated, one needed to practice a sensitive and patient gradualism, preserve what seemed valuable from the standpoint of "purity" but avoid the crudeness and clumsiness of willed human interventions into delicate organisms.[61] When Grimm asserted that the political and territorial unit must be anchored in the linguistic and cultural one, he did not rule out future geographic adjustments to further linguistic shifts, and when he urged caution against any organized campaigns of linguistic and cultural cleansing, he showed himself tolerant of past incursions and entanglements.

It is against the backdrop of these claims about language and nationhood that one can begin to understand the self-appointed political task of the philologist. Grimm believed that German philology, equipped with detailed knowledge of the distinguishing features of languages and nations with particular histories and locations, could help redraw the boundaries of Central Europe so that they would better reflect the actual geo-linguistic landscape. Territories ought to be determined by the homelands of linguistically defined peoples, not by the relative power of regionally dominant princes, the imperial expansion of strong states, or even by the civic attachment of a particular group to a state. To Grimm, the assembly of German historians, jurists, and linguists knew the cultural community most intimately, loved it most ardently, and was called to defend its integrity but do so without ignoring or seeking to annul a long history of importations and influences. As a self-consciously non-regional, proudly national institution, the association of scholars itself even seemed to foreshadow the future integration of larger German communities into one non-arbitrary political body.[62]

Given Grimm's argument, one might expect him to conclude his address with a final celebration of the philologist's indispensability to politics. Choosing a more cautious approach, however, he instead emphasized the separation of knowledge and rule, *Wissenschaft* and political battles. The meetings of the Germanists, he said at the end of his address, would not be able to make any decisions and they had to remain distant from "actual politics [*eigentliche Politik*]," although the questions that emerged in the fields of history, law, and linguistics "naturally and inevitably" would touch on political topics.[63] There were likely several reasons for Grimm's reticence: an equation of politics with decision-making, a concern for the particular character and integrity of research, and perhaps a tactical caution in anticipation of censorial interventions by authorities.[64] Yet the claim that scholarly pursuits must remain at a distance from politics clearly did not mean that they had no political consequences. Grimm's bundle of ideas – that linguistic boundaries could be precisely observed, that spoken languages defined peoples,[65] and that the geographic distribution of linguistically defined peoples ought to determine territorial borders – would, if implemented, have undermined the political order of his day. A German political body that would mirror a putative linguistic and cultural unity would entail the delegitimization of local princely rule in the plurality of German states, the dismantling of multinational configurations such as the Habsburg or Ottoman Empire, and a consequent destabilization of the European balance of power.[66] These potential implications were to some extent also debated at the conference. The philologist was a guardian of *national* self-determination, a figure whose expert advice could allow for the proper exercise of rule grounded in linguistic and cultural facts, but because of this national focus, the Germanist philologist was also a figure of disruption, even a harbinger of war.

Popular Sovereignty, National Particularism, and Territorial Rights

The Germanist congress of 1846 did not only feature discussions of grammar, Medieval German literature, German history, or legal antiquities; it was not a purely academic affair. The initial debate about the German character of the duchies of Schleswig and Holstein, as well as discussions about German migration to America on the third day of the Frankfurt congress or German settlements in Eastern Europe at the second Germanist congress in Lübeck in 1847, made it clear that the scholars were preoccupied with groups and lands, populations and territories, which were eminently political and geopolitical concerns. In his opening Frankfurt address, Grimm conveyed his belief that Germans formed one national community that ought to be unified and self-ruling, neither internally divided into many principalities nor dominated by a foreign power within a polyethnic empire, and that the location of that national community should dictate territorial borders. The congress was not just a first scholarly event at the national level, but a nationalist manifestation.

When Grimm posed his "simple" question – *what is a people?* – he believed that he could provide a definitive and authoritative answer as a scholar or disinterested *Wissenschaftler*; yet, he was aware that the question itself and the implications of his answer were not apolitical. The concern with what a people might be had become so urgent, so unavoidable, because the "people" had emerged as a central political figure during his lifetime,[67] for some even a unitary agent capable of empowering and constraining governments,[68] and it had to be recognized and even delineated sharply and convincingly for the sake of establishing a legitimate political order. In Grimm's view, the philologist stepped in to specify the people in an era in which such a specification had become absolutely necessary because of the political import of the concept – or fiction[69] – of the people. Philology, Grimm believed, could satisfy a pressing political need.

Born in 1785, Jacob Grimm came of age after the French Revolution, and he followed and participated in the politics of his day. To name just a few important episodes of his life that we will later revisit in greater detail, Grimm was a civil servant in his hometown Kassel under a French king in a French administration (1807–1814), worked as a delegation secretary for the restored Electorate of Hesse at the Congress of Vienna (1814–1815), lost his post as a state-employed professor when he challenged the decrees of a new king of Hanover together with a group of academics in Göttingen (1837), and went to Frankfurt as an elected representative in the first German parliament (1848). Grimm thus experienced firsthand the Napoleonic conquest of German principalities, the post-Napoleonic restoration and reordering of Europe, the long and frustrated struggle for constitutionalized monarchies throughout the German Confederation, and the attempt to establish as well as the failure to maintain the first German national parliament. While not an outspoken democrat[70] or especially interested in clearly defined liberal civil rights,[71] and certainly reluctant to consider a full-fledged alternative to royal power, Grimm believed that the legitimacy of any monarch ultimately depended on rule being sensitive to the culturally formed preferences and habits of a delimited people.

To Grimm, the king or prince did not "stand above" a people given shape solely through its subjection to a patrimonial or religiously justified government, but rather ruled legitimately by standing at the people's "helm," as its dedicated and knowledgeable guardian and fitting representative.[72] No prince was simply a "sovereign [*souverän*]," and the word itself was clearly French and hence, of course, "un-German."[73] Neither a champion of popular sovereignty enmeshed in post-revolutionary political philosophy nor simply an ethnic chauvinist with expansionary plans and little concern for the acceptance of the governed or subjugated, Grimm considered the national people the fundamental political unit, which must be properly accommodated and expressed in any valid order; politics should ultimately provide an appropriate external arrangement for a national group already revealed in language and culture.[74] The principle of monarchical rule was, for him, not in question, but a kingdom had to match the outlines of a nation, and a ruler ought to respect the nation's character and cultivate an interest in its cultural particularity. Ideally, a German king should think and feel like a German philologist, or at the very least use his position to promote the cultural and linguistic inheritance of the homeland rather than hold up foreign cultures as models and spend excessive sums on alien prestige objects such as Italian paintings or Greek statues.[75]

Grimm's position represented an alliance between a moderated or muted version of a post-revolutionary and hence more broadly popular politics, on the one hand, and historicist cultural particularism, on the other. Grimm did believe that rule could only obtain legitimacy when it was plausibly exercised in the name of people, but he also held that this now politicized people must first and foremost be construed as a historically formed linguistic and cultural community. It was the combination of these two principles that assigned a unique political task for the philologist: if rule had to reckon with the people, and the people was a historically formed linguistic collective, then the philologically trained scholar was especially well positioned to delimit it, which included tracing its spatial contours. The combined requirements of popular legitimacy and cultural-linguistic peoplehood entailed a philologization of politics. It was the philologist, Grimm believed, who could demarcate the people by clarifying and applying criteria for membership. In this way, the philologist would even be able to address a problem of determination that followed from the internal logic of popular sovereignty, for the idea of the people as the source of legitimate political authority had inevitably generated a question that proved quite hard to answer, namely the question of what a people *was*. This was of course precisely Grimm's question: *what is a people?*

How did the notion of popular sovereignty give rise to a problem of determination? A synoptic overview of the post-revolutionary preoccupation with the *boundary* of the people will help us understand the problem that Jacob Grimm sought to solve by philological means. The principal political organization of Grimm's place and time, early nineteenth-century Europe, was the state,[76] a relatively centralized entity, differentiated from other, subordinate organizations, with control over the means of physical coercion in a defined area, and generally headed by a king or prince.[77] The state was at its core a claimant or master of a territory,[78] and its size ultimately corresponded to its ability to hold on to land with military means. These spatial boundaries were not necessarily understood as rooted in the geographic distribution of a language or the ethnic character of a people, and they were ultimately determined by the state's capacity to defend the area.[79] Within this territory, its rule was meant to be unrivaled; it possessed sovereignty understood as the undivided and unchallenged right and ability to command.[80]

The French Revolution mounted a successful challenge to absolutism, the exercise of rule by a monarch in control of a centralized machinery of administration for connected activities such as taxation, diplomacy, and warfare. However, even as the revolution assailed royal rule, it did not dissolve the state's territorial integrity and let regions and districts revert into localism. Rather, new elites inherited the state's existing borders.[81] While personal rule by the monarch was transformed by a vision of collectively authorized rule, the paradigm of supreme command within a delimited space remained in place. The absolutist achievement of centralized command and territorial consolidation was seized and, in a sense, retroactively legitimized in the name of the people. Article 3 of the French Declaration of the Rights of Man and Citizen declared that the principle of all sovereignty resided essentially in the nation; no individual or group of individuals was entitled to a decision-making authority that was not ultimately derived from the people as a whole.[82] The declaration did not inaugurate a direct collective rule, but rather it installed the people as the figure with the ultimate power to establish and disestablish rule and the right to grant a mandate to the state's government.[83]

In the aftermath of the revolution, many educated and well-informed bourgeois subjects ceased to view royal rule as divinely ordained, with a king self-evidently standing above a population as its patrimonial lord.[84] The post-revolutionary public instead believed that the people could confer legitimacy on constitutions, regimes, and territorial boundaries.[85] But if the state ultimately derived its authority from the people, then the people had to be imagined as in some sense prior to that state and not as its product or effect. The appeal to the people in the context of undivided sovereignty implied the existence of unified and unitary community[86] that had existed *before* the constituted authority of the state and its agents,[87] a pre-political unity that had preceded but also would survive any given regime that aspired to rule in its name.

The people's boundaries could, according to this logic, not be the result of a decision made in the realm of politics,[88] because no king or government could ever possess the authority to impose or determine such boundaries. A people that would somehow have acquired a definite outline only through the ordering efforts of an apparatus or the commands of a king could also have been shaped in some other way and then contain other sets of members. In that case, political rule would have created the conditions of its own supposed legitimacy; the game would be rigged. Only an already existing collective could avoid entering into the circle in which political power defined or produced the human collective that then was asked to ratify its own subjection.[89]

In the age of popular sovereignty, then, the people's identity could not be an effect of a political imposition by a king with the right to rule over his subjects. Nor could the people's cohesion be a result of a democratic procedure, a conscious, voluntary, and fully collective decision to form a new people. This would generate another circle, for a people as a *demos* could not somehow have arrived at a resolution about its own contours and its own criteria of membership without already having presupposed these contours and criteria in the very act of the collective decision.[90] Again, the people must have already possessed a definite form and discernible outlines. In this way, post-revolutionary sovereignty required the people to be determinate rather than undefined, natural rather than fabricated, historically deep rather than recently conjured; the people had to possess its very own bounded unity before the advent of any regime claiming to represent it.

How, then, could the people be determined or discovered? How could one delineate its shape and unity without compromising the necessary fiction of its natural and independent character? In the early decades of the nineteenth century, nationalists believed they could answer this question. After the revolution, the necessity of specifying the boundaries of the people led them to identify the all-important but elusive *demos* with the cultural *nation* defined as a community of kin united by its language, shared culture, or ethnic traits.[91] Attention to a common language, common practices, customs, and traditions would help mark out a stable and exclusive community that had existed and would continue to exist in a recognizable form regardless of any one particular ruler or form of regime. The new legitimating fiction of the sovereign people could attain the requisite temporal depth and communal closure, but only when imagined ethnically and culturally as a nation.

As a collector of the words, tales, laws, and myths of the German nation, Jacob Grimm tirelessly promoted the nationalist resolution of the post-revolutionary boundary problem in the German context. For him, the people as a political unit should be understood as synonymous with the national community, the identity and coherence of which was abundantly manifest in its language, literature, inherited legal corpus, and ancient mythical beliefs. The people were, for Grimm, not a voluntary or contractual association,[92] and certainly not a unitary collective agent looking to expand and dominate its surroundings. Instead, it was an evolved, natural community whose proudest but also "most innocent" shared property, its language, could be expertly mapped by the philologist.[93] The urgent political question of what made a people could, Grimm thought, be conclusively answered, because the philologist could identify its borders grammatically and hence methodically and precisely. In a situation in which the idea of the people as sovereign fused with the idea of the people as a bounded nation,[94] the philologist scholar could advance into the position of an expert arbiter of state boundaries and claim that every regime would need philological support and advice.

Grimm ultimately relied on several interconnected ideas: heads of state only ruled legitimately in the name of the people; the contours of the people were determined by the shape of nationhood; nationhood could be traced by the philologist; and, finally, the state's area of exclusive jurisdiction should coincide with the existing national homeland. No territorial unit could, in Grimm's implicit view, be understood as the inheritable property of a dynastic king.[95] In the German context, this was a radical position, since it suggested the impracticality and redundancy of the remaining micro-principalities; the independently defined German nation should determine the shape of the state and not local princely rule.[96] However, the notion of popular-national sovereignty also generated a particular conception of a people's relationship to a tract of the earth, a kind of territorialization of the community.[97] Armed states were masters of territory, but the people was the ultimate source of the state's authority; combined, these two claims singled out the people as the exclusive master of a territory.[98] It was the nation, and not the king, dynasty, or government, that emerged as the legitimate possessor of an inalienable communal land[99] and the spatial frontiers of the state had to correspond to the boundaries of the people.[100] Any apparent arbitrariness to borders was eliminated, or concealed, once territories were viewed not as the results of a history of political conquest and conflict but as ancient habitats of national communities entitled to the land they occupied.[101] The external frontiers of a state could, in Grimm's view, be imagined as the natural edges of a distinct transgenerational community, as the outlines of the place where the national people was "at home."[102]

Grimm's 1846 Frankfurt address on the people encapsulated a nationalization of the sovereign political community and an associated culturalization or ethnicization of its territorial claims.[103] In Grimm's eyes, the right of any state to its boundaries was justified by the prior collective occupancy of a philologically circumscribed national people.[104] Posing the question of the people before his fellow Germanists, Grimm explicitly defined it as a nation bound together by the common language and surrounded by other groups with different although historically affiliated tongues. According to him, the nation was not the outcome of an imposition from a center of political agency or any kind of conscious decision but had grown naturally and spontaneously and could not be transformed at will. The nation presented the world with a common social life that did not emanate from or depend on rulers but whose integrity and spatial distribution should instead be respected by them. To enable such respect, Grimm also asserted that the people was eminently determinable and that the philologist could perform this determination, as well as defend and justify it, should it be denied or disputed. Specifically, he arrived at a subdivision of European peoples into geographically localizable groups (German, Dutch, French, English, Scandinavian, etc.) through his study of systemic grammatical shifts over time, which meant, to him, that the demarcation of peoples could claim for itself the validity and reliability of a scholarly finding. The philologist's empirically grounded delineation of nationhood on the basis of linguistic and historical fact, he assumed, protected the judgment from contamination by petty interests. Philological judgment only tracked independently specifiable linguistic and cultural properties of nations and in this way established the all-important pre-political ground for legitimate politics.[105] Modern rule by sovereign states required a delineation of the people in time and in space, and the discriminating philologist, Grimm thought, could identify a collective identity, a coherent, unified *Volk*, which would not be synonymous with tumultuous masses or a rowdy populace.[106]

To summarize the steps of Grimm's argument: genuine political legitimacy required a rule anchored in the people; the politically foundational people required definite cultural and spatial boundaries; the boundaries were given by the diffusion of languages in space, each one with a limited reach; linguistic tracing, which should dictate territorial boundary drawing, required finely tuned observations of lawlike grammatical patterns; and the epistemic authority to draw these boundaries was ensured by disciplinary methods. On the strength of this argument, Grimm's Germanist philologist stepped into the political arena, not to take charge, not to exercise power, not to question or subvert the monarchical order, but to demarcate the proper unit of constitutionally constrained but nonetheless continued, re-legitimated, and territorially consolidated royal rule. This explains why the first day of the Germanist congress was devoted not to linguistic findings, historical sources, methodological debates, or future collaborative projects, but to the dispute over the status of Schleswig and Holstein, to a conflict over land and habitats.

Recent historical scholarship has been uncomfortable with the entanglement of popular sovereignty and nationhood and has sought to challenge the notion that a revolutionary and more democratic age must allow nation-states to emerge from dissolving empires; empires were more adaptable and less doomed than previously acknowledged, and supposedly national peoples more mutable and unfinished.[107] Grimm himself was clearly a promoter of the story of national resurgence and imperial demise. His presentation of the politically active philologist was, it should also be added, a peculiarly German performance. Among the revolutionaries in France, many had indeed rejected the idea of bounded nations, each living its separate life under its own regime. The petty care for one's nation should not, Jacobins would argue, take the place of one's commitment to the greater brotherhood of humanity.[108] The logical aim of a revolution ought to be a morally unified world rather than an ethnically provincialized one, a rousing vision with supporters all over Europe, including the German principalities.[109]

It was precisely this universalist vision, however, that some Germans came to reject, among them Jacob and Wilhelm Grimm, who witnessed the French move into their hometown Kassel in 1806 and then lived and worked under the rule of Napoleon's brother Jérôme until 1813, with Kassel as the capital of the newly constructed Kingdom of Westphalia. The collapse of the Holy Roman Empire and the fact of French rule[110] convinced them and many of their generational peers that the universalist vision of humankind's liberation could end with a coercive regime installed by an arrogant power over more fragmented lands.[111] Nationalism was a resentful response to the condescension of an occupier,[112] and Jacob Grimm wrote in 1814 of the hatred that he considered the "natural response [*natürliche rückwirkung*]" to the coercive pressure of a foreign regime.[113] For the philosopher Georg Wilhelm Friedrich Hegel (born 1770) or the influential literary critic Friedrich Schlegel (born 1772), the French Revolution had been a formative and exciting historical moment,[114] but Grimm, born a little more than a decade later than these luminaries, was shaped more by the experience of the subsequent Napoleonic conquest and hegemony. To him, the supposed emancipation and progress of humanity had revealed itself, locally, as French domination over German lands.[115]

French rule certainly meant modernization – in the form of the dissolution of the Holy Roman Empire, the consolidation of many small principalities into larger units, the introduction of a rationalized legal code, as well as a more uniform and meritocratic system of administration.[116] Napoleon himself believed, with respect to Westphalia, that German populations would come to appreciate the benefits of the new order and approve of French rule.[117] Yet the perception of exploitative French rule motivated the Grimms to explore the particularity of their own nationality, insufficiently modern as it may have been. The brothers' entire philological output, the compilations of folktales, legends, heroic epics, myths, and legal antiquities as well as the construction of a record of linguistic change, was meant to demonstrate the existence of a Germanic cultural tradition expressive of an autonomous and distinctive social life. The recovery of the deep vernacular past was a reaction to a universalism that had arrived in the form of foreign superiority.[118]

Despite this apparently retrograde turn to the ancient past, Jacob Grimm was not simply a political conservative. Without endorsing a principle, he nonetheless implicitly accepted the premise that rule must be anchored in the people, hardly a reactionary tenet. By the 1840s, Grimm, once a locally oriented, Hessian patriot, had effectively come to support the construction of a larger and more centralized state, a state that would coincide with the larger German community: the extent of the nation demanded the elimination of autocratic micro-states.[119] As we have seen, however, Grimm continued to refuse politically enforced universalistic visions. In his hands, the philologically conducted nationalization of the people was meant to delimit rule and render it legitimate in a way that resisted the erasure of all cultural individuality in the name of a unified, undifferentiated humanity.[120] Grimm invoked the language and culture of the nation to give plausible shape to a people as a political unit, but he also asserted the nation's integrity against a form of rule that justified itself through claims to greater rationality and efficiency. Through this fusion of a post-revolutionary conception of sovereignty and national particularism, the rule of the people could only occur when ruler and ruled hail from the same cultural community, and, as the guardian of cultural and linguistic togetherness, the philologist emerged as the figure who best knew when this identity of ruler and subjects had been authentically achieved. Grimm believed that philology, a discipline that "naturally and inevitably" touched on political matters, could facilitate the formation of a legitimate government.

The Philologist at War

Nationalists such as Grimm propounded a modern geopolitical vision: Europe ought to be divided into states that would coincide with national peoples defined by their languages, common cultures, and shared histories. This was a challenge to the early nineteenth-century elite representatives of the old European order, few of whom attached any political significance to the nationality or ethnicity of broad segments of the population. Multilingual and multiethnic empires clearly did not stand to benefit from making language and nation the criteria of political boundary drawing:[121] the Habsburgs famously ruled over "Magyars and Croats, Slovaks and Italians, Ukrainians and Austro-Germans."[122] Ethnic settlement all over Europe was often quite dispersed,[123] and linguistic communities frequently overlapped spatially. Territories could be linguistically mixed, with diverse groups dwelling side by side rather than cleanly concentrated in separate areas.[124] The world was culturally messier than Grimm may have wanted to admit.

Grimm's equation of language and territory rested on several assumptions: that individuals, however polyglot, possessed one mother tongue; that they consequently belonged to one and only one people; and that the people constituted a fairly homogeneous and cohesive group that inhabited a definable area. This collective then qualified as the master of a territory, over which it possessed some form of collective ownership by virtue of its enduring occupancy.[125] Grimm's vision effectively implied the need to put an the end to actual multilinguistic regions and multinational co-dwelling, since the close coexistence of languages would impede the formation of a national polity.[126] Nationalists like Grimm tended to demand not just the devolution of empires but also at least implicitly the requirement of coercive forms of "depluralization"[127] or homogenization of linguistically and culturally varied territories. Philologists who put their scholarly knowledge of linguistic and cultural differences in the service of the nationalist cause ultimately called for sharper political and territorial divisions in a context where cultures shaded into one another and people were accustomed to complex patterns of language use such as bilingualism and diglossia.[128] The postrevolutionary shift in the conception of political legitimacy, exemplified here by Grimm's approach, redefined political membership and re-specified political collectivities, transformations that could not fail to unleash conflicts and impose exclusions.[129]

There were several culturally and linguistically jumbled areas in central Europe in Grimm's time, places with "soft borders" between populations,[130] and nationalists instigated hostilities in more than one of them. The most fervently debated sites of national conflict around the time of the Germanist convention in 1846, were, once again, the duchies of Schleswig and Holstein; the inhabitants of Schleswig spoke German and Danish in roughly equal proportions.[131] This area in between Scandinavia and Germany became the object of German but also Danish campaigns for nation building[132] and as such the primary location for a fairly novel type of antagonism, namely the one between competing nationalisms.[133] The German nationalists did not always honestly admit the reality of linguistically heterogeneous populations; many came close to denying that there were native speakers of Danish in Schleswig.[134]

The legal and political situation in Schleswig and Holstein was exceedingly complex. The duchies had been ruled by the Danish crown since

1460[135] but were locally nevertheless dominated by the landed aristocracy, which was German. Traditions and languages were entangled: the ruling Danish royal family was a German dynasty; German aristocrats and civil servants played an influential political and cultural role in Copenhagen, the Danish capital;[136] and German also served as the primary language in religious services, even for the Danish-speaking population of Schleswig.[137] Politically, the two territories were both divided and closely tied to each other. Holstein was part of the German Confederation, but Schleswig was not, and yet the two were united under Danish rule. According to German scholars, legal documents from earlier centuries established the indissoluble connection of the two duchies.[138] The discussion of rightful rule became further complicated with disputes over the principles governing the inheritance of the throne. Danish law allowed for succession along the female line, whereas Holstein, following an ancient Frankish legal code, did not. The matter of agnatic or cognatic succession came to the forefront in the 1840s since contemporaries could anticipate a future without male heirs descended from a Danish king; the Danish royal family faced a "serious long-term problem."[139] If female succession prevailed, the Danish crown could hold on to the duchies further into the future; if the inheritance was restricted to males in Holstein, however, Danish rule in the duchy might come to an end. As a result, the clashing campaigns for conversion of the duchies into either Danish or German national areas were partly conducted with obscure legal arguments.

The tangle of linguistic, cultural, legal, and political factors did not deter the Germanists gathered in Frankfurt in 1846. In fact, the philologists and jurists excelled precisely at mobilizing arcane linguistic and legal history to prove the essentially German character of Schleswig and Holstein and supply a scholarly justification for a nationalist challenge to Danish authority. As mentioned, the first day out of three was exclusively devoted to the topic and the agenda of the presenters was entirely partisan; speakers offered arguments against Danish rule to shore up an already existing consensus. Some of the academics who delivered speeches after Jacob Grimm's introductory address were even veterans of the Schleswig-Holstein conflict, men with family backgrounds in the area and a long history of making the case for German hegemony.

One of the most prominent of the five scheduled presenters was the historian and political scientist Friedrich Christoph Dahlmann (1785–1860), a close friend and ally of Jacob Grimm since their days as colleagues at the University of Göttingen in the 1830s. In Hanover, Dahlmann and Grimm had both protested King Ernst August's abrogation of the recently adopted constitution, both lost their positions and were exiled, and then both were celebrated and vilified as icons of German liberalism.[140] By the time of the Germanist convention, Dahlmann had fought for a national conception of the duchies for about three decades; he was truly an insider of the German nationalist campaign. Born in Swedish Wismar in 1785, he studied in Copenhagen and Halle; lectured in the Danish capital; and became a professor in Kiel, the university of Holstein, between 1812 and 1829, where he also served as the secretary of the deputation of the German nobility and clergy of Schleswig-Holstein.[141] In his youth, Dahlmann had been an intimate friend of one of German literary history's most passionate nationalists, Heinrich von Kleist (1777–1811), and both had been committed to German resistance to the French. During his long academic career, however, he emerged as a more moderate liberal nationalist who held that peoples should live in nationally based constitutional monarchies.[142]

As a representative of the landed aristocracy in their drawn-out tug of war with the Danish crown, Dahlmann had been tasked with the defense of the nobility's economic and political interests, which were not necessarily nationalist in character but often collided with those of a centralizing Danish crown.[143] In this position, however, Dahlmann had begun constructing historical arguments against the solidification of Danish power.[144] A classical philologist by training and a historian by profession, he retrieved and interpreted historical documents on the basis of which he argued that the aristocracy was independent from the Danish crown and that the arguably inseparable duchies therefore ought to enjoy autonomy.[145] He was a liberal nationalist using philological discoveries to deploy the duchies' aristocratic history against the Danish king.[146]

In Frankfurt am Main in 1846, Dahlmann went to the podium as one of the last to speak during the first day, and he chose to give a more personal and anecdotal presentation. The inhabitants of Schleswig did speak Danish, he conceded, but only a decayed dialect, and Luther's Bible German had spread peacefully throughout the region.[147] Even Danish speakers, he continued, went to German mass and studied in the German town Kiel, not in the Danish capital Copenhagen.[148] Dahlmann's sketch, self-serving as it may have been, fit Jacob Grimm's opening address. While Grimm posited the unity of language, people, and territory in Northern and Western Europe more generally, Dahlmann tackled the specific case under debate and argued that High German was firmly established as the predominant language of faith and learning in the churches and at the university, two key institutions. Dahlmann's argument for the German national character of Schleswig depended not on some census of the preferred language of all existing households but on the identification of genuine nationhood with the culture and language of the more educated strata.[149] Dahlmann believed that political rule should be coterminous with linguistic areas, in turn determined by the culturally dominant idiom. More generally, Grimm and Dahlmann held that the historical geography of languages should serve as the indispensable reference point for politics. The philologist and the historian both presented themselves as authoritative experts who could validly define nationhood, discriminate among peoples, evaluate their relative cultural predominance, and settle conflicting territorial claims.

Even so, Grimm and others balked when the convener of the conference, Dahlmann's son-in-law the jurist August Ludwig Reyscher (1802–1880), called upon the collective of Germanists to decide, in the manner of a "jury," that the duchies should cease to belong to the Danish crown.[150] The opponents to this suggestion pointed out that an assembly of scholars did not have the authority to pronounce a binding verdict on a legal and political question, and that the very attempt would vitiate the scholarly character of the event.[151] As chairman, Grimm himself adamantly resisted Reyscher's suggestion. The topic of Schleswig and Holstein was clearly political to the scholars themselves, and philological knowledge was obviously politically relevant knowledge, but an academic association, Grimm wrote in a newspaper summary after the congress, could not suddenly transform itself into a juridical body; it possessed no competence or right to make an outright political decision.[152]

For Grimm, however, this attitude of restraint was a question of context, venue, and authorization, and certainly not of opinion. Responding indignantly to a pro-Danish article in a Berlin newspaper in the spring of 1848, Grimm once again called Schleswig a German country, into which the Danes had "forced themselves."[153] Grimm also did not hesitate to vote for resolutions and encourage belligerence once he acted as an elected deputy in the national parliament in Frankfurt during 1848, the year of European upheaval. When the new Danish king, under pressure from mass protests in 1848, declared Schleswig a Danish territory and wanted to make its male inhabitants available for service in the Danish army, the Prussian army moved into Denmark.[154] By the end of April 1848, the Danes had been defeated on land, while the Danish blockade of the northern Prussian coastline continued.[155] The parliament in Frankfurt opened in May, with representatives from Schleswig and Holstein – a de facto recognition of their German status.[156] During the debates, Jacob Grimm, the expert philologist now turned parliamentarian, supported the campaign against Denmark and even advocated for a particularly aggressive position, namely continued warfare, to be concluded only when the Danish crown acknowledged all German claims. He added that the national parliament ought to declare that it would never tolerate the "intervention [*einmischung*]" of a foreign people in German national affairs.[157] Friedrich Christoph Dahlmann was also a leading parliamentarian and both Grimm and Dahlmann gave nationalist speeches;[158] the continuity with the first congress of the Germanists two years earlier was unmistakable.

Even so, the war over Schleswig disappointed the nationalists, among them Jacob Grimm. Leaned upon by Britain and Russia and suffering from the blockade by the superior Danish fleet, Prussia signed an armistice in Malmö, Sweden, in August 1848,[159] without the approval of the deputies in the German national parliament.[160] The majority of the parliamentarians recognized that they had no control over any military forces and had to accept the Prussian course of action; this meant endorsing the armistice.[161] To Grimm, this conclusion was deeply disappointing. Prussia, he wrote to his brother Wilhelm in Berlin, had simply committed an "an un-German action [*einer undeutschen handlung*]."[162] As always, the philologist believed himself competent to decide when regimes were acting in an appropriately German way. The Prussian action was un-German because it did not further the consolidation of Germany, and it constituted a betrayal of the German nationals in Schleswig. The so-called Elbe duchies would later be annexed by German forces, but only in the year 1864, and then by a Prussia led by Otto von Bismarck, who would become the first chancellor of a unified imperial Germany.[163] By the time of the second war in Schleswig, however, Jacob Grimm had already passed away; he died in September 1863.

Power and Knowledge in the Age of Nationalism

Jacob Grimm believed that philological knowledge qualified him for a crucial modern political task. In his view, the philologist could best distinguish between peoples and trace their supposedly natural borders to identify viable and legitimate territorial units of rule. The first Germanist convention, chaired by Jacob Grimm and dominated by professors with nationalist sympathies, was one public arena for the philologist aspiration to inform and guide political life,[164] and the interlinked discussions about the German territorial shape and constitutional form, national belonging and citizenship, continued in the Frankfurt parliament two years later.[165] Germany's geographical definition and basic political institutions were major topics of debate then, too,[166] and almost a tenth of the parliamentarians were professors; the two deputies Jacob Grimm and Friedrich

Christoph Dahlmann were joined by several of their Germanist peers.[167] As shown in the letter to the Prussian monarch Frederick William IV, however, Jacob Grimm also wanted to reach the ultimate political elite of his day and even hoped for the appearance of a philologically informed ruler, a philologist king.

Grimm's political philologist differs from other, more familiar representatives of knowledge, theory, and scholarship who have sought to make interventions in the political realm. He did not, for instance, set out to aid princes engaged in struggles over power with political know-how in the Machiavellian tradition. For this well-known type of advisor, history had served as a repository of valid examples of moral, prudential, or heroic behavior, a large pool of case studies for strategy geared toward the conquest and maintenance of state power.[168] In contrast, the nineteenth-century philologist of Jacob Grimm's kind treated history as the medium for the unfolding of national cultures that ought to achieve institutional expression at the level of the political order.[169] For Grimm, history did not serve as a collection of templates for advisable action but represented instead a process of evolution to which fundamental political arrangements must be adapted[170] – the nation was the ultimate anchoring reality for the state. The philologist did not provide counsel on the basis of an archive of human behavior[171] but instead wanted to delimit the unit of rule on the basis of researched insights into the collective's historicity and cultural individuality.

The political philologist also contrasts sharply with the *philosophes* who had gathered around the enlightened despots of the late eighteenth century. Absolutist rulers had famously invited secular and cosmopolitan thinkers to serve as tutors, correspondents, and advisors,[172] partly to create a stimulating court culture but also to draw on their assistance in the project of augmenting absolutist power through rational reform.[173] Exponents of the Enlightenment who wished to enhance the population's moral, physical, and economic well-being by means of pedagogy, planning, and continuous policing willingly entered into alliances with major European rulers intent on enlarging the state's authority and capacity.[174] In the 1760s, for example, a whole cohort of philosophers imagined themselves as the consultants of Catherine the Great of Russia.[175] From the perspective of the philologist with knowledge about the origin and evolution of individuated cultures over time, such a combination of philosophy and absolutist rule would be a recipe for a potentially arrogant treatment of national peoples. Viable rule, the philologist believed, depended not on the superior reason of a king in conversation with philosophers but on the linguistic and cultural *fit* of government and governed within the frame of national self-determination. The absolutely primary task of a German king was not to act prudently and not to love wisdom, but to act in a "German" rather than an "un-German" way, out of genuine attachment to the German nation. The king should not rely on the philosopher but the philologist.

Grimm's political philologist differed, finally, from the "intellectual," a term reserved here for authors who operated in the liberal public sphere and at least partly drew their income from the growing literary and journalistic market.[176] Intellectuals of the early nineteenth century met the demand of the reading public for poetry, anecdotes, satires, political reporting, entertainment, and opinion and hence stood apart from the apparatus of the state, which they confronted in the form of censorship. In Grimm's time, the intellectual was epitomized by the popular poet and correspondent Heinrich Heine (1797–1856), who wrote in German but spent long stretches of his life in Paris and had a Jewish background.[177] The intellectual's relatively independent position, and in Heine's case exilic location,[178] allowed for an unsparingly critical perspective on German political affairs, but such an autonomous standing and even extraterritorial vantage point could also provoke complaints about political incompetence, dilettantism, and aloofness.[179]

The difference between the philologist and the intellectual in the censored but nonetheless growing public sphere of the early nineteenth century should be apparent. The philological researcher embodied by Grimm typically occupied a post at a government-funded university and addressed political issues on the basis of specialist knowledge; his resource was expertise in a recognized discipline validated by a community of scholars. He possessed epistemic authority rather than moral charisma or artistic ability. The critical intellectual in Grimm's era was, by contrast, not infrequently an aspiring academic discriminated in or ejected from the university system[180] who succeeded in the public sphere thanks to a facility with genres of public speech and engaged the audience through appeals to their conscience and political interest. The intellectual was not an academically trained expert speaking to fellow experts as Grimm did in 1846, but rather a figure of the public speaking to the public. The ultimate aim of someone like Heine was also not to assume a position as a government expert or counselor close to the ruler, but to mobilize public opinion against concentrated power, a project that was quite foreign to Grimm. Yet Heine, our exemplary intellectual here, did at one point turn to the Prussian king, to Frederick William IV. In his long satirical poem

Germany: A Winter's Tale from 1844, he advised the king not to persecute poets but to "spare" them.[181] The advice was mingled with a threat: Heine added ironically that mercy toward poets was a tactically prudent move for the king who would otherwise become the object of their enduring ridicule.[182] In December 1844, the Prussian monarch issued an arrest warrant for the poet.

Grimm believed he possessed politically relevant knowledge, but he had little interest in offering strategic advice, formulating rational policy, or speaking truth to power. Instead, he and his colleagues among the Germanists focused on the historical emergence, geographical extension, and legal and political traditions of a distinct people – the German people – and claimed that their knowledge enabled them to uncover a reliable national basis for a future political order. The program was very much of its time. The political philologist was a transitional figure who appeared in an era of political reconfiguration, after the French Revolution, the dissolution of the Holy Roman Empire, the Napoleonic restructuring of German states, and the post-Napoleonic restoration, all dramatic developments that had challenged the legitimacy of old dynastic regimes and generated new and short-lived political units. In the first decades of the nineteenth century, lands changed hands and borders were adjusted multiple times, which eroded the sense of a legitimate and geographically settled system of rule.[183] It was in this situation that a philologist such as Jacob Grimm stepped in to supply a new and supposedly stable ground for future politics. Borders were to be determined not by unpredictable transactions and temporary alliances among kings or by military conquests and imperial hegemony, but by the historical homelands of national peoples. This new principle of boundary drawing led to further turbulence and war, such as in the case of Schleswig-Holstein, but the ultimate aim was the establishment of a non-arbitrary political map composed of sovereign nations.

In Grimm's view, disciplined examinations of the nation's historical space could plausibly ground national politics precisely because they were not shaped by the interests, or the whims, of absolutist rulers. Philologists such as Grimm and Dahlmann claimed to be able to provide fundamental orientation in the political realm not despite of but rather thanks to their strict adherence to methodological principles of research, institutionally sheltered at the university that recruited and promoted its members according to meritocratic criteria of aptitude and achievement.[184] A modern reader of Grimm and his peers is likely to spot biased research, conducted by nationalist professors interested in furthering their ideological agenda, but the scholars themselves saw no necessary tension between their commitment to research, on the one hand, and their dedication to national life, on the other. On the first day of the congress, the organizer August Ludwig Reyscher declared that the scholars were meeting to further "science [*Wissenschaft*]" *and* to honor the "fatherland"; he seems to have perceived no conflict whatsoever between these two objectives.[185] The deliberations instead reveal that the methods of scholarship, such as comparative grammar and a rigorous approach to written sources, were understood to guarantee objective findings about language, law, and history. The nation emerged most clearly and conspicuously in the medium of methodical, meticulous scholarship.[186] The philologist could help establish an authentically national and hence legitimate politics because the information about the German nation had been gathered and organized within an autonomous system of knowledge production.

Modern disciplinary knowledge could and should be put in the service of modern political legitimacy by negotiating a new, more fitting relationship between rulers and ruled – this was the underlying assumption of the politically vocal philologists. The 1846 letter to the Prussian king written by Grimm and signed by his colleagues encapsulated the attempt of the professional researcher to give "counsel [*ratschlüsse*]" to a head of state, however timidly and cautiously.[187] The philologist, Jacob Grimm believed, possessed knowledge of pivotal importance to the exercise of rule, but it was not knowledge of the practicalities of effective governance, the history of diplomacy and military strategy, and certainly not philosophical insight into principles of justice and virtue; it was methodologically sound knowledge of the historical integrity and distinguishing traits of the people as nation. As we shall see in the next chapter, this was a belief shaped by experiences early in Grimm's career, experiences that supplied the motivation for the first and most famous of Jacob and Wilhlem Grimms' projects, the collection of children- and household tales.

CHAPTER 2

Folk Hatred and Folktales
The Nationalist Politics of the *Children's and Household Tales*

The Brothers Grimm in Kassel, 1813

Toward the end of 1813, with Napoleon's armies defeated at Leipzig by a large coalition of Austrian, Prussian, Russian, and Swedish troops, the two Hessians Jacob and Wilhelm Grimm announced their contribution to the ongoing anti-Napoleonic war effort. Born in 1785 and 1786, they were still young men, in their late twenties. Throughout the fall, the military and political situation had been turbulent in the city, then the capital of the Napoleonic vassal kingdom of Westphalia.[1] In September 1813, Russian troops on their way through Europe arrived at the outskirts of the city. Surrounded by hostile contingents, the French king of Westphalia, Jérôme Bonaparte, decided to retreat; he had then ruled the constructed state since he was installed as its ruler by Napoleon Bonaparte, his older brother, in 1806. He did ride back into Kassel the next month, when Russian troops proved too weak to hold the city; after Napoleon's defeat in the massive battle at Leipzig in October 1813, however, Jérôme knew he could not hold on to Westphalia and fled to France.[2] The month after, the former German ruler of Hesse, the Elector Wilhelm I (1743–1821), returned to Kassel from Prague where he had lived in exile for more than half a decade.[3] The Grimms were in the cheering crowds as the old Hessian ruler and his entourage passed through the city gates. In an article a few years later, Wilhelm called 1813 the "year of redemption."[4] Napoleon's regime had come to an end, the Hessian ruler restored.

The first task of the Elector was to raise an army in the war-weary state where young men had been mobilized to fight in the large Napoleonic armies. Wilhelm I was obliged to call up almost 25,000 men for a battle with the French army whose commander refused to accept the terms set by his European enemies.[5] This final anti-Napoleonic mobilization was the cause to which the Grimm brothers publicly committed themselves in late 1813. In an announcement in an academic journal published in Heidelberg, the Grimms urged readers to sign up as subscribers for a forthcoming rendition of the Middle High German narrative poem *Der Arme Heinrich* and made it known that the generated funds would support voluntary corps.[6] Two of their brothers – the slightly younger Ferdinand and Carl Grimm – joined the Hessian troops;[7] Jacob and Wilhelm worked on an edition of an old German literary text, with the purpose of converting it into to a genuinely popular work, a "*Volksbuch*"[8] – that was to be their contribution. The Medieval-Germanic scholarship would serve a patriotic cause.

As the survey of local conditions in Kassel at the end of the Napoleonic wars indicates, Jacob and Wilhelm Grimm did not exactly live in Germany. They had grown up in Hesse-Kassel, a landgraviate of moderate size in the mosaic of the Holy Roman Empire. During their childhood, the small state was governed by a locally dominant autocrat, the landgrave Friedrich Wilhelm, who, to his great satisfaction, was elevated to the more prestigious position of an Imperial Elector in the Holy Roman Empire in 1803, albeit only three years before that empire was dissolved.[9] With roughly half a million inhabitants, the Electorate of Hesse was neither a negligible statelet nor a European power such as Prussia or Austria. It was overwhelmingly rural and had one significant town, which was Kassel, with a population of around 20,000. Eyewitness accounts from the time did not speak much of the region's prosperity; in the Grimms' lifetime, Hesse was still a land of "indigence in good years, hunger in bad."[10] Nor did it count as a renowned center of artistic or academic culture;[11] over their scholarly and sometime political careers, the Grimms would emerge as two of the most illustrious Hessians of their epoch.[12]

In the preceding century, the landgraviate's primary or at least most well-known "export industry" had been state-organized auxiliary troops,[13] Hessian contingents contracted out by the landgraves to fight campaigns for other powers.[14] A fairly small state, it nonetheless maintained a large and well-trained army, which provided men in the upper strata with career opportunities and the landgraves who collected subsidies from other kingdoms with financial independence from the Hessian estates.[15] In the eighteenth century, there were more soldiers per capita in Hesse than in the famously militaristic Prussia.[16] The practices of this "mercenary state" are known today primarily because almost 20,000 Hessians infamously served in the British war against the American revolutionaries,[17] an extension of a common practice at the time but one that was increasingly criticized. The notorious arrangement with the British brought in large revenues to the landgrave Friedrich II,[18] who died in the year Jacob Grimm was born, in

1785, but damaged the image of the Hessians, at least in the American sphere.

The brothers Grimm thus grew up in a relatively poor German principality governed by a debt-free regime,[19] a landgraviate shaped by the dominating presence of the military rather than by manufacturing, industry, or commerce[20] and ruled by a line of patriarchal autocrats with a declining international reputation; later historians have generally been critical and singled out the early nineteenth-century Hessian Electors' avarice, rigidity, and illiberalism.[21] In this setting, the Grimms were born into a family of local ministers and judicial officials, settled in Hanau, a region with some textile production.[22] Their father, who passed away when they were still children, had served as a local administrative official or district magistrate of the Hessian government, principally responsible for judicial matters in a collection of small towns and villages.[23] Exposed to the threat of downward mobility after the father's early death in 1796, the extended family managed to place the brothers in the main lyceum in the capital and from there they moved to the university in Marburg in 1802 (Jacob) and 1803 (Wilhelm), Hesse's one significant center of higher learning, with about 200 students.[24] In Marburg, hardly as great a university as the nearby Göttingen in Hanover,[25] both brothers studied law, the obvious choice at the time for anyone striving to obtain a position in public administration.[26] The Grimms were thus prepared for administrative and judicial careers in the family tradition and evinced an attitude of regional identification, attached to the landscape and traditions of their childhood, and reverent toward the patriarchal, patrimonial ruler,[27] the "father of the fatherland [*Vater des Vaterlandes*]."[28] When Jacob Grimm spoke about his *Heimat*, his homeland, the historian Johan Huizinga writes, he meant his particular province, electoral Hesse.[29]

For the young brothers Grimm with their focus on future careers in the Electorate, Germany did not exist as one single, integrated nation-state. Nor did they envision such a state in their early years; they would likely have balked at such a massive enterprise of political centralization in the heart of Europe. The Grimms believed that there were Germans and that they all belonged together, but as subjects of affiliated but still independent individual states, each with its own local traditions and specificities. The conquest or domination of one German state by another or military conflicts between German states, the young Jacob Grimm believed, were nothing but a "sin" and "perversion."[30]

In the first decades of the nineteenth century, however, the political order to which the brothers were accustomed was shaken by war, conquest, foreign domination, and multiple territorial reconfigurations. As young men in the era of the drawn-out and devastating Napoleonic wars, the brothers experienced a great deal volatility and uncertainty to which they responded with some degree of melancholic nostalgia.[31] Looking at their personal experience, the most consequential of the period's transformations was the already mentioned Napoleonic occupation of Hesse-Kassel and the surrounding states. After political miscalculations by the Elector Wilhelm I, who had ruled Hesse since the birth year of Jacob Grimm in 1785, Napoleon marched in and seized the country without a single battle in October 1806[32] – Hesse experienced a defeat without war.[33] The Elector himself escaped, first to his brother in Denmark and then to Habsburg Bohemia.[34] On Napoleon's orders, the Electorate was incorporated into the new and larger Kingdom of Westphalia, to be ruled by his inexperienced and compliant 23-year-old brother Jérôme as a model French state.[35] The German population now governed by the French regime would – this was Napoleon's intention[36] – come to see the many benefits of a more modern government. In a letter to his brother, Napoleon confidently envisioned that the subjects of his brother's rule would welcome the blessings of a more enlightened and meritocratic regime: "What the people of Germany impatiently desire is that men without nobility but of genuine ability will have an equal claim upon your favour and advancement, and that every trace of serfdom and feudal privilege ... be completely done away with."[37] The first German state to receive a constitution according to the French template, Westphalia was Napoleon's most ambitious attempt to put a French model of governance on display in German lands.[38]

To demonstrate the virtues of rational, efficient, and liberal French rule, the new Napoleonic regime reorganized local administration, staffed many of its top positions with French civil servants,[39] replaced currency and measurements, abolished privileged access of the nobility to certain government offices,[40] removed special taxes and occupational restrictions on Jews,[41] and promulgated equality before the law and freedom of religion.[42] Yet the administrative and legal transformation of Hesse was ultimately meant to serve its integration into a universal empire of the French, in which unfettered trade and administrative cohesion in Europe would strengthen Napoleonic superiority.[43] This imperialist agenda soon became clear to the German population, which found itself ruled by a French establishment that controlled key civil and military posts. To support the expansive military ambitions of Napoleon, the Westphalian inhabitants were forced to supply new and heavy taxes as well as thousands of men for war, so much so that even Jérôme, the puppet king, eventually pleaded with his brother to restrain the exploitation of the country's wealth and people.[44] Napoleon could speak of the blessings of modernization for the local population but focused on revenues and troops, taxation and conscription;[45] his regime was meant to eliminate feudalism and yet its modernity consisted primarily in the efficiency of its systematic resource extraction.[46]

In 1813, the brothers Grimm welcomed the dissolution of Napoleonic rule in Kassel with relief and even jubilation.[47] For them, an illegitimate regime finally came to an end. They had not, however, been vocal opponents to its rule. On the contrary, Jacob Grimm quickly found steady employment at King Jérôme's court. While Wilhelm Grimm's periods of frail health kept him at home during most of these years, Jacob served quite faithfully and successfully in the Napoleonic administrative system, in which French was a required language.[48] From late 1807 and on, he performed the role as Jérôme's court librarian and was, after a couple of years, also selected as an auditor at the meetings of the king's state council, a position meant to prepare promising young men for a future career in government.[49] By the time Napoleonic troops retreated from Westphalia, Jacob Grimm had served the French king longer than he had the exiled Hessian Elector. Nor was Jérôme's kingship toppled by any popular uprising, despite outbursts of local unrest a couple of times during the French reign, often led by veterans of the Hessian armies, some of whom had fought in America.[50] French rule was never seriously contested and ended because of Napoleonic losses on the battlefield.

Still, the brothers Grimm clearly felt uneasy about French dominance under Jérôme. In an autobiographical piece from 1835, Wilhelm Grimm recalled the initial shock and sense of indignity he felt at the Napoleonic occupation of his hometown about three decades earlier and spoke of his unease at encountering foreign people with foreign ways and hearing a "foreign, loudly spoken language in the street and pathways" of Kassel.[51] The retrospective comment might have been shaped by subsequent experiences and accrued political views, but Kassel did change dramatically under Jérôme Bonaparte: the city swelled from 20,000 to about 30,000 inhabitants as it became the seat of a French court and attracted new French and Francophone residents, only to shed most of this quickly added population after the Napoleonic retreat.[52] No other city, Wilhelm Grimm asserted, had experienced as many dramatic changes during the period.[53] In a similar account of his years as a librarian, Jacob Grimm did not linger on his visceral reaction but noted that the French king of Westphalia, although always friendly in his manner, nevertheless preferred to rely on his French civil servants, something that Jacob found "natural [*natürlich*]."⁵⁴ The French and Germans in Kassel politely conducted government business across cultural and linguistic lines and yet gravitated toward their conationals. These moments of discerned difference in the brothers' autobiographies might seem trivial but point to a political climate in which members of a German-speaking intelligentsia had begun to invoke cultural particularity to complain about the awkwardness and inappropriateness of foreign rule in German lands. The new French political and administrative elite thought they brought a superior and more equitable system of administration that would benefit the subjects, but to the Grimms, this elite clearly acted as a French regime and relegated German culture and language to a subordinate position.

The return of a German prince in 1813 and the abolition of a French-speaking administration did not necessarily satisfy Jacob and Wilhelm Grimm over the long term. With a steadily growing reputation in pan-German academic circles, the brothers would eventually grow quite frustrated in the stagnant environment of Kassel, complain about poor compensation, and resent the Hessian ruler's indifference to their accumulating achievements.⁵⁵ When they were recruited to the University of Göttingen at the end of the 1820s, one of the most prestigious German universities, they chose to relocate and crossed the border between Hesse and Hanover to begin work in a more urbane atmosphere, Jacob as professor and Wilhelm as university librarian. The brothers' expression of enthusiasm for the Elector's return in 1813 was also not motivated by a purely ideological passion for restored German cultural integrity in government. Their various efforts to welcome the Hessian Elector back to Kassel and help rebuild Hessian rule, including its military capacity, may have had something to do with their hopes for undisrupted employment. In the post-Napoleonic Hessian Electorate, Wilhelm Grimm obtained a position as a junior librarian whereas Jacob was dispatched as a secretary for the Hessian diplomatic mission to Paris and Vienna. The brothers Grimm were aspiring civil servants in a mid-size state who, in a moment of tumultuous regime change, sought to secure the favor of the returning traditional elite. As part of that effort, they drew on their scholarly expertise to produce a scholarly work – an edition of *Der arme Heinrich* – to raise at least symbolic funds for a mobilization effort that would let the Elector fulfil his obligations and achieve renewed European recognition as the legitimate ruler of his land.

Yet the sequence of regime changes had affected the political imagination of the brothers Grimm. Jacob and Wilhelm Grimm supported the returning Hessian ruler but did not necessarily share his conception of his role, and their interest in old Germanic works as well as circulating folktales was tied to their commitment to a new, cultural criterion for legitimacy. Having served a French regime in a quickly assembled dual-language kingdom, they had begun to envision a new kind of intimacy between ruler and ruled, one that a returning German prince would not automatically satisfy. In 1813, the Hessian Elector himself thought he was arriving to reclaim his patrimony, of which he had been deprived.[56] Even after the era of the French Revolution and Napoleonic reforms, most hereditary German monarchs viewed states and territories as their personal property, to be augmented or abandoned at will;[57] to the traditional elites, dynastic lineage was still the key to legitimacy.[58] The brothers Grimm, however, had come to believe in the virtues of a cultural fit between a ruler and a people with an independent, historically rich collective life, a people that could not change its inherited character according to the needs or whims of a regime. For German supporters of the French regime, the Kingdom of Westphalia was a "state without a past,"[59] unburdened and forward looking, but precisely this lack of historical and cultural foundation was a problem for the Grimms.

The brothers Grimm thus greeted the return of the Hessian Elector to Kassel with enthusiasm in 1813, but they had, through their experiences and studies during their twenties, already discovered the nation. Sensitized to manifestations of cultural difference under the Napoleonic regime, they saw even mild cultural frictions and separate languages as politically pertinent facts. Interestingly, Jacob Grimm's complaints about Jérôme Bonaparte did not principally take aim at his poor character or incompetence, and Grimm recognized the king's amiable nature and goodwill.[60] The French king, Grimm wrote to his friend the Romanticist author Achim von Arnim (1781–1831), failed to take an interest in the people, in a cultural sense. Jérôme never tried to learn German, Grimm noted, and lacked both "love and knowledge [*Liebe und Erkenntnis*]" of the German people.[61] Symptomatically, Jacob Grimm detested the queen of Westphalia more sharply, a German princess from Württemberg who behaved in an "un-German [*undeutsch*]" manner.[62] This requirement of genuine Germanness worked as a criticism of foreign rule, but Grimm's notion of a close linguistic and cultural connection between government and governed deviated from a purely dynastic or religious legitimation of monarchical rule and could thus potentially be applied to all forms of princely rule, even when the ruler was from a German house. For Grimm, any prince or king in Germany had to exhibit a new kind of proximity to a people and possess knowledge of and show genuine love toward its cultural character. Without such appreciation and affection, the rule would be awkward, brittle, unfitting, and illegitimate.

For the young Grimms, then, vernacular tongues and geographically concentrated cultures ultimately determined the boundaries of legitimate government, a principle that would be anathema to most traditional monarchs, who would have dismissed any linguistic limits to plans of expansion.[63] According to the brothers, the genuine father of the fatherland must speak the language of its inhabitants, and ruler and ruled should hail from the same people. In their implicit, still inchoate view, the exiled Hessian Elector did not exactly return to a scattered bunch of people who could now be properly re-subjected to their rightful patriarch: instead, he returned to a cultural whole with an independent existence, to a German people. The formerly patrimonial ruler appeared legitimate insofar as he stood in a more intimate cultural relationship to the population;[64] access to rule had become reserved for those who credibly represented a German cultural community, for those who could govern as non-alien figures with respect for the people's linguistic and ethnic cohesion. This people who now required some form of political recognition (if not democratic enfranchisement) was conjured, one could add, in the folktale collection that Jacob and Wilhelm compiled during the years of Napoleonic reign, the famous *Children- and Household Tales*. Folk narratives lovingly assembled, widely disseminated, and properly understood, the Grimms would even imply, could help prove and strengthen a cultural identity to which monarchical rule would have to adapt.

Military Mobilization and Folktale Collection

In the euphoria of 1813, Jacob and Wilhelm Grimm put their scholarship in service of the anti-Napoleonic cause; the sales of a translated edition of a medieval German narrative, *der Arme Heinrich*, would help raise funds for the war effort. In the announcement of their edition, Wilhelm Grimm suggested a somewhat strained analogy between the theme of the medieval manuscript and the hardships of the patriotic war against Napoleon. Like the knight in the poem who was to be cured of leprosy by the willing sacrifice of a virgin of modest background who longed for the afterlife, contemporary Hessians could, in this "happy time" of warfare, sacrifice their lives for their fatherland.[65] The preface to the actual volume continued in a similar vein. It recounted the scene of the Hessian men pulling the returning Elector's carriage through Kassel's gates in 1813 and then, a little later, raising their swords in anticipation of battle,[66] out of love and loyalty for the fatherland, unbroken by years of foreign domination; "Hessian blood will fight for the fatherland . . . !"[67]

The Grimms' exercise in patriotic crowdsourcing was not, however, an immediate success, or a success at all. About 150 people signed up to pay for the edition, the majority of them residing in Hesse, and most members of that regionally concentrated group were in some way personally connected to the brothers Grimm. The call to fund German sacrifice was heeded by the editors' social circle.[68] The translation was also delayed and only appeared in the summer of 1815,[69] when the Congress of Vienna had already taken place and the major battles for the future of Europe were over, at least for the time being.

The Grimms' delayed edition of *Der arme Heinrich* was not the only patriotic text published to raise funds for the Hessian war effort during the Wars of Liberation, and not the most rhetorically stirring. A volume entitled *War Poems of the Germans* [*Kriegslieder der Deutschen*] with thirteen poems and a versified dedication to German warriors represented an example of literature more directly in the service of war, from the same Hessian region.[70] Written by a poet with the pseudonym Veit Weber der Jüngere, the songs pursued two primary strategies to strengthen the resolve of the reader. One group of poems invoked values and attitudes that should motivate mobilization against the Napoleonic troops, such as "national pride,"[71] the defense of German freedom, and German imperial unity.[72] Another set was devoted to a sequence of stylized stations of soldierly experience: bittersweet departure from home, exhilarating advance, the evening before battle, the attack, and the victory. By combining the celebration of German ideals with a concatenation of glorified war scenes, the booklet sought to provide the reader with a vocabulary and narrative that rendered individual participation in war meaningful and promising. Like the Grimms' edition, it was a volume intended for the educated reader. A literary motto was attached to each poem, the majority of them drawn from the works of Friedrich Schiller, and one poem called for the defense of the freedom of German scholarship or *Wissenschaft*, celebrating the life of study and student camaraderie to which the educated young soldiers eventually would return.[73]

The Grimms' version of *Der arme Heinrich* and the war poetry of Veit Weber der Jüngere were two parallel efforts to stir the Hessian population and enlist the efforts of patriotic German subjects more broadly to fight the conscription-based French armies, the size of which were unprecedented in European history;[74] the Napoleonic wars inaugurated the age of massive *Volksheeren* [people's armies].[75] The authors also belonged to the same circle in Kassel. Behind the pseudonym Veit Weber the Younger one finds Paul Wigand (1786–1866), an old school friend of Wilhelm Grimm and correspondent of both brothers throughout several decades, who, like Jacob Grimm, worked in the administration under Jérôme Bonaparte[76] and would enjoy a long career as a locally based jurist and legal historian. In late December 1813, just before he left Kassel for Hessian diplomatic service, Jacob Grimm wrote a letter to Wigand, thanking him for the volume of war songs that he had just received as a gift.[77] In his response, Grimm also included the announcement of the brothers' own forthcoming medieval text, with the wish that Wigand subscribe and disseminate the news about the edition. In the final days of the "year of redemption," the two friends exchanged their respective contributions to the wartime propaganda efforts. The swap suggests an equivalency between the projects, and a shared purpose: the struggle against Napoleonic dominance. Jacob and Wilhelm Grimm as well as their friend Paul Wiegand all hoped for a French defeat.

The brothers published other collaborative works during this period, including the first editions of the world-famous *Children's and Household Tales*, the main source of their enduring worldwide reputation. The preparation dates of the two volumes of folktales even framed the Wars of Liberation. The preface to the first volume of tales is dated to October 1812, and hence it was compiled under Jérôme's reign, before Napoleon's defeat in Russia and the unraveling of French imperial power. The preface to the second volume was finished about two years later, in September 1814, and the book appeared in 1815, when the Congress of Vienna was underway; by that time, Napoleon had been vanquished and a quarter century of warfare had come to an end. The timing of the publications had little to do with war, as opposed to the Grimms' edition of *Der arme Heinrich* and their friend Wigand's martial poems. The Grimms' Berlin-based publisher Georg Andreas Reimer's main concern was to release the first volume of tales around Christmas time to ensure solid sales.[78] Compared with the edition of the medieval poem, the *Children's and Household Tales* was from the very beginning a book for families, despite its scholarly apparatus. If the edition of *Der arme Heinrich* had been dedicated to female members of the returning royalty, the Electress of Hesse and her daughter,[79] and was in this way associated with regime change, the *Children's and Household Tales* were dedicated to a friend, Achim von Arnim's wife Elisabeth (or Bettina) von Arnim (1785–1859) and her child, little Johannes Freumund von Arnim.[80] The readers of the folktale collection found themselves in a less political and more intimate, domestic sphere.

The prefaces to the folktale volumes spoke only in vague terms about contemporary turmoil and the end of a traditional world and did not enthusiastically greet the opportunity for sacrificial service to the fatherland. The tone was instead infused with nostalgia for plain German folk life, domestic sociability, peasant festivities, and countryside sceneries – placid vignettes unattached to any specific political occurrences. While Wilhelm Grimm argued that folktale motifs exhibited affinities with grander and more heroic genres such as ancient epics and myths,[81] he believed that the folktales themselves evinced simplicity and innocence of spirit.[82] The gathered tales, Wilhelm also indicated, constituted a fund of national literature in the sense that nothing in the tales had been borrowed from another tradition.[83] While the collection of tales was not a repository of martial values and attitudes, to be evoked with pathos in a popular struggle for recovered national German or local autonomy, they did represent a cultural space to be cherished and protected, the mundane but cozy places around the hearth and the kitchen, typically tended to by women. Initiated sometime in 1807, during the first years of Napoleonic occupation,[84] the collection may seem clearly separated from the events of war and political transformation, and yet they were presented as documents of a quiet, traditional life endangered by unspecified forces of change.

The war effort was in fact not far away from the minds of the brothers in the final phases of editing the first couple of volumes of tales. At the end of his own copy of the first volume, Jacob Grimm added a little note close to Wilhelm's final sentence in his preface. The date of completion for the introductory text, October 18, 1812, Jacob scribbled in the collection, was one year before the victory over Napoleon on the battle field outside Leipzig: "Precisely one year before the Battle at Leipzig [*Gerade ein Jahr vor der Leipziger Schlacht*]."[85] In a minimalist fashion, Jacob Grimm retroactively inscribed the first collection of household tales into the context of the anti-Napoleonic wars, and he even suggested that the folk narratives might be mysteriously connected with the military triumph over the French emperor. This would mean that the modest, the simple, and the neglected for him stood in a relationship to the geopolitical and world historical, an attractive idea to Jacob Grimm who was known for unfailing attention to apparently insignificant minutia and love for the small, non-prestigious, and provincial.[86] The noted coincidence of dates also ascribed to the collection a latent prophetic or even combative quality – the first little volume of gathered stories had anticipated the resurgence of the native over the alien, the German over the French.

Jacob Grimm himself thus indicated a relationship between the *Children's and Household Tales* and the large-scale military and political clashes of his time. Scholars have followed Grimm and long debated the nationalist value of history's most famous folktale collection. With their book, the Grimms certainly promoted a favorable public image of the creative vitality of common people,[87] but the publication and republication of the tales over time successfully established a cultural object of broad appeal to German readers who, with its help, could understand themselves as the collective inheritors of an old folk culture. By presenting the narratives as expressions of a German folk, the Grimms contributed to the plausibility of a unified collective German subject, a national community with a shared tradition. Out of cultural materials of sometimes quite different provenance including a number of tales from French Hugenot families and more aristocratic circles,[88] two bookish aspiring civil servants[89] managed to forge an image of a national rather than exclusively local folkloric literature. By conjuring a reassuring, sociologically underspecified vision of a vaguely rural and artisanal world,[90] they invited readers into a trans-regional, cross-class solidarity.[91] In this way, the Grimms converted brief stories people told now and then, here and there, into supposedly distinctive manifestations of the German people and its putative collective soul.

Again, however, the brothers released their collections of folktales alongside other projects in a broader *ensemble* of nationalist works meant to articulate and promote regional and pan-German self-assertion. It is in the context of a more comprehensive picture of genres that one can identify more precisely the ideological service that the collection started in 1807 performed through its carefully constructed hominess, modesty, simplicity, and innocence. The aim of the rest of this chapter is to reconstruct a set of nationalist genre preferences, or the elements of what one could call the nationalist *literary repertoire*. The combination of genres – folktale and military song, rustic vignette and hortatory announcement – that we have already encountered in the Grimms' and Paul Wigand's contemporary works exemplifies a recurring constellation of textual forms in the early nationalist public sphere. These forms were often-used literary means with which the Grimms and their contemporaries in German lands conjured a German people that had, it was argued, always existed in its particularity but was now in desperate need of preservation and military defense. The nationally defined people possessed a historically deep existence but must protect itself and fight against forces that might well annihilate it – that would be the statement that one could distill from the *combination* of genres that characterized early nationalist literary productivity, the peculiar coexistence of ventriloquized innocence and simplicity (folktales) with calls for struggle and sacrifice (war songs).

For the Grimms, then, military mobilization and folktale collection were to some extent complementary activities, and the first generation of German nationalists as a group coordinated propagandistic rhetoric and folksy narratives. The tales of the brothers Grimm were not an overtly political work on their own, but their distinct ideological meaning becomes visible in a broadened literary context. To understand this vital relationship between genres, however, one must first grasp the particular structure of German nationalist ideology in the Napoleonic period.

National Particularity and Statehood in Napoleonic-Era Nationalism

The Napoleonic period in Germany saw the emergence of a fairly coherent nationalist creed. Its development can be summarized in the following way: under the pressure of French occupation and mass war, an already articulated anthropological vision of humanity as composed of a plurality of culturally particular nations became a tool of rhetorical mobilization for resistance in the hands of intellectuals who began to imagine a new and ultimately popular basis for legitimate political rule; the exercise of power, they demanded, must be appropriately rooted in cultural particularity and assume the form of national autonomy. The early German nationalists, mostly Protestant German philosophers, historians, legal scholars, publicists, and educators, thus fused the Enlightenment idea of self-government as legitimate government with a conception of a naturally differentiated humanity to argue that culturally discernible peoples constituted separate units of rule.[92] Specifically, they reacted to French conquest and Napoleonic hegemony with its combination of administrative modernization and fiscal and military exploitation[93] by formulating a politicized anthropology,[94] a vision of collective self-determination on a cultural and linguistic basis.

Among the small, nationally oriented intelligentsia in various German lands dominated by the French, this rudimentary argument seems to have achieved the status of common sense, with the origins, benefits, and values of cultural plurality variously explained and justified, sometimes with reference to natural evolution, sometimes to divine providence.[95] Jacob and Wilhelm Grimm were highly conscious of the emerging nationalist conversation; they read, commented on, and occasionally crossed paths with some of the most prominent nationalist thinkers of the period, men about a decade or two older than they were. The two young Hessians were peripheral figures in relation to this forming nationalist discourse, and it was in any case hardly a mass-based movement until around the 1830s,[96] but the Grimms absorbed and frequently approved of the ideas and arguments they encountered in pamphlets and essays dedicated to the problem of legitimate modern rule, or more specifically to the question of who was entitled to rule over Germans.

By the end of the Napoleonic wars, Johann Gottfried Herder (1744–1803), whose major works were published in the late eighteenth century, had emerged as the most influential German-language thinker of cultural particularity. Seeking to resist both the authority of misconstrued classical models over a complex and evolving European literature and the perceived superiority of French civilizational achievements uncritically emulated by German aristocracies,[97] Herder had insisted that peoples and their cultures should not be ranked on one scale, according to their approximation of a supposed universal ideal. Instead, all human communities could and should be appreciated in their uniqueness, as distinctive embodiments of a plastic human capacity for development. In contrast to animals, Herder argued, humans were relatively unformed and only acquired definite traits through learning processes. Since humans spread out over the globe and interacted with diverse environments, their traits and skills would always be peculiar to them, molded by specific sets of circumstances, prepared for specific sets of problems, and finally also expressed in specific aesthetic forms.[98] There was, according to Herder, not one kind of excellence to be aspired to by all human beings at all times but competencies, virtues, and sensibilities that had evolved in response to different landscapes over time; "the good," he wrote in the mid-1770s, is "*distributed* across the earth."[99] Herder, one could say with only slight exaggeration, discovered the wondrous multiplicity of nations, peoples, and cultures and often jubilantly celebrated it.[100]

Herder had arrived at a vision of the fundamental elements of humanity, a textured "social ontology"[101] according to which humankind necessarily consisted of a plurality of peoples, each shaped by its own location and history, guided by its local values, and employing its native skills. Such a vision served to disable the application of a single (French) standard of cultural achievement onto a German sociocultural landscape well before French military conquest of German lands. In the resulting nationalized conception of the world, humanity appeared as a multiplicity of groups, each one held together by its shared language and culture rather than its members' political acceptance of some common sovereign power or contractual association with one another.[102] Human beings in the abstract, somehow untouched by a local geography and climate, beyond all historical contexts, did not exist; there were, Herder believed, only ever culturally individualized realizations of humanity.

As French military dominance extended over larger and larger territories after Herder's death, and Napoleon dispatched the old political arrangements of the Holy Roman Empire in 1806 to consolidate numerous German statelets into larger vassal kingdoms or satellite states, some educated Germans believed they faced a powerful wave of centralization and regimentation; all the world would be remade, it seemed, in the image of French rule. Under these conditions, even writers who had initially greeted the French Revolution as an inspiring liberation began to invoke the irreducibly national composition of humanity and give it a hardened political application. The cultural and linguistic contours of humanity, they now insisted, imposed constraints on legitimate rule, and French control over all of Europe was neither desirable nor viable. The key conceptual move consisted in the articulation of cultural particularity, *Eigenthümlichkeit*, and political independence, *Selbstständigkeit*. The primary task of each people, the Jena-based professor Heinrich Luden (1778–1847) pronounced in his well-visited lectures on the study of history (published in 1810), was to "to retain its independence [*Selbstständigkeit*], to remain free and autonomous from the rule of any other people, in order to retain the possibility of freely developing its particular [*eigenthümliche*] character."[103] In Luden's view, some form of universal imperial domination would run counter to the innermost mission of each historical community and consequently had to be resisted. The nation was not just a unique cultural community; it represented an ideal unit of rule. This politicization of cultural communities may have affected the way in which they were conceptualized: whereas Herder could understand cultural development and learning within but also across human groups as a ceaseless "Protean" process[104] in which traits, skills, and expressions flourished and vanished, the nationalists of the Napoleonic period assumed a greater degree of communal closure around a more stable set of shared traits, for the reason that culture had now become the ground of territorial and political claims. *Eigentümlichkeit*, particularity, they believed, had to be more sharply defined, and nobody would define it with greater precision than the grammarian Jacob Grimm.

The historian Heinrich Luden was well known as an opponent of French rule; writing in his exile in Russia, the Prussian statesman Baron von Stein (1757–1831) singled out Luden in a strategy paper as a dependable and popular scholar to be deployed in an anti-French public relations battle, along with other publicly recognized thinkers such as the theologian and nationalist preacher Friedrich Schleiermacher (1768–1834).[105] The historian Luden, however, was far from the only one to argue for the political salience of cultural distinctiveness. In an 1813 pamphlet that Jacob Grimm praised in a letter to his friend Paul Wigand,[106] the Munich-based reform-oriented jurist Anselm von Feuerbach (1775–1833), later known among other things for a book on the wild child Kaspar Hauser, narrated the course of events in Europe from the French Revolution to the present and noted the fragility of Napoleon's achievement. When peoples that were linguistically, culturally, and morally different nonetheless were forced into political unity, Feuerbach wrote, the result was a composite prone to dissolution.[107] Here again one can discern the principle of a necessary congruence between historical and cultural community and state extension, in the negative form of a reaction to overextended French rule about to lose its grip over the peoples of Europe.

This emphasis on the cultural distinctiveness of peoples was not only a matter of pragmatic convenience, as if rule simply became more cumbersome for all parties if conducted over cultural and linguistic rifts. It was, for some prominent voices, an urgent question of national survival, at least during the years of apparent French invincibility. Some argued that Napoleon's victories and the rule of his family did not just constitute evidence of foreign supremacy and humiliation to German states but would over time mean the complete extinction of German culture and therefore had to be resisted by the entire people. In an 1810 historical survey of the persistence of vanquished peoples, "About the Means of Maintaining the Nationality of Defeated Peoples," the Göttingen historian of antiquity Arnold Heeren (1760–1842), another figure noticed by the Prussian statesman Baron von Stein, claimed that peoples dominated by mightier powers frequently vanished from the records of history.[108] Disappearance was a terrible but realistic prospect. To determine the possibility of averting this fate, Heeren listed some of the defining features of nations and then assessed which ones were particularly vulnerable and which ones it would be most damaging to lose. A people's loss of its own language would be fatal, Heeren claimed, and lead to its dissolution. Luden echoed this sentiment in his lectures: the loss of independence for a people would surely threaten its particularity, expressed in religion, traditions, art, science, and law, which in turn would "annihilate [*vernichtet*]" the people; it would simply cease to exist.[109]

The poet, essayist, and historian Ernst Moritz Arndt (1769–1860), who was directly employed by Baron von Stein[110] and probably both the earliest and the most notorious champion of radical anti-French sentiment,[111] envisioned a similar fate for Germans: French rule, he stated in an 1813 pamphlet on the river Rhine as a border, would lead to the "effacement and extermination [*Auslöschung und Ausrottung*]" of German cultural particularity.[112] Jacob Grimm read Arndt's Rhine tract with approval in early January 1814 and wrote to Wilhelm that it contained much that was "right and true," although he did not consider it exhaustive from a scholarly point of view.[113] Like Arndt, Grimm believed that Germans needed to reconquer the left bank of the Rhine, but not primarily for military-strategic reasons, to fortify the defense of Germany, but because the region was simply not French. The population, Grimm claimed with definitiveness, "is and speaks German [*weil es deutsch ist und spricht*]."[114]

The professors and writers cited earlier – Luden, Heeren, Feuerbach, Arndt – saw cultural particularity and statehood as entwined. For this group born in the 1760s and 1770s, cultural and linguistic nationhood required and justified self-government, and the loss of independent statehood would entail cultural impoverishment or even cultural death. For some early nationalists, the shared worry about the menace of national erasure inspired nothing less than profound desperation. In his twelfth lecture in the *Addresses to the German Nation* held at the Academy of Sciences in Berlin during the early years of French occupation in 1807 and 1808, the philosopher Johann Gottlieb Fichte (1762–1814) discussed the German nation's means of persistence under foreign rule and argued that literature alone could not possibly sustain Germanness – only an independent state structure could.[115] A permanent alien occupation, Fichte predicted, would diminish German literature, for authors write to shape public consciousness, even to exercise a kind of rule in the realm of the intellect, and a language unconnected to a state would decay in public status, prove less attractive to authors eager to determine a shared future, and eventually deteriorate and perish.[116] Authorship could thus not be sustained without the promise of substantial moral influence guaranteed within a resilient political structure. In fact, Fichte continued, a nation shamefully unable to maintain its self-determination might very well give up its language, too, and simply merge with its evident masters.[117] This prospect of permanent political submission and collective cultural and linguistic extinction, however, must fill individuals with dread, because only the nationally defined people with its language and distinctive way of life held the promise of longevity, a kind of earthly eternity.[118] Individuals may die, Fichte argued, but a people as a whole appears to preserve the life form that shapes every person and to which he or she also contributes; it functions as the vessel of the individual's legacy. The erosion of national particularity and the effective dissolution of a distinct people under long-term foreign rule would thus deprive the members of a nation of their sense of futurity, of the permanence and meaning of their deeds and their legacy, causing them to look at the world in disgust and wish they would never have been born.[119] Like Arndt and other nationalists, Fichte expressed a fear of imminent cultural extinction. Jacob Grimm read Fichte's lectures with enthusiasm and, in a letter to Wilhelm, he wrote that a popular version of the lectures ought to be published for as broad an audience as possible.[120] To his mentor Friedrich Carl von Savigny (1779–1861), he declared that Fichte's *Addresses* was one of finest works ever written.[121]

In the Napoleonic era, then, an already established, Herderian vision of an internally plural humanity, once devised to challenge French and hence aristocratic cultural prestige, became more sharply politicized under the pressure of French conquest and rule. To this fairly small academic elite of politicized and radicalized Herderians,[122] humanity was not just variously embodied and hence naturally divided into distinct communities, but each community had the obligation and the right to ensure its continuity and resist its own demise. The nationalist writers of the period from 1806 to 1815 transmitted, in their tracts, lectures, and pamphlets, a more narrowly focused and rigidly instrumentalized anthropology, a politicized social ontology. Their concept of the nation itself represented an "arming of culture."[123] The core premise, inherited from cultural debates at end of the eighteenth century, was that humanity existed only in the form of a diverse ensemble of culturally particular peoples, and the shared discovery in the early nineteenth century, born of military and political collapse, was that such peoples were vulnerable and under threat and must defend themselves aggressively. Nationalists believed that nations could not possibly be invented on the spot, but that they could and must be protected.

This formula was explicitly articulated in the tract of another Herderian, the Prussian-born educator Friedrich Ludwig Jahn (1778–1852), mostly known for heading a nationalist gymnastic movement that spread across German lands, often eyed suspiciously by princes. Jahn deemed it impossible to engineer the qualities and virtues that characterized a particular people. Such qualities were instead always the result of the people's historically drawn-out and quiet process of coming together into eventual unity: "No thousand-year-old oak," he wrote, "ever grew in a hothouse [*Keine tausendjährige Eiche erwuchs im Treibhaus*]."[124] In fact, no missionary religion, no reformation, no great cause whatsoever could ever advance without allying itself with the energies of an already extant people. Jahn stood for an ethnicized approach to the world, in which political projects initiated by great individuals were dependent on the slowly and spontaneously evolved peoples who resolved to support them; Mohammed would have been nothing without the power of the Arab people, and Luther's achievement was enabled by the release of collective German energies.[125] Yet Jahn's 1810 tract *Deutsches Volksthum*, which outlined in greater detail than any of the writings of his contemporaries the appropriate regional divisions, legal arrangements, educational institutions, cultural celebrations, and linguistic conventions for a German future, clearly stated that nationality could be preserved through conscious organization.[126] Jahn's writings thus called for an active, even militarized, defense of a spontaneously evolved cultural substance. Both Wilhelm and Jacob Grimm met Jahn on some occasions, read his work approvingly, followed his activities, but thought him a little voluble. They were, in the end, primarily scholars, whereas Jahn was one of the most prominent organizers and propagandists of early German nationalism.[127]

This review of Fichte, Jahn, Arndt, Luden, and the others members of the small German nationalist intelligentsia reveals a nationalist pattern of argumentation. They all espoused the premise of a valuable plurality of distinct and bounded peoples but also pointed to the fragility and susceptibility of individual nations to military conquest and subjugation and called for their forceful defense. This line of reasoning implied a novel conception of political legitimacy. To this loose group of nationalists, the cultural character of a people in effect constituted a test of aptness for any political rule; regimes had to be culturally fitted to nations. This did not exactly entail a commitment to the active participation in politics by all citizens of a state, to full-fledged popular sovereignty and democracy; however, the nationalist rejection of foreign conquest and occupation relied on a vision of cultural consonance between the nationally defined people and its political elites. Governing competence or dynastic genealogy had to make room for a new criterion of legitimate rule, namely the shared nationhood of ruler and ruled. This greater accommodation of the people understood as a historically particular collective looks like an advance over traditional conceptions of royal sovereignty, but the emerging democratization of political discourse was entangled with an increasing demonization of a collective enemy. Nationalist propaganda often demanded a greater degree of representation of the German people in politics, but the political egalitarianism was coupled with an incitement of a general, popular hatred pitted against the collective enemy – a genuine folk hatred.

The entwinement of more inclusive politics and mobilization of collective affect was embodied in the figure of Ernst Moritz Arndt, the most widely disseminated nationalist author of the Napoleonic era, and probably one of the most prolific. His pamphlets, among them the February 1813 statement on the task of a Prussian militia, was printed in tens of thousands of copies,[128] and his poem "What Is the German's Fatherland? [*Was ist des deutschen Vaterland?*]," a lyrically virtuosic argument for German unification, came to epitomize the period's literary production.[129] Arndt excelled at the rhetoric that Paul Wigand and Wilhelm Grimm dabbled in, namely the call to Germans to do battle against French armies in the name of their shared national culture. However, Arndt did not just oblige his Prussian employers and encourage Germans to resist and fight the French emperor. Realizing that German rulers were pressured by massive, conscription-based Napoleonic armies and somewhat reluctantly had to drum up patriotic support in the larger population, he followed up the call for militia mobilization, approved by members of the Prussian administration, with further pamphlets on the importance of a national constitution that would allow all estates, including the peasantry, an expanded role in government. Arndt linked support for a more comprehensive enlistment of male Germans, a vision that never really came to pass,[130] to the redistribution of political influence away from the aristocracy and the clergy and toward the peasantry and bourgeoisie,[131] partly inspired by a Swedish model;[132] he was born in Swedish Pomerania, the son of an independent peasant.[133] He first made language the overriding criterion of political membership, helped define fellow nationals of all groups and classes as loyal and honorably masculine combatants in war,[134] and finally argued that readiness for sacrifice in battle entitled larger numbers of people not just to partake in the previously aristocratic reserve of military glory but to participate in the political process. Warfare on an unprecedented scale should also bring the nation closer to some form of representative government.[135] If military violence had to involve the entire people, then politics must, too;[136] the soldier should be a citizen, the citizen a soldier.[137]

Arndt combined his call for maximal mobilization of Germans, to be rewarded with expanded political participation, with a dark image of the French as an enemy nation. Political inclusion was thus tied to a more comprehensive form of national closure and stricter territorial and cultural exclusion.[138] For Arndt, nation had to stand against nation, people against people. In an infamous pamphlet from 1813 entitled "On Folk Hatred," Arndt argued that the natural and mild disinclination that conationals with a common culture and common language typically feel toward the character of another culture should be sharpened in a time of war and assume the form of collective hate, of *Volkshaß*.[139] Only such a shared passion with its galvanizing effect upon people would ensure a vigorous popular resistance to the military enemy.[140] In Arndt's view, the age of mass warfare inaugurated by Napoleon required mass affect. Every able man should take up arms to fight the populous foreign army, and every German national should be roused out of slumber and actively direct hatred not just toward a French imperial regime but the French as a collective.

Hate, however, would not just incite people and make them ready for active resistance to the enemy. As an enhancement of the natural but latent aversion of one culture to another, hate would render regrettably fluid cultural borders more permanent;[141] Arndt was drawn to hatred because it could serve to rigidify separations. Due to its conserving nature, the affect of hatred solved a pressing problem for Arndt, a problem that he shared with many of his nationalist peers, namely the perceived fragility of human cultural plurality.[142] Luden, Heeren, Fichte, and others believed that humankind was naturally differentiated and diversely realized, and yet particularities that comprised it were also always under threat and could face extinction – this was a central conundrum of early German nationalism. Collectively felt hatred would, Arndt believed, serve to fortify the cultural boundaries by making the people as a whole more unyielding, more determined to hold on to what they were and reject what was foreign: "proud and noble hatred" would "separate and hold apart" that which was "diverse and unequal."[143] In this way, folk hatred would stabilize the plural composition of humanity and do so in a way that would not require policing by a coercive agent. In 1813, Arndt stood for the most radical version of a politicized, indeed militarized Herderian social ontology. The defense of the people's distinctiveness had to be ensured by the people itself, by means of a collective affective barrier.

All nationalists of the period devoted themselves to the defense of national particularity, the forced erasure of which supposedly would deprive the people of its memory, identity, and orientation and despotically flatten the rich cultural topography of the world. In response to this challenge, Fichte urged the construction of a national apparatus of mass education,[144] which would over time strengthen and unify Germans as Germans, and Jahn introduced a long list of institutional and ritual supports for German peoplehood. Arndt, as we have seen, propagated popular hatred. These three projects appear as functionally equivalent; they were all meant to safeguard German particularity and, by extension, human cultural plurality. Arndt's aggressive solution differed mostly in that it required much less of an organizational, infrastructural investment. Incitement of popular hatred directed against the imperialist enemy was a quicker fix than educating all Germans in the Fichtean manner or structuring a shared culture according to Jahn's plan. The question with relation to the Hessian brothers Grimm, however, is what role their early philological project played in the nationalist imagination, alongside proposals for comprehensive institution building (Fichte), organized public life (Jahn), and collective hate (Arndt). What was the ideological meaning and purpose of a collection of humble folktales in the era of continental war and belligerent nationalism? How did the folktales, so carefully framed by the brothers as modest, natural, and innocent, fit into the structure of early nationalist ideology?

Folk Hatred – and Folktales

Jacob and Wilhelm Grimm read and discussed Fichte, Arndt, Jahn, and other nationalist authors, all of whom were a little older than they were, born in the 1760s and 1770s rather than the 1780s. They were familiar with the nationally oriented rhetoric of their time, had read the key nationalist pamphlets of the era, and occasionally wrote opinion pieces themselves on the necessary defense of German culture in journals of the era, most notably the *Rheinischer Merkur*.[145] Both brothers certainly wanted the French to retreat from Kassel and depart from all German lands, but they were young scholars and antiquarians, not publicists or pamphleteers, and their writings were not exactly expressions of passionate or strategic hatred. During his long work trips to France, Jacob Grimm reported that he wished to leave Paris as soon as he could and he did express a strong aversion to French law,[146] but the propagation of hatred seems like it would have been an alien endeavor to him, an excessive rhetoric, although he understood that hatred may be a reaction to oppression or "pressure [*Druck*]" by a foreign power.[147] What, then, could be the link between the nationalist vision of comprehensive mobilization and even collective hatred and the folktales gathered by the brothers Grimm throughout the period of French reign?

The political endeavors of Arndt and others were quite closely connected to the more scholarly efforts of the Grimms because the latter obligingly gave substance to key elements in the nationalist argumentation. The infinitely valuable collective particularity that nationalists like Luden, Arndt, and Fichte invoked must, at some point and in some way, also be exemplified. The distinctive ways of being, folk traditions, values, and expressions that defined the people and must be defended so vigorously also had to be demonstrated to exist – and to exist *prior to* the enterprise of an organized political and military defense of the nation. The fundamental assertion of collective cultural particularity required plausible documentation. This was the self-appointed task of Jacob and Wilhelm Grimm: their early collections and scholarly publications served to substantiate the politically indispensable claim to cultural and historical *Eigenthümlichkeit*.

The brothers and their peers among scholars reoriented humanistic study around the value of cultural particularity, or "own-ness," to use a more literal translation of *Eigenthümlichkeit*. Wilhelm Grimm very frequently invoked particularity in his texts,[148] and it was a more pervasive term in Jacob Grimm's works than the more famous concept *Volksgeist*, the people's spirit.[149] In an ambitious review of Old Norse literature published in an academic journal some five years after the end of the Napoleonic wars, Wilhelm Grimm articulated the broad Herderian shift toward nation-ness that he and his fellow German scholars had already performed: the purpose of humanistic study was to discern and preserve national particularity, he argued, rather than to perpetuate a shared European, classical heritage and hold it up as a universal normative model for all human self-cultivation. The "task of education," he wrote, "is not to assemble a collection of all retrievable samples of excellence" but instead "to promote the natural development of our own particularity [*Eigenthümlichkeit*]."[150] The study of the ancients was the key to self-understanding, Wilhelm Grimm admitted in his programmatic text, but because people remained shaped by their own origins and historical paths, scholars must turn away from a pantheon of decontextualized templates of classical greatness and instead fix their attention on the unfolding peculiarity of their very own culture. In his article, then, Wilhelm Grimm captured the nationalization of humanistic study and Germanic philology's focus on native particularity, but he also rendered his discipline compatible with nationalist politics, which depended for its plausibility on the existence of a historically anchored way of life, a national specificity.

Broadly speaking, nationalist propagandists such as Arndt worked in tandem with less obviously propagandistic scholars such as the Grimms, because the organized political and military defense of the people in its cultural particularity needed proof of that posited particularity, the spontaneous and distinctive cultural life of that people. There were certainly concrete ways in which Grimms' *Children's and Household Tales* figured on the periphery of a nationalist campaign, but the very notion of a document of authentic folk life alone occupied a crucial place in the nationalist logic of ideas. Early nationalism depended on scholarly validation, some robust supply of evidence for the people's ongoing, historical life. Such evidence could come in multiple forms, and early nationalism was inspired and sustained by a range of activities undertaken by amateur collectors, enthusiasts, and academics.[151] Philologists compiled dictionaries of living languages and dialects; ethnographers observed folk customs and festivities; folklorists transcribed and anthologized circulating songs, tales, and legends; literary scholars edited, updated, and published ancient or not-so-ancient manuscripts; collectors gathered rustic artifacts and put them on display, and so on. As Miroslav Hroch has pointed out, scholarly activities typically predated the formation of nationalist mass movements;[152] they constructed an object that an audience could then cherish, identify with, and swear to protect. Networks of scholars thus helped establish in an objective-seeming fashion the enduring and autonomous life of the national people, and the reality and distinctiveness of its expressions. This supposedly already well-defined collective constituted the all-important "pre-political ground" that justified the struggle for nationally circumscribed political power.[153] Early nationalism, one could claim, was a very scholarly ideology, even an ideology with a predilection for the literary; it relied for its persuasive force on collections of songs, tales, customs, legal relics, and all sorts of other material that rendered the national character legible.

The nationalist creed articulated by such figures as Arndt or Jahn thus reached out for ethnographic and historical scholarship: the political demand for national self-rule required a preexisting nation, and this nation and its history had to speak and display itself in compilations of rustic tales. The task and the achievement of the scholars who then captured the nation in its expressions were neither overtly political nor completely unpolitical but served a function in the nationalist argumentation. The scholarly projects took place in a pre-political space, as they furnished evidence of the nation's prior existence that could then be invoked as the basis for legitimate political rule. The Grimms' book of tales was not a pamphlet meant to rouse or amplify the anger of the people against a foreign occupation force, but it would be wrong to view it simply as a volume for the Christmas market, although it was certainly published with reading parents in mind and several of their friends and acquaintances greeted it as a perfect gift for children.[154] The collection instead served its political purpose precisely by *not* focusing on the explicit political consciousness of the nationally defined people but instead on its cultural productivity – its modest, simple, innocent, delightful, historically anchored communal life.

Were the *Children's and Household Tales* ever perceived as nationalist by contemporary readers? Not so much by the brothers' circle of friends, who treated the book as an anthology of stories for children and even faulted the brothers for having published too scholarly a collection, with too many unsuitable tales, but without the appeal of added visual imagery.[155] Over time, many of the canny suggestions from the early readers would also be implemented. After the success of the shortened English-language version published in London in 1823, scholarly notes were shed, brutal tales edited or omitted, and pictures added; the book may have been culturally German but the media strategy was imported from the English book market.[156] Yet the book's early publication history still circumstantially suggests that it participated in a broader nationalist project. The first publisher of Grimms' folktale collection, the Berlin-based Georg Andreas Reimer, was perhaps the premier nationalist publisher at the time of Napoleonic occupation and the Wars of Liberation. He supported the anti-Napoleonic struggle personally[157] and entertained connections with many of the most prominent nationalist writers. Reimer was a very close friend of the nationalist theologian Friedrich Schleiermacher, provided living quarters to Ernst Moritz Arndt once the nationalist writer had lost his professorship in Greifswald under French rule, and his house served as a gathering place for circles of German patriots.[158] Reimer also brought out several of the era's most influential nationalist statements, among them Arndt's poems and pamphlets such as "Catechism for German Soldiers" as well as a book on German gymnastics by Friedrich Ludwig Jahn.[159] A further relevant project housed by Reimer's company was the journal *The Prussian Correspondent*,[160] edited by a series of figures such as Schleiermacher and Achim von Arnim, and partly dedicated to war reporting; Wilhelm Grimm read it with interest and also contributed an anonymous report from Kassel in 1813.[161]

During the beginning of the nineteenth century, Reimer thus emerged as an important German-language publisher on nationalist topics,[162] and his receptivity to the folktale collection indicates its compatibility with the Romantic-nationalist profile of the catalogue as a whole. However, the

Grimms did not exactly approach Reimer because his positions harmonized with theirs; it was the writer Achim von Arnim who initiated the contact,[163] and Reimer published Arnim's tales and songs, along with works by Jean Paul, Ludwig Tieck, and the Schlegel brothers, all famous Romanticist authors. The mere co-presence of several different genres – Arndt's pamphlets and Grimms' tales – in the catalogue of one single publishing house does not imply any essential interconnection between them, some obvious alliance between the nationalist pamphlet, on the one hand, and the collection of folk materials, on the other. The correspondence between Grimms and Reimer was almost entirely pragmatic; they discussed, and eventually bickered, about adequate compensation.[164]

The constellation of complementary nationalist genres published by Reimer, however, did reappear in the works of more than one author. In the decisive year of 1813, Jahn published a succession of pamphlets written with the intent to marshal German forces against the French. "*An das deutsche Volk*," for example, exhorted all German men to take up arms against the "country-thief [*Länderräuber*]" and "people-annihilator [*Völkertilger*]" Napoleon.[165] Jahn also compiled an anthology of German "martial songs [*Wehrlieder*]" to encourage a more compact general resistance against foreign domination;[166] the first item in the anthology was unsurprisingly his former teacher Ernst Moritz Arndt's poem on the border-setting, boundary-drawing German language.[167] Yet Jahn was also interested in less propagandistic genres of literature. Already in his 1810 tract on national organization, he had called for collections of folktales and legends, even a "German *Thousand and One Nights*."[168] After Wilhelm Grimm had met Jahn in Kassel in March 1814, he related to his brother Jacob in a letter that the guest liked their *Children's and Household Tales* very much and that Jahn was planning a peacetime journey through German lands, all for the purpose of writing a history of German legends. Jahn, Wilhelm Grimm wrote, "knows the ways of the people well and is familiar with many legends and enjoyed our tales [*Er kennt die Sitten des Volks gut und weiß viele Sagen und hat Freude an unsern Märchen gehabt*]."[169]

A quick sequence of pamphlets and hortatory songs during wartime followed by a postwar project of folktale collection – this was also the pattern followed by the proponent of folk hatred, the publicist and poet Arndt. In the year 1813 alone, Arndt wrote a steady stream of pamphlets and gained the reputation of being the most strident anti-Napoleonic writer, an evangelist of German nationhood.[170] A survey of Arndt's places of publication for his war poetry in 1813 and 1814 shows that he sought to print and disseminate his nationalist songs at the shifting focal point of current military and political events[171] – as a publicist, he strove for maximum impact. After the Wars of Liberation, however, Arndt began to moderate his rhetoric of hate-filled repudiation.[172] In the period after the war, he also published a collection of folktales with Reimer in Berlin. In the preface to his 1818 collection, Arndt cited entirely personal motivations for his work.[173] He had lost nearly all his books during a transport across the Baltic Sea and suddenly deprived of his personal library, he turned to his memories of stories heard in his childhood and youth in Pomerania. The tales were not all of the fairy tale–type made paradigmatic by the Grimms, but often samples of the more locally rooted genre of the legend; even some of Arndt's obviously fantastic tales mentioned particular place names such as a village on Rügen.[174] Yet the book as a whole, and the further collection of tales Arndt published much later, was partly meant to advertise his self-image as a grounded man of the common people, who had grown up among modest peasants.[175]

Arndt's poem "What Is the German's Fatherland?" is perhaps the only poem to have survived the period of the Wars of Liberation, and it now serves to epitomize German nationalist poetry; most other similar publications from the period have, unsurprisingly, disappeared from view. The Grimms' *Children's and Household Tales* remains one of the most widely translated and disseminated works of literature, and it has certainly marginalized other German folktale collections. Yet the Grimms' little known publications in support of resistance to French rule as well as the forgotten folkloric projects of nationalist propagandists such as Jahn and Arndt suggest that nationalist authorship in the second decade of the nineteenth century was defined by a particular *spectrum* of genres. The proponents of nationhood and folk hatred, *Volksthum* (Jahn) and *Volkshass* (Arndt), set out to collect and transcribe folk narratives that could preserve and display the cultural presence of a German people invoked in the pamphlet literature. The more consistently dedicated scholars of folk literature and its connection to ancient mythic materials (Jacob and Wilhelm Grimm) occasionally linked their projects more directly to military mobilization, such as in the case of *Der arme Heinrich*. The constellation of different genres – war poem and folktale, aggressive pamphlet and local legend – appeared across several authorships and indicates a connection between genres of military mobilization and genres of cultural substantialization.

Early nationalism, one could say, spoke with two voices, both equally important. Wilhelm Grimm could celebrate the willingness of Hessian men to take up arms and do battle with imperial forces but also portray the quiet everyday life around the hearth where old stories would be told and retold. The pathetic and the martial could be combined with the ethnographic and antiquarian, although not in one and the same text, but distributed over genres expressive of different affects and attitudes. The supposed addressee of Paul Wigand's war poems was the educated young man excited by the prospect of military advances and victories, and the audience of the folktales gathered and collected by the Grimms around the same time was the traditional household, the family. Yet the genres belonged together as two strategies in the nationalist discourse. Arndt, Jahn, and Wigand were practitioners of the poetry and rhetoric of war and liberation, whereas Jacob and Wilhelm Grimm were devoted to the accumulation of folkloric materials. The propagandistic efforts of mobilization for the defense of national political autonomy stood in a relationship with the scholarly or semi-scholarly documentation of national cultural particularity in the form of legends and tales. Nationalism existed in the form of two connected clusters of values, articulated in two groups of genres: calls for military mobilization, martial sacrifice, and collective hatred, on the one hand, and collections of folk stories and vignettes of an endearingly simple traditional life, on the other.

The Nationalization of the Fairy Tale

The folktale collection of the Brothers Grimm was not an overtly nationalist work, prepared to stir fellow Hessians or Germans into immediate action, but it did occupy a definite place in the collective nationalist argumentation of the Napoleonic period. The book was meant to verify the existence of a particular people, to substantialize the notion of a native culture perceived to be under threat, alive and available yet vulnerable and in need of protection. This oblique but ideologically essential work of the collection for a wider nationalist project was discernible in Wilhelm Grimm's two prefaces, one from 1812 and one from 1814. Taken together, the two prefatory remarks established the tales as a genre that was both collective and indigenous. The collection, Grimm claimed, contained no individual voice but only the expressions of a whole people, and no foreign elements but only the expressions of a particular nation. *The Children's and Household Tales* was not the only or the first collection of folktales, but the brothers Grimm most resolutely nationalized the genre by framing it as the expression and joint property of a fatherland.

The first, 1812 introduction related how the tales had been sustained through a communal practice of oral storytelling sheltered by household spaces, and it attributed to the tales the qualities of purity, simplicity, innocence, and naiveté, all of which would be spoiled by an overly sophisticated treatment.[176] Wilhelm Grimm presented the tales as a non-individual artifact separated from any literary education, an authentic representation of non-elite cultural life. The traits ascribed to the tales also indirectly referred to the character of the national collective that told them: the tales were uncomplicated, straightforward, modest, simple – all terms from the lexicon of authenticity. The second text, from 1814, shifted the focus slightly to speak more explicitly of the tales as a people's poetry, *Volksdichtung*, and insisted not only on their soundness and vitality but also on their connection to deeper layers of specifically German or Germanic myth.[177] The tales were, Wilhelm asserted, German both in their origin and their development and nothing in them had been "borrowed" from adjacent national traditions.[178]

Scholars and critics have pointed out that the Grimm brothers acknowledged that the genre was not solely a German one and that the folktales of this world did not all spring from a German source. In the 1812 preface, Wilhelm wrote that no people could forgo fairy tales. In the context of all of the brothers' many books, the *Children's and Household Tales* even stands out as a work without the word "German" in the title.[179] In the long list of Jacob Grimm's works, which includes *German Legends*, *German Grammar*, *German Legal Antiquities*, and *German Mythology*, this looks like a conspicuous absence, almost a concession: the tales could not really be called German. Wilhelm Grimm's insistence that the tales had been drawn from a native tradition did not, to him, imply that the genre as a whole was exclusively German, for national particularity or *Eigenthümlichkeit* was not the same as singularity. The collected tales were authentically German yet not incomparable with folk narratives from other regions. On the contrary, the tales were necessarily *comparable*, because the particularity of the national and the German could only emerge through a series of contrasts with similar products from other national-cultural spheres. An ancient and therefore collective literary work was typically "both similar and dissimilar [*sowohl ähnlich als unähnlich*]" to works from other cultures and precisely for this reason "particular [*eigenthümlich*]."[180] According to the Grimms, national particularity must be understood as a discernible and profoundly valuable *inflection* of a shared human culture, not an incommensurable quality. Throughout his career as a scholar, Jacob Grimm would therefore welcome volumes with tales in other languages and still maintain the peculiarly national character of their own collection, since each national culture occupied a space in the ensemble of nations in the world.[181] In his prefaces, Wilhelm Grimm also discussed collections that had appeared in other European languages, such as French and Italian, and assessed them with varying degrees of criticism;[182] the genre was not everywhere the same, but similar stories did belong to many nations regardless of their perceived civilizational status, including African peoples.[183] Each nation possessed its very own tales, or rather its very own *versions* of tales, unmistakably national and yet not entirely alien to others; the fairy tales exhibited national specificity, but the genre was not bound to one culture only, as evidenced, perhaps, by the enduring worldwide success of the Grimms' tales.[184]

Wilhelm Grimm thus presented the folktales as samples of a world genre while maintaining the absolute national authenticity of the collection. The tales were German, neither fabricated with deliberateness by single authors with education and ambition nor shaped by any appreciation for a superior foreign creativity. Instead, they were the expression of a people understood as a culturally autonomous whole. This position has naturally come under an enormous amount of criticism in the scholarship on the Grimms. Commentators have pointed out that a whole group of tales came from France, inadvertently smuggled into the collection by informants with a Huguenot background, and it is clear beyond any doubt that Wilhelm Grimm edited, revised, and honed the tales, creating a smoother, more polished fairy-tale style in the process.[185] Contrary to the programmatic prefatory statements, the tales were in fact both cross-national and works of deliberate authorial craft.

What interests us here, however, is precisely the collection's indispensable role in the nationalist argument of the first two decades of the nineteenth century. When Wilhelm Grimm described the tales as expressions of a culturally and linguistically contoured people; an inheritance untouched by dominant foreign influences; and an entirely simple, modest, non-manipulative speech, he delivered to a modern national political project the image of an already existing people, enclosed in its own cultural life. The tales were the natural speech of the nation and as such evidence of its very existence. It was this submission of a literary proof of peoplehood that satisfied an inherent requirement of nationalist ideology, perhaps its most central need, namely that a people had to exist and had to have evolved autonomously and spontaneously rather than been conjured or constructed from above. The autonomous cultural unity that Wilhelm Grimm portrayed in the prefaces was the scholar's gift to the German nationalist project of the early nineteenth century; Grimm supplied literary proof of the pre-political ground for national self-rule.

The close association of the people with popular tales was not an invention of the brothers Grimm; it had been established long before the end phase of the Napoleonic era. The narrative of how the link came to be forged begins, again, with Johann Gottfried Herder. He was the writer who, in a sequence of texts from the 1770s, most decisively and influentially effected the relocation of prestige away from the refined and norm-conforming poetical products of a literary elite toward previously neglected artifacts of the common people.[186] Most fundamentally, Herder revised the cultural vocabulary by converting the raw, vulgar, and unrestrained – attributes associated with the people – into the vital, expressive, and dynamic. He also supplied a collection to render this relocation of cultural value more concrete. Herder's anthology of folk songs, the first volume published in 1778, established a canonical template for collections of popular national poetry,[187] and he also encouraged his contemporaries to prepare anthologies of folktales, although his call initially went unheeded.[188] The thinker most closely associated with the idea of a humanity composed of nations also introduced a genre supposed to demonstrate this plurality of communities in the field of literature.

After Herder, many other attempts followed to render the people legible, make it subject to literary documentation, and ultimately also move it into the realm of social and political claims. The most famous of these project is *Des Knaben Wunderhorn*, the collection of songs accumulated and creatively recomposed by Achim von Arnim and Clemens Brentano (1778–1842), two Romanticist authors who came to know Jacob and Wilhelm through their academic mentor in Marburg, Friedrich Carl von Savigny.[189] The Grimms even made contributions to Arnim's and Brentano's Romantic project[190] and would dedicate and rededicate the *Children's and Household Tales* to Arnim's wife Bettina.[191] The genre switch from folk songs to folktales had by this time already been made by other authors and amateur scholars, primarily by Johann Karl August Musäus (1735–85), who published *Folk Tales of the Germans* [*Volksmärchen der Deutschen*] in 1782.[192] Musäus's title captured the close connection between the narrative genre and the national subject: the tales belonged to the German people. Even though Musäus was a man of wit and presented the tales as fantasies that would satisfy the human desire for distraction, he still described them as native products and as such also as revelations of a national character.[193] By the time that the Grimms published their first collection in the early 1810s, then, folktales had been framed as emanations of a nationally defined people for at least three decades and Wilhelm Grimm's prefaces partly reiterated established assumptions.

Folktale collections were not always prepared to corroborate the existence of a German folk in a way that could support the crystallized nationalist argument. Both before and during the time of publication of the Grimms' *Children's and Household Tales*, similar narrative materials were assembled for other reasons than serving as evidence of a national folk life. A few years before the appearance of the Grimms' first volume, the pedagogue Albert Ludwig Grimm (1786–1872; no relation) published an anthology of tales, a book of which the Grimms were painfully aware since their own work was frequently confused with this 1809 volume entitled *Children's Tales* [*Kindermärchen*].[194] In his preface, explicitly addressed to parents and educators, Albert Ludwig Grimm mentioned that the tales came from the folk, but for him, the origin mattered much less than the contemporary addressee, namely children, who must be provided with cognitively suitable material.[195] The tales, he claimed, should be tweaked and honed through testing their effect upon a young audience, which meant that a supposedly native folk form should not be allowed to control future renditions; the story collection was not primarily meant as a proof of nationhood but should be used as a didactic instrument.

A collection from the year 1800 by Johann Carl Christoph Nachtigall (1753–1819), writing under the pseudonym Otmar, also carried the title *Folk Tales* [*Volcks-Sagen*]. It pursued a more antiquarian than pedagogical project.[196] In the introduction, Nachtigall placed the tales in the context of the history of peoples. The stories had to be retrieved from a variety of print and oral sources, and they could shed light on the conditions of earlier times as well as the character of differentiated peoples. Here we encounter a near-contemporary research-oriented overview of a variety of sources, paired with claims about the genre's historical and ethnographic value – again, many of the Grimms' assumptions were already in place. Although Nachtigall presented an inchoate cultural theory of folktales as popular narratives that reflected local circumstances including climate, geography, and political constitution, this initial claim was nonetheless subordinated to an overriding conception of every people's necessary trajectory through a series of cultural stages, *Kulturstufen*.[197] The education of each people, Nachtigall claimed, followed a similar path and the tales consequently embodied less a national essence unfolding over time than a particular stage of human development through which *all* peoples had to pass; hence, peoples without contact with one another would tell tales that exhibited striking resemblances. Nachtigall linked the stories to the people, the *Volk*, but not in a way that fit the nationalist position.

The Grimms, by contrast, purposefully devised their publication so that it suited the literary needs of a nascent nationalist program. Ethnographic collection and scrupulous editing had resulted, Wilhelm Grimm claimed in 1814, in a compilation of narratives that indexed the historical existence of a people with particular indigenous national characteristics, precisely the image of the people required for the nationalist argument. The collection, Grimm declared, was neither overedited to serve literary or pedagogical purposes alien to the material (in the manner of Albert Ludwig Grimm) nor presented as an emanation of the common people without regard for nationality (in the manner of Nachtigall), nor simply offered as a source of pleasant entertainment (in the manner of Musäus). Instead, the *Children's and Household Tales* were nationally focused and untouched by any extraneous pedagogical or aesthetic program. The supposed editorial restraint and the nationalist purpose went together, for the authentic voice of the people would only emerge by means of philological sensitivity to the integrity of the material. The more respect the collector showed toward the original form of the folk narratives, Grimm implied, the better they would serve the nation.

The achievement of the Grimms was not to discover the people's cultural productivity or introduce the folktale as a genre to the educated reading public – these were accomplishments of multiple predecessors. A look at earlier collections reveals instead that Wilhelm Grimm weakened the genre's association to pleasant distraction, pedagogy, or general non-national folksiness and framed the tales more clearly as an emanation of a nationally defined common people. By shedding various earlier programs of entertainment and education, Jacob and Wilhelm Grimm thus prepared the folktale for deployment in a forming nationalist ideology.

The Grimms' attempt to raise funds for the Hessian Elector's war effort toward the end of the Napoleonic wars may have been botched in multiple ways, but the brothers performed better in a genre that the nationalists Arndt and Jahn tried their hands on without doing particularly well, namely the collection of supposedly genuine folk narratives. The *Children's and Household Tales* was not an obviously political work, not even in its own day, and the tales themselves certainly did not transmit a nationalist message. By reuniting the genres of the folktale collection and the militant nationalist pamphlet that parted company after their intimate coexistence in the nineteenth-century public sphere, we can nonetheless come to see how the tales fulfilled an ideological function: they provided evidence of the people's cultural existence and in this way helped secure the imagined pre-political basis of the political claim to national autonomy. The folktale and the call for struggle were two distinct aspects of one interconnected discourse.

There were, however, different kinds of nationalisms in the German lands of the Napoleonic era. The playwright Heinrich von Kleist, a son of a Prussian military family and good friend of the Grimms' later colleague, friend, and ally Friedrich Christoph Dahlmann, was not known for his antiquarian interests and left behind no collections of folk materials, wrapped in assurances of a peculiar affection for the home-grown, local, and innocent. Kleist emerged as a passionate nationalist, but recent literary scholarship has shown how his works display the active work of preparation and even manipulation required for the people to embrace the nationalist struggle.[198] The Germanic hero Herrmann's victory in the quintessential German nationalist drama *The Battle of Herrmann* [*Die Herrmannsschlacht*] written in 1808, for instance, happens thanks to much plotting and deception and not through a simple activation of an already existing cultural identity. The dominant hero must work actively to ensure that the conflict he wants to provoke assumes the proper ethnic shape. Popular hatred is crucial for armed resistance, Kleist's play seems to suggest, but it is not somehow naturally rooted in an already present people; it must be incited and channeled.

In Kleist, then, we encounter a convinced nationalist author who did not coordinate the propagandistic and the folkloric, who did not produce works in genres of political mobilization as well as genres of cultural substantialization. Interestingly, Heinrich von Kleist was a favorite author of both of the brothers Grimm. In a letter from May 1816, Jacob Grimm wrote to Paul Wigand about a future collection of posthumous texts by Kleist: "Heinrich Kleist's [*sic*] posthumous work will be published this summer, edited by Tiek [*sic*], along with an account of his life. I will read it eagerly, although I don't usually read new literature with any interest."[199]

CHAPTER 3

The Prince of Germany
Wilhelm Grimm and the Philologist as Redeemer

Wilhelm Grimm

The brothers Grimm believed that respect for the spontaneously evolved cultural and historical collective, the nation, constituted the precondition for legitimate political rule. Even when some people ruled over others within the nation, like still ruled over like – German over German, French over French. Rule across national borders, by contrast, appeared culturally detached and obtrusive, shorn of natural acceptance. This vision of the evolved cultural basis of legitimate political rule relied for its plausibility on evidence of the independent historical existence of a steady communal life, on the existence of a cultural record. The discovery, preparation, and presentation of such a record was the task of scholars – ethnographers, linguists, or the collectors of folktales and legends – who could point to the origin, historical development, geographical extension, and enduring particularity of the nation's shared cultural practices. To the Grimms, political rule worked best, or only worked, when it fused with the long cultural history of a circumscribed population, but this history was not just generally known and cherished but must be explored, preserved, and transmitted in and by scholarship. To the scholars, political legitimacy had a *philological dimension*, and rulers ought to listen to philologists, who were the most informed and reliable custodians of the people's culture.

This nationalist argumentation entailed a heightened conception of scholarly work and the vocation of the philologist. Jacob and Wilhelm Grimm did not argue that philologists should exercise power directly. This was the domain of traditional rulers, such as the prince tied to the country by long tradition and genealogy. They did believe, however, that the judgment of the philologists ought to matter in some way to political regimes, because only philological discernment could uncover the historical foundation of rule and delimit its proper extent; it could detect what was national and what was foreign and hence settle the proper borders of governance. The philologists were the guardians of the cultural particularity that a people and its rulers should share and could connect them to one another more intimately and enduringly.

Over his career, Jacob Grimm emerged as a minor political figure – not a politician but an icon of German cultural unity in conflictual political contexts. It was Jacob Grimm who served as the chair of the semipolitical Germanist association and was voted in as a delegate to the national parliament in Frankfurt in 1848. Hence, Jacob Grimm, and not his less publicly active brother, embodied the role of the politically present philologist. Nevertheless, the quieter, less prolific, and in some ways politically more cautious and conservative Wilhelm Grimm also developed a vision of the philologist as the facilitator of a national cultural awakening. He partly did so, however, in a more literary form, especially in his prefaces to the *Children's and Household Tales*. To understand Wilhelm Grimm's conception of the philologist's vocation, his metaphorical, even encrypted representation of the scholar as the nation's redeemer, we must first reconstruct his vision of German cultural antiquity and autonomy as well as both brothers' training in the historicist legal study pioneered by their teacher Friedrich Carl von Savigny.

Natural Poetry and National Life

In his early studies of German epic literature such as the *Nibelungenlied*, the young Wilhelm Grimm often stated his belief in the absolute, undiluted Germanness of ancient German literature. The authentically collective and national rather than individual quality of this early poetry rested, he asserted, on its being a manifestation of the actual historical experience of an entire community rather than the artifice of single poets who happened to express themselves in a particular language. There was such a thing as an essentially national collective literature, a wondrous epic voice that emanated naturally from a tribe rather than any individual singer in that group.[1] To obtain legitimacy, the ruler and the state had to be sensitive to the collective body of the nation – this was the core nationalist thesis – but at the historical heart of this nation, Wilhelm Grimm believed, there was a completely *communal* poetry, a poetry untouched by deliberate individual composition, spontaneous and self-organizing to such a degree that it bridged any divide between the cultural and the natural. A community that had spoken or rather sung in such poetry had also been completely authentic and not shaped by narrow individual interest or elite organization and thus it constituted the historical basis for a determinate, non-arbitrary unit of political life. This conception of national poetry was more or less in place in Wilhelm Grimm's work in the first decade of the nineteenth century, even before the publication of the first volume of fairy tales in 1812.

The brothers Grimm were not the only ones to turn to an ancient literary tradition at a time of political volatility and perceived foreign domination, and their early careers coincided with a growing scholarly interest in ancient Germanic poetry, best exemplified by the *Nibelungenlied*. This epic poem about the vortex of rivalries and bloody battles among noble families during the Migration Period had been rediscovered in 1755[2] and would become the centerpiece of German literature syllabi in the early nineteenth century.[3] Writing in his brother Friedrich Schlegel's journal *Deutsches Museum* in 1812, the prominent Romanticist critic and scholar August Wilhelm Schlegel (1767–1845) claimed that German soldiers marched into battle during the Wars of Liberation carrying copies of the epic.[4] For Wilhelm Grimm as well as for other critics and readers, *Nibelungenlied* served as a widely accepted object of cultural pride in an uncertain present, and a means to consolidate national consciousness. The sheer age of the epic material satisfied the nationalist craving for temporal depth and cultural integrity that could serve as evidence of the nation's antiquity, an important source of communal worth.[5] In the competition for status with greater European literary powers such as France but also with classical languages, a game in which the currency of time and antiquity was of utmost importance, recovered indigenous poetry from ancient times was vital to the project of enhancing the prestige of the national literature; the older a culture, the more distinguished it was.[6]

The *Nibelungenlied* not only satisfied the general cultural-nationalist desire for a deep vernacular past; it also exemplified the most grandiose of literary genres, the *Iliad*-like heroic epic,[7] which recounted in a large narrative format heroic deeds of a warrior culture. Every aspiring nation, Johann Wolfgang von Goethe (1749–1832) had stipulated, needed a national epic, and Germanists like Wilhelm Grimm worked quite hard to fill the category for their own nation.[8] This search for a national epic often ran into obstacles and conflicts, since ancient works did not quite fit with modern states. The Old English epic *Beowulf*, for example, was clearly a Germanic literary work in the broad sense and discussed as such by Wilhelm Grimm.[9] Yet *Beowulf* could be claimed by more than one contemporary nation. Rediscovered in England by the Icelandic-Danish archivist Grímur Jónsson Thorkelín (1752–1829) in 1787, the poem is a narrative about Scandinavian peoples – Danes,

Geats, and peripherally Swedes – written in the language of North Germanic tribes who invaded the British Isles.[10] So to whom did it properly belong? To Germans, to the English, or to the Scandinavians, three groups who were all speakers of Germanic languages? There was less confusion surrounding *Nibelungenlied*, which partly explains its centrality to Germanists. Yet Wilhelm Grimm and others knew well that its language, Middle High German, was not easily accessible to readers of modern German. *Nibelungenlied* was a Germanic epic not entirely comprehensible to contemporary Germans, and scholars debated the merits of translations and modernizations.[11]

Wilhelm Grimm ranked the *Nibelungenlied* as a great epic on par with Homer,[12] an oft-repeated move in the struggle for literary prestige.[13] The Greek epics were richer and possessed greater elocutionary elegance, Grimm claimed, but they lacked *Nibelungenlied*'s profound representation of an inexorable fate that pulled everything with it;[14] August Wilhelm Schlegel engaged in similar comparisons with Homer.[15] Yet it should be added that Grimm made no claims about the contemporary political import of the ancient national character to be found in the surviving manuscripts. In his 1807 review of a recent translation of the *Nibelungenlied* by the scholar and soon-to-be professor Friedrich Carl von der Hagen (1780–1856), Wilhelm Grimm almost seemed to downplay the present significance of the past epic and ancient German literature as a whole.[16] The Germanic epic, Grimm wrote, ranked as high as Homer in terms of literary quality, but it was also culturally "just as foreign and just as close" as the Homeric epics and could not be directly reintroduced as an epic for Germans living today – it was indisputably great as a literary work but belonged to its time.[17]

Grimm did not quite see the *Nibelungenlied* as a repository of German ideals and attitudes. Hagen, the target of the highly critical review, had argued that the epic put on display a national ethic, with characters who exhibited "hospitality, decency, probity, loyalty and friendship unto death, and humanity, mildness, and magnanimity in battle [*Gastlichkeit, Biederkeit, Redlichkeit, Treue und Freundschaft bis in den Tod, Menschlichkeit, Milde und Großmuth in des Kampfes Not*]."[18] The German epic embodied values, prescribed norms of social behavior, and legitimated action.[19] In his 1807 review, in contrast, Grimm celebrated the *Nibelungenlied* and considered it the gravitational center of an ancient German canon but did not suggest that it enshrined the virtues of a German national character.

What interested Wilhelm Grimm about the *Nibelungenlied* were not necessarily its political and moral values but rather its origin and mode of transmission. For him, the epic poem did not primarily show that

Germans were particularly heroic or upstanding, but its evolution, its philologically reconstructed history, suggested something more fundamental: that Germans belonged together. This idea appeared in a programmatic article from 1808 about the origin of ancient German poetry and its relationship to the affiliated Nordic tradition, a topic to which Grimm would return throughout his scholarly life; the text constituted a kind of nucleus of his thought.[20] Grimm's text was published in a scholarly venue, a series of volumes edited by two Heidelberg professors, the theologian Karl Daub (1765–1836) and the philologist, Orientalist, and archaeologist Carl Friedrich Creutzer (1771–1858), which bore the simple title *Studien* and came out for about half a decade, from 1805 to 1810. The articles on philosophy, theology, history, language, and literature were long and ambitious, meant for an initiated rather than general audience. Wilhelm Grimm's contribution was no exception and claimed about eighty pages in his collected minor writings; we see him here as a young, ambitious scholar, not the popular storyteller and collector of folktales.

The political message of Grimm's article on German and Nordic poetry was fairly explicit: the cultural life of a nation, Grimm declared, had to be grounded in its very own historically evolved character or "nature" and nothing was more "unfortunate [*misslich*]" than when this culture was damaged and marginalized by the intrusion of another, foreign one.[21] This was a bold statement in 1808, when Jérôme Bonaparte ruled over the newly constituted kingdom of Westphalia and the administrative elite residing in Kassel spoke French. The focus of the article was not properly national politics, however, but the origin and development of a genuinely national poetry understood as the expression of a people. Grimm set out to prove the exclusive national origin and continued national life of a literary inheritance, encapsulated in the greatest of the Germanic heroic epics, which of course was the *Nibelungenlied*.

According to Grimm, the literary tradition, and with it the source of a central canonical work, was bound to a nation as a whole. To nationalize a literature in this way, he first denied that heroic poetry should be regarded as completely mythic, without any historical kernel. Instead, he maintained that poetry and history were intertwined and that the songs joined into one epic cycle represented the actual deeds of heroic men during the Migration Period of the fourth to the sixth centuries, the era of the *Völkerwanderung*.[22] Poetry, he maintained, was not complete invention but followed closely upon or even originated in heroic action, like celebration immediately followed victory.[23] Ancient song was first and foremost testimonial.[24] The commitment to the mimetic and empirical quality of art was in this case also a nationalist commitment, because the entwinement of poetry with history meant that the epic could not have been imported from elsewhere – it served as a commemorative representation of the deeds of German men and women, of Siegfried and Kriemhild.²⁵ The *Nibelungenlied*, Grimm claimed, stood "firmly on German ground."²⁶

This fully German epic poetry was also, Grimm continued, a completely *collective* artifact. While he did not necessarily believe that the long and complex verse narrative of the Germanic epic was the direct result of collective authorship,²⁷ he argued that the extended constructions were composed of many shorter, older songs and that these smaller elements had once circulated among a larger collective and could not be attributed to any individual. The uncoupling of the songs from individual creativity may seem mysterious, but Grimm, influenced by the classicist Friedrich August Wolf's (1759–1824) 1795 study of the rhapsodic tradition in ancient Greece,²⁸ insisted that such folk songs had always existed in manifold and geographically distributed variants, and that each poem was always fully absorbed into a drawn-out process of modification, addition, and subtraction that made it impossible to trace it back to one single creator; like history as a whole, the poems could not be the work of one human being.²⁹ Songs continued to change with each new performance and thus ended up having a more decentralized and "distributed authorship."³⁰ Wilhelm's seemingly speculative claims were grounded in a scholarly account of how memorized songs and narratives circulated among many minds dispersed over time and space; existed in multiple, morphing versions; and hence possessed an existence detached from any one creative author.

The *Nibelungenlied* was a national epos not only because it celebrated the deeds of the heroes of a particular ethnicity but also because it emanated from the nation as a collective: people sung songs organized according to a shared form, these songs were later amalgamated into larger cycles by a class of still-anonymous singers, and even the resulting literary structures remained quite malleable and modifiable.³¹ The national epic that was later transposed into writing and solidified into a finite number of versions was, for hundreds and hundreds of years, a dynamic collective process. Grimm called the epic an ongoing "mobile and adaptable" literary form that would sound "different in every mouth."³² For him, the plot and the figures of the German epic were national in the sense that they portrayed heroes from an ethnic community, and the multiple performances were national in the sense that they were developed and varied by a transgenerational collective.

Grimm thus combined a claim about the historical veracity of literature with a claim about the dynamic of oral transmission to anchor the epic form in communal, tribal life. The result was a perfect example of nineteenth-century "bardic nationalism," a bundle of values and intellectual practices developed by literati in other areas of Europe as well.[33] In Britain, for example, Scottish, Irish, and Welsh antiquarians reacted to imperial dominance by reconstructing indigenous histories of bards who could be presented as the icons and mouthpieces of suppressed cultures.[34] In a similar vein, Wilhelm Grimm argued that there was such a thing as a completely German literature, neither rooted in cultural materials shared by multiple peoples nor the isolated creation and property of individual poets. This fully German literature was an epic poetry sung and ceaselessly re-sung by the members of a people constituting a coherent and culturally autonomous whole.

The resulting "national poetry [*Nationalpoesie*]" was of such great significance to Wilhelm and Jacob Grimm[35] because it ultimately grounded their vision of an entirely natural and hence non-arbitrary national existence. In the ancient poetry of the people, no single, isolated artist had imposed poetic form upon linguistic matter, bending material according to an individual "consciousness and intention [*Bewusstsein und Absicht*]."[36] Poetry instead emerged freely out of the collective and articulated itself, organized itself, in a way that even seemed to transcend the customary polarity between willful fabrication and natural growth[37] – creation was natural and nature creative. True epic poetry, Jacob Grimm even stated in a long letter to the author Achim von Arnim in May 1811, was self-generating; it was poetry that created itself, sprung out of an autonomous process of "self-making [*Sichvonselbstmachen*]."[38] Wilhelm Grimm similarly preferred impersonal formulations: a song or an epic had once "composed ... itself [*es hat sich ... gedichtet*]."[39]

While the Grimms' account of spontaneous literary production and their enthusiasm for the non-individualized, non-intentional creativity has been criticized for its nebulosity and even absurdity,[40] it underpinned an entire argumentative edifice. For the Grimms, political rule achieved legitimacy insofar as it traced the outlines and respected the integrity of a preexisting ethnic community, a community that was precisely not the effect of conscious political arrangement, conquest, or coercion. Again, however, there had to be a credible record of such a community, some kind of artifact, some kind of poetry, that could point to its existence since ancient times and disclose its particularity. Yet the authentic poetic materials recovered by the self-restrained philologist could not themselves be objects of ingenious individual artifice, no matter how accomplished, because that would risk reintroducing a literary version of intention and arrangement, or at least purely individual genius, at the very heart of collective national life. The expressive national poetry could not be a willed and constructed literary form or the possession of a singular poet; instead, it would have to have emerged as a natural effusion of the collective. At the core of the Grimms' commitment to the nation, one finds a special kind of poetry, said to be completely autogenetic and non-individual. The wonder of folk poetry revealed that the ancient singing collective of the nation even belonged to the order of a self-articulating nature, and the task of the philologist was to present this poetry carefully and faithfully, without any distortion. The utterly authentic non-individual poetic voice could sound again in the present and help reconstitute the nation, but only thanks to the mediation of the philologist.

Literary History, Social Fragmentation, and the Philologist's Task

According to Wilhelm Grimm, the German epic was the completely spontaneous and fully collective expression of a natural tribal community and as such evidence of a primordial German togetherness. The story of literature after the first heroic and nation-grounding era of communal song, he would then admit, was one of increased individualization or even atomization, and also of increased foreign influence. Wilhelm and Jacob Grimm were quite reticent when it came to articulating their implicit commitment to a philosophy of history,[41] a genre of their time, but they did assume that cultures tended to progress toward greater sophistication and abstraction but lost some of their initial energy and sensualism – such was the path of the human spirit.[42] In the case of the *Nibelungenlied*, its growth into a more elegantly composed work of considerable length, organized by more professionalized singers, also involved a loss of its original intensity. This was an unavoidable development, pictured by Wilhelm Grimm as a trade-off rather than as a form of decline.

Yet there was a sense in which this progression toward increased gracefulness threatened the distinctly *national* character of the epic. Over time, and especially with the introduction of writing, the production of poetry turned into a specialized task carried out by more professional singers who reworked inherited materials to give them the stamp of individuality. This literary history presupposed a rudimentary sociological account of how stratification and specialization grew out of a less complex social organization. In Wilhelm Grimm's conception, the original songs of the national epic emerged in something of an undifferentiated, non-atomized collective, whereas the poetry of the German Middle Ages, the period from about the twelfth century on, was cultivated by groups of trained performers, who moved in the same circles as a societal elite of noblemen and even princes.[43] The poetry that came out of this later social setting could be more ornate and show traces of bookish learning, which also distanced the cultural products from the mass of people; it was typically these more erudite individual composers of poems who would be prone to imitate foreign patterns. The individual poet was, Grimm wrote, more agile and could advance culturally and intellectually more easily "through foreign aid" than the more inert collective, for which the importance of a shared legacy tended to outweigh any excitement about novelty.[44] Increased individualization in the realm of literature thus more frequently led to the integration of foreign ideas, Grimm argued, because the single literate poet was more inclined to reshape poetry according to templates and styles from other, more sophisticated traditions. Grimm thus painted a picture of increasing fragmentation of the national literature, a process that had started in the Middle Ages. The technique of writing and the crystallization of a socially differentiated class of literate men with cosmopolitan learning entailed poetic individualization, accompanied by a certain degree of cultural denationalization.

Like his brother Jacob, Wilhelm Grimm spoke of the resulting divergence between the ancient national epic and the later art of poetry in terms of a dichotomy between natural and artful poetry, *Naturpoesie* and *Kunstpoesie*.[45] The former referred to the spontaneous and jubilant response by the undifferentiated tribal people to the intensity of their collective ethnic life of vivid perceptions and daring actions; the latter named the results of deliberate design by individuals tasked with the composition of pleasant and entertaining poetry for the consumption of affluent non-poets. Understood more neutrally as a descriptive distinction rather than as a tool of nostalgic valorization, the terms captured how the performance of poetry became a particular function or office and the higher degree of reflexivity and rhetorical consciousness that tended to develop around a more clearly delineated and delegated task. The terms "natural poetry" and "artful poetry" referred to distinctive poetic styles but ultimately rested on a sociological sketch of an increasing and irreversible division of labor in the realm of artistic creation.

This literary-historical narrative in both Jacob and Wilhelm Grimm's works also indicated the culturally essential task of the nineteenth-century philologist. It was the philologist, the scholar who surveyed the epochs of natural and artful poetry and studied the shifting conditions of composition, who then also appeared as the guardian of the nation's genuinely non-individual voice in an age of individualization and fragmentation. Scholars of the Germanic past, such as Wilhelm and Jacob Grimm, and not contemporary creative authors, could put present-day Germans in touch with the literary legacy that grounded their shared cultural belonging. The philologist presented and protected the documents of natural poetry in an age of late artful poetry.

In Wilhelm Grimm's long article on ancient German and Nordic poetry, the philologist thus ultimately stepped forward as the figure who could best represent the heroic ethnic past embodied in the culturally autonomous national epic. The scholar could not deliver a manual for action to the contemporary public; Wilhelm Grimm never made the case for the philologist as a teacher in matters of heroism. Yet the philologist did have, he believed, a crucial role to play in the awakening of the German nation, one rooted in his special guardianship of the collective natural poetry of the past. Great poets could produce wonderful poetry in the present, but the philologist understood and could point to the inimitable, even unwritable natural poetry that had once emanated from the collective and would forever function as a reminder of the nation's original cohesiveness.

To understand this redemptive role, one must reconstruct more fully Wilhelm and Jacob Grimm's shared conception of the historically oriented scholar. Both brothers were well acquainted with an already established ideal of scholarship according to which the interpretive researcher most fully appreciated the national past and was called to prevent the excesses of unmoored and despotic political regimes indifferent to the nation's cultural substance. This conception of the pivotal role of the researcher and academic belonged to their teacher and mentor, Friedrich Carl von Savigny, one of the period's most prominent legal scholars.

Friedrich Carl von Savigny and Professorial Authority

In the spring of 1815, Wilhelm published a very critical review of a recent pamphlet by a Bavarian jurist and professor of law, Nikolaus Thaddäus von Gönner (1764–1827). The background to this skirmish was an ongoing debate on the future shape of law in German lands. The French Revolution, the Napoleonic invasion and occupation, the dissolution of the Holy Roman Empire, the consolidation of German statelets into fewer and larger political units, and the internal German attempts at modernizing reform had provoked wide deliberations on the character and extension of German legal codes;⁴⁶ the entire legal and normative order was under discussion.⁴⁷ Some prominent legal experts argued for the introduction of a more rationally organized and coherent nationwide code that would allow for greater German unity and facilitate commercial activity, whereas others saw the call for a new code as disruptive of settled ways of life and advocated for a more gradual cultivation and clarification of existing sources of law;⁴⁸ the crafting of an entirely new law code would amount to a revolution. Wilhelm Grimm belonged to the latter camp.

Grimm was not a legal thinker and his position in the review in the short-lived journal *Rheinischer Merkur* was entirely derivative. He only presented an argument in defense of his former teacher and slightly older friend Friedrich Carl von Savigny, who was the authority on legal matters in his personal circle, but who had also emerged as one of the most influential jurists of the time after the 1803 publication of his book on the Roman legal sources on the concept of possession in contradistinction to property. The brothers had studied with Savigny in Marburg, Hesse, between 1802 and 1804, and Jacob Grimm served as his assistant on a research trip to Paris in 1805.⁴⁹ Savigny and the Grimms corresponded throughout the decades and eventually ended up in the same city, in the Prussian capital Berlin, after 1841. Over time, the former students emerged as important interlocutors, whose preoccupation with the *Volk* influenced Savigny.⁵⁰ Yet the friendship was not without stresses: the Grimms came from a modest background of local officials, while Savigny was a member of a noble family, cultivated an aristocratic appearance, and enjoyed an illustrious legal and administrative career. Shortly after the Grimms had relocated to Berlin, Savigny was named high chancellor, a title for a select number of elite officials working under the king, and was also appointed Prussian minister for legislative revision.⁵¹ His patrician manners and skeptical attitude toward the brothers' more liberal politics would occasionally disappoint Jacob Grimm, and the alienation from the former mentor's high society world of rigid snobbery would come through in a curiously ambivalent 1850 public homage to the former teacher.⁵²

Wilhelm Grimm's 1815 review, entitled "On Legislation and Jurisprudence in Our Time [*Über Gesetzgebung und Rechtswissenschaft in unserer Zeit*]" took its name from the reviewed book, which in turn was directed at Savigny's prior 1814 publication with the title "On the Vocation of Our Time for Legislation and Jurisprudence [*Vom Beruf unserer Zeit für Gesetzgebung und Rechtswissenschaft*]";⁵³ the titles all mirrored one another. Again, Grimm restated a position that agreed with Savigny's view rather than construct an original one. The argument Grimm did make, however much as it relied on an already articulated argument in an ongoing legal debate, aids our understanding of his conception of the people's cultural productivity, the integrity of its national particularity, and ultimately also of the culturally crucial task of the philologist who could rediscover and help preserve this particularity.

Law, Grimm argued in his review, was embedded in the communal existence of a people. Legal norms were even analogous to languages or customs: while they clearly developed over time, they seemed to have always already emerged, which meant that changes were always only modifications to an existing corpus. For Grimm, the people had not created the law, if creation meant an identifiable intentional act in time and space that marked the transition from a lawless condition to a lawful one. The law, he wrote, was rather *aufgewachsen mit dem Volk*, grown with the people, steadily accompanying them on their path.[54] The authority of law for the people in fact depended on its familiarity, on its quiet and constant accretion without noticeable manipulations by individuals or segregated groups; law was legitimate thanks to its cultural intimacy, its *Nähe* or closeness.[55] Much like the ancient German poetry of which Grimm was an expert, legal norms were not the result of recognizable individual stipulation but rather an expression of an ongoing and fully collective life, and this collective life of course possessed a national *Eigenthümlichkeit*, a discernible particularity.[56] Yet this idea of the people as the ultimate source of law did not amount to an endorsement of the revolutionary concept of collective legislation or popular sovereignty. It was rather an argument against any kind of imperious declaration, even if made in the name of a popular sovereign; legitimate law was the result of an always ongoing incremental growth and had no absolute beginning.[57]

The occasion for this explication of a gradualist and nationally oriented understanding of the foundations of legitimate law was a tract that argued a contrary position, the intervention by Thaddäus von Gönner. In Grimm's summary, Gönner did not believe that law ought to rest on the relics of an unenlightened age or popular prejudice. Instead, positive law should be the result of the legislative efforts of a ruler, who received assistance from an elite of administrative and legal experts. The all-important guide for legal norms, however, was human reason; the legal code should be derived from law of reason, the *Vernunftrecht*.[58] The aim of any regime should be, Gönner argued, to distill law from reasoning and deliver to the people a coherent legal code that would regulate its activity in a consistent and just manner, without concessions to local prejudice and quixotic old ways.

Wilhelm Grimm found fault with every aspect of this picture. He considered it arrogant in its disregard for centuries-old local habits and authentic collective wisdom, disruptive of cherished and stabilizing traditions, damaging to legal authority sustained by familiarity, and plainly despotic in its elevation of the ruler and an elite over the people. A rational law intellectually available to some governing clique, above all to the ruler, he deemed little more than a transparent rationalization of arbitrary rule. Just and enduring law, Grimm believed, could not be formulated in isolation from the people to then be "poured over it."[59] The ruler must instead remain bound by an evolved corpus of legal norms rooted in the life of the entire national community.[60] If not, the king or prince would force upon the people a legal code that was insensitive to its particular life and violated its social complexity.[61] That which had been fabricated by men in the present, the Grimms' teacher Savigny had asserted, would never obtain the same public legitimacy as that which had emerged slowly and steadily over a people's history.[62]

To Grimm, the implementation of a new code derived from reason and hence free of the debris of accumulated prejudice would only serve to institute the sterile domination of a people by a ruler. A sudden, top-to-bottom erasure of habit and tradition would not amount to liberation but rather the institutionalization of heteronomy justified by reference to universal reason. The conception of a universal reason here was very much part of the perceived problem, because it was antithetical to the appreciation of the actual texture of a world with its manifold embodied and historically shaped communities. A people did not achieve a state of freedom by transcending the local conventions and norms that set it apart from others to live under laws fully transparent to rational, non-provincial thought; such transcendence in fact eliminated that which had come to define a people and hold it together. A people instead obtained or rather preserved its genuine freedom when it was allowed to live its particularity, which in the legal realm meant abiding by laws that emerged through an incremental externalization of its unique character, without abrupt compulsion.[63] Law was legitimate when it was culturally and socially *fitting*, which it could only be if it crystallized the particular spirit of a unique people in history rather than approximated some context-independent, rational ideal. The attempt to introduce an entirely new law, Savigny himself had stated, would be as foolish as calling for a new language for a population; such a break with the past was not humanly possible and the very attempt involved dangerous "self-deception [*Selbsttäuschung*]."[64] Neither a regent nor a revolutionary should be permitted to clear away the traditions of the people as if they were nothing but a dead mass; such abruptness and overconfidence would amount to despotism.[65]

It should be apparent why Grimm eagerly embraced the conception of law as a slowly evolving, collectively produced, and nationally particular corpus – it perfectly matched his vision of ancient German poetry. The non-imposed, evolved, national legal norms that expressed and defined the community ran parallel to the poetry that emanated from the community in a self-organizing, self-making aesthetic form. Yet Grimm left out of his critique of new legislation an account of the role of the jurist in relation to the communally rooted law. How were ambiguities clarified, the code updated, and cases decided on the basis of this historical understanding of legal norms? Savigny, whom Grimm was defending, did supply an answer to this question. The historical view of the law, Savigny believed, should prohibit the departure from existing traditions in the form of an arrogantly devised princely or popular code, but it also secured an eminently influential role for the legal scholar. To Savigny, it was first and foremost the historically conscious jurist who could clarify the law and guide its application by methodically exploring, ordering, and expounding extant sources. New legislation was deficient compared with the scholar's careful and rigorous scrutiny and explication of already established law, and the historical accretion of law itself contained the solutions to legal problems[66] – when carefully examined by scholars; legislation could emerge "out of legislation."[67] To Savigny, the historical attitude to societal life and the fidelity to tradition ultimately supported professorial leadership in the realm of law.[68] Valid law did not grow out of political power but could emerge from the university, from faculties of law populated by jurists trained in the methods of legal-historical interpretation.[69]

Savigny argued that law could be augmented not by prescription but through the historical community's interpretation of its own, particular path,[70] and that this interpretation could be responsibly performed by rigorously educated jurists. In this vision, the professoriate emerged as the vanguard of German legal unity.[71] There were legal scholars and philosophers who argued against Savigny's position, which seemed to imply that the state of law in Germany hinged on the proper scholarly preparation of available legal manuscripts. The well-being of the German people, Savigny's main adversary Anton Friedrich Justus Thibaut (1772–1840) pointed out, should not have to rely on the helpfulness of librarians and completeness of archives,[72] and ancient law may well be too fragmented, scattered, and unsystematic to prove useful for a forward-looking society.[73]

The philosopher Georg Friedrich Wilhelm Hegel was also critical: Savigny, Hegel claimed, denied the educated nation its right to legislate, which was nothing less than an insult to its maturity, autonomy, and dignity.[74] In addition, the practical conservatism of Savigny's program was unmistakable: as a dominant university jurist and high Prussian civil servant, Savigny consistently invoked historicity to stifle liberal reform attempts.[75]

Savigny claimed that the university-trained and university-employed scholar should protect and cultivate the law and ensure that the people remained close to its evolved particularity, sheltered from the arbitrariness that would accompany historically insensitive codification efforts. What did the brothers Grimm think about the philologist? Could the philologist assume a similarly prominent role as the law professor vis-à-vis the development of a national literary and even political culture, as the custodian and interpreter of a particular national past? With Savigny's argumentation as an example, one could imagine parallel efforts to elevate the philologist to some socially central position, as the figure who could carry the people's past into the present and maintain and manage the definition of its national essence.

Interestingly, Wilhelm Grimm did not quite make an overt argument for the philologist as the guardian of national culture, not in the review at least. He loyally summarized and endorsed Savigny's gradualism but did not touch on the legal leadership of the professoriate that Savigny's argument was designed to support.[76] Both brothers were aware of the multiple analogies between legal and literary history that emerged from Savigny's account and were, as we shall see, very keen to point them out in their letters to their mentor, and yet they dealt only in passing with the implications for their own vocation.

The Grimms' immediate responses to their teacher's 1814 intervention in the German debate on codification were nothing but enthusiastic. In letters sent by Jacob Grimm in October 1814 and Wilhelm in December of the same year, they highlighted the many points with which they wholeheartedly agreed. Jacob wrote that he believed that law surrounded and accompanied by local popular habit and settled expectation would be viable for a people, as opposed to law that expressed the will of the ruler.[77] Savigny considered the Napoleonic legal code imposed in the occupied territories an instrument of domination;[78] in letters written from his work journey in France in 1814, Jacob expressed approval for the French political philosopher Benjamin Constant's (1767–1830) idea that the modern despot violated cultural particularity when he strove to impose legal and administrative homogenization.[79] As did other thinkers and scholars of the late

Romantic era, Jacob Grimm viewed centralization, homogenization, and the concomitant erasure of historically grown diversity as veritable evils.[80]

Unsurprisingly, both brothers were also very attracted to Savigny's explicit analogies between law and language, introduced to suggest that valid law was not the result of deliberate design guided by reason, created at a specific, identifiable moment. In the page-by-page commentary Jacob Grimm sent to his former teacher, he emphasized how language was never the outcome of conscious invention and that the attempt to construct a law for a people was as preposterous as to want to construct a new language for it.[81] The outcome of such legislative efforts could not possibly gain broad support. Wilhelm Grimm for his part highlighted the secretive, non-individual origins of folk poetry as analogous with the beginnings of law and said that he wished to present the history of poetry in such a way that it emerged as an entirely shared property of the people, a *Gemeingut*.[82] Both brothers, then, focused on the analogies between law, literature, and language that tied these fields and disciplines together.

However, the brothers also lingered on how both the history of law and poetry had to be understood in terms of societal differentiation, in which particular tasks were increasingly delegated to specially trained groups. Wilhelm wrote to Savigny that societies moved from a condition in which every man participated in legal decision-making to a stage in which educated judges carried out this function, just like poetry ceased to be the collective activity of the people as a whole and became the office of bards.[83] Jacob similarly drew a parallel between judges and singers as part of an account of how the heightened focus on what he called the "technical" element of basic activities (judging, singing) lead to the erection of a hierarchy of different functions performed by figures separated from the people.[84]

Despite the broad agreement with Savigny and numerous elaborations of their mentor's ideas, the brothers' response to his work did not include a statement on the role of the literary philologist in comparison with the university-trained juridical expert. In the letters to Savigny, Jacob mentioned the brothers' collaborative project of collecting tales and legends[85] and Wilhelm stated their intention to write about the origins of folk poetry, but they did not follow Savigny's example and elaborate upon the philologist's dignified vocation in the present day. Neither of them clarified the mission and the status of the scholar who recovered a history of national expressivity and by doing so made available the proof of a people's ancient togetherness, the documents of its invaluable particularity. Savigny introduced the figure of the professorial guardian of the law; given the similarities, one would expect Jacob and Wilhelm Grimm to portray the philologist as the guardian of the national literature and culture, tasked with its proper presentation and interpretation, and even accorded the authority to define national particularity – but they did not explicitly touch on the subject. Despite this apparent reticence, Wilhelm Grimm did have an exalted view of the philologist's task as the legatee of a fully national and natural poetry, a view he formulated in the same period as his programmatic text on the origin of ancient German poetry (1808) and his Savigny-inspired review (1815). This conception can be found not in the reviews and essays on poetry and law or the letters to Savigny, however, but in prefaces to the *Children's and Household Tales*.

Wilhelm Grimm's Cultural Manifesto

Savigny sent each brother a copy of his intervention in the German codification debate. In his December 1814 letter to Savigny, Wilhelm Grimm did not just provide his enthusiastic response but also reciprocated the gift by sending along his own most recent publication, the second volume of the *Children's and Household Tales*.[86] In a subsequent letter, Savigny thanked him for the book and mentioned how he and his children had enjoyed reading from it;[87] for the older mentor, the brothers' collection was meant for the family, for a father and his children. That is, after all, what the title suggested. Nevertheless, Grimm's two prefaces to the collection, one written in 1812 and one two years later, also constituted a manifesto.[88] The texts declared the importance of the tales for German national culture and called for a general reevaluation of folkloric inheritance but also, more surreptitiously, indicated the crucial task of the literary collector and scholar in the present day: the figure who rescued and reintroduced the stories of the folk, the philologist, would also reawaken the nation. Grimm did have an idea of the philologist's mission and status that matched Savigny's conception of professoriate leadership in the realm of law.

Wilhelm Grimm's concern in his two framing remarks to the *Children's and Household Tales* was cultural prestige. He set out to elevate folk culture in relation to traditionally esteemed forms of art, and by so doing also elevate German culture in relation to other, more highly regarded countries and cultures that had come to define civilizational achievement. The prefaces together sought to bring about a two-step, strategic redistribution of cultural value, an operation that also shifted the status of the collector and editor of folktales. If the assembled tales were not simply meant as tools of edification for children and sources of light entertainment for adults but would rather help strengthen Germany's position in a European cultural space, then the compiler no longer appeared as a pedagogue or a witty man of letters, but as a very different and much more significant figure.

As collectors and editors of tales, the Grimms did not strive to appear as authors in their own right – this was simply not the model for their writing. Despite honing a particular fairy-tale style over the decades, a very carefully crafted idiom of simplicity and artlessness,[89] Wilhelm Grimm would claim that they had retrieved the stories of the folk from the household spaces where they were shared to then make them available without distorting manipulations. In the realm of the faithfully sustained cultural inheritance from which these tales emerged, both brothers believed, there had been no authors in the modern sense – the poetry was entirely natural and entirely national. Among the people, in ancient times, creation had been a completely collective process, impossible to analyze in terms of distinguishable individual contributions. However, the brothers also did not step in to continue the premodern intergenerational storytelling chain; they salvaged and sustained the ancient narrative material, but by scholarly means. In doing so, they did not necessarily wish to serve only as near-invisible collectors, whose names were meant to fade away once the voice of the people had been adequately transcribed and could speak out of a book, and yet they would not admit to being literary thieves plundering a collective heritage for their own glorification.

To use Jacob and Wilhelm Grimms' own favored dichotomy, their aim was to introduce redeemed examples of natural poetry into the literary realm now organized around artful poetry. Yet their own transfer operation, and hence the *Children's and Household Tales* as a collection, belonged to neither of these two categories: it was neither the unproblematic continuation of a fully social and national narrative practice that occurred spontaneously and unconsciously – *Naturpoesie* – nor the inspired or learned literary work crafted by an individual author with artistic and ultimately also legal control of his or her creation – *Kunstpoesie*. Instead, their task was precisely to construct a passageway between these two artistic, historical, and ultimately also social paradigms and in this way restore to present consciousness an appreciation of the greatness of a forgotten native past. The Grimms saw themselves as facilitators, but this was not necessarily a modest role, since the recuperative, mediating mission on the threshold between historical periods (ancient vs. modern times), social configurations (undifferentiated vs. functionally differentiated community), and media systems (oral vs. print transmission) was meant to change the cultural game in which Germany seemed like a lesser, impoverished player than other, neighboring cultures, notably that of the French occupier. By reconnecting the era of individual artifice, of *Kunstpoesie*, to the neglected treasures of an age of collective poetry, *Naturpoesie*, the long course of German literary development, and by extension the fate of German cultural nationhood, would seem different and more glorious. With a historically unique and politically consequential redemptive intervention, the philologist would uncover the depth of the national culture.

In the prefaces, Wilhelm Grimm performed a series of interlocking reevaluations. He first made a case for the value of the tales themselves, then for their significance to a fuller, more adequate understanding of German literature and its ancient history, and, finally, for the worth and greatness of that German literature in a nationalized struggle for literary eminence.[90] If only the neglected and misunderstood folktales could be allowed to move closer to the realm of literature without having to shed their peculiar form, then German literary history would appear more complete. If German literary history could be better reconstructed or perhaps even healed in this manner, then its antiquity and particularity could be more fairly appreciated and no longer viewed as deficient compared with the paradigmatic European traditions. The tales were, Wilhelm Grimm claimed, "rich in themselves"[91] and deserved appreciation, but they also pointed to the "richness of German poetry" more generally,[92] and the collection of tales, which was sufficiently extensive or sufficiently "rich" for publication,[93] could restore and enhance the awareness of this national opulence. Wilhelm Grimm followed the prototypical agenda of the historicist intelligentsia in the Romantic era: salvaged cultural remains would help regenerate national consciousness, and the "artifactualization" of previously neglected folkloric forms[94] would support the "vernacularization" and nationalization of literary culture.[95]

Let us follow the argument a little more closely. The tales, Grimm wrote, were lovely; their intrinsic quality was the starting point of his reevaluation. The positive terms he selected to characterize the tales formed a cluster: the stories were absolutely pure and for this reason wondrous, the situations they represented were disarmingly simple, and the narrative tradition as a whole exuded the robust health and vitality of the people.[96] This particular jargon of authenticity is familiar and its objective transparent: it was supposed to subvert a dominant hierarchy between the civilized and the vulgar, the refined and the coarse. The tale's obvious lack of sophistication was not a deficiency, but rather a virtue, since the simple, wholesome, and naive could be of greater value than the overcomplicated and the artificial.

Grimm did seem to anticipate that the tales were not quite ready for the standard literary assessment applied to masterpieces in the realm of artful poetry, and he even tried to place the stories beyond the reach of regular literary criticism. One should not argue against those who question the tales' literary worth, he wrote, but rather preserve them from review altogether. Their loveliness was of a sort, he continued, that immediately activated one's protective impulses. In part, this was because they simply did not belong to the literary system constituted by authors who wrote books to be discussed critically in journals by critics upon their release to the reading public. The folktales instead possessed the particular charm of the preliterary and should be appreciated on their own terms rather than subjected to literary evaluation. Their specificity could be preserved in German, but not, he argued predictably, in French, because the French literary language had achieved such an advanced state of elegance and polish that it could no longer capture the rustic, popular idiom.[97] Stories told in French automatically exhibited finely honed dialogue and epigrammatic remarks, thanks to the smoothness and wit inherent to this highly developed literary language. Grimm sought to place the *Children's and Household Tales* in a liminal space, neither inside nor outside of literature: their charm could be appreciated but they should not be judged poetical or unpoetical. They could not directly compete with actual literary works and hence did not contest the obvious French literary supremacy, but they did indicate how that sophisticated linguistic universe was in fact bound and enclosed, unable to integrate speech that lived outside of it.

Placed at the boundary of literature in this way, the tales could also help restore a more complete sense of an ancient German poetry that was available only in fragmentary form and had regrettably been neglected. The immediately endearing tales, Wilhelm Grimm claimed, contained or even consisted of traces of grand epic poetry, much of which has been lost. Unbroken popular traditions of oral transmission had been able to retain that which had been lost by scholarly, courtly, or clerical elites. An altogether marginal genre, simple children's and household tales, had ironically functioned as a protective vessel for the most grandiose genre of them all, namely ancient heroic poetry. Children's and household tales had functioned as such a protective context precisely *because* of their marginality, because of their lack of significance or their invisibility in the domain of official, public culture. The high and the solemn from a vanished era had survived in the low and charming, shards of masculine heroism in domestic spaces coded as feminine. The Grimms' publication of the tales was meant not only to highlight their intrinsic delightfulness and relativize French literary supremacy but also to help the German reading public regain fragments of its ancient poetry, relics of a greatness that should constitute the principal object of German literary studies and even serve as the foundation of German culture as a whole.

Wilhelm Grimm's conception of the neglected folktales as a repository of ancient poetry and mythology was in urgent need of some proof. His preface did provide examples of how scenes, episodes, figures, and beliefs that belonged to the realm of epic poetry appeared in folktales, but in a kind of miniature form. Most centrally, he identified *Dornröschen* or the fairy-tale figure of Sleeping Beauty, in deep sleep for a hundred years after being pricked by a spindle, with Brunhilde sleeping behind a wall of fire in the *Nibelungenlied*, Grimm's key specimen of German epic poetry endowed with unquestionable majesty and depth.[98] Yet it was not the case that the folktale had preserved a trace of *Nibelungenlied*, but that both stemmed from a now lost, ancient source.[99] The example seems to have been a favorite one of the brothers; it reappeared in Jacob Grimm's massive *German Mythology* from 1844, a work that again welded folk customs and pagan mythology to bestow upon a vanishing rural culture the somber aura of religion.[100] When Jacob Grimm addressed the topic of myth's survival in marginal, neglected genres, he, like his brother, pointed to *Dornröschen*, Sleeping Beauty, as a memory of a Valkyrie.[101] This and other examples were meant to convince the readers that transcribed tales, primarily from the Grimms' own region, Hesse, could help fill gaps in the nation's literary and cultural history and thereby enhance the reputation of the fatherland. More or less local ethnographies of folk storytelling could uncover a lost national greatness, the modest "domestic space" opened up into a grandiose "national space."[102]

Wilhelm Grimm presented the collected tales as worthy evidence of German cultural endurance. Such survival over the ages for him counted as self-evident capital in the struggle for literary eminence on the European stage. Germany was just as culturally wealthy as nations such as France, although proofs of its literary wealth had been hidden in unexpected places such as neglected folktales.[103] The German nation seemed to suffer from a relatively weak high-literary tradition, but once the collected tales had been properly reevaluated, or properly positioned vis-à-vis the literary field, Germans would be able to make a better case for the antiquity of their poetry; the preliterary oral tradition functioned as evidence of a very old but fragmented heritage of collective poetry.

As if this frame would not provide a sufficiently strong justification for the work of assembling and disseminating the folktales, Wilhelm Grimm's preface added yet another layer of legitimation. The time for his procedure of literary-historical restoration was running out, he also claimed, because the age of storytelling itself was coming to an end. Fewer and fewer old women told stories in the previously protected domestic spaces, Grimm claimed, as the socio-narrative practice had come under threat by a more sophisticated but also emptier culture of conversation and refined interaction.[104] That the tradition was threatened by the "industrialization and urbanization"[105] or "economic modernization,"[106] as is sometimes claimed, could hardly be the case in nonindustrialized Hesse of the early nineteenth century, and Wilhelm Grimm did not make any such claim or suggestion; he only very vaguely sketched the threat to old traditions. Whatever the cause, the decline of storytelling meant that an important avenue of access to the age of ancient heroic poetry was closing down. The self-appointed task of the Grimms was therefore not only to use humble tales to reconstruct German literary history but to do so before it was too late, before the tales themselves disappeared. The rediscovery of ancient German poetry in the neglected realm of the folktale was part of an urgent rescue operation. The encounter with the tales was meant to kindle the public's appreciation of the wonderful treasures of ancient German poetry, help found the rigorous study of the origins of German poetry,[107] and ultimately undermine the prejudiced view of German culture as too poor to be meaningfully compared with the French, but all of this, Grimm stated, had to happen immediately.

Such was the articulated rationale for the folktale collection, explained in the two prefaces composed in 1812 and 1814. What was, against this background, the task and position of the scholars vis-à-vis the storytelling tradition that they were trying to save and glorify, excavate and elevate? What was the role of the philologist exactly, in relation to the narrative practice of storytellers, on the one hand, and the German public, on the other? Again, the brothers were not creative authors like their friends Clemens Brentano and Achim von Arnim who had put together the folk song collection *Des Knaben Wunderhorn* (1805–8) but remained committed to the production of novel imaginative literary works. Nor were the Grimms simply storytellers in a generational chain of storytellers. They were collectors and compilers of supposedly vanishing tales, certainly also scholars knowledgeable about wider cultural and mythological contexts, and all in all respectful guardians of a hidden national cultural wealth. In light of Wilhelm Grimm's account of the imminent loss of the stories that preserved traces of epic poetry, they also implicitly presented themselves as mediators between distinct modes of retention and transmission who wanted to manage the replacement of one medium by another. By collecting tales, they converted a vulnerable oral tradition into print and yet sought to frame this tradition as essentially alien to the new medium, not to be judged by critical standards attached to it. They were also two young men who replaced what they themselves indicated was a long succession of female storytellers. Yet by representing the genre of the folktale as a cluster of traces that pointed to the forgotten existence of other, awe-inspiring and dignified genres, Wilhelm Grimm also indicated that the public's interest and admiration should ultimately be directed at this distant majesty, which was now about to be represented for the benefit of contemporary national culture. The brothers did not create the tales nor did they simply pass them on, but they rescued them from disappearance, remediated[108] and re-gendered them, with the final aim of redeeming the ancient heritage lodged in them.

Wilhelm Grimm had no simple name for the philologist's essential position, or for this complex transitional activity on the threshold between historical and artistic periods. In the prefaces, however, he did offer the reader an account of the philologist's vocation – the philologist was nothing less than a redeemer of national being. He delineated this mission and revealed the scope of his scholarly ambition by means of an image rather than by explicit argument. We can only understand Wilhelm Grimm's self-conception as collector, editor, and scholar, then, if we are attentive to the imagery that these texts present.

The Prince of Germany

In 1816, after publishing their first volumes of folktales, Jacob and Wilhelm Grimm put out a collection of German legends. In the preface, written by Jacob Grimm rather than by Wilhelm, the work of collecting legends was likened to the child's joyful discovery of hidden birds' nests in the woods. In both cases, the finder had to proceed carefully and attentively and treat the material with utmost sensitivity: "here, too, with the legends, one must quietly lift up the leaves and cautiously bend away the branches so as not to disturb the people and to watch, in secret, the wondrous but modest natural landscape, nestled in itself and fragrant of foliage, meadow grass and freshly fallen rain" [*es ist auch hier bei den sagen ein leises aufheben der blätter und behutsames wegbiegen der zweige, um das volk nicht zu stören und um verstohlen in die seltsam, aber bescheiden in sich geschmiegte, nach laub, wiesengras und frischgefallenem regen riechende natur blicken zu können*]."[109] The process of collecting legends was a little like bird watching or eavesdropping; one had to tread with care, not announce one's presence or rudely overwhelm the material. If only the philologist exercised sufficient attentiveness, patience, and restraint, he would have the opportunity to witness a humble but marvelous hidden world of the people and to share this glimpse with others.

When picturing his work as a philologist, Jacob Grimm imagined standing silent before a natural boundary that both hid and sheltered something infinitely precious. Wilhelm Grimm's 1812 preface to the first volume of the folktales featured a similar image of protection. His text opened with a picture of hedges and the safety they could offer against ravaging storms. This image of shielding greenery introduced one of the main ideas of the preface, namely that of preservation – the preservation of culture over time despite fragmentation and forgetting, and the preservation of a great literary heritage in the pockets of marginal narrative practices. The question of Wilhelm Grimm's 1812 preface was the following: What had safeguarded the folktales, and with them the traces of a magnificent ancient Germanic culture?

> Wir finden es wohl, wenn Sturm oder anderes Unglück, vom Himmel geschickt, eine ganze Saat zu Boden geschlagen, daß noch bei niedrigen Hecken oder Sträuchern, die am Wege stehen, ein kleiner Platz sich gesichert und einzelne Aehren aufrecht geblieben sind. Scheint dann die Sonne wieder günstig, so wachsen sie einsam und unbeachtet fort, keine frühe Sichel schneidet sie für die großen Vorrathskammern, aber im Spätsommer, wenn sie reif und voll geworden, kommen arme, fromme Hände, die sie suchen; und Aehre an Aehre gelegt sorgfältig gebunden und höher geachtet, als ganze Garben, werden sie heimgetragen und Winterlang sind sie Nahrung, vielleicht auch der einzige Samen für die Zukunft. So ist es uns, wenn wir den Reichtum deutscher Dichtung in früher Zeiten betrachten und dann sehen, dass von so vielem nichts lebendig sich erhalten, selbst die Erinnerung daran verloren war und nur Volkslieder und diese unschuldige Hausmärchen übrig geblieben sind. Die Plätze am Ofen, der Küchenherd, Bodentreppen, Feiertage noch gefeiert, Triften und Wälder in ihrer Stille, vor allem die ungetrübte Phantasie sind die Hecken gewesen, die sie gesichert und einer Zeit aus der andern überliefert haben.[110]

When a storm or some other calamity from the heavens destroys an entire crop, it is reassuring to find that a small spot on [by] a path lined by hedges or bushes has been spared and that a few stalks, at least, remain standing. If the sun favors them with light, they continue to grow, alone and unobserved, and no scythe comes along to cut them down prematurely for vast storage bins. But near the end of the summer, once they have ripened and become full, poor devout hands seek them out; ear upon ear, carefully bound and esteemed more highly than entire sheaves, they are brought home, and for the entire winter they provide nourishment, perhaps the only seed for the future. That is how it all seems to us when we review the riches of German poetry from earlier times and discover that nothing of it has been kept alive. Even the memory of it is lost – folk songs and these innocent household tales are all that remain. The places by the stove, the hearth in the kitchen, attic stairs, holidays still celebrated, meadows and forests in their solitude, and above all the untrammeled imagination have functioned as hedges preserving them and passing them on from one generation to the next. These are our thoughts after surveying this collection.[111]

What does a hedge do? A hedge offers protection; Grimm's word was *sichern*, to render secure.[112] In Grimm's fairly convoluted and flowery opening paragraph, modest domestic spaces, recurring traditions of celebration, a quiet agrarian landscape with pastures and woods – that is to say, an entire traditional context of life – had safeguarded and saved the children's and household tales, like a hedge or a row of bushes near a road could protect at least one small spot where some of the growing crop could be preserved from ravages. In Grimm's telling, a traditional lifestyle, centered on the hearth, had managed to maintain German folktales, and these tales in turn had carried in themselves shards of the Germanic epic tradition. Not for long, however, since "the custom of telling tales" was "on the wane";[113] past practices of preservation were coming to an end and the "hedges" would cease to exist.

The 1812 opening implied that Wilhelm and Jacob Grimm could carry out their redemptive cultural work because someone or something – a transgenerational sequence of storytellers, household narrative practices – had surrounded a treasure with a "protective shell,"[114] preserving it for future retrieval. Unlike Jacob Grimm's portrayal of the cautious collector, however, Wilhelm Grimm did not explicitly mention the figure of the witness in his opening; he did not include, in this part of the text, anything about anyone standing at the hedge, cautiously bending away twigs so as to get a better view. This absence is a little curious. The folklore scholar Marina Warner has suggested that the Grimms' famous collection staged a "crucial encounter" between the folk, on the one hand, and intellectuals or scholars, on the other.[115] Yet in Wilhelm Grimm's opening metaphoric passage, one side of the encounter remained a little in the dark, namely the collector. In his preface to the *German Legends*, Jacob Grimm spoke explicitly about the philologist making discoveries and peering through a boundary, like someone searching for birds or watching people from a distance; Wilhelm Grimm likewise spoke about a protective boundary but did not mention an observer.

Read together, though, Wilhelm Grimm's two prefaces did indicate that someone was standing at the protective hedge at the very moment of its untangling or unraveling. In the 1814 preface, Grimm prominently adduced the similarity between *Dornröschen* [Brier Rose] or Sleeping Beauty and Brunhilde as evidence of the genealogical relations between the folktales and ancient Germanic poetry. The protective hedge around the princess in the famous fairy tale was like the wall of flames around Brunhilde and the similarity suggested, both Jacob and Wilhelm Grimm believed, a common ancient source. The story of the Sleeping Beauty is a very familiar one. After being pricked by a spindle, the princess falls asleep for a hundred years, both shielded and imprisoned by a hedge of thorns that grows every year and covers and conceals the castle, to keep out curious intruders. She is eventually woken up when the prince arrives and finds that he can move through branches that part for him of their own accord. The hedge in the tale does not guard possessions but shelters the figure who sleeps, until the day has come for her and all the kingdom to rise, the day that the right one arrives at the hedge. The image of the hedge, the protective but ultimately *dissolving* boundary, involves not one but a couple of figures: one who sleeps behind the hedge and the other who walks up to it and passes through it. The hedge in Grimm's preface can be read in light of the folktale's hedge of thorns, introduced by Grimm himself, and the more complete picture that then emerges does locate two figures at the barrier, one on either side. With the supplemented or completed image, one can identify the scholar as the one who stands before the hedge, just like Jacob Grimm portrayed the collector as standing behind branches in the woods, getting a glimpse of what they were concealing.

When there is a hedge in the folktale, there is a sleeping figure behind it but also a hero before it, who will come at the right moment to move through the barrier that opens. What was long hidden will at that moment appear again and what was dormant stirred to life. Wilhelm Grimm never told this story of reintroduction and indeed resurrection, but strands of it were undeniably present in his texts. Reconstructed with the help of the folktales mentioned in the prefaces as well as Jacob Grimm's affiliated imagery, we can imagine Wilhelm Grimm's collector and philologist as the figure standing before the now unraveling hedge to retrieve the treasures that had been shielded but also hidden from view, quietly protected but also not fully known.

According to Wilhelm Grimm, the protections of tradition were disappearing, which put the tales – the hidden treasures – at risk; the previously safeguarding hedges would soon be a thing of the past. It was precisely this decline of the protective folk life that called forth the necessity of preserving the tales and making them available in some other way – this was after all part of the rationale of the folktale collection. In a sense, the text's half-hidden imagery of timely arrival at a dissolving boundary best captured the role of the collecting scholar; Wilhelm Grimm's philologist occupied the position of the figure before a protective but now disintegrating barrier. Buried in the prefaces with its imagery of shielding hedges was even something of an allegory of cultural awakening, in which the collector-editor appeared at just the right moment for the public reemergence or even resurrection of a cultural life long hidden but maintained by common people in their modest domestic spaces. The transcription and publication of the folktales was, in this frame, an entirely legitimate undertaking, and perhaps also a perfectly timed one. The Grimms could not be accused of stealing the tales or exploiting the tellers, the prefaces indicated, because they had not come to violate a sheltered location or steal the narrative treasures of the people, but to witness the reappearance of a richness previously hidden. The retreat and even dissolution of traditional life, which seemed so regrettable to Wilhelm Grimm, coincided with the philologist's retrieval and public display of forgotten treasures, which presumably was an occasion to be celebrated. In this way, the transition from local folk practices to the collector's and editor's work of restoration, synthesis, and dissemination was inscribed into the imagery of the preface – and justified by it.

Wilhelm Grimm's prefaces to the volumes of folktales, then, contained a sort of encrypted narrative of self-justification, cast in an imagery of preservation and discovery that appeared across more than one text. This was a narrative that outlined, by means of a key image of protection or "securing [*sichern*]," the transitional role of the collector-editor who could facilitate the contact between a sustained but also long-concealed cultural past and a tumultuous present, manage the shift from resilient but stubbornly local and now endangered oral traditions to a print-based mode of national distribution, and connect the collectivism of age-old popular storytelling practices with the contemporary literary sphere. The prefaces indicated that little known folk traditions had long guarded the remains of ancient German poetry, but that these remains could and should now be introduced to a public so as not to become lost – at the right moment and by the right person. That person, tasked with a unique recuperative and mediating mission at a particular epochal juncture, namely the retrieval and release of a German cultural heritage in a period of fading folk culture, was none other than the philologist. Whenever there is a hedge in the folktale, there is also a hero or redeeming prince, and in relation to the previously protected folktales and their hidden riches, the philologist Wilhelm Grimm surreptitiously slipped into the role of the prince of Germany.

Wilhelm Grimm developed a particular conception of the philologist's mission. He was, like his brother, trained and inspired by Savigny, the influential scholar and civil servant who broke with the dominance of the natural law tradition in the German legal world, headed the historical school of jurisprudence, and argued for the legal leadership of the historicist professoriate. For Savigny, jurists ought to tend to the law, piece together its sometimes scattered and disordered parts, clarify its structure, and guide its application so that the people could continue its historical life undisturbed and uncoerced by a supposedly enlightened regime. Savigny, one could say, argued against the rule of a philosophizing king in favor of the historically oriented jurist – the scholar was the guardian of law. Together with his brother, Wilhelm Grimm shifted attention from law to literature and argued that ancient German poetry constituted a collective historical substance that marked out the Germans from other peoples. As the legal scholar carefully and rigorously maintained the law of the people in its particularity, the philologist explored and disseminated knowledge of a once spontaneously self-generating, communal poetry – a purely natural and national speech – that represented an authentic record of the people's past cohesiveness. It was the philologist who mediated between the nation's intensely collective past and the more dispersed and differentiated society of the present. The Grimms, one could say, were neither traditionalists nor modernists, because they were focused on guiding and managing the *transition* from a now declining traditional and localized folk culture to the modern, integrated cultural space of the nation. That was their all-important task of scholarly mediation.

What was it that Wilhelm Grimm's philologist knew, or knew and did? He claimed to know the nation, that it existed and existed naturally, that it possessed historical depth and cultural autonomy, and that it should not be unfavorably compared with or dominated by other nations, given its naturalness, antiquity, and particularity. This national knowledge was not self-evident, but rather the result of patient exploration and retrieval and hence methodical discovery, and it could be made available so that the present age, the contemporary public, could come to understand its prehistory of vibrant expressivity and declare its cultural independence with greater confidence. This meant that the philologist was the figure who could stir Germany to life. Wilhelm Grimm subtly pictured himself as the prince of Germany, but then a folktale prince rather than an actual ruler, a self-appointed redeemer of a slumbering national culture at a particular juncture in time.

In Wilhelm Grimm's vision, the philologist roused the previously dormant and half-hidden narrative culture, restored it and released it, made it public in the age of print and in doing all this enabled the nation's return to literary greatness. Revered authors such as Goethe or Schiller created canonical literary works that enhanced the status of German culture in the European space, but, according to the Grimms, the nation still needed diligent experts on the natural poetry of the people, the poetry that once had sprung spontaneously out of the tribal collective and survived in fragments and marginalized genres. Only the philologist could assume this custodianship of ancient poetry, since he respected its self-organized form, collected and edited it with the utmost care rather than treat it as raw material on which to impose an artistic will. By reconnecting the densely communal ancient history to the precarious national present, the philologist could lay claim to a kind of cultural leadership and seek to perform a redemptive function in a transitional time. National revitalization depended on the facilitating practice of scholarship in the form of a respectful recollection of the past, and the results of this scholarship were the medium of the nation's encounter with its own historical identity.

For all his emphasis on cultural redemption and revitalization, however, the young Wilhelm Grimm had no developed understanding of how the philologist could relate to any actual ruler. The philologist's task, according to his half-hidden programmatic statements, was directed toward a German readership, a people that ought to develop a richer self-understanding. Jacob Grimm, by contrast, reflected more on the philologist's location in between the nationally defined people and the political regime. It was not enough for the philologist to return to the German people the particular and collectively owned culture that belonged to it; one also had to make the ruling elite attentive to this culture, with the hope that princes and kings would respect and love it. Having worked under the king of Westphalia and then going on to an intermittent and reluctantly pursued amateur political career, Jacob Grimm was perhaps more attuned to the question of how to mediate between the ruler and the ruled, the king and the people. This task of political mediation is the object of the next chapter.

CHAPTER 4

Love of the Fatherland and Fatherly Love
Jacob Grimm's Political Thought

The Scholar in Politics

Jacob Grimm would often claim that he preferred the quiet, even reclusive existence of a scholar,[1] and yet he found himself in the midst of decisive political events more than once in his life and could observe, often closely, dramatic developments as they unfolded in major European cities, such as Paris, Vienna, Berlin, or Frankfurt. At moments, he was caught up in central political occurrences of the first half of the nineteenth century, some of which distracted him from his work, disrupted his career, tore him away from his home, and pushed him into exile but also heightened his reputation and made him a figure of national renown. You could tell a story about Grimm in which he repeatedly stumbled onto the scene of politics, found himself entangled in spectacular events, and became an icon of political struggles, only to withdraw again into scholarship when he had reached the point of exhaustion.

However, Grimm's political positions were generated through the relationship of philological scholarship – its animating spirit and defining purpose, its methods and results – to political rule. For Grimm, philology meant love of the word, and, in the case of *German* philology, loving dedication to the vernacular spoken in and by the German nation. He did claim that his work in the field of German or Germanic Studies, a field he co-created and promoted over decades, embodied and expressed a love for the fatherland. The aim of Grimm's project of rendering politics more philological meant to infuse rule with similar respect and love: the exercise of power should limit itself to the boundaries already set by the national vernacular and always be guided by loving devotion to the nation, its character, and its past.

Grimm's politics were at the same time transformational and frustratingly vague, ambitious and curiously limited. Grimm believed himself to have a philologically grounded notion of the extent and shape of the unit of rule; the philologist could settle boundary disputes by delineating nations. Yet his philological nationalism was fairly reticent about the question of the right system of governance *within* the established unit. He certainly envisaged a more important role for the nationally defined people in politics but never called for some form of popular rule. He still believed in traditional monarchical order as the guarantee of governmental stability and unity but would no longer accept royal indifference to national integrity. Hesitant to take sides in ideological conflicts within the nation and seemingly unwilling to specify the ultimate source and bearer of political sovereignty – the monarch or the people – Grimm wished that the ties of understanding and solidarity across hierarchies in the linguistic and ethno-cultural community would guarantee political harmony; the frequent invocations of love papered over inevitable tensions.

Jacob Grimm's Political Biography

How did Jacob Grimm end up in Paris, Vienna, Berlin, and Frankfurt? Paris was the capital of defeated, post-Napoleonic France, Vienna the birthplace of a restored continental order, Berlin the center of the rising power of Prussia, and Frankfurt the site of the first democratically elected German national assembly. What brought Grimm to these cities at various points between 1814 and 1848, just as they were the focal points of consequential political events and developments?

After the Wars of Liberation fought against Napoleon, Jacob Grimm, then in his late twenties and living in Kassel, applied for the job as the secretary of the Hessian diplomatic mission to the anti-Napoleonic allies. He was given the position and quickly joined the troops on a drawn-out march toward Paris.[2] In the loud and intimidating French capital, he supported the representation of Hessian interests and tried to recover the books and artworks taken from the Hessian court and brought to Paris as part of Napoleon's effort to make the city the majestic cultural center of a vast French empire.[3] As a librarian under the French regime in Westphalia, Grimm had been forced to assist with the systematic confiscation of valuable books;[4] after the wars, he would make not one but two trips to Paris to retrieve them, along with paintings by artists like Rembrandt and Rubens.[5] Wilhelm Grimm was also peripherally involved in this effort to reverse Napoleon's campaign of cultural conquest and concentration. In late 1815, he published a brief, anonymous magazine report about the ongoing restitution in Kassel and regretted the absence of paintings by, for instance, Leonardo da Vinci. They were the Elector's rightful property, Wilhelm Grimm claimed, but added that the loss offended all Hessians and Germans;[6] the interests of the ruler apparently coincided with a national cause.

After his time in Paris, Jacob Grimm also travelled with the Hessian legation to the Habsburg capital Vienna,[7] to be present at the European congress as the boundaries of states were settled and an international system of peace constructed after a quarter century of continent-wide warfare.[8] In this position, Grimm clearly took a direct interest in politics and wrote articles urging German lands to collaborate and respect one another; conflicts "in Germany among Germans [*in Deutschland unter Deutschen*]" would be a grave sin, a symptom of corruption beyond measure.[9] Yet he failed to please some of his superiors in the small Hessian diplomatic contingent, who wanted him to intercept information about diplomatically relevant developments in Viennese venues rather than write editorials and spend time with scholars and poets in the city.[10] The mutual irritation was unsurprising; the congress, a grandiose meeting place for large numbers of visitors representing the European royalty and nobility,[11] was not the most congenial environment for a young scholar from a modest civil servant background.

The young Grimm's wish for trans-German political concord that would manifest the cultural and linguistic unity of all German-speaking peoples was also at odds with the deals struck among the traditional European aristocratic and royal elites. For figures such as the leading Austrian diplomat Klemens von Metternich (1773–1859), the restoration and consolidation of royal authority combined with regularized diplomatic communication among traditional European political elites were the keys to stability and peace, not the unification of national peoples and their induction into politics.[12] According to the conservative analysis, popular revolution had fatally destabilized governance and unleashed the unconstrained ambitions of a tyrant, which had led to a long period of European-wide destruction.[13] To contain such chaos, princes ought to be firmly in power over their areas, and in permanent contact with one another, to stifle local rebellions and prevent geopolitical instability. The "restorative federalism" of the German Confederation,[14] a bundle of about forty independent German states, was supposed to be sufficiently strong to withstand French military aggression but not stand as one centralized German-national state of excessive might.[15] Jacob Grimm did not at this time demand a single nation-state, but he was alienated by how aristocratic cliques conducted negotiations about the future of all Germans in disregard of actual populations.

Grimm had neither fascination nor talent for a diplomatic career and resigned from his post as secretary in 1815; the string of visits to centers of European politics as a civil servant on various diplomatic expeditions came to an end. Yet he continued to serve the government in Hesse as a librarian, and also a somewhat reluctant part-time censor, from 1816 to 1829,[16] a long stretch of relative quiet and productivity.[17] Jacob Grimm and his brother were content with their calm situation, even though their relationship to the princely government deteriorated over time, especially after the succession of Wilhelm II (1777–1847), the son of the old Hessian Elector, who was willfully ignorant of the Grimms' scholarly achievements and eventually promoted dilettantes over the more qualified brothers.[18] Disappointed, both Jacob and Wilhelm Grimm left Kassel in 1829 for posts at the university in Göttingen, a town in the larger kingdom of Hanover, north of Hesse, ruled in so-called personal union by the British monarch; George III, whose father and grandfather had spoken German, was king in two kingdoms, The United Kingdom and Hanover. In Göttingen, Jacob Grimm assumed a post as professor and librarian at one of the finest universities in Germany, a rank it had achieved at least partly because of the historical Anglo-Hanoverian communications and relatively light and liberal rule by the distant British court.[19] Göttingen was also where Grimm was to take a more explicit and controversial political stance, no longer an observer of German and European politics, but – temporarily and not terribly enthusiastically – a key character.

The background to the political events in Göttingen was the struggle over constitutions, a struggle central to the *Vormärz* era, the period from the Congress of Vienna in 1815 to the European-wide revolutions of 1848. To many people in the circles of the brothers Grimm, constitutionalized monarchies seemed the proper political form of the age. After the revolution, monarchy was on the defensive, compelled to justify itself anew,[20] but many educated professionals in German lands nonetheless feared its complete dismantling; the lesson of the French Revolution seemed to be that regicide entailed chaos, dissolution, and the rise of upstart oppressors. In this situation, German liberals in the post-congress period typically championed constitutions that would fix and stabilize the rule of the monarch, render kingship a position within an articulated system that included elements of popular representation, and secure basic liberties for citizens no longer defined exclusively as the subjects or dependents of a paternal king. Such constitutions would put an end to unconstrained, absolutist rule but do so without decapitating the monarch.[21] The constitutional documents would set some moderate and moderating limits to royal power – allow for representative assemblies and define rights such as freedom of the press and opinion – but not undermine traditional authority. German liberalism in fact largely coincided with such a call for constitutional monarchism,[22] in which a hereditary king would continue as the head of state in charge of executive and legislative power but nonetheless allow for more cooperative decision-making procedures.[23]

Such reformist demands seemed modest; the monarch would, after all, remain firmly on the throne and the collective of citizens would not exercise sovereign power.[24] More conservative figures even insisted that the king would only issue a constitution that he could then also revoke, and that constitutional monarchy consisted in the king's gracious self-restraint and willingness to rule in a legal state removed from pure personal patrimonialism.[25] Yet the very idea of popular representation did convert the ruler into one party in an ongoing negotiation.[26] The king would no longer rule over a kingdom understood as his exclusive possession but would instead have to act in concert with the people, at least minimally, in accordance with procedures specified in a constitutional document,[27] although one typically issued by the sitting dynasty. The result was a dualist vision of rule, and numerous attempts to imagine mediations between kingship and popular freedom.[28]

The middle-aged Jacob Grimm was in many ways a typical representative of the age, in that he piously spoke of the need for harmonious interaction between the prince and the people.[29] Specifically, Grimm invoked the benefits of a common German nationhood uniting the king and his subjects. In a nationally circumscribed state, he hoped, shared cultural belonging would constitute a basis for a mutual trust and accommodation between the monarch and the citizens, but later commentators have generally remained skeptical. Constitutionalized monarchy was, many have claimed, marred by unresolved oppositions[30] and represented a transitional and ultimately impossible combination of absolutism and parliamentarism.[31] In this view, the constitutional monarchy was a compromise formation,[32] a constellation of contradictory elements in which the source of ultimate authority remained undefined. The political form was, the historian James Sheehan writes, characterized by a "persistent obscurity about the ultimate locus of power," and a shared care for the nation did not clarify the situation.[33]

In the late 1830s, the kingdom of Hanover became the site of an emblematic conflict over a constitution and Jacob Grimm played a leading part. It was in the university town of Göttingen that a rigidly traditionalist king with an absolutist understanding of his prerogatives clashed with educated professionals in state service, a group to which Grimm belonged. The background to the conflict was complicated. With the ascendance of Queen Victoria to the British throne in 1837, Hanover's personal union with Great Britain ended, since the law of the German kingdom did not permit female succession. William IV could be the ruler of both Britain and Hanover; Queen Victoria could not. Instead, Victoria's uncle Ernst August (1771–1851), the Duke of Cumberland, succeeded to the Hanoverian throne; he had studied in Göttingen in the 1780s and, returning as the king, he became the first ruler to actually live in Hanover in more than a century.[34] However, Ernst August was over 65 years old at the time and had the reputation of an archconservative military man.[35] Shortly after his arrival in his kingdom, he dissolved the parliament and abrogated the most recent and quite modern constitution, which had been adopted in 1833, partly drafted by the political philosopher and historian Friedrich Christoph Dahlmann, close friend of the brothers Grimm.[36] In a report back to England, Ernst August wrote that he had "cut the wings of this democracy."[37] The professors, and among them Jacob and Wilhelm Grimm, had, as was usual, sworn an oath of allegiance to the suddenly suspended constitution as servants of the state,[38] and they balked at the king's imperious demeanor. In a sense, both sides, the king and the group of professors, believed that the other had acted rashly, beyond the bounds of their legitimate space of action, and called for a return to an earlier condition. The king, a defendant of royal preeminence, thought the recent constitution arbitrary and illegal, imposed without his consent,[39] while the professors deemed the sudden revocation of the constitution a brazen autocratic action in defiance of an appropriately balanced system of rule. In Hanover, the compromise of constitutional monarchy seemed to come apart as a new king simply annulled the recently adopted constitution.

To voice resistance, the Grimms' colleague Dahlmann wrote a letter of protest signed by six other Göttingen professors, among them the brothers Grimm, addressed only to the board of the university.[40] After the protest had been unintentionally leaked and circulated widely by Göttingen students, King Ernst August responded by discharging the professors, and Jacob Grimm, Dahlmann, and the younger literary historian Georg Gottfried Gervinus (1805–71) were compelled to leave the kingdom.[41] In the meantime, the protestation letter reached the general public; newspapers reported on the affair; and, over time, there were even campaigns collecting funds in support of the professors. In some camps, the Grimms and their peers were celebrated as heroic defenders of the constitutional order. The brothers worried more about the arbitrary initiative of the ruler inattentive to the life of the people and cared less about the actual content of the constitution,[42] but their stance against the king electrified liberal students.⁴³ Even though Grimm and his peers often cloaked their unbroken commitment to the Hanoverian constitution in the language of Protestant religious piety and humble fidelity, the collective action of the professorial circle had demonstrated that civil servants no longer simply served the king.⁴⁴

With Jacob Grimm ejected from Hanover, the brothers felt offended, even wounded, and they were certainly anxious about their future, but they were eventually invited to Berlin as members of the Prussian Academy by King Frederick William IV, who ascended to the throne in 1841, and proceeded to rehabilitate a series of censored and maligned nationalist academics, among them Ernst Moritz Arndt and Christoph Dahlmann. The brothers Grimm were recruited to Berlin thanks to the tireless lobbying work of Bettina von Arnim, to whom the brothers had dedicated their *Children's and Household Tales*.⁴⁵ The recruitment was of course approved by the Prussian monarch but kept as discreet as possible because of the king's family ties to the Hanoverian ruler: Ernst August was the brother-in-law of Frederick William's father, William III.⁴⁶

The 1840s spent in Berlin was to be the decade of Jacob Grimm's most direct participation in the political process, as a parliamentary delegate in the first German national assembly, the Frankfurt parliament. In early 1848, revolutionary conditions in large cities and rural spots all over Europe and Germany, among them Berlin, seemed to suggest the possibility of a momentous political transformation. Urban crowds rioted, workers went on strike, farmers occupied land and refused to render services to lords, and insurgents clashed with armed forces on the streets of Vienna and Berlin, causing Metternich to flee the Habsburg Empire and the Prussian army to retreat from the capital.⁴⁷ The cascades of unrest set off by a sequence of poor harvests and recession-like years that aggravated pauperization put severe pressure on governments all over Europe, causing many to crumble.⁴⁸ European monarchies, among them those in German states, seemed unable to defend themselves against rapidly spreading mass rebellions.⁴⁹

In this situation, prominent German liberals gathered in March 1848 to call for the formation of a national parliament that would exercise greater power than any previous German assembly and yet cooperate with princes amenable to reform.⁵⁰ The aim of those involved was initially not to dissolve the forty or so sovereign German states to create one unitary national state. Their plan was instead to establish a national parliamentary institution that would communicate with the circle of German rulers⁵¹ and then discuss and resolve the interlinked questions of Germany's future political order, federative structure, and territorial extent. Should Germans live in a monarchy or perhaps in a future republic, a federative union or a unitary state, and what areas should be incorporated as German? The dominant groups within German liberalism remained committed to the continued existence of a monarchical executive,[52] but one compelled to interact with a democratically elected assembly that represented a uniform body of citizens.[53] Elections took place all over Germany in May 1848, allowing all adult and independent male citizens to vote, restrictions that were differently interpreted in different German lands.[54]

Following political developments from Berlin, Jacob Grimm took part in a series of preelection meetings and eventually did travel to Frankfurt as an elected delegate, but then as a representative for a constituency in the Rhineland where he replaced Ernst Moritz Arndt who had an alternative seat.[55] A member of an academic elite, Grimm was in many ways a typical Frankfurt parliamentarian. Around a tenth of the delegates were professors, and administrative and judicial officials as well as lawyers were in a majority; businessmen, industrialists, and landowners were less well represented.[56] Once an observer in Paris and Vienna and an exiled defender of the constitution in Hanover, it would seem that Jacob Grimm had finally become a political actor as a delegate in an assembly striving for political influence in all of Germany. Grimm, now well over 60 years old, began service as a parliamentarian.

In the actual building where the parliament started its work in late spring of 1848, the Paulskirche in Frankfurt, Jacob Grimm was even placed in a symbolic spot in the very middle and enjoyed the reputation as an icon of German unity.[57] He did submit proposals and speak to the assembly and even emerged as an occasional radical, arguing not for the abolition of kingship but for the elimination of noble ranks in Germany.[58] The nobility was a historically significant class, Grimm conceded, but the practice of knighting distinguished citizens was no longer necessary and produced absurd linguistic results, a sure symptom of the obsolescence of feudal gradations. The noble name "Heinrich von Kronberg" made some sense – Heinrich came *from* Kronberg – but not "Johann Wolfgang von Goethe," since Goethe was not a location.[59] In Grimm's implicit view, monarchy should be retained in German lands but no longer rest on the social and political dominance of an aristocratic elite. Instead, kings should rule as unifying figures over a destratified, more egalitarian national community.[60] For Grimm, an individual's birth and genealogy were still decisive, but only because they guaranteed *national* membership, not hereditary noble status;

the concept of nationhood required a form of governance based in equality under law.⁶¹ Grimm's motion was voted down.

Eventually, Grimm left the parliament early and returned to Berlin. Worried about his health and ultimately indifferent to the everyday business of politics, Grimm departed from Frankfurt before the parliamentary session came to a close.⁶² He was also deeply discouraged by the Prussian government's truce with the Danish king in late August 1848,⁶³ an armistice that concluded the conflict over Schleswig and Holstein and simultaneously demonstrated that the parliament did not control the military or foreign policy.⁶⁴ Grimm did not want to speak out against the decision of his king,⁶⁵ and yet felt he had to follow his conscience and retreat from an assembly that accepted the end of the Prussian campaign against Denmark and harmed the national cause.⁶⁶ Disappointed, Grimm wrote to his brother in Berlin that the Prussian government had failed Germany; it had committed "an un-German action [*sich einer undeutschen handlung schuldig gemacht*]."⁶⁷ Grimm traveled from Frankfurt to Berlin in October 1848 and in November, large Prussian forces loyal to the king marched into the capital; took control of major streets, squares, and buildings; and stifled any resistance in the city⁶⁸ – it was a monarchist *coup d'état*.⁶⁹ The next year, the German national assembly was dissolved, effectively powerless against German princes who could still count on the support of their armies as well as the administrative and judicial bureaucracies.⁷⁰

Paris, Vienna, Göttingen, Berlin, and Frankfurt – these cities were stations in Jacob Grimm's political biography, as the sites of tumultuous, even epochal events, and in some cases stages for an increasingly public role. After stepping down as a Frankfurt delegate and returning to Berlin, Grimm did not cease to observe or comment on politics in the following decade, and there were further political incidents in the lives of the brothers as well as further proclamations from Jacob Grimm.⁷¹ Yet his most intensive involvement and his most widely recognized moments as a representative of the German constitutional and nationalist movement were in the past.

At the end of his life, Jacob Grimm could look back on an at least intermittently political career. He had served as a Hessian official in post-Napoleonic Paris tasked with the recovery of stolen art, a somewhat disgruntled and underpaid secretary at the Congress of Vienna,⁷² emerged publicly as a principled professor taking a stand against an autocratic king in Göttingen to then reappear, ten years later, as a widely venerated delegate in the German national parliament. The sequence of events and places could be read as a story of gradual national-liberal emancipation neatly embodied by the biography of one famous scholar. Grimm started out as a civil servant in the stagnant, absolutist Electorate of Hesse, became widely known as a defender of the constitution standing against the rigid Hanoverian king, and finally went to Frankfurt as an elected representative of the German people. Jacob Grimm's career would then instantiate a narrative of a frequently frustrated but nonetheless slowly progressing process of liberalization and democratization, in which educated and propertied groups in Germany demanded, and tried to seize, a greater political role vis-à-vis traditional princely rulers. Grimm's life was a long journey, from a mid-size and fairly provincial principality to a more integrated national arena, from service in absolutist conditions to the first German parliament.

In the Service of the King

Yet this story of Grimm's political biography does not capture his enduring, professional relationship to power as it was exercised in early nineteenth-century German lands. Jacob Grimm was employed, deployed, promoted, rejected, and recruited many times, almost always by an incumbent elector or king, for whom he could appear as a promising or insufficiently subservient servant of the state, a useful administrator-scholar, or an impertinent one. Together with his brother, Grimm experienced more than once just how much it mattered exactly who governed the lands where he lived and worked. The Elector Wilhelm I of Hesse, Jérôme Bonaparte King of Westphalia, the Elector Wilhelm II of Hesse, Ernst August I King of Hanover, and finally Frederick William IV of Prussia – each of these rulers in some way decided Grimm's professional situation, his tasks, and his status, for the simple reason that he was working in administrative and academic capacities for princely states. Like many other university-educated professionals employed in the administrative or judicial bureaucracy, Grimm's chief wish was to reform the state and educate the rulers on which he relied for secure employment and perhaps also a sense of existential comfort in an era of accelerated change.[73] While he hoped that the age of "unlimited power [*unumschränkter Herrschaft*]" of princes who treated states as their patrimonial possessions would come to an end,[74] he could also express the worry that the resolute separation of powers would fragment monarchical authority, weaken its reputation, and fatally destabilize governance.[75]

There was nothing extraordinary about Grimm's professional service to a string of rulers in smaller or larger German principalities. Eighteenth- and nineteenth-century German states and statelets relied on academically trained professionals who "wrote histories, compiled statistics, edited government directories, compendiums, handbooks, public affairs newspapers, and journals, gave special instruction to court residents and their children, censored private publications, even served on diplomatic missions."[76] Many items on this list apply directly to Jacob Grimm. He served as the court librarian and archivist under Jérôme Bonaparte in Kassel; a secretary, censor, and librarian under the first Hessian Elector; a librarian and professor in Göttingen; and an academy member and funded lexicographer in Berlin. Jacob Grimm himself never worked as a tutor at the court, but Wilhelm Grimm did, trying to teach the Hessian Elector's indifferent and apathetic son in the early 1820s.[77]

In this light, Jacob Grimm emerges as a fairly typical early nineteenth-century figure, the academically trained government employee, sometimes a scholar-administrator with particular tasks and sometimes a professor in the state-supported university system; a university post effectively meant working as a state servant tasked with the education of further generations of state servants.[78] Grimm came from a family of civil servants bound to the personal rule of the local landgrave and continued in that tradition;[79] while he insisted on the dignity and independence of the well-educated, professional, and incorruptible bureaucrat, he remained a salaried official in states headed by princes. For most of his life, he was a "servant of the state [*staatsdiener*]" working in some administrative or academic capacity under a "prince [*fürst*]."[80] The laws that regulated civil service increasingly granted bureaucrats greater autonomy, and Grimm insisted on the entitlement of civil servants to stable employment as well as their right to relinquish their positions should they so wish.[81] Yet during Grimm's lifetime, the administrative apparatus clearly remained an instrument of monarchs who selected, promoted, and in some cases dismissed bureaucrats.[82]

Despite his posthumous fame as the coauthor or coeditor of the world's most widely available collection of folktales, Grimm was in his own time not an author making a living in the book market and the public sphere; he was in some sense not even primarily a professor with the university as his natural professional home.[83] Instead, he was a professional with a legal and historical education who remained in close and direct contact with princes and monarchs and depended on employment in the state. He certainly always remained at a distance from other sectors of society, such as agriculture, private enterprise of any kind, or early industry. While he occasionally and very publicly appeared as a politicized civil servant and parliamentary delegate, he stayed close to the orbit of one or the other prince or king. Grimm was, after all, trained for and belonged to the organizational arm of state power, and his welfare depended on reliably discharging duties to princes; he had no experience of democratic governance and did not really believe in its viability; he wanted an "alert popular element [*waches volkselement*]," but not a democracy.[84] Grimm's life was at all times enmeshed with the princely and monarchical state.

This overview suggests a slightly different story than the one of gradual emancipation. Throughout his career, Grimm looked like a professional who managed to survive an unpredictable sequence of changes at the top:[85] he lost his position under the Hessian Elector but was hired by the new French king installed by Napoleon, only to find employment again in the restored Electorate after Napoleon's demise. He left Kassel for Göttingen after being ignored at the Hessian court but eventually ended up in Prussian Berlin, recruited by the Prussian ruler after refusing to comply with the actions of the Hanoverian king. The 1840s may have been Jacob Grimm's decade of vigorous political participation, including his work in the first German national parliament, but since Frederick William IV of Prussia had been personally involved in the rehabilitation of both brothers in 1841, giving them new official positions of security and prestige, Grimm believed he stood in a relationship of strong personal loyalty and obligation to the king.[86] This attachment to the institution of monarchy was not merely a private stance, but something he was happy to announce to the public. When presenting himself to the voters in his assigned parliamentary district in 1848, he assured the electorate in a newspaper note that he was a staunch antiradical: "I stand for a free, united fatherland under a powerful king, and against all republican desires [*republikanische Gelüste*]."[87]

For both Jacob and Wilhelm Grimm, the historically long-lasting institution of kingship understandably loomed large in their political imagination. They could grumble and protest about clumsy, indifferent, arrogant monarchs and take a stand against a king's rash suspension of a constitution supposed to temper royal power, but they did not question the fundamental necessity and rightness of monarchical government. At crucial junctures, they benefited from royal recognition and protection. Yet monarchy did not fully define their political horizon, for there was of course also the nation, the German nation, to which Grimm was singularly devoted as a scholar. Politically, Grimm aimed for a reconciliation between a strong monarchy and a constitutionally protected people, a reconciliation enabled by nationhood understood as a community of mutual affection. Grimm's political vision of a philologically informed king ultimately embodied his wish for an enduring connection between the nation he loved and the king he served.

Politics and the Love of the Fatherland

As a civil servant in an age that took steps toward the mixed form of constitutional monarchy, Jacob Grimm did not glorify kingship as divinely ordained. Few German thinkers invoked divine right in the post-revolutionary nineteenth century, not even leading conservatives, who instead spoke of the "monarchical principle," a term for the monarch's unified control over the legislative and executive functions of the state understood as a guarantee of order.[88] Grimm seemed to accept such a concentration of functions in the hands of a royal head of state, such a non-separation of powers,[89] and never understood monarchy as a historically superseded or deficient form of rule. He was neither a sycophant monarchist fearful of any degree of popular involvement nor a committed republican. Instead, he hoped for a new form of mediation between monarchical rule and popular freedom and dignity,[90] an "alert popular element" somehow integrated into the nation's politics, but in no way a full-fledged democracy without a royal head.[91] To achieve political balance, princes should adopt constitutions that would regulate their actions vis-à-vis the citizens, Grimm thought, but above all, kings should relate respectfully and even lovingly to the culturally and linguistically defined people and accept a given, natural, non-malleable, territorially limited ground for their rule. This knowledge of and love for the nation could be appreciated, even judged from the outside – by a philologist.

For Grimm, the nation was a community of love, and philological research devoted to the national community was a labor of love, a patient attempt to retrieve, order, and publicize literary materials that would constitute a restored cultural object of collective reverence. Together with Wilhelm Grimm, whose major philological study was an inventory of the ancient Germanic tradition of epic narrative, Jacob sought to bequeath an entire tradition to his contemporaries – German grammar, German myths, German laws, German legends, German tales. The research output served to construct large repositories that could serve as tangible proof of the existence of a German people as a linguistically distinct, self-enclosed, and self-generating *Volk*, a people with ancient roots, a collective subject to which political rule must show sensitivity and pledge fidelity.

Importantly, Grimm understood this life-defining attempt to resurrect a German vernacular culture as an expression of love; the word *liebe* often figured in his vocabulary when it came time to justify or summarize his decades-long enterprise. In an autobiographical account written for a history of Hessian men of letters from 1831, Grimm wrote that love of the fatherland, *liebe zum vaterland*, was implanted in all the Grimm siblings early on without anyone actually speaking about it – it was simply woven into their modest family life.[92] He returned to the theme at the end of the narrative, just before a bibliography of his writings, to add that the bulk of his texts were dedicated to the history of Germanic language, poetry, and law and in this way explored the common fatherland, a work he called dignified and solemn.[93] He viewed the results of his scholarly labor as acts of devotion, but the tomes with linguistic, historical, and ethno-cultural material were also meant to "nourish" the "love" for the fatherland.[94] The purpose of Grimm's scholarship was not merely to expand historical learning, or to distill out of the past some directly applicable principles for present societal life, but to express and facilitate attachment and affection.

Love – love for the fatherland – was the motivation for and objective of Grimm's research. At the second national meeting of Germanists in Lübeck in 1847, a member of the association gave a toast to Jacob Grimm as the field's most prominent and wide-ranging scholar and the association's president, a man who single-handedly had founded the study of Germanic grammar. Moved to the point of tears, almost unable to speak, Grimm replied with a declaration of love for Germany and the absolute supremacy of this love in the hierarchy of his passions and loyalties: "*ich liebe mein vaterland, mein vaterland ist mir immer über alles gegangen* [I love my fatherland, my fatherland has always gone above everything]."[95] Grimm was a nationalist in the sense that he publicly expressed love for the fatherland, a love that exceeded any other attachment in his life, an allegiance more sacred than all other ties.

The invocation of love was partly a gesture of its time. Grimm was a figure of the Romantic period, an age known for multiple philosophies of love. Romantics such as Friedrich Schlegel, born in 1772, a little less than a generation before Grimm, believed that the rationalism of Enlightenment thought and the apparent legalistic character of Kantian ethics had fatally reduced the significance that love had held for morality in the Christian tradition.[96] Community, Schlegel believed, was principally formed through bonds of love and not through the commitment of reasoning minds to noncontradictory maxims or the discovery of shared interests.[97] The young Hegel, a contemporary of Schlegel and later his bitter critic, saw in love the avenue toward reconciliation between self and other, subject and object. In love, you become united with what seems different and distinct, as the loving self both surrenders itself to another and finds or rediscovers itself expanded and enriched by someone or something outside of itself. In this way, love releases humans from their narrow self-attachment and parochialism, creates unity with others, and helps heal a world apparently riven with division and conflict.[98] Around 1800, then, love emerged as an element in a conceptual vocabulary meant to remedy the insufficiencies of a philosophy focused on the faculty of reason; rational insight alone could not determine how people ought to act ethically, relate to one another, unite and remain unified, and it certainly could not supply enough motivation and energy for an ethical life.

Jacob Grimm did not give love a central role in a philosophical project, as he had no philosophical project of his own, but his repeated statements of love for the fatherland indicate that he privileged a community of loyalty sustained by bonds of affection over any other principle of cohesion, such as the shared subjection to a wise patrimonial ruler or the contractual agreements of self-interested individuals.[99] His insistence on love of the fatherland aligned with a more traditional patriotism, the premodern and certainly pre-Romantic doctrine of *amor patriae*, which stipulated the natural inclination and fundamental obligation to defend one's country, to which one owed one's moral formation and religious education;[100] traditional patriotism, too, held that a vigorous civic life depended on an affective basis.[101] However, in the texts of Jacob Grimm, love emerged as a fundamental principle of connection, without which *any* social life would remain arid and brittle; love would bind people together more effectively and more authentically than any other attitudes.[102] In this sense, Grimm was a Romanticist.

Grimm's rhetoric of love emerged early in his writing career. In an 1811 treatise on the social and poetic continuity between German court poets and city poets, the young Jacob Grimm suggested that the state apparatus should not fear the proliferation of exclusive and close-knit guilds, associations, and corporations such as universities within its bounds. Seeking to reconcile – or to obfuscate – the difference between smaller face-to-face communities and the less personal structure of a state,[103] Grimm argued that sub-state associations would not necessarily divide loyalty and fragment authority so much as they would multiply people's connections to one another. There would be no tension between local community and supra-local state, Grimm concluded, where "love dwells within love."[104] Such growth of love within love presupposed that the state itself already inspired love among its subjects. Without the halo bestowed upon it by the inner affection of subjects, the state would, Grimm claimed, seem like an alien and "miserable establishment [*elende Einrichtung*]."[105] The word for a genuinely loved state, Grimm also wrote, was *Vaterland*, and what defined the fatherland was the unity of hearts prepared to die for it – humans prepared to abandon their individual lives for what constituted their common collective life.[106] In the early tract on medieval poetry, then, the "fatherland" was Grimm's name for a polity insofar as it served as a treasured existential shelter and an encompassing realm of love for multiple smaller communities of love housed within it. Love for the fatherland was a consistent attitude of Grimms; he spoke of it in the early 1810s, the early 1830s, and the late 1840s, across venues and genres, in his early scholarly treatises, his brief notes toward a scholarly biography, and at ceremonial occasions late in his career. The rhetoric of love did not change, although the object of this love was quietly scaled up from provincial Hesse to a Germany yet to be unified; like the term *Heimat*, the "fatherland" proved a fairly elastic concept, able to render collectivities of various size emotionally accessible.[107]

The Romanticist Jacob Grimm preached love and the nationalist Grimm specified, and respecified, its ultimate target, but what was the "fatherland" and why did it figure, for Jacob Grimm, as the object of a profound and predominant love? The *father*-land, the word itself, relies on the "metaphorical infusion of biological descent into spatial location,"[108] a spatial location that the mature Grimm believed he could delineate with scientific, grammatical means. The notion attributes parentage to territory and binds people to a supposedly generating and sustaining place to which they belong and to which they are entitled. The notion of a fatherland also indicates that conationals are each other's kin – Grimm cared deeply about lateral relations, the "*collateralen*" that constituted a fraternity, a "brotherhood [*brüderschaft*]," and together formed a unit, even a tribe.[109] Not coincidentally, the two brothers Jacob and Wilhelm had very consciously and effectively made themselves known as the *brothers* Grimm.[110] The fatherland was thus the bounded, territorial-familial community into which linked and like individuals were born. It gave life to human beings who therefore had to thank it for their very existence; it was land understood as the source and support of fraternal, communal being.[111] When Grimm announced a love for the fatherland that exceeded all other attachments, he can be said to have expressed pious reverence for what he perceived to be his origin, something that preceded and enveloped him, and even gave him life. To claim indifference to the nation as fatherland would be to reject the very source of one's existence, to deny and hence betray the matrix and foundation of individual being.

Through his statements of love for the fatherland, Grimm attended to what he believed constituted the ground of his own existence, although he located this ground not in a divine being or in identifiable ancestors but in a historical community, not in the Father or the fathers but the fatherland. Against this backdrop, Grimm's philological work can be construed as an attempt to foster love as the appropriate attitude to a quasi-sacred source of present life. It was a philology dedicated neither to the prestigious classical heritage that still dominated gymnasiums and universities of Grimm's day nor to the scriptures of his Protestant environment, but one that instead applied the instruments of scholarly methodology to what Grimm called the "unremarkable, even despised conditions and particularities of Germany,"[112] which was his "country of birth."[113] Grimm's work was an initially counter-canonical philology that required the difficult retrieval and restoration of previously neglected textual sources, and then the further illumination of those texts by reference to an even less valued non-textual "folk tradition [*volkstradition*]."[114] The ultimate aim of this counter-canonical enterprise was to establish shared and stable objects of love, in effect a new collection of quasi-sacred texts that could lay claim to the kind of respect owed to traditional ancient and religious textual sources.[115] If love for the German nation in Grimm's view amounted to piety toward an origin, his reconstructive and redemptive philological work constituted a systematic attempt at consecration; the supposedly unremarkable and even despised, the profane and even trivial, merited the same kind of philological attention as deeply revered classical and religious sources, since it belonged to the nation.[116] Grimm's scholarship aimed to accumulate, catalogue, and disseminate as much material about the nation as was possible across the fields of language, literature, law, and religion, all to render more plausible the sense that nationhood represented the true reality of history and social life, one that demanded not only attention but affection and devotion. Philology was a disciplined practice of love dedicated to the nation as a community of love.

After this lengthy exploration of nationalist pathos, one might impatiently ask what kind of politics was implied by the rhetoric of love, or what political order would best embody and sustain the solidarity that Grimm understood as the source of authentic and lasting community. Grimm had little interest in declarations of devotion and sacrifice that went beyond the national border but also little genuine understanding for divisions or conflicts *within* the nation. For him, love denoted unity, a sense of community much more profound than any temporary agreements among agents with otherwise separate interests.[117] Needless to say, this vision diminished any appreciation for contentious politics conducted within the envisaged national space. He may have celebrated the plethora of associations and corporations as transgenerational communities of interest, mutual self-help, and familiarity, but he was uneasy about modern political parties, movements, and ideologies standing against one another and often evasively tried to appeal to an underlying unity as the basis for mutual understanding. The nation, in Grimm's view, should be a regionally and culturally varied but politically non-factionalized and only quietly stratified community of love, represented and guarded by a king.

When Grimm faced conflicts between radical critics and conservative defenders of the crown, as he inevitably did, he invoked the underlying commitment of all to the German nation. When confronted with the tension between princely power and constitutional constraint, he imagined the appearance of a *loving king* who would govern in accordance with the spirit of the people. In moments of conflict, then, Grimm retreated to assumptions about an extra-political and extra-juridical, entirely natural harmony guaranteed by nationhood. In this implicit vision, the battle lines of the age, between liberals and conservatives, between the king and the people, faded in a haze. The main principles of Grimm's political thinking seem to have been an aversion to conflict within the national space and the presumption of a unity that preexisted political conflict and negotiations. Yet the notion of love did serve as a criterion of confident, even aggressive judgment. Since devotion to the nation emerged as a requirement and source of legitimacy, Grimm could, as the self-appointed guardian of national being, sharply reject rulers who seemed lacking in love as well as dismiss combative political factions as overly rigid, narrowly focused, and even rude and repulsive. Jérôme Bonaparte lacked love for and knowledge of the German-speaking subjects, Grimm had written to Achim von Arnim, and clearly meant it as a definitive critique. The unloving king had no rightful claim to rule.

The Politics of National Unity

Grimm repeatedly explained that he viewed his linguistic, literary, and historical studies as a humble labor of love. Insofar as these scholarly studies yielded a principle of geopolitical boundary drawing, however, the sincere devotion to nationhood broke with the existing political organization in Central Europe. In his commitment to the nation as the relevant political unit, Grimm effectively demanded an end to state formations that extended across and below the supposed national space; he stood for the dissolution of the empire, the consolidation or at least federative bundling of myriad principalities, but also the opening up of the walled city – the program was fairly ambitious.

The question here is whether the philologist's care for the bounded integrity of the German nation ever involved political responsibilities and positions other than the initial determination of proper cultural and linguistic borders for the sake of legitimate rule. Did Grimm envisage the retreat of the philologist, once the ground for the exercise of rule had been defined? Or did he believe that the nation committed him to further opinions or programs, even to a post-revolutionary ideology, such as liberalism or conservatism, including a critique or defense of kingship?

In their day, Jacob and Wilhelm Grimm were typically seen as liberals, especially because of their insistence, in Göttingen, on the integrity of a binding constitution in the confrontation with a king who annulled it. In his treatment of the "age of revolution," the historian Eric Hobsbawm even singles out the brothers Grimm as prominent examples of authors who galvanized German liberals with their defiant stance.[118] After the conflict in Hanover, the liberal German-language press of the day certainly celebrated Jacob and Wilhelm Grimm and their colleagues as principled and courageous constitutionalists.[119] In Leipzig, a group of publishers even raised voluntary contributions for the seven protesters, to compensate for their suddenly canceled salaries.[120] Yet it is instructive to see how Jacob Grimm sought to depoliticize the protest[121] and generally eschewed ideological labels. In letters to his patrician and more conservative mentor Friedrich Carl von Savigny around the time of the French July Revolution in 1830, he assured his friend that he did not necessarily sympathize with the advocates of a constitution for Prussia and approved of it insofar as it would strengthen the love of the nation or the "national feeling [*nationalgefühl*]" among the general population.[122] Grimm's ultimate concern, here as elsewhere, was the unifying love for the fatherland, the *vaterlandsliebe* of all.[123] In another letter from the same year, Grimm even briefly appeared as an unprincipled political Romantic, just as attracted by the colorful pomp of monarchy as by the intrepid decisiveness of protesters and revolutionaries.[124]

Rather than forcefully and unequivocally take sides for monarchy or republicanism, Grimm preferred to speak about the harmonious adjustment between rulers and ruled. German princes, he wrote to Savigny, should relinquish claims to unconstrained domination,[125] calm their fear of a politically interested population, and embrace the current enthusiasm for the nation. It ought to be the princes' task, he wrote, to stimulate the people's devotion to their own nation, at the very least by supporting initiatives in the realm of scholarship, his own domain.[126] Grimm neither argued for the defense nor the complete abolition of princely rule but was primarily concerned with its adaptation to the national character of the population, as disclosed by Germanist scholars.

The rejection of explicit terms in the letters to Savigny may partly have been an attempt to placate a mentor wary of political turbulence, but ideological ambivalence was a fairly consistent feature in Grimm's writings. In an 1819 letter to his childhood friend Paul Wigand, Grimm confessed that incompatible political philosophies nonetheless appeared to him to possess some element of truth; he could appreciate both calls for restoration of an old order and demands for the introduction of liberal constitutions that would limit princely power.[127] Displaying some self-insight, he then also expressed relief over the fact that he stood far away from the difficult art of governing, in which consequential decisions had to be made under multiple constraints.

Such vacillation was not just amateurishness admitted only in letters to close friends and colleagues but marked Grimm's public statements as well. He had, he wrote in his long commentary on his own dismissal in Göttingen, no theory of the state [*staatsrechtliche theorie*] and none to support.[128] He was familiar with the ideological oppositions of his day but could not quite take sides. Who does not, he asked, in some regard sympathize with "constitutionalist and the legitimists, the radicals and the absolutists," as long as they were all decent and honest?[129] The orthogonal positions all had their virtues, and all had their flaws. In another comment, Grimm claimed that he found constitutionalists overly hasty and pedantic in their eagerness to do away with the evolved particularities of a social order [*hergebrachte und angestammte ordnung*], but that the absolutists presumed an unnatural degree of societal immobility – both camps failed to appreciate the virtues of gradualism.[130] As the list of conflicting positions suggests, Grimm was not ignorant of the divisions of his time and had certainly read a number of works of political philosophy, such as texts by Johann Gottlob Fichte, Karl Ludwig von Haller, Benjamin Constant, Adam Müller, and of course the writings of friends and colleagues such as Friedrich Christoph Dahlmann and Ernst Moritz Arndt.[131] However, in public as in private, he abstained from committing himself to any sharply defined doctrine regarding the optimal political order; his frequently professed *vaterlandsliebe* did not permit him to take sides in a battle over the character of political rule in Germany as long as all ideological combatants were German.[132]

Grimm was confident and even strident in debates about the *boundaries* of Germany but more diffident when it came to declaring support for one or the other vision of political order within the nation. Border settlement seems to have been the one task that the philologist was prepared to assume. As Michael Freeden has pointed out in his work on ideologies, nationalism is ideologically thin. It stands for a prioritization and positive valorization of a particular group that endows its members with an identity and claims their undivided loyalty.[133] The importance of this commitment to the nation as the fundamental component of humanity becomes obvious in an international setting: the world must be remade so that each people is given statehood; multinational empires, independent cities, and traditional principalities must all make room for a universalized nationalism, and the nation-state represents the most mature and most viable political form. Once the nation's independence has been established, however, the nationalist agenda appears underspecified.[134] After securing self-determination at the level of the nation, it is relatively quiet about liberties and rights for individuals within the new framework; despite its emphasis on the pseudo-kinship of conationals, it does not in itself generate a position on the optimal or just distribution of scarce goods within the community. Nationalism can combine with other ideologies. It can, for instance, make common cause with liberals in the pursuit of national self-governance or with conservatives in the attention to national history as a constraint upon the pace or direction of change – Jacob Grimm displayed both attitudes – but this adaptability only reveals the relative leanness of nationalist thought.

Jacob Grimm's vision encapsulated the radical character of early nineteenth-century nationalism but also its relative political reticence. He insisted on Germany's right to rule over itself as a nation of affiliated tribes united by a culture and a language, internally diverse but not fragmented, free from the oppression of an alien nation, and held together in some federal form. When the discussion moved to the precise political structure of the self-determining nation or potential catalogues of civil rights, however, Grimm often chose to convey ambivalence and indecision.[135] His statement on basic rights in the German national parliament was brief and unspecific and concluded with a salute to the hallowed German ground or territory; he felt more comfortable with the pathetic invocation of German unity than with the determination of particular rights.[136] He did not propagandize for any one side in the conflict between constitutionalists and absolutists, liberals and restorationists, and he typically had little to say about the procedures for determining a legitimate leader. He was, finally, so indifferent to socioeconomic structures, disparities of wealth, and pervasive penury that one may wonder what he was referring to when he spoke about the German "people"; it appeared as a figure abstracted from current social conditions and stratifications.[137] The "social question" that began to be discussed in Germany around 1840[138] and became so central to the upheavals of 1848[139] seems to have been largely alien to Grimm, although the widely discussed problem of pauperism cannot have been completely shielded from his view: in 1843, the family friend and ally Bettina von Arnim published a book dedicated to the Prussian king that included a report on the topic of poverty and incarceration in Berlin.[140] Bettina von Arnim, too, sought to capture the attention of the Prussian king, but with news about abject misery on the fringes of the capital.

It is entirely possible to pick out comments and positions in Grimm's writing and connect them with contemporary camps and ideologies. He had to refuse the term "constitutionalist" actively because he did stand up for an extant constitution in Göttingen. He did believe that there were limits to princely power and that a ruler should be responsive to the people, although not by governing according to popular will, but, more vaguely and indirectly, in consonance with the people's spirit, as it was expressed in cultural-historical objects of philological interest. While having to work in a commission for censorship in Kassel, he often preferred to choose the most tolerant option,[141] partly because of time constraints and other pragmatic concerns but also partly because a coercive intervention would, he thought, do more harm than good.[142] As mentioned earlier, in one of his more radical moments in 1848, he suggested the abolition of any legally enshrined recognition of noble status in Germany. No achievement for the fatherland, Grimm argued, required acknowledgment in the needlessly ostentatious form of knighting.[143] One senses here Grimm's dislike for social hierarchies *within* the national space, although he hardly grasped class-based politics. Such examples suggest that Grimm at least on occasion could envision a more egalitarian community, so long as the individual subjects were equal by virtue of their shared national membership. Grimm's anti-aristocratism was not necessarily fully or self-consciously democratic, but in its focus on the fraternal relationships among conationals, it did break with feudal stratification and paved the way for a more democratic conception of the population.

At the same time, Grimm might strike us as having a conservative temperament. He placed trust in the slow evolution of institutions and attitudes rather than intrusive attempts to steer a society toward an abstractly formulated ideal. He seems to have wanted to pull away from loudly proclaimed programs and characterized the young husband of his friend Paul Wigand's daughter as "a little too glaringly liberal."[144] The problem for Grimm here did not simply lie in the political stance but in the fervor and rigidity with which it was espoused and promoted; liberals appeared to him as strident "screamers."[145] This predilection for the modest and the muted was also apparent in his critique of the most vocal and radical collective carrier of early nineteenth-century German nationalism, the university fraternities. The *Burschenschaften* were, he wrote to Wigand in a letter from 1831, far too obstinate and solemn for his taste, unnaturally stiff in their commitment to principles.[146] A major demonstration for German national republicanism and the free press with thousands of participants, the so-called Hambacher fest in 1832,[147] Grimm dismissed as nothing less than revolting.[148]

Grimm celebrated the self-regulating organism over the voluntary intervention by some empowered agent, whether that agent was a traditional monarch with means of coercion or a modern factional association. Language, to name the obvious instantiation of such an organism, could refresh itself, shed old forms but compensate for losses, and evolve without the deliberate and discernible intervention of any one speaker or group.[149] It was with an eye to such examples of quiet self-correction and self-regulation that Grimm expressed skepticism and occasional disdain for explicitly formulated and aggressively pursued political programs; only that which grew of its own accord was truly viable. Even so, such Romanticist organicism remained ideologically ambiguous.[150] Grimm typically argued for greater self-determination over decision-making from above and the importance of a unifying nationality over rigidly separated castes; these attitudes were compatible with the politically liberal critique of both absolutism and corporate society. However, he also generally showed a preference for evolved institutions and conventions over fascination with novel designs, which hints at his affiliation with the Romanticist counter-Enlightenment.[151]

Grimm was outspoken when it came to defining the nation and settling claims over lands and populations, but more elusive when it came to declaring his beliefs about the state's political organization. This was due, one could say, to his particular brand of philological nationalism. He paid professional scholarly attention to historically developed communities of language and culture, which he thought allowed him to make definitive claims about the boundaries of legitimate rule; he knew where the line ran between the native and the foreign, the German and the non-German. The intervention or dominance of a national community by a "foreign people [*fremden volkes*]" certainly constituted a clear violation of its dignity, an unnatural denial of the fundamental reality of separate nations.[152] When a potentially invidious issue emerged within the national space, however, in clashes between republicans and restorationists, liberals and conservatives,[153] Grimm's vocabulary of unity and growth appeared a little less decisive, and this was noted in his time. Decades after 1848, the year of revolution, the German novelist and journalist Theodor Fontane recalled one of Jacob Grimm's speeches as simultaneously evocative and vacuous: "And then the old Jacob Grimm went up to the podium … and said something or other about Germany, something quite general, which in any real political assembly would have made people call out 'get to the point.' But these words were not uttered by anyone, because everyone was touched and moved by the sight."[154] This vagueness of the philologist, gently mocked by Fontane, was symptomatic; the Germanist scholar cared about the lingual and territorial unit of the nation but had few specific proposals to offer for its political future. As long as everyone engaged in political debates within a clearly defined and closed national discursive space, however, the nationalist had succeeded; the boundary had been drawn.

The Philologist King – the Loving King

Jacob Grimm wanted to be remembered for his love of the fatherland, not his attachment to a city, loyalty to a leader, or passionate engagement for a principle such as liberty or justice. Yet this love seems only to have been weakly generative politically and left many issues unaddressed. With its hyperalert concern for the borders of the collective unit, nationalism goes only so far ideologically once those borders have been determined and fortified. To cite a formulation from the political philosopher F. M. Barnard, Grimm concentrated on one aspect of political legitimacy, namely the "where" of legitimate government, and paid less attention to the "who" and the "how."[155]

Grimm's commitment to the nation as the legitimate unit of rule was not entirely empty politically speaking. A ruler who is also a conational will, so the implied nationalist argument goes, be more likely to cherish and help cultivate the shared national culture, which constitutes the highest value and priority for nationalists. In the figure of the Prussian king, who had experienced the anti-Napoleonic wars, liked to read historic romance novels, and was called a Romantic on the throne,[156] Grimm may briefly have felt that he encountered a ruler with some genuine interest in German culture, although he had often been wary of Prussian ambitions to dominate other German lands without respect for an internally diverse German ethnic and linguistic community.[157] The presumed ties of solidarity and common horizon among conationals, nationalists typically believe, also make the national leadership more inclined to promote the well-being of the subjects, or at least better able to understand the preferences of the culturally particular people.[158] When rulers and ruled hail from the same nation, their habits and interests are more likely to align. An imperial elite, by contrast, is more likely to ignore the dominated people's character or misunderstand the culturally separate subjects.[159] To speak of an ethnic or cultural dimension of political legitimacy may have its limited justification, although Grimm never quite expounded it.

Yet such a general, tacit assumption about the value of a hierarchy *within* the nation rather than *across* different ethnic or linguistic groups hardly answers the questions Grimm and his peers faced in the age of constitutional monarchy. In the post-revolutionary period, the idea of popular sovereignty was by no means universally embraced, but it could also not be completely suppressed; it loomed as a liberating or menacing vision and formed the backdrop to the national specification of the people as the only proper unit of any rule, independent of the structure of leadership. Among moderate liberals, however, the long-lived and symbolically potent institution of monarchy seemed to guarantee political stability and executive consistency in a volatile age, despite the erosion of its theological justifications.[160] For all their fervor, even radical nationalist propagandists such as Ernst Moritz Arndt and Friedrich Ludwig Jahn did not necessarily wish to dismantle royal rule.[161] However, the many resulting attempts to forge a mixed constitution that integrated strong royal leadership while securing basic rights and allowing for popular influence remained contradictory and unsatisfactory. Grimm himself experienced how traditional rulers in Austria and Prussia were chased out of their capitals by uprisings motivated at least partly by the demand for a constitution, and of course he was himself exiled by a king whose first act was to abrogate an already adopted constitution. The key political form of Grimm's era, the constitutional monarchy, seemed like an incoherent compromise between post-revolutionary and traditional rule. It typically could not subdue the battle for power or answer the question about the "final and absolute" authority.[162]

The Philologist King – the Loving King

Radicals who argued for the foundation of a German republic and conservatives who called for a complete restoration of absolutist monarchies all hoped to resolve the dualism of constitutional monarchy – by eliminating it. Grimm's peers among the moderate liberals, however, devised various means of resolution. Wilhelm Eduard Albrecht (1800–76), one of Grimm's colleagues in the professorial group who defied the annulment of the Hanoverian constitution in 1837, sought to remove sovereignty from the king as well as from the people and argued instead that it belonged to the impersonal state.[163] In Albrecht's view, the king was merely an "organ" of the state construed as a juridical person whose workings were specified in a constitutional document;[164] hence, neither the monarch nor the people possessed ultimate authority. Facing the same dilemma, Grimm suggested another, nonjuridical resolution to the conflict between princely power and popular autonomy. Shared nationality, understood as a thick tissue of homogeneous preferences and affective ties among conationals, would serve to bridge divisions. In the tension between royal and more democratized rule, between princely and popular sovereignty, cultural affiliation and national solidarity would help the monarch adapt his rule to the peculiarities of his own people and allow it to flourish according to its innate characteristic. However, this did not exactly help define the ultimate locus of decision-making. Facing the tension between paradigms of sovereignty and rule, one could say that Grimm opted for imprecision and wishful thinking, but it is clear that the widespread vision of a dual political power, a strong and authoritative monarchy as well as a fully awakened nation, compelled Grimm to search for some preestablished accord between the king and people.[165] Ethnic and cultural likeness as the basis for consonance and affection would, Grimm thought, ensure that rule remained unobtrusive and flexible vis-à-vis the population and that this population in turn would endorse and cherish its ruler.

For Grimm, these tensions of constitutional monarchy were not abstract possibilities. As mentioned, he was himself an agent and icon in the most famous constitutional struggle of the *Vormärz* period. In his 1838 public statement on the dismissal from the professorship in Göttingen, Grimm modestly indicated the utility of a constitution for a country, a set of fundamental laws to regulate the relationship between the ruler and the people. According to him, the "basic law of the state [*staatsgrundgesetz*]" could serve to inhibit abuses.[166] It could not really contribute to the kingdom's flourishing, however, for its use value was entirely negative and regulatory. Grimm also downplayed the value of the Hanoverian constitution in particular by saying that he did not want to comment on its specific virtues; many found flaws with it, he reported, and some thought it too democratic. Like all constitutions, it was an earthly creation and thus an impermanent and fragile thing, a mere "contract" between human agents.[167] Such a contract, however, should not be canceled as soon as a new ruler ascended to the throne; this would entail too much inconstancy and insecurity for the country. Instead, established constitutions ought to be respected and only be replaced or modified when both parties agreed on the terms; the king, Grimm concluded, ought to refrain from unilateral action. Grimm did not dispute the right of monarchs to rule, but he viewed them as partners in a relationship of mutuality and negotiation, without the prerogative to treat the nation as an object of command. In a strange rhetorical operation, Grimm managed both to downplay the sanctity of a constitution and to insist on the limits to the king's right to revise or suspend it.

From Grimm's Romanticist standpoint, a contract was an arrangement between self-interested parties for the maintenance of their relationship, and, as such, it failed to inspire; it was expedient but did not signify attachment. What did inspire, bring warmth, and foster intimacy was, as always, love, and the paragraph on the constitution in Grimm's statement then somewhat hastily concluded on that note: "genuine blessings flow, however, from the prince's pure love for his land [*der eigentliche segen geht allerdings von der reinen liebe des fürsten zu seinem lande*]."[168] The constitution existed to contain violations of the relationship between ruler and ruled, but its functionality, Grimm thought, was no replacement for genuine affection. Only a loving king would ensure the harmony between the ruler and the people and smooth the tensions in a traditional monarchy rendered constitutional.

Affectionate attachment was not the most traditional of royal attributes, and the suggestion that the king love the nation rather than show dominant strength and supreme wisdom might have been understood as a symptom of monarchy's subtly reduced status. Regardless of how much Grimm celebrated royalty, a loving king was likely too emotionalized a figure for staunch restorationists.[169] Yet the king's love for the nation might not be identical with the philologist's devotion, even in Grimm's own account. In Grimm's formulation, the prince's pure love for *his* land – *zu seinem Lande* – might still refer to the ruler's paternal concern for his subjects,[170] his well-meaning, well-intentioned care for *his* inheritance, and not just his attachment to the nation as the most prominent of conationals. Grimm invoked love to imagine a natural equilibrium between the king and the national people, but love itself was an ambiguous concept that could house both the new and the old, the philologist's passion for the nation as a community of love and the ruler's paternalist affection for his patrimony, love of the fatherland and fatherly love. Grimm's quietly traditionalist formulation about the love of the ruler for his land did not unambiguously picture the king as yet another member of the nation, and it at least alluded to the notion that the land constituted royal property. It remained unclear whether the country should be seen as the prince's fatherland or his father's land. Grimm's invocation of love did not so much resolve the tension between the people and the king as encapsulate it.

CHAPTER 5

The Mother Tongue at School
Jacob Grimm and the Institutions of Nation Building

The Nation and the Mother Tongue

In the modern age, political rule obtains legitimacy when it is sensitive to and grounded in the people – this was a premise shared even by the politically cautious Jacob Grimm and his peers among the moderate liberals and constitutional monarchists in the first half of the nineteenth century. However, this post-revolutionary conception of political legitimacy introduced a problem of delineation. What were the boundaries of the people, in the name of which rule could secure legitimacy? How could anyone draw clear lines around the collective self of collective self-rule? In the face of these difficulties of definition, nationalists like Grimm stood ready to supply an answer to the question of the appropriate political unit, its coherence and integrity. The national people, they claimed, was already naturally given, bound together as it were by a shared history, a homeland, a common culture but, above all, a language with ancient roots, a medium of mutual understanding that constituted indisputable proof of its natural cohesiveness. An absolutely minimal nationalist requirement for legitimate rule was thus that whoever ruled spoke the people's language. Linguistically and culturally, like should rule over like. The figure able to discern the linguistic and cultural boundaries of the people with scientific precision was, finally, the grammarian or philologist.

Yet if the philologist was to determine the true boundaries of the collective by studying the borders of languages and divide up speakers into non-overlapping groups, it should not be possible to gain entrance to a people by working deliberately to learn its language. Such opportunities would render the people too porous and confound the delineation. Only *native* speakers, those for whom the language was a "mother tongue," were guaranteed inclusion. National belonging was reserved for individuals who had absorbed their language in a particularly natural way, as evidenced by their easy mastery, free from any touch of foreign awkwardness. When the philologist separated peoples from one another, then, he would listen only to mother tongues. This delimiting and restricting function of the mother tongue, the one special language learned early and unconsciously and therefore spoken authentically and effortlessly, borrowed its plausibility from images of the maternal body, icons of the mother caring for and nursing a child who imbibed both its first nourishment and its language through a close familial relationship.[1] In the nationalist imagination, the political legitimacy ensured through the self-rule of the nationally defined people rested upon an iconography of the singularly intimate mother-child relationship. In Germany around 1800, the book market saw a stream of tracts and primers on maternal education, in which the mother was presented as the proper, indeed irreplaceable source of the child's linguistic ability and alphabetization; basic cultural skills were not to be taught formally by some authority but transmitted in the medium of motherly love.[2]

Jacob Grimm frequently invoked the concept of the mother tongue and painted scenes of the child learning the language from the loving mother. "The first words," he stated in his 1851 lecture on the origin of language held in Berlin, "the baby hears at the maternal breast, spoken by the soft and gentle voice of the mother."[3] The mother alone, he also wrote, conveyed "most indelibly [*unvertilgbarsten*]" our sense of "home and fatherland."[4] In a preface to his friend Vuk Karadžić's Serbian grammar, he spoke of the gift of language that everyone receives or "sucks in" with the "mother's milk."[5] The uniquely local subtleties and variations of a dialect, he wrote in an essay on the German comic author Jean Paul, were absorbed with the *muttermilch* [mother's milk] and would remain foreign to every stranger.[6] For Jacob Grimm, everyone had a mother tongue, the language learned first and most intimately. Latin had served as the language of the clergy and the professoriate, and French had been the language of courtly circles, but German had truly belonged to the mothers, partly because they had always been less educated.[7]

Even in Grimm's age, however, language was not learned exclusively in the mother's embrace and from the mother's mouth. The standardized, codified national tongue, typically spoken by millions of individuals over several provinces, had already begun to be taught in the institutional infrastructure of primary education, through schooling mandated by the state. The children of the nation spoke the same language and lived in an area of mutual comprehensibility that made them a people partly because they had all been exposed to a similar curriculum, taught by instructors going through similar forms of teacher training; "schools," a historian of culture states simply, "removed children from their local and familiar culture."[8]

Nationalists of Grimm's era understood that the school served as an indispensable instrument of nation building,[9] and yet they preferred the image of the mother whispering to her child over the image of the schoolteacher instructing his pupils, for an honest recognition of mass schooling could suggest that the nation represented a willed political project rather than a natural, pre-political ground. The emphasis on mass instruction instead of motherly speech could disturb the conception of legitimacy according to which political rule must respect the given boundaries among entirely naturel communities. For Jacob Grimm specifically, the recognition that nationhood was partially the outcome of large-scale schooling efforts would also sideline the figure of the philologist, whose political vocation depended on the importance of mediation between the natural community of the people and the ruling elite. A full account of schooling and its effects would force him to admit that a people could to some extent be *made* by top-down institutional means rather than discovered by means of philological research.

Living in the era of a massive expansion of increasingly state-supervised primary schooling, Grimm commented on the early nineteenth-century push toward universal literacy within German-speaking territories. He welcomed the prospect of gradual unification, linguistic and therefore also political, but believed that it would likely have to occur at the expense of regional linguistic variation. Grimm, both an advocate of political unity on a linguistic basis and an expert on indigenous folk traditions rooted in particular localities, was thus caught in a bind. He was compelled to reconcile his political support for the advancement of one unifying national language with his deep appreciation of provincial and often opaque local speech, and he had to resolve the tension between the implementation of a politically crucial transregional linguistic standard and the unplanned evolution of a genuine folk idiom. To return to the nationalist mother-child iconography, Grimm's writings had to find some way of harmonizing a powerful institutional tool of nation building – universal schooling – with the predilection for the icon of intimacy and naturalness that helped separate speakers into authentic and inauthentic ones – the maternal body. Grimm was in other words forced to present a plausible relationship between the iconography of the mother from whom language could be soaked up naturally and the image of the teacher who taught a regimented, standardized language at school.

The Mother Tongue and the Rise of Mass Schooling

In 1849, Grimm gave a lecture on institutions of education in the Prussian Academy of the Sciences in Berlin. He had joined the academy as a regular member in 1832, when he lived in Göttingen, but once he had relocated to Berlin, he gave more than twenty lectures, from 1842 to 1859, mostly on philological topics.[10] Work on the immense German dictionary, *Grimms Wörterbuch*, was begun under the auspices of the academy.[11] The 1849 lecture, however, treated a different and more sociological theme, namely the completed modern educational system as an organized series of credentializing institutions.[12] Its title simply lists three institutions without any mark or conjunction – "school university academy [*schule universität akademie*]"[13] – and the lecture that followed suggested that they constitute an ascending sequence of levels.[14] First all children attend schools to learn elementary required skills; then a smaller number of students are admitted to universities to explore fields of knowledge of their own choice; and, finally, an exclusive group of university-educated scholars gather in academies to exchange research findings. School, university, and academy appeared as interlocking institutions, each focusing on a particular step: teaching, teaching and research, and research alone.

Each of these institutions, Grimm believed, also stood in a unique relationship to the German nation, or ought to stand in one. The university, Grimm observed, had long provided German-speaking lands with a transregional institutional network and was widely recognized as a particularly German achievement, even the envy of other nations.[15] In addition, the universities in Germany were very much bases for the propagation of nationalist ideas in nineteenth-century German lands[16] and themselves reinforced national unity with the help of national scientific journals and national professional congresses such as the first Germanist convention in 1846. In contrast, Grimm deemed the academy, a body typically sponsored by a court, an import from French culture that did not quite tie the German states together.[17] In the lecture to his peers in the Prussian academy, Grimm called for a new German national academy, an institutional body that would recognize that the enterprise of science had become a national rather than a regional, principality-based endeavor.[18]

The link between the school and the nation was a little more complex, and Grimm did not laud primary education or call for its complete national extension. If anything, he approached state-mandated schooling as the relative novelty that it was, acknowledging its rapid rise in Prussia and elsewhere in German lands during his lifetime without granting it an inevitable existence. His observations conveyed an historical reality. Schools were in no way a nineteenth-century invention: hundreds of schools were established in Prussia in the 1730s and there were school-compulsion laws in the eighteenth century.[19] Still, military defeat in the Napoleonic wars had contributed to a renewed and intensified effort to extend public education. At the same time, the focus on religious conformity under church supervision was gradually replaced by state-organized schooling with the aim of creating a literate and loyal citizenry.[20] In his 1849 lecture, Grimm was clearly concerned with this current form of state-organized schooling.

Grimm's attitude to the rise of mass schooling was ambivalent to say the least. He opened his reflections on the school with a question, a fundamental one, namely whether schooling was or was not necessary: "Must human beings go to school? [*Musz denn der mensch zu schule gehen?*]"[21] His answer to this question was negative. Human beings did not in fact have to go to school, since they could learn plenty of things at home, all that they really needed, from their parents, their siblings, and their neighbors. The son of the farmer learned to work on the farm, the daughter in the household learned how to run it, and both learned how to speak the language of their family and environment. No pedagogically informed instruction outside of the familial unit and hence no public institution staffed by a distinct group of instructors were necessary for children to learn the tongue spoken by the parents, the language that could legitimately be called the mother tongue and gave them community membership.

Yet human beings did go to schools in early nineteenth-century Germany and Grimm knew well the rationale behind near-comprehensive and compulsory primary education, namely the achievement of universal literacy. Despite his preference for local and familial contexts of learning, Grimm hesitantly appreciated the value of the specifically modern project of mass learning. The basic aim of mandatory schooling was, Grimm reported, to ensure that all children "without exception" learn how to read and write in a medium of communication with a wide, national reach, skills that had become so vital that Grimm did not quite feel the need to outline their particular purposes.[22] His silence indicates perhaps that literacy no longer possessed one exclusive function, such as the religious one of basic access to the Bible, but instead constituted a general requirement in the institutional and media landscape of the day. In the late eighteenth and early nineteenth centuries, more and more institutions and activities presupposed literacy: the military and navy supplied officers with manuals and maps, merchants dealt with contracts and accounts, the legal profession as well as any encounter with it obviously involved paper work, as did state administration, and the volume of newspapers, periodicals, pamphlets, handbooks, and novels increased rapidly.[23] Grimm had to admit, however, that the language that the pupils were supposed to learn to read, write, and properly speak in school as future members of a literate national citizenry was not exactly the mother tongue, but rather the language of the schoolteacher, which in no way ranked as of superior quality. Teachers even routinely abused the native rules of language, the *angeborne sprachregel*, Grimm claimed.[24] Compulsory primary education organized by German states had become inescapable, Grimm conceded, but for those who cared about language or the integrity of the mother tongue, this institutionalized teaching did not constitute an advance.

Grimm recognized the modern necessity of teaching rudimentary reading and writing, and he did express support for the idea of a single national language. The unity of a *written* German language, Grimm announced in a preface to the 1822 edition of his *German Grammar*, could not come at too high a price,[25] for it served as a continual reminder of a shared German descent and functioned as an indispensable medium of the present German community. Such unity could be achieved without the introduction of mandatory schooling, but the school introduced reading and writing in this language to the totality of the nation's children. Even when it was taught imperfectly, instruction in and use of German across all institutions of education, from primary school to the university, represented for Grimm a triumph of the national over the foreign and the classical.[26] Grimm had arrived at a compromise position: he was not convinced of the quality of mass education and regretted the diminished linguistic role of the home and the family, yet he understood the great value of schooling to the project of nation building.

Many decades before his lecture to the academy in Berlin and some years before he commenced his grammatical studies, however, the young Jacob Grimm had been much less willing to accept the intrusion of teachers in the spontaneous familial process of language learning. A letter that he wrote as a young man to Friedrich Carl von Savigny evinced a more principled resistance to instruction in German to German-speaking children. Educational reform, he wrote in 1814, may well damage the natural linguistic competence fostered in small-scale communities. To learn a language at school, Grimm reasoned, was to learn to apply a set of rules, whereas the language spoken at home was learned naturally, without the mediation of explicitly stated conventions. Those who went to school, Grimm continued, learned to read and write their supposed "mother tongue [*Muttersprache*]" through a codified form and could begin to view German as if it were a foreign language, while being deprived of their local dialect.[27] It was appropriate to learn Latin or Greek in school, since the acquisition of these traditionally taught languages would not upset the automatic absorption of local speech, but that which was already one's own should not be presented, through formalized teaching, as if it came from without. The native, *das einheimische*, did not amount to a kind of knowledge or defined skill to be acquired; it should come as naturally as breathing.[28] In Grimm's view, then, teachers turned the native German tongue into something alien. Even in the 1819 preface to the first volume of the German grammar, he wrote that school instruction could interfere with the "free development of the child's capacity for language [*die freie entfaltung des sprachvermögens*]." The sounds of the "fatherland," he continued, enter the child with the "mother's milk [*muttermilch*],"and not through the instruction of the schoolteacher.[29]

When Grimm spoke to the academy in Berlin about schooling roughly three decades later, however, the early opposition to the teaching of German had faded. He continued to believe that inadequately trained schoolteachers were likely to corrupt young speakers with their faulty teaching of grammar, but he no longer argued against primary education. It was evidently not too late to pose a fundamental question in a more philosophical vein – "must human beings go to school?" – and yet much too late to demand that society dismantle its institutions of schooling. Even by the second decade of the nineteenth century, after Grimm's letter to Savigny, the great majority of both German liberals and German conservatives had come to accept mandatory schooling as a basic feature of society and an instrument for (liberal) reform and formation or (conservative) social control.[30] The educable masses and the schooled society were no longer, as in the eighteenth century, visions or ideas, but a reality to be shaped or modified rather than eliminated.

With no hope for limits to the school system and its curriculum, Grimm instead marveled at its sheer scale. There were, he mentioned in his academy address, 15 million people in Prussia, and about 30,000 schoolteachers, roughly one for every group of 50 pupils, according to his calculations. The other German-speaking lands employed around 50,000–60,000 teachers, a figure that Grimm believed may be larger than in other European countries and hence testified to the pan-German commitment to schooling: "Germany," he concluded, "is a country of school masters."[31] All in all, Grimm believed that about 80,000–90,000 schoolteachers contributed to the rise and dominance of a more or less uniform national language, numbers that appear in modern-day scholarship as well.[32] Whether or not the teachers guarded or corrupted the authentic mother tongue, the trend toward universal schooling was irreversible.

Against this backdrop, Grimm ceased to question the institution of the school and chose instead to focus on the political fights that had emerged within it or over it. In the mid-nineteenth century, there were a number of conflicts. First of all, schoolteachers themselves complained about their situation. As a group in society, they were struggling to obtain higher compensation and enhanced professional reputation and met with multiple obstacles, such as the gulf between schoolteachers and credentialized academics, the subordination of teachers under local pastors, poor teacher training, and the reluctance of local communities to pay for instruction.[33] As a state servant well aware of his societal location, Grimm stood firmly against the schoolteachers' desire for elevated prestige. In his lecture, he indicated that he wanted to maintain the comparatively low status of the elementary schoolteachers, against the efforts of the group's more restless and radical representatives, whose alleged ties to communists he deemed quite plausible.[34] (Only about 1 percent of schoolteachers were actually politically involved.[35]) As a delegate to the Frankfurt assembly in 1848, Grimm reported, he had found himself inundated with schoolteacher petitions for higher pay and improved legal standing, both of which he considered unsuitable to the important but still cognitively modest schoolhouse tasks. Human beings had to go to school and hence tens of thousands of primary schoolteachers had to be employed and paid; yet this stubborn fact about modern society did not, Grimm believed, need to be glorified in a way that would suggest any meaningful social proximity of local schoolteachers to the well-educated instructors and professors in the much more selective and demanding institutions of the gymnasium and the university.

In some way, the gradually fading importance of Latin in higher education, symbolized by Grimm's own advocacy for Germanic philology, was blurring the social border between the learned man and the simple teacher. Knowledge of Latin had traditionally drawn a conspicuous social boundary around the men of letters in European society,[36] and hence Grimm's lifelong efforts to enhance the aura of the vernacular served to soften the line between the erudite elite and low-level teachers. Yet it was clearly important to Grimm to maintain the social barrier, proud as he was of his position as a professional working for the state. Despite the rise of state-mandated schooling and dedicated teacher seminars in the nineteenth century, the teacher remained a low-status figure compared with the prestigious circle of university professors;[37] Grimm had no interest in changing this. The schoolteacher, he insisted, did not need or deserve the status of a civil servant.

By 1849, then, Grimm had partially overcome some of his anti-institutional impulse, his radical emphasis on the natural, the native, and the local, and accepted an accomplished fact: schools and schoolteachers were everywhere, in every German land, province, and village. Germany was well on its way to becoming a society of schools or what the historian Thomas Nipperdey has called a schooled over over-schooled society, *verschulte Gesellschaft*, in which school attendance had been installed as a nonnegotiable obligation for all.[38] Yet Grimm had clearly not overcome his social bias against schoolteachers and was not willing to grant them higher status. Nor did he think that the mere ubiquity of the school suddenly rendered the institution a more appropriate vessel for the mother tongue. For Grimm, the separation between the genuine mother tongue and the schoolmaster's taught idiom remained in force. Even so, the older Grimm tried to reduce the contrast between the polar figures of the mother and the teacher. Rather than posit a clear opposition between the family and the school, he now searched for some way to draw them closer to each other.

The schoolteacher was not the mother and yet, it turns out, not far removed from the maternal body. In his academy lecture, Grimm likened the schoolteacher to the figure of the *Amme*, the wet nurse, the woman who provides the child with nourishment and comfort, breastfeeds it and cares for it, but is not the birth mother: "a teacher, who like a wet-nurse [*amme*] holds the breast toward the infant, pours in the simple food of the first knowledge into the child, nourishes, prepares and instructs it in all things."[39] This image of breastfeeding was not a slip on Grimm's part but an attempt to give the teacher a place in relation to the nationalist imagery of the mother tongue. The pupil, Grimm continued, would even learn at the breast of the teacher, absorbing the "first milk [*ersten milchs*]" of learning.[40] In the 1849 lecture, then, the teacher had begun to morph into something like a mother. Grimm tried to justify this peculiar blending of disparate figures with linguistic material. Hallowed words for teaching and instruction in classical languages, Grimm pointed out, derived from ancient terms for wet nurse; the position of the teacher as an acceptable substitute for the mother had an ancient pedigree.[41]

Grimm's metaphor of the wet nurse was meant to sanctify the local teacher, without granting him a more elevated social status vis-à-vis instructors at the higher levels of teaching and research. He intended to establish the teacher's relative nearness and closeness rather than his intrusiveness and strangeness and did so with the help of imagery that clearly feminized this figure: the teacher was not the mother, but a close approximation – and hence at a remove from the male civil servant. Following the logic of his image, we could say that the children would not exactly learn a mother tongue at school, but the tongue of their *surrogate* mother. After the introduction of state-mandated education in the mid-nineteenth century, after the establishment of school houses in each and every German town, all of which provided training in reading and writing of a transregional language, the population would learn to write and perhaps also to speak neither a genuine mother tongue nor an essentially foreign language, but some close approximation of what Grimm considered the most natural idiom: a surrogate mother tongue.

Grimm's attempt to mediate between the mother tongue and the school took the form of a trope: teaching in the era of mass schooling inevitably involved the supplementation or replacement of the mother. The addition of the wet nurse to the iconography of the maternal represents a kind of compromise image. The ideological motivation for this argument by imagery ought to be clear. If the age of mass schooling put pressure on the iconography of the mother-child relationship supposed to anchor the intimacy of the mother tongue that protected exclusive national membership, then the unity of the nation, and with it the idea of legitimate political rule, could be preserved by the expansion of the maternal. When the nationalist conception of the mother tongue as the basis for natural national membership was brought into contact with the undeniable fact of mass schooling, the teacher had to be converted into a motherly figure.

Mandatory Schooling and Military Service

Must human beings go to school? Grimm's answer to the question was no, if humans were simply supposed to learn to speak their mother tongue, but the answer was yes if they were to become members of a nation of millions of people; the answer was emphatically yes if they were to become loyal subjects of a state willing to take up arms to defend its integrity. In an early nineteenth-century Germany shaken by Napoleon's victories, mass schooling emerged as a potentially effective means of forging a more compact and disciplined citizenry, just as it had long been an institutional device of ecclesiastical authorities to ensure conformity with religious dogma.[42] To this day, mass education remains a preferred instrument for governments that want to "indoctrinate previously unschooled populations into a coherent, shared national identity and establish a common, durable, national loyalty that supersedes previous ethnic, family, and kinship ties, inoculates the population from external agitation, and ensures resistance to alien rule."[43] In his study of nationalism, the sociologist Ernest Gellner even ranks the importance of the state's monopoly over the means of instruction higher than its monopoly over the means of coercion, for the former establishes a common standard of linguistic proficiency and cultural competence that facilitates uniformity and communicative ease across a large region and in that process builds a widely shared attachment.[44]

One can ask, though, attachment to what? Conationals, Gellner claims, are not necessarily loyal to the same king or the same God but rather to the same school culture, which formed them and to which they owe their social membership and employability in an anonymous but culturally standardized society. This may have been an intuition shared by nineteenth-century government elites who found themselves increasingly reliant on armies raised by conscription. Facing the threat of defeat and dissolution, they set out to expand the school system to provide a public good to a population on which it now depended militarily but also to homogenize that population's varied local cultures and give a consistent national shape to its allegiances.[45] Schooled subjects were given the opportunity to achieve literacy and numeracy, skills of increasing utility within a national territory, but they were also introduced to standardized narratives meant to foster a uniform cultural identity that could underpin mass loyalty. In this way, the school system represented a sort of historical bargain between rulers and populations.

Early German nationalists in Grimm's intellectual milieu did observe the close link between universal schooling and state loyalty, between the obligation to attend school and the obligation to fight for the country.[46] The school as an instrument of national military preparation appeared in Fichte's *Addresses to the German Nation*, which, as we know, the young Grimm hailed as one of the finest books ever written.[47] A system of national education supervised by the state rather than the church or local authorities, Fichte claimed, would undoubtedly be a costly enterprise and yet he promised it would prove an exceptionally wise investment in the state's future military capacity. With great confidence, Fichte envisaged a straight path from the state schools to the military barracks; a properly and uniformly schooled people would be a people ready for mobilization, unyielding in war.[48]

Fichte was hardly the first to tout the link between schooling and loyalty, and discussions of a school system took place among governing elites in the Holy Roman Empire as early as the 1770s.[49] Around the time that he gave his nationalist lecture series in French-occupied Berlin, Prussian elite reformers had begun to explore very seriously the possibility of a large-scale schooling expansion and reform. After Napoleon's humiliating defeat, they, too, considered investments in primary education a means to winning future wars. Schools could increase incentives to fight by linguistically integrating and instilling patriotism in an otherwise scattered, culturally fragmented, and hence reluctant population. Every citizen should receive a measure of instruction, the Prussian king advised after the Franco-Prussian treaty of Tilsit in the summer of 1807, through which Prussia was stripped of almost half of its territories and people.[50] Post-defeat schooling efforts did have noticeable effects: literacy rates in Prussia were very high prior to 1800, but illiteracy became negligible in the male cohort born between 1837 and 1841, the period just before Grimm arrived in Berlin.[51] European military rivalry drove the expansion and consolidation of schooling.

Grimm exhibited no overt enthusiasm for arming whole peoples in his lecture on educational institutions in 1849, but he did think of the school curriculum as a means to reduce foreign influence on German culture. He also chose to convey this view in martial rhetoric. Cultural and literary accomplishments, he wrote, must be achieved with one's "own weapons [*eigenen Waffen*]," that is, in and with the national language rather than a classical or transnational one.[52] The emergence of German as a fully developed literary language, which had culminated in distinctive masterpieces such as Goethe's poems, justified the desired dominance of the vernacular across the institutions of learning, including the university. Yet the idea of a nation in arms was also present in Grimm's account of national education, although it was lodged in the lecture's imagery. He called the tens of thousands of schoolmasters throughout Prussia and the rest of Germany a vast "army [*heer*]" of teachers and mandatory primary education the *heerstrasze für alle kinder*, the "great military road for all children."[53] At the level of metaphor at least, Grimm associated the agents of instruction with the massive armies that first appeared in the Napoleonic age. If nothing else, sheer scale allowed for an association between the modern mandatory school and the modern conscription-based military.

When one surveys the various images of the instructor in Grimm's lecture, one could say that he pictured the individual schoolteacher as both a surrogate mother and a member of a military-scale collective, both a wet nurse and a foot soldier. This split characterization of the teacher in the schooling system, distributed over the pages on primary education, is not an unfortunate case of mixed metaphors but reflects the ideological construction of nationhood. The national subjects taught at school were the potential members of a future army ready to do battle for their nation: as Fichte stated explicitly, one prominent ideological aim of education, perhaps the most prominent, was to generate a loyal national citizenry. At the same time, the national language had to remain a mother tongue, that is, the linguistic criterion of this national membership had to be naturalized in such a way that the national collective, however large and dispersed, retained the semblance of a familial community. The schoolteachers of the nation indirectly prepared the children for the defense of the state and must in this capacity plausibly stand in for the mother as the icon of symbiotic intimacy, because only the caring, nourishing maternal body guaranteed the depth and authenticity of national belonging. Given nationalism's double preference for the maternal and the martial, it is fitting that Grimm's schoolteacher appeared, over the course of his lecture, as both a substitute mother and an infantry soldier. The teacher who cared for the children like a wet nurse was also a member of a vast army.

National Schooling and the National Archive

Through a constellation of metaphors, Grimm captured the double task of the school to sustain the idea of an intimate linguistic communion and community across generations and to prepare large cohorts for duties in the service of the state. The schoolhouse was a substitute home as well as the first station on the way to military service. If Grimm expressed only lukewarm enthusiasm for schooling, it was, again, because of its deleterious effect on unique local habits of speech. It was primarily as a scholar of folk tradition that he deemed the price of mandatory education high. The young Grimm noticed how schooled children tended to unlearn the dialects that may have been almost entirely incomprehensible to German speakers of other regions, and the older, distinguished member of the Prussian academy speaking in 1849 remained aware of the fact that the schoolteacher's standardized tongue amounted to an assault on local cultural integrity in the very varied German lands.

To root out dialects and replace them with a purified national idiom was not infrequently an expressed aim of education and Grimm understood and regretted this fact.⁵⁴ Grimm viewed schooling as accompanied by the threat of a future retreat and even extinction of linguistic variety, a process that did take place during the nineteenth century.⁵⁵ Apprehensive of a cultural uniformity enforced by a coercive state eager to dissolve the semi-opacity of local communities and integrate them into a larger collective, Grimm knew that the language of the schooled nation was never introduced into a linguistic vacuum but did damage to existing linguistic subgroups for the sake of their greater transparency and availability to a centralized authority.⁵⁶ Of all the coercive simplifications of social life enforced by the modern state, James Scott writes in his anarchist treatment of the statehood, "the imposition of a single, official language may be the most powerful" – and such an imposition is made possible not least by means of universal schooling.⁵⁷

Grimm's hesitant stance toward schooling was rooted not only in his appreciation of cultural and linguistic individuality but also his own scholarly concern for intact research material. He noted in his lecture that the academic achievements of his own fields, comparative grammar and mythology, depended on attention to scorned idioms, allegedly unsophisticated languages, and neglected folk traditions, which helped uncover a more complete picture of linguistic and cultural change.⁵⁸ For Grimm, dialects embodied the charms of regional diversity, but they also preserved archaic linguistic forms with greater fidelity than the language of the elites in centers of learning and administration.⁵⁹ From the point of view of the grammarian and cultural historian, local variation must thus be salvaged, not flattened out. The achievement of national literary and cultural greatness did require the spread of a standardized literary German throughout educational institutions, but this very process marginalized and endangered the local material that was necessary for the comparative grammarian's exploration of linguistic history. A comprehensive German school system that would teach all its pupils to read and recite Goethe poems, Grimm's prime example of canonical vernacular literature, would at the same time contribute to the elimination of the richness of local dialects and speech patterns and hence attenuate connections to the past and deprive grammatical studies of clues.

The nationalist cause of achieving German literary and cultural greatness and promoting national loyalty was thus at odds with the academic's interest in saving the linguistic diversity that would help uncover the nation's history. Yet where we can discern an obvious tension between nationalist and localist causes, or a conflict between the aims of national-literary competitiveness in a European cultural space, on the one hand, and antiquarian or scientific motives, on the other, Grimm chose instead to see a coordinated process of nation building. He believed that the school system could contribute to both the homogenization of the vernacular *and* the preservation or linguistic remains for scholarly purposes.

What reconciled Grimm to the reach and penetration of the school system was at least partly the problem of retrieving and collecting materials for study. Several times over his career, Grimm sought to initiate large-scale collaborative projects of folklore collection to expand the archive of neglected and endangered traditions of German poetry. He was not the only one or the first to want to do so: Clemens Brentano and Achim von Arnim had similarly sought to cover all German regions with a "net of collection."[60] In 1811, one year before the two brothers Grimm published their very first volume of folktales Jacob Grimm drafted a call for materials, including traditions, legends, fairy tales, proverbs, poems, or really any fragment of a genuine folk literature that would allow him and others to gain a richer view of old German poetry.[61] In the call, Grimm made apparent why a few scholars alone could not complete such an enterprise. The desired materials, and especially the purest samples of folk literature, treasures undistorted by any "false enlightenment," would likely be found in the most remote and hidden regions of Germany – in high mountains, closed valleys, and small villages unconnected to major routes.[62] For this reason, only a great number of geographically dispersed collaborators would ever be able to gather the necessary volume of valuable folk expressions. Since specificity and locality were of utmost importance, Grimm also encouraged the future volunteers to transcribe dialects faithfully, without correcting perceived errors made by uneducated informants. The collectors must also note the precise place of transcription; only in this way would scholars be able to piece together a more comprehensive image of the variegated cultures of Germany. For reasons of completeness, Grimm expressed the hope that he would be able to recruit a knowledgeable liaison in every single German landscape.

The large numbers of eager amateur collectors never materialized, at least not to serve Grimm's preferred research project, but the early vision of an associational infrastructure for collecting folk materials resurfaced in his lecture on the school, university, and academy. Grimm saw that the thousands of German schoolteachers could not but help to serve as agents of cultural and linguistic homogenization, insofar as they would teach a more uniform national language across different provinces. At the same time, he believed the school system that put a teacher in every village might also allow for more systematic collection of linguistic and narrative materials so valuable to research in the field of Germanic Studies.[63] Schoolteachers could be asked to record and pass on local speech and tradition from all corners of the German-speaking lands to a center of study and research. The mass of teachers clearly contributed to the consolidation of German across regions but they could also be preparing the "artifactualization" of folk culture, the conversion of oral tradition and local habits into objects of scholarly investigation.[64] The arrangement and ordering of such materials, already conducted with exemplary zeal by Grimm himself, would in turn provide the nation with a cultural-historical depth that would otherwise be lost.

Grimm imagined the schoolhouse as the site for a process of exchange of great value to the gigantic project of nation building. Schoolteachers were primarily tasked with the dissemination of an increasingly widely read and understood national tongue, but, ideally, they should also transfer now-endangered folkloric forms to some center of research devoted to the excavation of the varied national past. The rural idioms, local dialects, and circulating folk narratives that Grimm knew would likely vanish over time, not the least because of mass schooling, could nonetheless be preserved and moved into the archives of properly trained researchers, thanks to the cooperative efforts of schoolteachers everywhere. If this would come to pass, the myriad of local mother tongues that would soon cease to be spoken could at least be transcribed and eventually put on display in anthologies and studies of German linguistic history, much like the magnificent historical objects that modern states no longer have actual use for, such as royal insignia, are not discarded but moved into the space of the museum to support the constitution of a shared historical identity. The art critic and theorist Boris Groys has claimed that museums, and by extension anthologies of linguistic and literary materials such as the ones Grimm produced, can be seen as tools of cultural recycling in that they convert materials marginalized by supposed historical progress into building blocks for a common historical identity.[65] Royal symbols cannot quite be used in a modern republic, but they can be displayed in glass vitrines as tokens of a shared past. For Grimm, the school emerged as a potential instrument of cultural recycling on a massive scale, since teachers everywhere could help record and save the cultural and linguistic legacy that schooling was ultimately meant to smooth out and replace.

Grimm viewed mass schooling as a crucial institutional device for nation building thanks to a double function, a possible bidirectional traffic between the peripheral school and the centers of state administration and state-funded research. In his vision, the numerous lowly agents of the growing German system of schooling were at work on supplanting dialects with standardized German, and yet they would also much more efficiently and comprehensively than any small group of scholars be able to capture local speech, to be examined and presented as historical evidence of the emergence of a unified (surrogate) mother tongue. In Grimm's view, the army of German teachers spread out over all the provinces would prepare their pupils for a national future and also help retain for this increasingly unified people the relics of a textured, diverse national past. The teachers would help save the dialects that they would gradually eliminate.

For Jacob Grimm, the philologist was a figure uniquely able to mediate between a national community and a political regime; the philologist could remind the German people of its own historical depth and the richness of its own language but was also best suited to the task of informing the king of the boundaries and character of the nation. The people needed philologically prepared opportunities for self-recognition, and the monarch needed philologically informed guidance about the extent and substance of the only viable and acceptable unit of rule in the modern era, namely the national people. Yet the school would seem to threaten the key mediating role of the philologist, since a state-organized educational system could forge linguistic and cultural unity over a vast territory. Schooling could *produce* a national people eventually ready to defend the state and would not necessarily need a philologist to trace the outlines of an already given wholeness whose integrity should be respected. In the age of comprehensive primary education, nations could be made rather than found, an awkward situation for the philologist devoted to the careful study of the naturally evolving, lovingly transmitted mother tongue and its natural geography. As we have seen, however, Grimm still found a way to insert the figure of the philologist into the institutional structure of the schooled society, partly by suggesting that the school system with its vast number of teachers could be turned into a supply line for the researcher eager for access to a great wealth of material from an infinitely valuable but superseded stage of national culture. For Grimm, the school would not be a threat to the German philologists but a support, not the end of all political-philological efforts but, at least during a transitional period, their best possible source.

CHAPTER 6

The Names of the Barbarians
The Philologist, the Tribe, and the Empire

Ethnic History and the Modern Nation

In the fall of 1848, Jacob Grimm published *The History of the German Language* [*Geschichte der deutschen sprache*]. It was a sort of final statement of Grimm's, a 1,000-page work on linguistic and ethnic history, the last large work that he would write. Grimm would later call the book his finest accomplishment.[1] It was certainly one of his most explicitly nationalist works. In the preface, Grimm celebrated heroic German accomplishments: the Germanic tribes of the first millennium, he declared, had thrown off the yoke of Roman domination, decided the victory of Christianity in Europe through their conversion, and stemmed the influx of Slavic peoples into the western parts of Europe.[2] In this way, the ancient tribes had asserted their autonomy and held their territory – they had been "undefeatable [*unbesiegbar*]."[3]

As the title of the work declared, however, its topic was linguistic history and as such related to Grimm's other, earlier, and more famous scholarly accomplishments in the field of grammar. In this late study, Grimm reviewed the historical evolution of Germanic languages to mine it for clues about the historical evolution of the Germanic tribes, especially in the first millennium, from their appearance in Roman textual sources through the Migration Period to a phase of relative stability in the early Middle Ages. *The History of the German Language* was devoted to diachronic grammatical development but also to ancient Germanic ethnic life, which according to Grimm had been historically varied and geographically diffused but nonetheless coherent and continuous. The tongues of the manifold Germanic tribes had all grown from the same "trunk [*stamm*]" and the modern descendants of tribes – Bavarians, Hessians, Franks, and so on – belonged together in one single nation;[4] local variability did not preclude historically anchored unity.[5] Grimm realized that German unification in his own day would bring forth an entirely new political entity in

Europe, but he argued that it would be rooted in a preexisting family cluster of ethnic communities;[6] such references to the diverse but associated German tribes as constituents of a coherent nation were in fact commonplace in contemporary political discourse.[7] By late 1848, Grimm had already publicly introduced the philologist – or introduced himself – as the figure who could expertly answer the question "what is a people?" However, *The History of the German Language* converted the central premise of Grimm's philological politics – shared language tracked nationhood – into its key methodological assumption: the study of Germanic dialects allowed the scholar to retrieve an ancient ethnic history that would enrich the people's collective self-understanding and allow the king in Berlin to grasp the proper future unit of government, which was not "old Prussia" but a unified Germany – a Germany "reborn."[8]

Significantly, the speedily composed work[9] made this argument in the year of revolution, in 1848, when Grimm believed that the prospect of German *einheit* ["unity"] was drawing closer.[10] While Grimm had written the book in 1847, he did not halt its publication when revolutionary events escalated in 1848; instead, he deemed its message all the more relevant.[11] He dated his preface in Berlin on March 11, 1848, only a few days before the outbreak of violent unrest in the city, and finished his shorter dedication to his colleague and Göttingen ally the literary historian and publicist Georg Gottfried Gervinus on June 11 in the same year, when both served as delegates in the first German national parliament.[12] As the dates of the two introductory texts indicate, the book really was finished and published during a tumultuous time. In the late summer and early fall of 1848, Grimm's Frankfurt letters to his brother Wilhelm in Berlin mixed discussions about the political campaign for German conquest of Schleswig and Holstein with mentions of the book's publication process.[13] Grimm's study of ancient Germanic linguistic and ethnic distinctiveness as well as tribal political and cultural self-assertion belonged to the year of the (defeated) revolution and (failed) national unification.

Commenting on the dramatic surrounding circumstances, Grimm also announced that he had written an utterly political book. In the four-page dedication to Gervinus, he called his work "political through and through [*durch und durch politisch*]," intended for readers who wished to understand the task and the dangers facing the "fatherland."[14] It was political in that it excavated linguistic and tribal history for the purpose of validating national unity in the form of an integration of multiple German lands into a coherent constitutional order under a German ruler. Grimm's plan was to have his brother Wilhelm send the two volumes to Frederick William IV of Prussia for perusal in September 1848 – the philologist was yet again eager to reach the king and deliver to him the philological justification of German unification.[15] Yet after having advocated for continued war against Denmark even after Prussia had signed an armistice accepting Danish annexation of Schleswig, Grimm nonetheless hesitated. He suspected that his own insistence on an unremitting struggle for German unity throughout 1848 might have alienated the king: "Now it could be that I have angered him [Frederick William IV] and he won't look at the letter and the book [*jetzt kann es kommen, dass er mir zürnt und brief und buch nicht ansieht*]."[16]

Grimm's resolutely nationalist work, however, written with the intent of strengthening the nation by proving its rooted unity and integrity, also showed how the philologist consistently had to assume an extra-tribal, extra-ethnic vantage point. Most of the sources that Grimm relied on to describe the Germanic tribes were Roman, and Grimm even admitted that the principal tools of philology, comparative grammar chief among them, were born of empire, a political formation that strove for hegemony partly by means of surveying and categorizing various ethnic communities and assembling and studying their languages. There was no access to the barbarians unmediated by empire. Politically, Jacob Grimm was a nationalist, but epistemically, he hailed from the imperial realm, and he quietly acknowledged the tension. The philologist, the guardian of nationhood, was an imperial figure.

Nationalist Dreams and Nightmares

To write about ancient German ethnic history, Grimm knew, was to write about barbarians, the peoples beyond literate civilization. Many other scholars before Grimm had written histories of the barbaric German populations,[17] and throughout the nineteenth century, figures across the political spectrum engaged in speculations about primitive society, including Karl Marx,[18] who would read *The History of the German Language*.[19] Grimm did take note of a few contemporary colleagues, for instance, Johann Kaspar Zeuss's (1806–56) work on the Germans and their neighboring tribes from 1837.[20] In this context, Grimm's declared methodological intervention lay in his systematic attention to the correlation between linguistic development and tribal life, including tribal migration in the final centuries of the Roman Empire.[21] A novel kind of ethnographic history could be written, Grimm claimed, on the basis of observations of patterns in language use, because the lexicon and grammar of Germanic tongues provided a record of collective life underexplored by historians. In relation to the discipline of history, linguistic study afforded a fresh starting point.[22] For Grimm, though, this transition from diachronic linguistics into the realm of history also represented a satisfying completion; he wrote that he had always wished to move "from words to things [*von den wörtern zu den sachen*],"[23] from the grammatical development of German to the historical reality of German-speaking communities. The titles of the forty-two chapters reflected the program articulated in the preface. For the most part, sequences of chapters on phonetic and grammatical phenomena, such as the "sound shift [*die lautverschiebung*]," were followed by sequences of chapters on different tribes, such as the Goths, Franks, Hessians, and Bavarians.[24] The purpose of the book was not to trace linguistic development for its own sake but to use the record of that development to survey the internal diversity of Germanic tribal life, establish the long and interconnected histories of multiple groups, and ultimately prove the resilient cohesiveness of the present-day German people, its unity-in-diversity over time.

As Grimm set out to reveal the proper boundaries of the modern political unit by exploring the historical affiliation of the present-day descendants of ancient Germanic tribes, he also pointed out the two enemies of a nationally based geopolitical order: the artificial, shrunken principality and the artificial, swollen empire. In the year 1848, Germany was an "unnaturally divided fatherland [*widernatürlich gespaltnen vaterland*]," still afflicted by the "unauthorized division of princes [*unbefugte theilung der fürsten*]."[25] To Grimm, language history revealed the connections of multiple German dialects and therefore issued in a call to unity against patrimonial rulers who treated populations as their "movable property [*fahrender habe*]."[26] At the same time, language imposed a definite outer limit on political rule, a line that must not be transgressed by imperial ambition. Grimm's concise principle of international politics read: "speakers of a foreign tongue should not be conquered [*anders redende nicht erobert werden sollten*]," at least among sufficiently large and "prevailing [*waltenden*]" peoples.[27] Empire building was illegitimate because it departed from the principle of national-linguistic integrity, although not all nations were equally viable and some would not escape hegemony; tiny nation-states for small peoples would remain as impracticable as the tiny German principalities.[28] Speaking of Europe in 1848, the year of revolutions, Grimm did see the national "principle [*grundsatz*]," which had always been so obvious to the "linguistic researcher [*forscher in der sprache*]," finally gain ground around him – it seemed "at last to permeate the world more and more [*endlich die welt zu durchdringen*]."²⁹ In his view, the nationally oriented philologist had been a visionary of contemporary European geopolitics.

The History of the German Language corroborated political statements Grimm had made in other works and venues. For him, two simple propositions identified the nation as the proper unit of politics: mutually intelligible speakers should neither be divided internally nor dominated by regimes from other linguistic groups. In his prefatory remarks, however, Grimm admitted that the borders of a linguistic area could shift as languages developed further in time. He closed his dedication to Gervinus by envisaging a bright but distant future in which conflicts among Germanic nations such as Denmark and Sweden would come to an end and different Germanic languages would ultimately begin to merge into one, possibly through processes of modern standardization and intensified communication; Grimm did not expound further. German national unification might one day be followed by an even greater Germanic supra-regional unification. Some borders, however, would likely never fade, namely those between Germanic, Romance, and Slavic languages.³⁰ These were the three language groups in Europe, Grimm stated, and hence the three ultimate units of European sociocultural life,³¹ and the tenacious inner grammatical structure of their languages would prevent them from blending into one another.

While a community could expand due to linguistic convergence within a family of languages, it could also lose ground, at least recently conquered ground. Grimm's reconstruction of tribal history was partly an account of irreversible losses afflicting Germanic Europe. There had been, Grimm reported, a number of Germanic tribes that at some point had ceased to speak a wholly Germanic language and ended up shedding their inherited identity during their advances and adventures – his examples included the Franks, the Burgundians, the Lombards, and in some way also the Anglo-Saxons.³² The fates of these groups served as a warning to Grimm's contemporaries: Germanic Europe could very well continue to shrink and dissolve, a prospect of cultural contraction he found truly menacing. Each of Grimm's aims – the recollection of past Germanic achievements, the delineation of present German unity, the future consolidation of German identity – was haunted by fears of cultural oblivion, territorial fragmentation, and national diminishment.

This concern with threats to nationhood indicated a deeper nationalist dimension of *The History of the German Language*. The book offered something of an existential justification for the preoccupation with the national past. The recovery of a long Germanic history, Grimm believed, would shore up a collective identity that alone could safeguard experiential meaning even in a volatile modern world. The nation's knowledge of its own achievements and its own outlines was so important, because this knowledge could guarantee a sense of continuity and integrity that in turn would endow present-day events with significance. Without specifying the source or character of the threat, Grimm nonetheless spoke with some horror about a great wave that could drench all individual countries in a "bottomless sea of generality [*bodenlosen meer einer allgemeinheit*]."[33] The menace he feared was not necessarily an apocalyptic disaster, some violent conflagration such as a continental war, but a sinister spread of uniformity across a previously varied cultural topography. Enemies such as petty autocrats and rapacious empire builders threatened the nation, but Grimm also had vaguer apprehensions of a future process of homogenization that would ultimately erase individuated national being.

Grimm's worry about cultural dissolution revealed his commitment to a theory of collective identity over time. In his nightmare vision, a reckless indifference to history, on the one hand, and deplorable cultural homogeneity, on the other, implied each other. The danger that Grimm imagined was not necessarily domination at the hands of a more powerful people or state, but that a narrow, even "self-serving [*selbstsüchtigen*]" focus on the present and its concerns could erode a historically shaped collective identity and empty life of meaning.[34] To reject history was to turn away from one's temporally extended formation and thus to choose, inexplicably for Grimm, alienation from oneself. Disinterest in the collectively shared identity incrementally built up through a shared historical life was, to him, not even a coherent attitude. One could not enjoy and affirm one's present existence, Grimm seemed to imply, without first recognizing the importance of the past, since complete indifference to one's history meant that one willingly ceased to embody a continuous, coherent, non-punctual center of experience. Nations were differentiated communal human identities formed in history and sustained by recollection, and such recollection framed and bestowed meaning upon whatever people did, encountered, and experienced as communities; resilient and bounded cultural and linguistic particularity was the precondition for a collective existence charged with genuine purpose. The problem with the Germanic tribes that had gradually abandoned their language such as the Franks or the Burgundians, Grimm claimed, was not simply that their linguistic and cultural defection had prevented greater Germanic hegemony in Europe; the problem was that they had drifted apart from their fellow tribes and indeed forgotten their *own* origin and cultural character. The problem, then, was that they had "largely lost themselves [*groszentheils sich selbst verloren*]" and that their troubles and triumphs presumably carried less existential weight, even for themselves, because of their truncated present identity.[35] They were no longer themselves, and in a future "bottomless sea of generality [*bodenlosen meer einer allgemeinheit*]," a global condition of cultural flatness, everybody would have lost themselves.[36]

Today many readers would simply reject Grimm's endeavor to recall past achievements and detect collective boundaries for the purpose of preserving an exclusive collective personality, but the project of *The History of the German Language* also suffered from inconsistencies on its own terms. Grimm's seemingly crisp delineation of the national political space stood in tension with his own compressed account of historical Germanic accomplishments in the very same prefatory remarks, specifically his celebration of tribal expansion in the era of the weakened Roman Empire. Foreign rule was unacceptable, he stated, and yet he glorified Germanic ventures and resettlements all over Western Europe – in Gaul, Britain, Spain, and so on – as advances that brought freedom to new areas[37] rather than condemn them as illegitimate campaigns of conquest. In his affirmation of tribal migration across large distances into lands occupied by others, Grimm contradicted his anti-imperial nationalist principles. If he disapproved of foreign rule and yet approved of territorial occupation by the Goths, Vandals, Lombards, Angles, Saxons, Jutes, and Franks, he might be seen to condemn permanent colonial domination over other peoples but not to condemn some form of ethnic removal, where one people, moving as a compact "mass [*masse*],"[38] pushed another one out of a particular space. Grimm would then implicitly hold that it was wrong for one nation to rule another, but not exactly wrong for the Anglo-Saxons to set out on a large-scale land-grabbing operation and marginalize or even annihilate the Celts on the British Isles, since such a removal would not have resulted in a long-term cultural and linguistic hierarchy among two or more coexisting peoples.

Even when Grimm wanted to commemorate the waves of tribal advances of the first millennium as spectacular events that testified to the explosive force of Germanic peoples, his comments on linguistic abandonment indicated that such settlements on already occupied land had negative effects – for the invading Germanic groups. The result of too forceful a march into new territories had not infrequently been permanent self-alienation – the Franks, Burgundians, Visigoths, and Lombards had lost their Germanic tongues and hence their Germanness in the process of moving into new areas. Even if Grimm did not explicitly admit that Germanic migration and expansion was as illegitimate as systematic empire building, he noted that tribes that had ventured into formerly Roman territories did not, in the end, strengthen the Germanic hold over Europe. Instead, they all seem to have crossed some invisible line, some linguistic boundary between the Latin and Teutonic worlds, and shed their languages.

In light of these arguments, one can distill Grimm's nationalist principles in the following way: never dominate another linguistic group, never tolerate domination by another linguistic group, never dissolve the ties to your linguistic kin, never let rulers artificially cut you off from your linguistic kin, but also make sure not to venture too far away from your fellows into alien linguistic areas, because you might then lose your own culture, mired as it will be in a foreign one. The most adventurous tribes had pushed Germanic languages the farthest geographically but also eventually stopped speaking those languages. Grimm did not want to reject Germanic migration but did suggest that territorial advances might attenuate tribal identity – tribes had never, he implicitly conceded, been untouched by the process of migration and perhaps did not even constitute perfectly self-reproducing population groupings, forever impervious to foreign influence.[39] Expansion could result in illegitimate domination of other ethnic groups but also in the dilution and loss of one's own language and culture – this was Grimm's stubbornly *nationalist* argument against any enterprise of territorial encroachment.

The Turn to the Tribe

In 1848, the year of transnationally connected upheavals,[40] Grimm focused as much as ever on the nation, made a historically and linguistically supported case for German national unification, and advanced criteria for how to settle the borders of nations and specify the collective self of future self-rule. The Germany he envisioned was not, he argued, the result of some arbitrary segmentation of populations but an ancient and natural being that had long existed, in the form of a plurality of affiliated tribes. Cultural unity and solidarity, this implied, were not state impositions or intellectual fabrications but a real legacy of the past, and the philologist was its guardian. Grimm made one further political move, namely to turn against a powerful tradition in political philosophy, or against political philosophy altogether. *The History of the German Language* focused on the barbarians rather than the empire, the tribe rather than the city. In so doing, Grimm's nationalism broke with the history of political thought and its preoccupation with the constitution of the polity – he was, as always, exclusively interested in constructing a plausible narrative of historical identity.

Jacob Grimm was not uninformed about current political events and not uninterested in debates in political philosophy; he knew how political thinkers wrote and thought, what issues they tended to focus on, and what concepts they tended to use. As mentioned before, one of his closest friends and allies was Friedrich Christoph Dahlmann, a prominent member of the Göttinger Sieben and a fellow parliamentarian in Frankfurt, who much like Grimm wanted to balance monarchical government with representation of the educated middle classes in the frame of a mixed constitutional order.[41] Contrary to the Germanic philologist Grimm, Dahlmann was a scholar in the tradition of political thought. In his most influential work of political thought, *Die Politik, auf den Grund und das Maaß der gegeben Zustände zurückgeführt* ["Politics, traced back to the ground and measure of the given conditions"] from 1835, one can recognize the persistence of the classical tradition.[42] Dahlmann began by critically discussing social contract theory and then launched into a review of the major forms of government – monarchy, aristocracy, and democracy – followed by an analysis of the political structure of Athens, Sparta, and Rome. A separate chapter was devoted to modern government, paradigmatically embodied in the British political system. In the historical overview of canonical political thought placed later in the book, he showed his preference for a more pragmatically oriented Aristotle over Plato's political ideals and summarized the contributions of the most prominent political thinkers of the modern age, Hobbes, Locke, Montesquieu, and Rousseau. Dahlmann's work would to this day be recognizable as an introduction to central issues and thinkers in European political thought. The focus on basic constitutional forms, the overview of historical examples and decisive thinkers, as well as the discussion of the fundamental problem of legitimate power and the right to resist, marked it as a standard work.

Dahlmann certainly cared about historical particularity,[43] the predominant concern of Jacob Grimm. Throughout *Die Politik*, he returned to the focus on constitutional viability and stated his preference for careful examinations of how different political orders suited specific historical contexts. In line with this pragmatic focus, Dahlmann also made the case for an empirically supported debate, for a school of political thought that would take the particular conditions of any given country into account, its constitutional traditions, historical development, geographic location, and demographic profile. Such a turn to historical particularity did not constitute a break with the tradition – Dahlmann identified with Aristotle, Montesquieu, and Burke. Grimm, by contrast, considered his work on linguistic and ethnic history an utterly political text, and yet it contained not a shred of the materials dealt with by Dahlmann. Grimm's historical work may have been political, but it cared about the tribe rather than the city, the *Stamm* rather than the *polis*. Its central classical figure was not Aristotle but Tacitus, whose *Germania* had been rediscovered in the late fifteenth century.[44]

What sort of conception or vision of politics could be derived from the study of tribal Germanic populations as they appeared in the historical record? Grimm was well acquainted with the image of the Germanic barbarian in European intellectual and cultural history since Tacitus, and certainly not the only German intellectual who returned to *Germania*.[45] To name one prominent example, Fichte had the habit of reading out passages from Tacitus's text around the time he composed the *Addresses to the German Nation*.[46] A premise of this Roman, Tacitean tradition was that the Germanic tribe had emerged as a separate and continuous form of communal life in opposition to Roman civic life.[47] In this discourse, the barbarians did not live in cities but in sparse villages composed of isolated houses[48] and were culturally unsophisticated, socially incapable of self-discipline, and quite possibly ungovernable.[49] Yet these weaknesses, obvious from a Roman horizon, were also strengths, because the apparent wildness could be understood as a primordial form of freedom. The tribal members feared nothing more than enslavement and fought to the death to retain their status as free men.[50] The barbarians would never willingly yield to a foreign ruler, and as virile warriors, uncorrupted by the temptations of civilization, they refused to transfer the duty of military defense to professionalized contingents.[51] This defiant barbarity, tied to a life in the forest rather than urban centers, was synonymous with resistance to governance by some centralized power, however competent and beneficial; tribes embodied a primeval demand for self-governance. In *The History of the German Language*, Jacob Grimm extended this tradition and claimed that the indomitable Germanic tribesmen had challenged the declining Roman Empire.[52]

Grimm also preserved the ambiguity of barbarian wildness, which connoted both lack of self-restraint and irrepressible dynamism; the Germanic migrations were a "violent eruption [*heftiger ausbruch*]" that nonetheless testified to the barbarians' courage and proud spirit.[53] In a peculiar attempt to identify the barbarian ethos in the tendencies of linguistic development, Grimm even asserted that the second sound shift, which differentiated the High German tongue from other Germanic languages, exhibited the adventurousness of the "vanguard" high-German tribes.[54] Yet he also associated the sound shifts, the documentation and schematization of which had made him famous as a grammarian, with a certain lack of control; even if sounds organized themselves in new ways, they had for a moment become completely "unsettled."[55] In a speculative vein, Grimm suggested an analogy between tribal unruliness and phonetic transformation: "in a certain way, phonetic shifts appear to me as a kind of barbarism and descent into wildness, which other, calmer peoples would have resisted ... even in the innermost sounds of their language they [the Germans] pushed forward."[56] Going from "*t*ooth" to "*Z*ahn" had been, Grimm suggested, an expression of dynamism and explosiveness; he embraced the classical, Tacitean image of barbarism and transported it into his linguistic analysis.

Yet Grimm did not argue for a politics somehow modeled on tribal life or a collective return to its virtues. While his accumulated materials conveyed his deep fascination for an archaic age shimmering forth in the words of ancient Germanic languages, he did not offer his findings to the public as parts of a directly applicable political agenda for his own day. The tribe or clan was not, for Grimm, a model of immediate relevance as a form of human organization, the "general assembly of [German] warriors"[57] not a prefiguration of more democratic order. In Tacitus's *Germania*, the tribes possessed their own leadership structures and procedures for making collective decisions. Tacitus portrayed regularized bonds of loyalty and gift giving between chieftains and retainers as well as recurrent assemblies of weapon-bearing men who settled legal and political matters of collective import.[58] Peers of Grimm such as the constitutional historian Georg Waitz (1813–86) even argued that the system of limited monarchy had roots in a particularly Germanic conception of kingship reconciled with popular freedom and public election by acclamation.[59] Grimm made no such arguments. *The History of the German Language* simply did not focus on fundamental questions such as the right form of government, the election of leaders, the just distribution of goods, or any other issue commonly associated with political thought. It was precisely what it declared to be: a historical tableau of "collective origin."[60] To Grimm, the diachronic depth of the German community, its sheer continuousness as a linguistically specifiable cluster of groups, was the supreme political or rather pre-political fact. Whether or not the community should be ruled as a monarchy, republic, or democracy mattered less than that it should enter politics as an already extant national body whose outlines were most expertly traced by the philologist. The German people arrived to contemporary politics as a unit that should never be sliced or torn apart by elites who waged wars, conducted negotiations, and signed treaties. Its already existing cohesion simply constituted the ultimate reality for politics, the inescapable anthropological foundation of *any* contemporary order.

In his eager efforts to validate German unity by means of an excavation of tribal history, Grimm thus bracketed questions of political forms, but the ultimate results of this philological search for indigeneity, contemporary critics of nineteenth-century nationalist scholarship have asserted, were altogether spurious. To begin with, the ungoverned, undomesticated, and uncaptured[61] Germanic tribes that Grimm described had all been characterized as such by imperial observers and hence from within civilization, the world of Roman city life;[62] the major sources on barbarian origins, customs, deeds, settlement, migration, and political organization were Roman or Latin. "[A] people exists," one modern-day scholar writes, "when the literate world takes notice of it" and in the case of the Germanic barbarians, it was the Romans who took notice of them.[63] Most influential was, again, Tacitus's *Germania*, but ethnographic scholars also consulted the geography by the Greco-Roman Claudius Ptolemy, Julius Caesar's work on the Gallic wars, and Jordanes's history of the Goths.[64] For an exclusively textual scholar such as Grimm, with no access to an archaeological record, knowledge of barbarian history relied on non-barbarian sources. Such sources, one should add, were frequently unreliable: "[I]f Cornelius Tacitus was ever on the Rhine," one contemporary classicist states, "he discloses no sign of it in the *Germania*."[65]

Present-day scholars have furthered questioned whether Germanic groups really existed as pre-constituted, natural communities merely registered by literate witnesses, or whether they instead reflect imperial attempts to give some shape to culturally fluid crowds of people at the northern borders.[66] Caesar's division of Celts and Germans into separate ethnic macro-groups was not, scholars suggest, made with linguistic and cultural differences in mind; it was a distinction between potentially civilized and uncivilized groups drawn for political and military purposes.[67] Those barbaric peoples, the historian Patrick Geary has claimed, likely also assembled for the first time in the Roman borderlands and did not arrive to the empire already constituted elsewhere. When groups launched attacks on the imperial armies or attempted to break into more prosperous areas, they were quite often confederations or alliances among disparate communities brought together for military and political ends and coalescing around a rising leader.[68] Units crystallized through interactions at the imperial edges rather than reaching it fully formed; ethnogenesis itself was partly a border phenomenon. Along the same lines, the agrarian historian James Scott argues that state and non-state peoples always related to one another and indeed coevolved. Non-state peoples congregated at the frontiers of much wealthier states to supply slaves, cattle, and fur in exchange for artisanal and luxury goods – or built alliances to plunder their wealthier neighbors.[69] This continually developing complementarity leads Scott to reverse the temporal order of the civilized state and the barbarian tribe. Grimm and his peers may have thought of tribes as primeval units, but early states, Scott claims, typically generated so-called barbarians around them. The tribes recorded in the Roman sources were not clumps of pure primordiality but shaped and even constituted in an ongoing relationship with the empire.

The interaction between Romans and barbarians was clear to many nineteenth-century scholars. In his 1825 account of the German people, the historian Heinrich Luden stated that the division of Germans into tribes could reflect "particularities [*Eigentümlichkeiten*]"[70] and thus have some grounding in a cultural and ethnic reality, but he conceded that the identification of units according to some distinctive feature likely satisfied a need for clarity and overview in the confusing mass of barbarians, a need he attributed to the scholar but also the Roman imperial observer. The surviving designations and descriptions could therefore not be presumed to match actual barbarian communities and their forms of life. For a historian of the German people, this situation was a cause of frustration. Luden noted that tribes were mentioned in Latin texts but were not characterized at any length and sometimes seemed to vanish as quickly as they made an appearance,[71] and he even expressed doubts about the tribal names as sources of any meaningful, verifiable knowledge.[72] The sheer multiplicity of groups seemed to suggest that the late Roman Empire had not really confronted a single undefeatable Germanic enemy, but something more like a "dust cloud of fragmented peoples of varying ethnicities."[73]

As we shall see, even Jacob Grimm quietly acknowledged the elusiveness of the barbarians and the overreliance on outside, imperial sources. He admitted that he never quite had access to the barbarian tribe directly and hinted at the implications of this awkward fact, primarily in his recurring reflections on the names of the barbarian tribes. For Grimm, too, the names of ethnic groups were not enduring emblems of tribal self-assertion but rather relics of encounters; they testified to past interactions *between* communities close to the imperial realm rather than the spontaneous self-expression of any Germanic ancestors. Even in Grimm's nationalist work, the purely indigenous Germanic tribes tended to recede from view in the course of the philological investigation. His programmatic turn to the Germanic tribe revealed itself to be a turn to the imperial space in which they had first appeared.

The Names of the Barbarians

Grimm's analyses of names and their origins and meanings took up a very large part of most of his chapters on individual tribes, sometimes because little else was known about those tribes and their languages other than their names.[74] For Grimm, the names were an important source of information – and sometimes the only source. The Marcomanni, to pick one example, meant "border people," *marka* being a word for frontier or border and *manni* a word for men. Grimm pointed out that this name likely designated a tribe that lived in the vicinity of other, alien peoples, perhaps close to large forests, since forests separated peoples from one another.[75] Sometimes, such linguistic discussions of the meaning and origins of names even made up the bulk of entire chapters. Grimm's chapter on the Franks opened with a brief paragraph on the historical appearance and mighty reputation of the tribe but then immediately launched into an explanation of the meaning of the name; *Frank*, Grimm stated, meant free. Yet he continued the discussion of alternative derivations for about six pages,[76] after which he moved on to another tribal name, the Sigambern, and its possible context of origin and meanings. Could not the heroic names of Sigi, Sigmund, and Sigfried, Grimm wondered, be related to the name of the Sigambern?[77] A chain of further tribes was then introduced toward the end of the chapter, such as the Usipeten, Tencterer, and Bructerer, but Grimm reported that very little or nothing was known about these peoples; only their names had survived.[78] This lack of information was nothing unusual. From the language of the Vandals, Grimm wrote, nothing remained but Vandal names, and of course the name of the tribe itself.[79]

Sometimes Grimm sought to decode these names with the aid of his grammatical knowledge, such as his table of Germanic sound shifts. The tribe that Roman sources called Chatten, he claimed, could be continuous with the Hazzi or the Hessians, the people of Grimm's home region in Germany; *Ch* (as in Chatten) had turned into *H*, and *TT* into *ZZ* and *SS*.[80] At other times, it is a little harder to follow Grimm as he associated various names and peoples with one another and located them in particular landscapes and regions, surrounded by neighboring groups. The Rhoxolani, according to the Greek and Roman sources, were a Sarmatian people or a Scythian tribe, each considered Eurasian or Iranian. Grimm reviewed the available ancient documents, such as texts by Strabo and Jordanes, which placed the warring Rhoxolani outside of the Roman Empire, in close contact with Germanic peoples. Then he added that Finns call Swedes Ruotsalainen, Estonians call them Roostlane, and the Norwegian sami used the name Ruotteladzh, similarities that he believed may point to some identity between peoples at the eastern and northern periphery of Europe.[81] Grimm clearly delighted in association and speculation, linking seemingly floating names to present-day peoples and countries.

As revealed by these samples, *The History of the German Language* did not conceal that little remained of the barbarian tribes beyond their names, nor did it deny that those names had mostly been recorded in non-barbarian Roman sources. For a linguist like Grimm happily focused on minutiae, the presence of the names of Germanic tribes and not much else even seems to have stimulated rather than constrained scholarly productivity. The Grimm biographer Ulrich Wyss views *The History of the German Language* as an account of the exhilarating pursuit of minimal clues about numerous tribal communities now forever lost. To illustrate the arcane quality of the book and its taste for the recondite and the exotic, Wyss lists some of the lesser-known tribes that Grimm introduced in his book: "Bastarnen, Gepiden, Skiren ... Rugiern, Herulern, Avionen, Alanen, Hunen, Vandalen, Semnonen, Triboken, Nemeten, Vangionen, Armilausi, Markomannen, Quaden, Sigambern, Gugernen, Ubiern, Chamavanen, Bructeren, Tencterern, Usipeten, Batten, Canninefaten, Tubanten, Hermunduren, Marsen, Dulgubinen, Angariern, Haruden, Sturmaren, Ambronen, Chauken, Langobarden, Burgunden, Mugilonen, Buren, Navarnahalen, Victohalen, Reudingen, Suardonen, Aestiern, Guttonen, Gothinen, Tectosagen, Roxolanen."[82] There were myriad tribes, many of whom remained very elusive, as all that had really survived of them were the tribal names.

Since names constituted perhaps the central material of his work, Grimm early on provided a general discussion of their typical sources and function. In line with his etymological interests, he first clarified that name, or the German *Name*, derived from the verb *nehmen*, "to take," originally signified that which had been received as a gift.[83] As a rule, Grimm pointed out, people do not give themselves names: "nobody attaches a name to himself, but it is attached to him by others [*keiner legt sich seinen namen selbst bei, sondern er wird ihm von andern beigelegt*]."[84] This was true for individuals, who were given their names by parents or relatives, but also of collectives. Each community, Grimm believed, was typically named by other, neighboring ones.[85] The urge to name another group, he asserted, was even stronger than the need to give oneself a name; every tribe named those whom they encountered and ended up named by them.[86]

Grimm returned to these initial arguments, first presented in the long section on the laws and customs of ancient peoples, in the chapter on "Germanic Peoples and Germans [*Germanen und Deutsche*]," the very final segment in the book and one of obvious, overarching importance. Discussing the "names of peoples [*volksnamen*]," he reiterated the core idea that no ancient people had named itself but rather had received its name from others, ethnically affiliated or more "alien [*fremde*]" neighbors[87] and then suggested three principal sources for those who named others: names were given with reference to an ancestor or heroic figure, a salient feature of the people as a whole, or finally the place and landscape with which they were associated, although such names did not seem very suitable for roaming barbarian tribes. Examples of each category followed, with a slight emphasis on names that encapsulated some prominent property, either with regard to the people's appearance or their character. The name *Langobard* (Lombards) referred to the long beards of that people,[88] whereas *Friesen* (Frisians) pointed to the people's status as free from the domination of others.[89] A name such as the latter, Grimm added, was a mark of honor; it testified to the admiring recognition of those who had encountered the tribe.

Grimm clearly held that the tribal names he gathered and interpreted were never generated from within the communities themselves but rather attached to them by observing others. There were few or no proud acts of autonomous self-naming. As a consequence, the surviving names may often have come from a dialect or even a language not spoken by the tribes themselves, but from the language of a neighbor or even an imperial power. The Bavarians, for instance, were a Germanic people, but the name was of Celtic origin.[90] Grimm's reasoning even led him to an unexpected conclusion: the one word with which the tribe was most intimately associated, and in some cases the *only* word that had survived its historical disappearance, did not typically belong to its dialect or native tongue. The inference might seem peculiar, but some of Grimm's contemporaries arrived at a similar conclusion. In his book on the Germans and their neighboring tribes, Grimm's fellow philologist Johann Kaspar Zeuss stated that peoples did not name themselves in their own language, at least with regard to the names for bundles of related tribes, such as the Celts, Germans, Wends, or Slavs.[91] Historians knew tribes by the names given to them by others, in tongues only half-known or possibly alien to those tribes themselves, and in many cases scholars had almost nothing beyond precisely those names.

Grimm thus knew that the names could not be taken as vehicles of barbarian self-expression but represented the attempts of other groups to name a foreign community, attempts then recorded in non-barbarian Roman sources intended to bring order into a confusing ethnic terrain. The name of any tribe did not reveal to him the tribe itself in its immediacy; it was a designation from the outside, a mark of an encounter, typically picked up by interested imperial authors and preserved in a text. Grimm himself even explored how the medieval literary record consisted of traces of past cultural confrontations that had a distorting or mythologizing effect on the appearance of peoples. While most chapter titles of *The History of the German Language* pointed either to grammatical features such as sound shifts or weak verbs or tribes such as the Goths or the Franks, a late chapter, the twenty-seventh, stood out: its topic and also its title was *die edda*, by which Grimm referred both to the Icelander Snorri Sturluson's medieval prose work on Norse mythology and the older collection of Norse poetry with mythic content.[92] Grimm deemed these texts to be singular works, which described the system of pagan belief in a highly credible way.[93] Yet their greatness alone did not warrant their inclusion in *The History of the German Language* as the only literary works to receive any treatment in a book on linguistics. Grimm turned to the *Eddas* because they vividly confirmed his intuition that ancient peoples emerged in the eyes of others and were named by them. Behind the medieval Norse depiction of a mythological universe with dwarfs and giants, each with its own characteristics – the dwarves were nifty yet unreliable, the giants lumpish and reckless but also loyal and sensible[94] – Grimm detected stories of confrontations between Germanic peoples and a series of alien others, such as Finns, Sami, and Sorbs. In the tales of dwarfs and giants, he claimed, one could discern "marginalized, old inhabitants of the land who retreat before the immigrating tribe [*zurückgedrängte, vor dem einwandernden stamm ... weichende alte landeinwohner*]."[95] The mythological sources presented transformed versions of cultural encounters with unknown and intermittently hostile groups; the Norse myths revealed an ancient history of interethnic confrontations.

In the *Eddas*, Grimm thus believed he had found Germanic observations of other peoples and the attempt to name them and characterize them in ways that were obviously imaginative, creative, at times even grotesque. He did not explicitly infer from this that the Roman texts he mined for information about Germanic tribes were similarly fantastical, but they were. (In *Germania*, Tacitus reported that behind the barbarians, among groups living even farther away from the Roman border, one would find monstrous human-animal hybrids.[96]) When Grimm set out to dig as deeply as he could into the available sources about Germanic peoples, he found a linguistic and literary history of cultural encounters in which tribes and ethnic groups appeared through the eyes of others, in the idioms and languages of others, named and portrayed elusively through guesswork, projections, and fantastical storytelling. Grimm confidently introduced the barbarian tribes as the validating ancestors of a unified Germany, but he implicitly acknowledged that ancient peoples mostly emerged in fictional narratives about past cultural confrontations, as experienced and encapsulated by others. The Germanic tribes had been seen and imagined from the outside rather than the inside.

The work that Grimm considered the joyously written summation of his career as well as a scholarly case for German unity was partly, one could say, about the challenges and limits of philology. Grimm admitted that he did not have an account of the internal constitution and habits of the Germanic tribes so much as an account of encounters among groups, and that he did not possess a genuine record of the tribes left behind by themselves so much as the fragmentary, frequently unreliable, and even extravagant testimonies of strangers. The tribal units invoked by Grimm to anchor the nation in an ancient history never spoke for themselves but were instead instruments or even fictions of foreign observers. The delineation of peoples, already implicit in the acts of naming and the characterizations, was often performed from the vantage point of the city with its non-tribal, civic life. Who, then, was the philologist, the researcher with the task of tracing the contours of tribally rooted peoples to deliver bounded nations to the world of contemporary politics? Removed from the tribe in time, forced to rely on non-barbarian sources, attending to names that expressed not the groups themselves but were given by their neighbors or enemies, the philologist himself seemed constantly to slip into the position of an external observer. In fact, Grimm took one further step in his discussion of his materials and methods by implying that philology itself was a discipline born of empire. The philologist did not just rely on imperial sources; the guardian of nationhood was unthinkable without the long history of non-national, alien rule.

Imperial Knowledge

Jacob Grimm claimed with great seriousness that German philologists would be especially successful if they dedicated themselves to Germanic languages and literatures. A German national would arrive at the most perceptive and profound insights, he believed, when working on documents in his own language, because of the greater interpretive availability of native materials over foreign ones: "We naturally rely on our fatherland," Grimm claimed at the 1846 Germanist convention, "and with the gifts that we have inherited, there is nothing that we can learn to grasp as securely and profoundly [*auf das vaterland sind wir von natur gewiesen und nichts anderes vermögen wir mit unsern angeborenen gaben in solchen maasze und so sicher begreifen zu lernen*]."[97] Everyone was born into and immersed in one specific culture, and the inescapable socialization predisposed the scholar to grasp the historical products of his or her own culture more intimately than those of others. Just as the human mind could more easily penetrate the products of humanity than the mute objects of nature, Grimm thought, artifacts from one's own nation were more easily and authentically understood than those from other cultural realms. Speaking to his peers gathered at the conference of Germanists in Frankfurt, Grimm put this point in martial vocabulary: "the human in language, literature, law, and history is closer to our hearts than animals, plants, and elements; with those same weapons, the national triumphs over the foreign [*mit denselben waffen siegt das nationale über das fremde*]."[98]

Grimm's insistence on the importance of cultural closeness was meant to shift scholarly attention away from the traditionally revered classical culture to the hidden and misunderstood greatness of the vernacular and the national. An anecdote told by the poet August Heinrich Hoffmann von Fallersleben (1798–1874) captures this desired reorientation toward the German. Fallersleben is now probably most known, if known at all, as the author of Germany's national anthem,[99] but he was also a prolific scholar of Germanic literature. As a young classicist, he visited the city of Kassel to inspect antique sculptures in its museum, built with funds from the profitable business with Hessian military contingents. While in Kassel, Fallersleben encountered Jacob Grimm and reported that the older Grimm brother asked him a question that made him abandon classical studies and devote himself to the study of the Germanic languages and literatures. The simple but consequential question, put by Jacob Grimm, read: "but is not your fatherland closer to you [than Italy and Greece] [*Liegt Ihnen Ihr Vaterland nicht näher*]?"[100] By posing this question, Grimm did not dispute the beauty of the artifacts Fallersleben wished to see or the greatness of the classical tradition, but the choice of an object of study, the older scholar suggested, should not be determined by the attraction of aesthetic excellence. What mattered instead was one's closeness to the subject matter. The particular construction of closeness that Grimm sought to promote was of course national belonging. Only a nationally grounded intimacy with the object of scholarly attention could incite the necessary passion and motivation as well as ensure the greatest possible hermeneutic access. The German-born philologist should, Grimm believed, always first consider becoming a Germanist.

The central claim of Grimm's philological politics was that the philologist alone could accurately trace the contours of the people and hence supply modern politics with a much-needed unit of legitimate rule. Grimm's statements on the particular proximity of the German scholar to German materials might seem to suggest that the philologist would also be able to discern the substance and the outlines of his *own* nation better than anyone else, since he could perceive the culture and its boundaries most clearly. The German philologist, Grimm would then be suggesting, was especially close to the German nation, knew the German language and culture better than anyone else, and could also speak about its borders with the greatest authority.

In *The History of the German Language*, however, Grimm did not make this claim. In his own exploration of tribal history on the basis of the fragmentary linguistic record, he showed that the character and contours of each tribe were in some way always surmised from an external vantage point. He admitted, at least implicitly, that the ancient Germanic tribe was something of a fantastical beast, often spotted or imagined from inside the city to which the barbarians themselves did not belong. The name of a tribe had never been triumphantly called out from within the community, there had been no or few acts of autonomous self-designation, and all the philologist could do was try to decode the labels affixed to tribes and peoples by neighbors and hegemons, admirers and enemies.

In Grimm's view, the philologist was the one who could best disentangle peoples so that they could begin their separate political futures. Judging by the argument in *The History of the German Language*, however, this figure did not simply belong to one nation and one nation only but inhabited an implicitly imperial position, since he hovered above several peoples, studied them, learned their names from imperial sources, and necessarily observed them from some cultural distance. Grimm made the imperial character of the philologist most apparent in his discussion of the origins of comparative grammar, the disciplinary tool that in his view helped him distinguish peoples from one another and ultimately allowed him to envision a future geopolitical space on the basis of an appreciation of systematic linguistic differences. *The History of the German Language* asserted that the methodically acquired knowledge of multiple languages had only become historically possible within an empire, even within the realm of "world domination [*weltherrschaft*]."[101] It was the Romans, Grimm wrote in his ethnic history, who had possessed the "richest material for linguistic comparison [*das reichhaltigste material zu sprachvergleichungen*]" thanks to their contact with captured kings, priests, and warriors and subordination of entire foreign peoples, although they failed to develop modern comparative grammar.[102] If the Romans had never moved linguistics forward despite their domination of defeated tribes and assimilation of disparate territories, another empire had facilitated precisely that achievement. In an essay from 1851, some three years after the completion of *The History of the German Language*, Grimm pointed to the origin of comparative grammar in the British Empire.[103] He did not mention William Jones by name, the imperial judge and scholar who discovered patterns of similarity across Sanskrit, Greek, and Latin and conceived of "Eastern" poetry as strongly expressive rather than mimetic.[104] He did, however, point out that British rule of India – *die herschaft* [sic] *der Briten* – allowed for comparisons that laid the foundations for the science of language as he knew it.[105] Modern empire building, and hence "domination" or "rule" far across national lines, established the conditions for the study of multiple expressive cultural traditions of poetry as well as the subtle laws of language as they operated in diverse tongues.[106] Nonclassical literary studies and comparative grammar had, according to Grimm, unmistakably imperial origins.

In Grimm's mature view, the philologist could sort out peoples and tongues, divide them with precision, and produce a map of nations for a more stable, just, and peaceful order, in which conationals were assembled rather than internally divided or dominated from abroad. In this envisioned geopolitical order, like would finally rule over like, kings belong to peoples. Yet philology as a discipline depended, as Grimm acknowledged, on the possibility of transcending the single community of the nation and conducting comparisons of several languages and traditions of poetry. For Grimm, the philologist's very existence implied an international dimension above nationhood, from which the distinctiveness of each nation could be studied and understood. This dimension had, Grimm added, historically been the imperial expanse. The philologist did not belong to the nation, but had appeared in the realm of the empire thanks to a position of dominance and management in a multinational, multiethnic, and multilingual domain.

More than most scholars, Jacob Grimm contributed to the transfer of value from the classical languages to vernaculars and strengthened the idea that linguistic and cultural distinctions among those vernaculars were coterminous with the outlines of national communities. In Grimm's hands, comparative philology and literary studies turned into political instruments that could help create an order of nation-states. In the conception of Jacob and Wilhelm Grimm, the philologist was even tasked with the heroic mission of redeeming and revivifying the slumbering voices of the nation, releasing them into the present, and reclaiming the nationally defined people from the grip of autocrats and imperialists, from arrogant and ignorant regimes. At the same time, Grimm did not deny that philological work was completely dependent on comparative analyses of multiple languages and traditions, and that the polyethnic empire had been philology's condition of possibility. Crucial philological sources and tools had emerged through a distinctly imperial awareness of multiple peoples, multiple languages and their interrelations. When Grimm sought to find his way to the core and origin of German being, the ancient tribe as a purely indigenous community, he found himself in the position of an outside observer, even an imperial one.

Conclusion

The lives and careers of Jacob and Wilhelm Grimm coincided with a dramatic reorganization of political space in Central Europe. The brothers were born in 1785 and 1786 as subjects in a midsize principality in the mosaic of the Holy Roman Empire but would witness how drawn-out continental war, foreign occupation, and multiple territorial reconfigurations transformed their familiar context. They packed up everything to move away more than once, from their hometown Kassel to Göttingen in the kingdom of Hanover and, finally, to Berlin, the large capital of Prussia. When Jacob Grimm passed away in 1863, German unification was less than a decade away. To a significant degree, the brothers themselves contributed to a form of cultural consolidation. They tirelessly collected and promoted German antiquities and folkloric materials and made them available for mass circulation, insisted on linguistic and cultural criteria for political belonging, and claimed that philology could disentangle peoples and territories from one another with scientific precision. Skeptical about the relevance of traditional nobility, Jacob Grimm even argued for some moderate leveling of social gradations within the national space. The ideal was one nationally defined people under one king rather than a plethora of feudally stratified populations. In this way, the brothers Grimm sought to prepare the cultural, social, and political "closure" around a national form that they believed they could delineate.[1] In response to the dissolution of the old order of their childhood and early youth, they embraced national communities as the basis for new, non-arbitrary political units and introduced technical-grammatical criteria for settling the borders of appropriately sized future states.

Over his career, Jacob Grimm became an increasingly active figure on a national stage in the process of construction: he published in newspapers, chaired a national association of scholars, and became a deputy in the first national parliament. In this way, he emerged as an agent and embodiment of the trans-local and trans-regional scope of politics. He used his opportunities to speak publicly to define German nationhood rather than envisage more clearly and distinctly the constitution of a new political form. His political mission was first and foremost to establish the *contours* of the nation and less to transform its internal political organization. As we have seen, this program in no way involved dismantling monarchy but rather aimed to nationalize dynastic kingship, to nudge the ruler himself to endorse a national foundation for the state, respect linguistic borders, and in this way become a "philologist king." Jacob Grimm could praise the wisdom, justice, and strength of monarchs but wanted to add to this traditional catalogue of virtues an exclusive love for the nationalized people.

It is already widely known today that the Grimms sought to restore a historical folk culture to highlight and reinforce a collective German identity, but their orientation toward monarchy as the still-dominant political system of their day meant that the philologists faced a two-sided task of persuasion: regular people in their varied localities had to begin to understand themselves as members of a larger, imagined unit with sharp outer edges – the nation – but the king also had to begin to prioritize national affection and attachment over dynastic, non-national links to aristocracy and royalty. Encouraged and supervised by philologists as experts on national being, both the people *and* the political elite had to grasp the all-important political value of cultural likeness and come to appreciate their mutual, cross-hierarchical affinity.

The Grimms' commitment to the culturalization and nationalization of politics was rooted in their socialization and class context. They were educated sons in a family of petty officials who set out to find employment in a small state ruled by a patrimonial regime; although a series of disruptions compelled them to leave their home, they always remained within the milieu of state administration or state-sponsored academia. Intensely attached to their province as proud Hessians, they nonetheless relocated successfully, taking up new positions as university-trained civil servants prepared for archival and educational tasks. As their trajectory indicates, they were sufficiently educated and mobile not to have their lives narrowly defined by local opportunities and constraints. Without a patrician background, however, they never felt at ease in urbane circles or outside of German lands and never embraced a cosmopolitan outlook. While polyglot as scholars, they favored the vernacular, and even though they cherished their Hessian dialect, they celebrated the unified and unifying national language. Their work consisted in gently fusing local cultural environments into a single national space, all the while adamantly defending this now nationally defined particularity against the threat of non-national, imperial homogenization. They were nationally employable clerks, working for a succession of states headed by traditionalist electors and kings, and stayed within the compass of German-speaking lands. As such, the Grimms were vanguard representatives of an educated middle class composed partly of journalists, schoolteachers, lawyers, and officials who stood to gain from unified national spaces and typically "manned the battle-lines of linguistic nationalism."[2]

In a sense, the brothers Grimm wanted to remake the world in their own image: everyone should understand themselves as members of a nation living in one continuous national space under a king. While they did not view their project as a magnification of their socially shaped preferences, they clearly developed an exalted conception of the philologist's mission: it was the task of the Germanist scholar to remind the people of their shared roots and cultural cohesion as well as to advise rulers on the scientifically discernible, nonnegotiable borders of this people. Their chief means of cultural influence was a series of collections. The philological collector and editor could represent the community to itself by assembling and making available its neglected treasures of national expressivity, treasures that could focus and reinforce the love of the nation for its history and character. The philologist, and not the creative artist, could properly tend to the nation's particularity, its evolved "own-ness" or *Eigenthümlichkeit*, and convert it into legible artifacts such as the *Children's and Household Tales* that could then function as plausible instantiations of a collective cultural property or *Eigenthum*.[3] For the Grimms, shared national identity was exemplified and sustained by a kind of fictional joint ownership over collective literary resources. The resulting repositories of shared narratives and cultural traditions were eminently political objects, but often because their content was politically innocent. Through their display of supposed naturalness, these curated collections documented the already existing and self-sustaining cultural togetherness of the popular community that should be respected by the political elite.

Each chapter of this study has reconstructed an aspect of this philological-political project. According to the Grimms, philologists could, thanks to their grammatical expertise, trace the boundaries of languages in space and reliably designate speakers as members of a fraternal collective in a sustaining fatherland; study and promote an intergenerationally transmitted mother tongue that tied people together and anchored their insider status in early intimate socialization; and, finally, follow this mother tongue back to the idioms of a cluster of related tribal communities, whose spontaneous collective song had survived not only in textual fragments of heroic epics but also in the marginal folktales and legends that now must be salvaged and disseminated within the nation's borders. Having experienced the military and diplomatic remaking of states in their youth, the Grimms developed a series of interlinked practices such as grammatical discernment and textual collection and transcription to claim that the modern scholar could best watch over the integrity of the communal linguistic and cultural substance of the people.

Most of the commentary on nationalism is severely critical of its beliefs and symbols. The academic entrepreneurs of early nationalism such as the brothers Grimm, critics point out, accumulated piles of cultural debris to build a spurious collective identity designed for the purpose of muting class antagonism and excluding newly defined minorities from political enfranchisement. Much of this study has also been devoted to detecting the limits and contradictions of the Grimms' project. The authentic folktale was very much an editorial product in which cross- or non-national tales were instrumentalized for political purposes, the mother tongue depended on politically mandated institutionalized schooling, the tribal community was a projection of the imperial imagination, and the philologist a figure with an inescapably imperial perspective on languages and groups.

The sociologist Ernst Gellner has listed some contradictions between nationalism's self-image and its actual character: the ideology

> claims to defend folk culture while in fact it is forging a high culture; it claims to protect an old folk society while in fact helping to build up an anonymous mass society. ... It preaches and defends continuity, but owes everything to a decisive and unutterably profound break in human history. It preaches and defends cultural diversity, when in fact it imposes homogeneity.[4]

Yet the tensions between continuity and discontinuity, diversity and homogeneity, rustic folk culture and bookish scholarly culture were addressed by the Grimms themselves. The brothers knew well that local dialects were receding, that collective traditions of storytelling were coming to an end, that the Germanic tribes were all long gone and that almost nothing had survived of their cultures, that old grammatical forms tended to erode, and Jacob Grimm even suspected that smaller Germanic languages such as Icelandic would fade away in some future of intensified linguistic convergence.[5] Against the background of these insights, the Grimms' aim was not exactly to preserve an authentic culture but to represent the surviving materials of the past and make them available under new social and media conditions, an intervention that, in the case of oral tradition, might even hasten the decline of previous forms of cultural transmission.

In this light, the brothers did not simply preach continuity and diversity while imposing modernity and homogeneity. Rather, they tried to manage the transition from past to present, from local community to anonymous society, by reconstructing and protecting cultural particularity in the guise of, or at the level of, consolidated nationhood. Their projects of collection and dissemination consisted in designing a set of tangible compromises between a threatened cultural world and the tendencies of political centralization, societal modernization, and linguistic standardization. The underlying question of their work thus reads: what forms of individuality can be preserved at all under the current conditions, and with what means? From this perspective, the German nation they conjured was not necessarily the only authentic form or the most optimal one under all circumstances; the Grimms were aware of too many ongoing, unavoidable transformations and losses. Instead, the nation emerged as a form in which a significant degree of linguistic and cultural particularity could still be preserved and defended, thanks to its compatibility with a fortified, sovereign state under philologically informed monarchical leadership. The guiding concern of the Grimms was to promote cultural and linguistic particularity as the object of affection and source of existential meaning, and if nationhood was not the only imaginable kind of cultural individuality, it was clearly the most viable and resilient one – the one that could survive. They knew that old, homey provinces with all their local charms were politically feeble but believed that vast continental-imperial domains were too domineering and too colorless. Only the nation combined emotional attractiveness with future political strength, the promise of identity with the promise of stability. With this in mind, Jacob and Wilhelm Grimm sought to persuade both the people and the king of the importance of nationhood and also to shape this nationhood so as to suit a more centralized political rule over a more uniform society.

Notes

Introduction

1. Jacob Grimm, *Kleinere Schriften*, vol. 8, edited by Eduard Ippel (Gütersloh: C. Bertelsmann, 1890), 430.
2. Jürgen Storost, "Jacob Grimm und die Schleswig-Holstein-Frage: Zu den Kontroversen von 1850," *Brüder Grimm Gedenken* 8 (1988): 64–80; 64; William Carr, *Schleswig-Holstein, 1815–1848: A Study in National Conflict* (Manchester: Manchester University Press, 1963), 199.
3. Jacob Grimm, *Kleinere Schriften*, vol. 8, 430.
4. Jacob Grimm, *Kleinere Schriften*, vol. 8, 430.
5. For a critique of Grimm's questionable speculations about tribal history in the region, see Kurt Erich Schöndorf, "Noch einmal: Jacob Grimms Theorie von der Besiedlung Jütlands in der germanischen Frühzeit oder von den Grenzen der Germanistik," *Spurensuche in Sprach- und Geschichtslandschaften: Festschrift für Ernst Erich Metzner*, edited by Andrea Hohmeyer et al (Münster: LIT, 2003), 37–51; 43.
6. Jacob Grimm, *Kleinere Schriften*, vol. 8, 430.
7. Jacob Grimm, *Kleinere Schriften*, vol. 8, 431.
8. Leo Strauss, "Plato," *History of Political Philosophy*, edited by Leo Strauss and Joseph Cropsey (Chicago: Rand McNally & Company, 1963), 7–63; 29.
9. Malcolm Schofield, *Saving the City: Philosopher-Kings and Other Classical Paradigms* (London: Routledge, 1999), 35.
10. Strauss, "Plato," 31–32.
11. Plato, *Republic*, translated by Benjamin Jowett (New York: Barnes & Noble, 2004), 255.
12. Strauss, "Plato," 42; Plato, *Republic*, 255.
13. Plato, *Republic*, 255.
14. Strauss, "Plato," 10 and 30.
15. J. G. A. Pocock, *The Machiavellian Moment* (Princeton, NJ: Princeton University Press, 1975), 20.

16. Schoefield, *Saving the City*, 40.
17. James Turner, *Philology: The Forgotten Origins of the Modern Humanities* (Princeton, NJ: Princeton University Press, 2014), x.
18. Hans Blumenberg, "Wirklichkeitsbegriff und Staatstheorie," *Schweizer Monatshefte: Zeitschrift für Politik, Wirtschaft und Kultur* 48.2 (1968): 121–46; 125.
19. Ernest Gellner, *Nations and Nationalism* (Oxford: Blackwell, 1983), 1.
20. See Chapter 4.
21. Plato, *Republic*, 231.
22. Hans-Ulrich Wehler, *Deutsche Gesellschaftsgeschichte 1700–1815*, vol. 1 (Munich: C. H. Beck, 2008), 47.
23. Perry Anderson, *Lineages of the Absolutist State* (London: Verso, 1974), 250.
24. Perry Anderson, *Passages from Antiquity to Feudalism* (London: Verso, 1974), 165.
25. Wilhelm Bleek, *Vormärz: Deutschlands Aufbruch in die Moderne: Szenen aus der deutschen Geschichte 1815–1848* (Munich: C. H. Beck, 2019), 37; Theodor Schieder, "Partikularismus und Nationalbewußtsein im Denken des deutschen Vormärz," *Staat und Gesellschaft im deutschen Vormärz*, edited by Werner Conze (Stuttgart: Ernst Klett Verlag, 1962), 9–38, 23.
26. Fritz Valjavec, *Die Entstehung der Politischen Strömungen in Deutschland 1770–1815* (Munich: R. Oldenbourg, 1951), 346; James Sheehan, *German Liberalism in the Nineteenth Century* (Chicago: University of Chicago Press, 1978), 8.
27. Hartwig Brandt, "Die 'Germanisten' des Vormärz zwischen politischer Theorie und praktischer Politik," *Zur Geschichte und Problematik der Nationalphilologien in Europa: 150 Jahre Erste Germanistenversammlung von 1846*, edited by Frank Fürbeth (Tübingen: Max Niemeyer, 1999), 77–84, 82.
28. Robert Berdahl, *The Politics of the Prussian Nobility: The Development of a Conservative Ideology 1770–1848* (Princeton, NJ: Princeton University Press, 1988), 241.
29. Andreas Wimmer, *Waves of War: Nationalism, State Formation, and Ethnic Exclusion in the Modern World* (Cambridge: Cambridge University Press, 2013), 1 and 4.
30. Benedict Anderson, *Imagined Communities: Reflections on the Origin and Spread of Nationalism* (London: Verso, 1991), 85
31. John Breuilly, "On the Principle of Nationality," *The Cambridge History of the Nineteenth-Century Political Thought*, edited by Gareth Stedman Jones and Gregory Claeys (Cambridge: Cambridge University Press, 2016), 77–109; 100.
32. Jacob Grimm quoted in Helge Bech, "Jacob Grimm und die Frankfurter Nationalversammlung," *Euphorion* 61.3 (1967): 349–60, 352.
33. Michel Foucault, *The Government of Self and Others: Lectures at the Collège de France 1982–1983*, translated by Graham Burchell (New York: Palgrave Macmillan, 2008), 294–95.

34. David Blackbourn, *History of Germany 1780–1918: The Long Nineteenth Century* (Oxford: Blackwell 2003), 97.
35. Heinrich Heine, *Historisch-kritische Gesamtausgabe der Werke*, vol. 9, edited by Manfred Windfuhr (Hamburg: Hoffmann und Campe 1987), 11–12.
36. Louis Snyder, *The Roots of German Nationalism* (Bloomington: Indiana University Press, 1996), 51.
37. See for instance Roland Feldmann, *Jacob Grimm und die Politik* (Kassel: Bärenreiter Verlag, 1970).
38. See for instance Ewald Grothe, "Die Brüder Grimm und der Liberalismus," *Jahrbuch zur Liberalismus-Forschung* 15 (2003): 65–89.
39. See for instance the irreverent Klaus von See, *Die Göttinger Sieben: Kritik einer Legende* (Heidelberg: C. Winter, 1997).
40. See for instance Maria Tatar, *The Hard Facts of the Grimms' Fairy Tales* (Princeton, NJ: Princeton University Press, 2003), 20; Donald Haase, "Feminist Fairy-Tale Scholarship," *Fairy Tales and Feminism: New Approaches*, edited by Donald Haase (Detroit, MI: Wayne State University Press, 2004), 1–36; 10–14.
41. Jack Zipes, *The Brothers Grimm: From Enchanted Forests to the Modern World* (New York: Palgrave Macmillan, 2002), 13; Jack Zipes, *Fairy Tales and the Art of Subversion: The Classical Genre for Children and the Process of Civilization* (New York: Wildman Press, 1983), 46–47.
42. David Hopkin, *Voices of the People in Nineteenth-Century France* (Cambridge: Cambridge University Press, 2012), 20–21.
43. Jürgen Osterhammel, *Die Verwandlung der Welt: Eine Geschichte des 19. Jahrhunderts* (Munich: C. H. Beck, 2009), 849.
44. James Brophy, *Popular Culture and the Public Sphere in the Rhineland, 1800–1850* (Cambridge: Cambridge University Press, 2007), 34.
45. Jürgen Osterhammel, *Die Verwandlung der Welt*, 829; David Barclay, *Frederick William IV and the Prussian Monarchy 1840–1861* (Oxford: Clarendon, 1995), 6–7; Wolfram Siemann, *Vom Staatenbund zum Nationalstaat: Deutschland 1806–1871* (Munich: C. H. Beck, 1995), 34.
46. Ernst-Wolfgang Böckenförde, *Recht, Staat, Freiheit: Studien zur Rechtsphilosophie, Staatstheorie und Verfassungsgeschichte* (Frankfurt am Main: Suhrkamp, 1991), 252.
47. Michael Freeden, "Is Nationalism a Distinct Ideology?" *Political Studies* 75 (1998): 748–65; 751.
48. Erika Benner, "Nationalism: Intellectual Origins," *The Oxford Handbook of the History of Nationalism*, edited by John Breuilly (Oxford: Oxford University Press, 2013), 36–52; 37.
49. John Breuilly, "On the Principle of Nationality," 78.
50. Ernest Gellner, *Nations and Nationalisms*, 119.

51. Avishai Margalit, "The Moral Psychology of Nationalism," *The Morality of Nationalism*, edited by Jeff McMahan and Robert McKim (Oxford: Oxford University Press, 1997), 74–87, 74; Isaiah Berlin, *The Crooked Timber of Humanity* (Princeton, NJ: Princeton University Press, 2013), 263.
52. Erika Benner, "Nationalism: Intellectual Origins," 37.
53. David Miller, "The Ethical Significance of Nationality," *Ethics* 98.4 (1988), 647–62; Thomas Hurka, "The Justification of National Partiality," *The Morality of Nationalism*, edited by Jeff McMahan and Robert McKim (Oxford: Oxford University Press 1997), 139–57; Dany Rodrik, "Who Needs the Nation-State," *Economic Geography* 89.1 (2012): 1–19.
54. Jacob Levy, *The Multiculturalism of Fear* (Oxford: Oxford University Press, 2000), 7.
55. Benedict Anderson, *Imagined Communities*, 10–12; Lloyd Kramer, *Nationalism: Political Cultures in Europe and America* (New York: Twayne, 1998), 65.
56. Ulrich Hunger, "Gründung oder Prozess: Die Entwicklung der wissenschaftlichen Germanistik, ein Werk Jacob Grimms?" *Jahrbuch der Brüder Grimm-Gesellschaft* 5 (1995): 153–76; 157.
57. Herfried Münkler and Grit Straßenberger, *Politische Theorie und Ideengeschichte: Eine Einführung* (Munich: C. H. Beck, 2016), 59.
58. John Connelly, *From Peoples to Nations: A History of Eastern Europe* (Princeton, NJ: Princeton University Press, 2020), 149.
59. Jacob Grimm, *Geschichte der deutschen Sprache*, vol. 1, *Werke*, vol. 15, edited by Maria Herrlich (Hildesheim: Olms-Weidmann, 1999), 4.
60. Robert Prutz (1816–1872) quoted in Michael Ansel, *Prutz, Hettner und Haym: Hegelianische Literaturgeschichtsschreibung zwischen spekulativer Kunstdeutung und philologischer Quellenkritik* (Tübingen: Max Niemeyer Verlag, 2003), 163.
61. Ulrike Haß-Zumkehr, "Das Deutsche Wörterbuch von Jacob und Wilhelm Grimm als Nationaldenkmal," *Nation und Sprache: Die Diskussion ihres Verhältnisses in Geschichte und Gegenwart*, edited by Andreas Gardt (Berlin: De Gruyter, 2000), 229–46; 230.
62. Benedict Anderson, *Imagined Communities*, 71.
63. Benedict Anderson, *Imagined Communities*, 4.
64. George Iggers, *The German Conception of History: The National Tradition of Historical Thought from Herder to the Present* (Middletown: Wesleyan University Press, 1988), 6.
65. Kenneth Minogue, *Nationalism* (London: Batsford, 1967), 59–60.
66. Sarah Pourciau, *The Writing of Spirit: Soul, System, and the Roots of Language Science* (New York: Fordham University Press, 2017) 21.
67. Sarah Pourciau, *The Writing of Spirit*, 22.

68. Jacob Grimm, *Kleinere Schriften*, vol. 4, edited by Karl Müllenhoff (Berlin: Ferdinand Dümmlers Verlagsbuchhandlung, 1869), 73.
69. Frederick Beiser, *The German Historicist Tradition* (Oxford: Oxford University Press, 2011), 13.
70. Jacob and Wilhelm Grimm, *Briefe der Brüder Grimm an Savigny aus dem Savignyschen Nachlaß*, edited by Wilhelm Schoof and Ingeborg Schnack (Berlin: Erich Schmidt Verlag, 1953), 165.
71. Jacob and Wilhelm Grimm, *Briefwechsel zwischen Jacob und Wilhelm Grimm*, Briefwechsel Kritische Ausgabe, vol. 1.1, edited by Heinz Rölleke (Stuttgart: S. Hirzel Verlag, 2001), 308.
72. Einar Haugen, "Dialect, Language, Nation," *American Anthropologist* 68.4 (1966): 922–935; 925.
73. Jacob Grimm, *Kleinere Schriften*, vol. 4, 73.
74. Jacob Grimm, *Deutsche Grammatik 1 (1870), Werke*, vol. 10, edited by Elisabeth Feldbusch and Ludwig Erich Schmitt (Hildesheim: Olms-Weidmann, 1989), xiii.
75. Pierre Rosanvallon, *Democracy Past and Future: Selected Essays*, edited by Samuel Moyn (New York: Columbia University Press 2007), 54.
76. Andreas Wimmer, *Waves of War*, 4.
77. Louis Snyder, *The Roots of German Nationalism*, 43–51.
78. Donald Sassoon, *The Culture of the Europeans: From 1800 to the Present* (London: Harper Press, 2006), 78.
79. Wilhelm Hansen, "Die Brüder Grimm in Berlin," *Brüder Grimm Gedenken*, edited by Ludwig Denecke and Ina-Maria Greverus (Marburg: N. G. Elwert, 1963), 227–307; 272.
80. Jacob and Wilhelm Grimm, *Briefwechsel zwischen Jacob und Wilhelm Grimm, Dahlmann und Gervinus*, vol. 2, edited by Eduard Ippel (Berlin: Ferdinand Dümmlers Verlagsbuchhandlung, 1886), 46 and 74.
81. Jacob and Wilhelm Grimm, *Briefwechsel zwischen Jacob und Wilhelm Grimm, Dahlmann und Gervinus*, vol. 2, 39.
82. Priscilla Robertson, *Revolutions of 1848: A Social History* (New York: Harper & Row, 1960), 109.
83. Patrick Eiden-Offe, "Dichter, Fürst und Kamarilla: Heinrich Heine berät Friedrich Wilhelm IV. Notiz zum Wintermärchen," *Rat geben: Zu Theorie und Analyse des Beratungshandelns*, edited by Michael Niehaus and Wim Peeters (Bielefeld: Transcript, 2014), 275–300; 285–287; Barclay, *Frederick William IV*, 68.
84. Walter Bußmann, *Zwischen Preußen und Deutschland: Friedrich Wilhelm IV. Eine Biographie* (Berlin: Goldmann, 1990), 374–379.
85. Wilhelm Hansen, "Die Brüder Grimm in Berlin," 277.

1 The Philologist King

1. Katinka Netzer, *Wissenschaft aus nationaler Sehnsucht: Verhandlungen der Germanisten 1846–1847* (Heidelberg: Winter, 2006), 83.
2. *Verhandlungen der Germanisten zu Frankfurt am Main am 24., 25., und 26. September 1846* (Frankfurt am Main: J. D. Sauerländer's Verlag, 1847), 5.
3. Hans-Ulrich Wehler, *Deutsche Gesellschaftsgeschichte 1815–1848/49*, vol. 2 (Munich: C. H. Beck, 2008), 406; Andrea Wulf, *The Invention of Nature: Alexander von Humboldt's New World* (New York: Vintage Books, 2015), 231.
4. *Verhandlungen der Germanisten zu Frankfurt am Main am 24., 25., und 26. September 1846*, 3.
5. Uwe Mewes, "Das Fach deutsche Sprache und Literatur an den deutschen Universitäten im Jahr 1846," *Zur Geschichte und Problematik der Nationalphilologien in Europa: 150 Jahre Erste Germanistenversammlung von 1846*, edited by Frank Fürbeth (Tübingen: Max Niemeyer, 1999), 85–103; Rainer Kolk, "Zur Professionalisierung und Disziplinentwicklung in der Germanistik," *Wissenschaft und Nation: Studien zur Entstehungsgeschichte der deutschen Literaturwissenschaft*, edited by Jürgen Fohrmann and Wilhelm Voßkamp (Munich: Wilhelm Fink, 1991), 127–40; 129.
6. Katinka Netzer, *Wissenschaft aus nationaler Sehnsucht*, 79.
7. William Carr, *Schleswig-Holstein*, 21 and 23.
8. William Carr, *Schleswig-Holstein*, 293–317.
9. *Verhandlungen der Germanisten zu Frankfurt am Main am 24., 25., und 26. September 1846*, 11.
10. Jürgen Habermas, "Was ist ein Volk? Bemerkungen zum politischen Selbstverständnis der Geisteswissenschaften im Vormärz, am Beispiel der Frankfurter Germanistenversammlung von 1846," *Zur Geschichte und Problematik der Nationalphilologien in Europa. 150 Jahre Erste Germanistenversammlung von 1846*, edited by Frank Fürbeth (Tübingen: Max Niemeyer, 1999), 23–39; 24.
11. Moran Mandelbaum, "The Fantasy of Congruency: The Abbé Sieyès and the Nation-State Problematique Revisited," *Philosophy and Social Criticism* 42.3 (2016): 246–66; 246.
12. *Verhandlungen der Germanisten zu Frankfurt am Main am 24., 25., und 26. September 1846*, 11.
13. Eberhard Lämmert, "Zurück zu den Anfängen? Die kulturwissenschaftliche Weite der Germanistik von 1846," *Zur Geschichte und Problematik der Nationalphilologien in Europa. 150 Jahre Erste Germanistenversammlung von 1846*, edited by Frank Fürbeth (Tübingen: Max Niemeyer, 1999), 7–22; 9.

14. John Edward Toews, *Becoming Historical: Cultural Reformation and Public Memory in Early Nineteenth-Century Berlin* (Cambridge: Cambridge University Press, 2004), 343–44.
15. Jürgen Trabant, *Europäisches Sprachdenken von Platon bis Wittgenstein* (Munich: C. H. Beck, 2003), 247.
16. Steffen Martus, *Die Brüder Grimm: Eine Biographie* (Berlin: Rowohlt, 2009), 316.
17. John Edwards Toews, *Becoming Historical*, 350; Stefan Jurasinski, *Ancient Privileges: Beowulf, Law, and the Making of Germanic Antiquity* (Morgantown: West Virginia University Press, 2006), 24–28.
18. John Edwards Toews, *Becoming Historical*, 355; George Williamson, *The Longing for Myth in Germany: Religion and Aesthetic Culture from Romanticism to Nietzsche* (Chicago: University of Chicago Press, 2004), 110.
19. Ulrich Hunger, "Gründung oder Prozess: Die Entwicklung der wissenschaftlichen Germanistik, ein Werk Jacob Grimms?" 175–76.
20. Jacob Grimm, *Kleinere Schriften*, edited by Karl Müllenhof (Berlin: Ferdinand Dümmlers Verlagsbuchhandlung, 1864), vol. 8, 149.
21. John Edwards Toews, *Becoming Historical*, 355.
22. Tim Blanning, *The Pursuit of Glory: The Five Revolutions That Made Modern Europe 1648–1815* (London: Penguin, 2007), 336.
23. *Verhandlungen der Germanisten zu Frankfurt am Main am 24., 25., und 26. September 1846*, 11.
24. *Verhandlungen der Germanisten zu Frankfurt am Main am 24., 25., und 26. September 1846*, 11.
25. *Verhandlungen der Germanisten zu Frankfurt am Main am 24., 25., und 26. September 1846*, 17.
26. Rudolf Grosse, "Volk und Nation bei Grimm und seinen Nachfolgern," *Zeitschrift für Phonetik, Sprachwissenschaft und Kommunikationsforschung*, 38.5 (1985): 481–88; 481–82.
27. Jürgen Trabant, *Europäisches Sprachdenken*, 251; Michel Foucault, *The Order of Things: An Archaeology of the Human Sciences* (New York: Random House, 1970), 286–87.
28. Tuska Benes, *In Babel's Shadow: Language, Philology, and the Nation in Nineteenth-Century Germany* (Detroit, MI: Wayne State University Press, 2008), 125.
29. Frans von Coetsem, "Grimm's Law: A Reappraisal of Grimm's Formulation from a Present-Day Perspective," *The Grimm Brothers and the Germanic Past*, edited by Elmer Antonsen (Amsterdam: John Benjamins Publishing Company, 1990), 43–59; 43–44.
30. Tuska Benes, *In Babel's Shadow*, 126; John Edwards Toews, *Becoming Historical*, 366.

31. Joep Leerssen, *National Thought in Europe: A Cultural History* (Amsterdam: Amsterdam University Press, 2018), 189–90.
32. Jan Puhvel, *Comparative Mythology* (Baltimore, MD: Johns Hopkins University Press, 1987), 191.
33. Hans Frede Nielsen, "Jacob Grimm and the 'German' Dialects,'" *The Grimm Brothers and the Germanic Past*, edited by Elmer Antonsen (Amsterdam: John Benjamins Publishing Company, 1990), 25–42; 30.
34. *Verhandlungen der Germanisten zu Frankfurt am Main am 24., 25., und 26. September 1846*, 12.
35. *Verhandlungen der Germanisten zu Frankfurt am Main am 24., 25., und 26. September 1846*, 11.
36. *Verhandlungen der Germanisten zu Frankfurt am Main am 24., 25., und 26. September 1846*, 11.
37. Jürgen Habermas, "Was ist ein Volk?" 27.
38. Jacob Grimm, *Kleinere Schriften*, vol. 1, 37.
39. Holger Pedersen, *The Discovery of Language: Linguistic Science in the Nineteenth Century*, translated by John Webster Spargo (Bloomington: Indiana University Press, 1931), 240 and 261.
40. Sarah Pourciau, *The Writing of Spirit*, 53.
41. Jacob Grimm, *Kleinere Schriften*, vol. 8, 414; Sarah Pourciau, *The Writing of Spirit*, 53.
42. See Chapter 2.
43. See Chapter 4.
44. *Verhandlungen der Germanisten zu Frankfurt am Main am 24., 25., und 26. September 1846*, 18; Günter Wollstein, *Das Großdeutschland der Paulskirche: Nationale Ziele der bürgerlichen Revolution 1848/49* (Düsseldorf: Droste Verlag 1977), 32.
45. *Verhandlungen der Germanisten zu Frankfurt am Main am 24., 25., und 26. September 1846*, 18.
46. Günter Wollstein, *Das Großdeutschland der Paulskirche*, 32.
47. Katinka Netzer, *Wissenschaft aus nationaler Sehnsucht*, 52.
48. *Verhandlungen der Germanisten zu Frankfurt am Main am 24., 25., und 26. September 1846*, 18.
49. Hans-Ulrich Wehler, *Deutsche Gesellschaftsgeschichte 1815–1848/49*, vol. 2, 399–402.
50. Günter Wollstein, *Das Großdeutschland der Paulskirche*, 23–97.
51. Katinka Netzer, *Wissenschaft aus nationaler Sehnsucht*, 120.
52. Jürgen Storost, "Jacob Grimm und die Schleswig-Holstein-Frage," 68.
53. Jacob and Wilhelm Grimm, *Briefwechsel zwischen Jacob und Wilhelm Grimm*, edited by Heinz Rölleke (Stuttgart: S. Hirzel Verlag, 2001), 395.
54. Jacob Grimm, *Kleinere Schriften*, vol. 8, 402–4.

55. Jacob Grimm, *Kleinere Schriften*, vol. 8, 398.
56. Berthold Friemel, "Jacob Grimms unpreußische Ansichten über Polen und Sachsen," *Brüder Grimm Gedenken* 10 (1993): 68–81; 68–69.
57. Jacob Grimm, *Kleinere Schriften*, vol. 8, 400.
58. *Verhandlungen der Germanisten zu Frankfurt am Main am 24., 25., und 26. September 1846*, 12.
59. *Verhandlungen der Germanisten zu Frankfurt am Main am 24., 25., und 26. September 1846*, 16.
60. *Verhandlungen der Germanisten zu Frankfurt am Main am 24., 25., und 26. September 1846*, 16.
61. *Verhandlungen der Germanisten zu Frankfurt am Main am 24., 25., und 26. September 1846*, 14.
62. *Verhandlungen der Germanisten zu Frankfurt am Main am 24., 25., und 26. September 1846*, 17; Hans-Ulrich Wehler, *Deutsche Gesellschaftsgeschichte 1815–1848/49*, vol. 2, 406–7.
63. *Verhandlungen der Germanisten zu Frankfurt am Main am 24., 25., und 26. September 1846*, 18–19.
64. Katinka Netzer, *Wissenschaft aus nationaler Sehnsucht*, 40.
65. Jacob Grimm, *Kleinere Schriften*, vol. 1, 271.
66. Hans-Ulrich Wehler, *Deutsche Gesellschaftsgeschichte 1815–1848/49*, vol. 2, 675; Harm-Hinrich Brandt, "The Revolution of 1848 and the Problem of Central European Nationalities," *Nation-Building in Central Europe*, edited by Hagen Schulze (Leamington Spa: Berg, 1987), 107–34; 128.
67. Francis Cheneval, *Demokratietheorien* (Hamburg: Junius, 2015), 86.
68. Edmund Morgan, *Inventing the People* (New York Norton & Co., 1988), 58.
69. Chris Thornhill, *The Sociology of Law and the Global Transformation of Democracy* (Cambridge: Cambridge University Press, 2018), 127.
70. Jacob and Wilhelm Grimm, *Briefwechsel zwischen Jacob und Wilhelm Grimm*, 745.
71. Jacob Grimm, *Kleinere Schriften*, vol. 8, 438–39; Hartwig Brandt, "Einleitung," *Restauration und Frühliberalismus 1814–1840*, edited by Hartwig Brandt (Darmstadt: Wissenschaftliche Buchgesellschaft, 1979), 1–84; 14.
72. Jacob Grimm, *Kleinere Schriften*, vol. 8, 404.
73. Jacob Grimm, *Kleinere Schriften*, vol. 8, 404.
74. John Edward Toews, *Becoming Historical*, 371.
75. Jacob Grimm, *Kleinere Schriften*, vol. 4, 120.
76. Jürgen Osterhammel, *Die Verwandlung der Welt*, 867; Perry Anderson, *Lineages of the Absolutist State*, 16–17.
77. Charles Tilly, "Reflections on the History of European State-Making," *The Formation of National States in Western Europe*, edited by Charles Tilly (Princeton, NJ: Princeton University Press, 1975), 3–83; 27.

78. István Hont, "The Permanent Crisis of a Divided Mankind: 'Contemporary Crisis of the Nation State' in Historical Perspective," *Political Studies* 42.1 (1994): 166–231; 172.
79. István Hont, "The Permanent Crisis of a Divided Mankind," 188.
80. István Hont, "The Permanent Crisis of a Divided Mankind," 180; Andreas Kalyvas, "Constituent Power," *Political Concepts: A Critical Lexicon*, edited by J. M. Bernstein, Adi Ophir, and Ann Laura Stoler (New York: Fordham University Press, 2017), 87–110; 88.
81. István Hont, "The Permanent Crisis of a Divided Mankind," 183.
82. Bernard Yack, "Popular Sovereignty and Nationalism," *Political Theory* 29.4 (2001): 517–36; 519.
83. Bernard Yack, "Popular Sovereignty and Nationalism," 519; Hagen Schulze, *States, Nations and Nationalism*, translated by William E. Yuill (Oxford: Blackwell, 1996), 154–55.
84. Eric Hobsbawm, *The Age of Revolution: 1789–1848* (New York: Vintage, 1962), 59; Karl Möckl, "Hof und Hofgesellschaft in den deutschen Staaten im 19. und beginnenden 20. Jahrhundert: Einleitende Betrachtungen," *Hof und Hofgesellschaft in den deutschen Staaten im 19. und beginnenden 20. Jahrhundert*, edited by Karl Möckl (Berlin De Gruyter, 1990), 7–15; 9.
85. Margaret Canovan, *The People* (Cambridge: Polity, 2005), 1.
86. Hannah Arendt, *On Revolution* (London: Penguin, 2006 [1963]), 147; Jacob Levy, *The Multiculturalism of Fear*, 16–17.
87. Bernard Yack, "Popular Sovereignty and Nationalism," 523; Albrecht Koschorke, Susanne Lüdemann, Thomas Frank, and Ethel Matala de Mazza, *Der fiktive Staat: Konstruktionen des politischen Körpers in der Geschichte Europas* (Frankfurt am Main: Fischer Taschenbuch Verlag, 2007), 262.
88. Paulina Ochoa Espejo, "Populism and the Idea of the People," *Oxford Handbook of Populism*, edited by Cristobal Rovira Kaltwasser et al. (Oxford: Oxford University Press, 2017), 607–28; 607.
89. Paulina Ochoa Espejo, "Populism and the Idea of the People," 610.
90. Francis Cheneval, *Demokratietheorien*, 86–87.
91. Arash Abizadeh, "On the Demos and Its Kin: Nationalism, Democracy, and the Boundary Problem," *American Political Science Review*, 106.4 (2012): 867–82; 876; Duncan Kelly, "Popular Sovereignty as State Theory," *Popular Sovereignty in Historical Perspective*, edited by Richard Bourke and Quentin Skinner (Cambridge: Cambridge University Press, 2016), 270–96; 295.
92. Erika Benner, "Nationalism: Intellectual Origins," 41.
93. *Verhandlungen der Germanisten zu Frankfurt am Main am 24., 25., und 26. September 1846*, 11.

94. Hugh Seton-Watson, *Nations and States: An Enquiry into the Origins of Nations and the Politics of Nationalism* (Boulder, CO: Westview Press, 1977), 445.
95. Margaret Moore, *A Political Theory of Territory* (Oxford: Oxford University Press, 2015), 23–25.
96. Stefan Breuer, *Der Staat: Entstehung, Typen, Organisationsstadien.* (Hamburg: Rowohlt, 1998), 196–98.
97. Andreas Wimmer, *Nationalist Exclusion and Ethnic Conflict: Shadows of Modernity* (Cambridge: Cambridge University Press, 2002), 54.
98. Bernard Yack, "Popular Sovereignty and Nationalism," 526 and 527; István Hont, "The Permanent Crisis of a Divided Mankind," 172.
99. Bernard Yack, "Popular Sovereignty and Nationalism," 527; Jacob Levy, *The Multiculturalism of Fear*, 198.
100. Margaret Canovan, *The People*, 3.
101. Jürgen Habermas, "Was ist ein Volk?" 27.
102. Étienne Balibar, "The Nation Form: History and Ideology," *Becoming National: A Reader*, edited by Geoff Eley and Ronald Suny (Oxford: Oxford University Press, 1996), 132–49; 139.
103. Andreas Wimmer, *Nationalist Exclusion and Ethnic Conflict*, 55.
104. Anna Stilz, "Nations, States, and Territory," *Ethics* 121.3 (2011): 572–601; 574–75.
105. Arash Abizadeh, "On the Demos and Its Kin," 869.
106. Richard Tuck, *The Sleeping Sovereign: The Invention of Modern Democracy* (Cambridge: Cambridge University Press, 2016), 266.
107. Jeremy Adelman, "Empires, Nations, and Revolutions," *Journal of the History of Ideas* 79.1 (January 2018): 73–88.
108. István Hont, "The Permanent Crisis of a Divided Mankind," 210–11.
109. Eric Hobsbawm, *The Age of Revolution*, 78.
110. Steffen Martus, "Moderne Traditionalisten: Die Brüder Grimm und ihre Zeit," *Expedition Grimm*, edited by Thorsten Smidt (Kassel: Sandstein Verlag, 2013), 17–27; 21–22.
111. Tom Nairn, *The Break-Up of Britain* (London: NLB, 1977), 96.
112. John Connelly, *From Peoples to Nations*, 58.
113. Jacob Grimm, *Kleinere Schriften*, vol. 8, 398.
114. Steffen Martus, "Moderne Traditionalisten," 21.
115. Tom Nairn, *The Break-Up of Britain*, 338.
116. Tim Blanning, *The Pursuit of Glory*, 668.
117. Tim Blanning, *The Pursuit of Glory*, 668.
118. Tom Nairn, *The Break-Up of Britain*, 100–101.
119. Stefan Breuer, *Der Staat*, 196–98.
120. Jacob Grimm, *Geschichte der deutschen Sprache*, vol. 1, 3.

121. Christopher Clark, *Iron Kingdom: The Rise and Downfall of Prussia, 1600–1947* (Cambridge, MA: Harvard University Press, 2006), 487.
122. Benedict Anderson, *Imagined Communities*, 83.
123. Harm-Hinrich Brandt, "The Revolution of 1848," 109.
124. James Brophy, "Which Political Nation? Soft Borders and Popular Nationhood in the Rhineland, 1800–1850," *Nationhood from Below: Europe in the Long Nineteenth Century*, edited by Maarten van Ginderachter and Marnix Beyen (Houndmills: Palgrave Macmillan, 2012), 162–89; 170.
125. István Hont, "The Permanent Crisis of a Divided Mankind," 172; Jacob Levy, *The Multiculturalism of Fear*, 70.
126. Bernard Yack, "Popular Sovereignty and Nationalism," 527; James Brophy, "Which Political Nation?" 170.
127. Dieter Gosewinkel, "Staatsbürgerschaft–ein Relikt europäischer Rechstkultur," *Merkur* 70.810 (2016): 18–30; 23.
128. Joep Leerssen, *National Thought in Europe*, 185.
129. Andreas Wimmer, *Waves of War*, 4 and 115.
130. James Brophy, "Which Political Nation?" 162.
131. William Carr, *Schleswig-Holstein*, 318; Richard Evans, *The Pursuit of Power: Europe 1815–1914* (London: Penguin, 2016), 199.
132. Hans-Ulrich Wehler, *Deutsche Gesellschaftsgeschichte 1815–1848/49*, vol. 2, 399–400.
133. Hans-Ulrich Wehler, *Deutsche Gesellschaftsgeschichte 1815–1848/49*, vol. 2, 401; Günter Wollstein, *Das Großdeutschland der Paulskirche*, 30.
134. Günter Wollstein, *Das Großdeutschland der Paulskirche*, 309.
135. Katinka Netzer, *Wissenschaft aus nationaler Sehnsucht*, 107.
136. Katinka Netzer, *Wissenschaft aus nationaler Sehnsucht*, 109.
137. William Carr, *Schleswig-Holstein*, 318.
138. Katinka Netzer, *Wissenschaft aus nationaler Sehnsucht*, 108.
139. William Carr, *Schleswig-Holstein*, 199.
140. Wilhelm Bleek and Daniela Lülfing, "'Meinem edelen und mannhaften Freunde Jakob Grimm, dem Bruder Wilhelms, in Dank + Liebe gewidmet.' Das Fragment einer politischen Biographie Friedrich Christoph Dahlmanns," *Jahrbuch der Brüder Grimm-Gesellschaft* 3 (1993): 11–28; 7–8; Steffen Martus, *Die Brüder Grimm*, 392; see Chapter 4.
141. Katinka Netzer, *Wissenschaft aus nationaler Sehnsucht*, 89–90 and 110; Bleek and Lüfling, "Das Fragment einer politischen Biographie," 11 and 13.
142. Marcus M. Payk, "Dahlmann, der Konflikt um Schleswig-Holstein und die 'Konstitutionalisierung der Nation' in Deutschland 1815–1850," *Friedrich Christoph Dahlmann: ein politischer Professor im 19. Jahrhundert*, edited by Thomas Becker, Wilhelm Bleek, and Tilman Mayer

(Göttingen: Vandenhoeck & Ruprecht, 2012), 105–17: 109; Wilhelm Bleek and Daniela Lüfling, "Das Fragment einer politischen Biographie," 11–12.
143. William Carr, *Schleswig-Holstein*, 50 and 206; Günter Wollstein, *Das Großdeutschland der Paulskirche*, 25; Katinka Netzer, *Wissenschaft aus nationaler Sehnsucht*, 110.
144. Katinka Netzer, *Wissenschaft aus nationaler Sehnsucht*, 113.
145. William Carr, *Schleswig-Holstein*, 51.
146. William Carr, *Schleswig-Holstein*, 53.
147. *Verhandlungen der Germanisten zu Frankfurt am Main am 24., 25., und 26. September 1846*, 41.
148. *Verhandlungen der Germanisten zu Frankfurt am Main am 24., 25., und 26. September 1846*, 41.
149. Brian Vick, *Defining Germany: The 1848 Frankfurt Parliamentarians and National Identity* (Cambridge, MA: Harvard University Press, 2002), 149.
150. *Verhandlungen der Germanisten zu Frankfurt am Main am 24., 25., und 26. September 1846*, 50; Katinka Netzer, *Wissenschaft aus nationaler Sehnsucht*, 116.
151. Katinka Netzer, *Wissenschaft aus nationaler Sehnsucht*, 117.
152. Jacob Grimm, *Kleinere Schriften*, vol. 7, edited by Eduard Ippel (Berlin: Ferdinand Dümmlers Verlagsbuchhandlung, 1884), 576.
153. Jacob Grimm, *Kleinere Schriften*, vol. 8, 432; Helge Bech, "Jacob Grimm und die Frankfurter Nationalversammlung," 356.
154. Richard Evans, *The Pursuit of Power*, 199.
155. William Carr, *Schleswig-Holstein*, 293.
156. Günter Wollstein, *Das Großdeutschland der Paulskirche*, 38.
157. Katinka Netzer, *Wissenschaft aus nationaler Sehnsucht*, 129; Grimm Kl. Schr. 8, 438.
158. Günter Wollstein, *Das Großdeutschland der Paulskirche*, 45 and 47.
159. Richard Evans, *The Pursuit of Power*, 199.
160. William Carr, *Schleswig-Holstein*, 263.
161. Christopher Clark, *Iron Kingdom*, 493.
162. Jacob and Wilhelm Grimm, *Briefwechsel zwischen Jacob und Wilhelm Grimm*, 769.
163. Richard Evans, *The Pursuit of Power*, 253.
164. Katinka Netzer, *Wissenschaft aus nationaler Sehnsucht*, 273.
165. Mark Hewitson, *Nationalism in Germany, 1846–1866: Revolutionary Nation* (Basingstoke: Palgrave Macmillan, 2010), 48.
166. Brian Vick, *Defining Germany*, 23.
167. Peter Wende, "Der 'politische Professor,'" *Historisierung und gesellschaftlicher Wandel in Deutschland im 19. Jahrhundert*, edited by Ulrich Muhlack (Berlin: Akademie Verlag, 2003), 25; Steffen Martus, *Die Brüder Grimm*, 453.

168. Reinhart Koselleck, *Vergangene Zukunft: Zur Semantik geschichtlicher Zeiten* (Frankfurt am Main: Suhrkamp, 1989), 38–66.
169. Jürgen Fohrmann, "Grußwort anlässlich des Gedenkbandes zum 150. Todestag von Friedrich Christoph Dahlmann," *Friedrich Christoph Dahlmann: ein politischer Professor im 19. Jahrhundert*, edited by Thomas Becker, Wilhelm Bleek, and Tilman Mayer (Göttingen: Vandenhoeck & Ruprecht, 2012), 9–10; 9.
170. Ulrich Muhlack, "Der 'politische Professor' im Deutschland des 19. Jahrhunderts," *Materialität des Geistes: Zur Sache Kultur – im Diskurs mit Ulrich Oevermann*, edited by Roland Burkholz, Christel Gärtner, and Ferdinand Zehentreiter (Weilersvist: Velbrück Wissenschaft, 2001), 185–204; 197.
171. Thomas Macho, "Was tun?" *Think Tanks: Die Beratung der Gesellschaft*, edited by Thomas Brandstetter, Claus Pias, and Sebastian Vehlken (Zürich: Diaphanes, 2010), 59–85; 79–80.
172. John Gagliardo, *Enlightened Despotism* (New York: Thomas Y. Crowell, 1967), 21.
173. Fritz Valjavec, *Die Entstehung der Politischen Strömungen in Deutschland*, 22.
174. John Gagliardo, *Enlightened Despotism*, 91–93; Fritz Valjavec, *Die Entstehung der Politischen Strömungen in Deutschland*, 22.
175. Larry Wolfe, *Inventing Eastern Europe: The Map of Civilization on the Mind of the Enlightenment* (Stanford: Stanford University Press, 1994), 309.
176. Hans-Ulrich Wehler, *Deutsche Gesellschaftsgeschichte 1815–1848/49*, vol. 2, 532–40.
177. Jürgen Habermas, *Eine Art Schadensabwicklung: Kleine Politische Schriften*, vol. 6 (Frankfurt am Main: Suhrkamp, 1987), 36–46.
178. Susan Bernstein, "Journalism and German Identity: Communiques from Heine, Wagner, and Adorno," *New German Critique* 66 (1995): 65–93; 71.
179. Jürgen Habermas, *Eine Art Schadensabwicklung*, 42.
180. Philipp Felsch, "Antiakademismus," *Zeitschrift für Ideengeschichte* 11.3 (2017): 113–20; 117; Wolfgang Eßbach, *Die Junghegelianer: Soziologie einer Intellektuellengruppe* (Munich: Wilhelm Fink, 1988), 131 and 253.
181. Patrick Eiden-Offe, "Dichter, Fürst und Kamarilla," 275.
182. Patrick Eiden-Offe, "Dichter, Fürst und Kamarilla," 284.
183. Fritz Valjavec, *Die Entstehung der Politischen Strömungen in Deutschland*, 346.
184. Charles McClelland, "Die deutschen Hochschullehrer als Elite 1815–1850," *Deutsche Hochschullehrer als Elite*, edited by Klaus Schwabe (Boppard am Rhein: Harald Boldt Verlag, 1988), 27–53; 30–31.
185. *Verhandlungen der Germanisten zu Frankfurt am Main am 24., 25., und 26. September 1846*, 9.

186. Anthony D. Smith, *The Ethnic Origins of Nations* (Oxford: Blackwell, 1986), 172.
187. Jacob Grimm, *Kleinere Schriften*, vol. 8, 431.

2 Folk Hatred and Folktales

1. Glenn Lamar, *Jérôme Bonaparte: The War Years, 1800–1815* (Westport, CT: Greenwood Press, 2000), 103.
2. Glenn Lamar, *Jérôme Bonaparte*, 104.
3. Steffen Martus, *Die Brüder Grimm*, 224–25; Ursula Rautenberg, *Das "Volksbuch vom armen Heinrich": Studien zur Rezeption Hartmanns von Aue im 19. Jahrhundert und zur Wirkungsgeschichte der Übersetzung Wilhelm Grimms* (Berlin: Erich Schmidt, 1985), 108.
4. Wilhelm Grimm, *Kleinere Schriften*, edited by Gustav Hinrichs, vol. 1 (Berlin: Ferdinand Dümmlers Verlagsbuchhandlung, 1881), 542.
5. Philipp Losch, *Geschichte des Kurfürstentums Hessen 1803 bis 1866* (Marburg: N. G. Elwert, 1922), 81.
6. Wilhelm Grimm, *Kleinere Schriften*, edited by Gustav Hinrichs, vol. 2 (Berlin: Ferdinand Dümmlers Verlagsbuchhandlung, 1882), 504.
7. Steffen Martus, *Die Brüder Grimm*, 228–29; Jacob Grimm, *Kleinere Schriften*, vol. 1, 12–13.
8. Wilhelm Grimm, *Kleinere Schriften*, vol. 2, 504.
9. Peter Wilson, *The Heart of Europe: A History of the Holy Roman Empire* (Cambridge, MA: Harvard University Press, 2016), 655; Philipp Losch, *Geschichte des Kurfürstentums*, 8; Gregory Pedlow, *The Survival of the Hessian Nobility 1770–1870* (Princeton, NJ: Princeton University Press, 1988), 11.
10. Frederik Ohles, *Germany's Rude Awakening: Censorship in the Land of the Brothers Grimm* (Kent, OH: The Kent State University Press, 1992), 14.
11. Frederick Ohles, *Germany's Rude Awakening*, 92.
12. Heinrich von Treitschke, *History of Germany in the Nineteenth Century*, translated by Eden Paul and Cedar Paul (Chicago: University of Chicago Press, 1975), 186–87.
13. Charles Ingrao, *The Hessian Mercenary State: Ideas, Institutions, and Reform under Frederick II, 1760–1785* (Cambridge: Cambridge University Press, 1987), 134.
14. Rodney Atwood, *The Hessians: Mercenaries from Hessen-Kassel in the American Revolution* (Cambridge: Cambridge University Press, 1980), 7–21.
15. Charles Ingrao, *The Hessian Mercenary State*, 130 and 127.
16. Jeremy Black, *European Warfare 1660/1815* (New Haven, CT: Yale University Press, 1994), 221.

17. Charles Ingrao, *The Hessian Mercenary State*, 3.
18. Charles Ingrao, *The Hessian Mercenary State*, 137.
19. Philipp Losch, *Geschichte des Kurfürstentums*, 11.
20. Gregory Pedlow, *The Survival of the Hessian Nobility*, 11; Hellmut Seier, "Der unbewältigte Konflikt: Kurhessen und sein Ende 1803–1866," *Die Geschichte Hessens*, edited by Uwe Schultz (Stuttgart: Konrad Theiss, 1983), 160–70; 161.
21. Heinrich von Treitschke, *History of Germany in the Nineteenth Century*, 180; Winfried Speitkamp, "Das Kurfürstentum Hessen und sein Ende 1866," *1866: Vom Deutschen Bund zum Deutschen Reich*, edited by Bernd Heidenreich and Evelyn Brockhoff (Oldenburg: De Gruyter, 2017), 69–85; 69.
22. Steffen Martus, *Die Brüder Grimm*, 14 and 16.
23. Steffen Martus, *Die Brüder Grimm*, 25; Jack Zipes, *The Brothers Grimm*, 3.
24. Jack Zipes, *The Brothers Grimm*, 6.
25. Frederik Ohles, *Germany's Rude Awakening*, 17.
26. Theodore Ziolkowski, *German Romanticism and Its Institutions* (Princeton, NJ: Princeton University Press, 1990), 70–71.
27. Jacob Grimm, *Kleinere Schriften*, vol. 1, 3.
28. Philipp Losch, *Geschichte des Kurfürstentums Hessen*, 80.
29. Johan Huizinga, *Men and Ideas: History, the Middle Ages, the Renaissance*, translated by James S. Holmes and Hans van Marle (New York: Meridian books, 1959), 143.
30. Jacob Grimm, *Kleinere Schriften*, vol. 8, 402; Berthold Friemel, "Jacob Grimms unpreußische Ansichten über Polen und Sachsen," 69.
31. Peter Fritzsche, *Stranded in the Present: Modern Time and the Melancholy of History* (Cambridge MA: Harvard University Press, 2004), 143–50.
32. Philipp Losch, *Geschichte des Kurfürstentums Hessen*, 35.
33. Ernst Weber, *Lyrik der Befreiungskriege (1812–1815): Gesellschaftliche Meinungs- und Willensbildung durch Literatur* (Stuttgart: J. B. Metzlersche Verlagsbuchhandlung, 1991), 213.
34. Philipp Losch, *Geschichte des Kurfürstentums Hessen*, 34.
35. Glenn Lamar, *Jérôme Bonaparte*, 56.
36. Helmut Berding, *Napoleonische Herrschaft und Gesellschaftspolitik im Königreich Westfalen: 1807–1813* (Göttingen: Vandenhoeck & Ruprecht, 1973), 20.
37. Quoted in Alexander Mikaberidze, *The Napoleonic Wars: A Global History* (Oxford: Oxford University Press, 2020), 286.
38. Helmut Berding, "Das Königreich Westphalen als napoleonischer Modell- und Satellitenstaat (1807–1813)," *Modell und Wirklichkeit: Politik, Kultur und Gesellschaft im Großherzogtum Berg und im Königreich Westphalen 1806–1813*, edited by Gerd Dethlefs et al. (Paderborn: Ferdinand Schönigh, 2008), 15–29; 17.

39. Nicola Todorov, "The Napoleonic Administrative System in the Kingdom of Westphalia," *The Napoleonic Empire and the New European Political Culture*, edited by Agustin Guimera and Peter Hicks (Basingstoke, UK: Palgrave Macmillan, 2012), 173–85; 176.
40. Helmut Berding, *Napoleonische Herrschaft*, 21.
41. Alexander Mikaberidze, *The Napoleonic Wars*, 287.
42. Philipp Losch, *Geschichte des Kurfürstentums Hessen*, 50.
43. Alexander Mikaberidze, *The Napoleonic Wars*, 288.
44. Glenn Lamar, *Jérôme Bonaparte*, 101.
45. Michael Rowe, *From Reich to State: The Rhineland in the Revolutionary Age, 1780–1830* (Cambridge: Cambridge University Press, 2003), 8.
46. Alexander Mikaberidze, *The Napoleonic Wars*, 292.
47. Jacob Grimm, *Kleinere Schriften*, vol. 1, 12.
48. Claudie Paye, *"Der französischen Sprache mächtig": Kommunikation im Spannungsfeld von Sprachen und Kulturen in Königreich Westphalen 1807–1813* (Munich: Oldenburger Wissenschaftsverlag, 2013), 59–67.
49. Steffen Martus, *Die Brüder Grimm*, 141.
50. Ute Planert, "Resistance to Napoleonic Reform in the Grand Duchy of Berg, the Kingdom of Westphalia and the South German States," *The Napoleonic Empire and the New European Political Culture*, edited by Agustin Guimera and Peter Hicks (Basingstoke, UK: Palgrave Macmillan, 2012), 148–59; 152.
51. Wilhelm Grimm, *Kleinere Schriften*, vol. 1, 11.
52. Frederik Ohles, *Germany's Rude Awakening*, 17; Claudie Paye, *"Der französischen Sprache mächtig,"* 48.
53. Wilhelm Grimm, *Kleinere Schriften*, vol. 1, 11–12.
54. Jacob Grimm, *Kleinere Schriften*, vol. 1, 11.
55. Steffen Martus, *Die Brüder Grimm*, 312.
56. Philipp Losch, *Geschichte des Kurfürstentums Hessen*, 80.
57. Abigail Green, *Fatherlands: State-Building and Nationhood in Nineteenth-Century Germany* (Cambridge: Cambridge University Press, 2001), 62.
58. Perry Anderson, *Lineages of Absolutism*, 38.
59. Claudie Paye, *"Der französischen Sprache mächtig,"* 25.
60. Reinhold Steig, *Achim von Arnim und die ihm nahe standen*, vol. 3 (Stuttgart and Berlin: J. G. Cotta'schen Buchhandlung, 1904), 31.
61. Reinhold Steig, *Achim von Arnim*, 280.
62. Reinhold Steig, *Achim von Arnim*, 280
63. Perry Anderson, *Lineages of Absolutism*, 32.
64. Monica Wienfort, *Monarchie in der bürgerlichen Gesellschaft: Deutschland und England* (Göttingen: Vandenhoeck & Ruprecht, 1993), 171.
65. Ursula Rautenberg, *Das "Volksbuch vom armen Heinrich,"* 108.

66. Wilhelm Grimm, *Kleinere Schriften*, vol. 2, 505.
67. Wilhelm Grimm, *Kleinere Schriften*, vol. 2, 505.
68. Ursula Rautenberg, *Das "Volksbuch vom armen Heinrich,"* 111.
69. Ursula Rautenberg, *Das "Volksbuch vom armen Heinrich,"* 112.
70. Veit Weber der Jüngere, *Kriegslieder der Deutschen* (Kassel: Germanien, 1813).
71. Veit Weber der Jüngere, *Kriegslieder der Deutschen*, 11.
72. Ernst Weber, *Lyrik der Befreiungskriege*, 225.
73. Veit Weber der Jüngere, *Kriegslieder der Deutschen*, 20–21.
74. Tim Blanning, *The Pursuit of Glory*, 628.
75. Mark Hewitson, *The People's Wars: Histories of Violence in the German Lands 1820–1888* (Oxford: Oxford University Press, 2017), 73.
76. Steffen Martus, *Die Brüder Grimm*, 185.
77. Jacob and Wilhelm Grimm, *Briefe der Brüder Grimm und Paul Wigand*, edited by E. Stengel (Marburg: N. G. Elwert, 1910), 157.
78. Steffen Martus, *Die Brüder Grimm*, 220.
79. Wilhelm Grimm, *Kleinere Schriften*, vol. 2, 505.
80. Wilhelm Grimm, *Kleinere Schriften*, vol. 1, 317.
81. Wilhelm Grimm, *Kleinere Schriften*, vol. 1, 330.
82. Wilhelm Grimm, *Kleinere Schriften*, vol. 1, 322.
83. Wilhelm Grimm, *Kleinere Schriften*, vol. 1, 332.
84. Heinz Rölleke, "Grimms Märchen," *Kinder- und Hausmärchen gesammelt durch die Brüder Grimm: Vollständige Ausgabe auf der Grundlage der dritten Auflage (1837)*, edited by Heinz Rölleke (Frankfurt am Main: Deutscher Klassiker Verlag, 1985), 1151–77; 1155; Heinz Rölleke, *Die Märchen der Brüder Grimm* (Munich: Artemis, 1985), 32.
85. Wilhelm Grimm, *Kleinere Schriften*, vol. 1, 328. Note that the editor of Wilhelm Grimm's minor writings includes this.
86. Jacob Grimm, *Kleinere Schriften*, vol. 1, 18 and 27.
87. John Gagliardo, *From Pariah to Patriot: The Changing Image of the German Peasant 1770–1840* (Lexington: University Press of Kentucky, 1969), 147.
88. Heinz Rölleke, "Grimms Märchen," 1157.
89. Heinz Schlaffer, *Die kurze Geschichte der deutschen Literatur* (Cologne: Anaconda, 2013), 67–73.
90. David Hopkin, *Voices of the People in Nineteenth-Century France*, 13.
91. David Hopkin, *Voices of the People in Nineteenth-Century France*, 20–21.
92. Elie Kedourie, *Nationalism* (New York: Frederick A. Praeger, 1960), 9; Hugh Seton-Watson, *Nations and States*, 445.
93. Tim Blanning, *The Pursuit of Glory*, 550 and 568; Michael Rowe, *From Reich to State*, 55.
94. Karen Hagemann, *Revisiting Prussia's Wars Against Napoleon: History, Culture and Memory* (Cambridge: Cambridge University Press, 2015), 105–6.

95. Heinrich Luden, *Einige Worte über das Studium der vaterländischen Geschichte* (Jena: Akademische Buchhandlung, 1810), 10; Ernst Moritz Arndt, *Ueber Volkshaß und ueber den Gebrauch einer fremden Sprache* (Leipzig, 1813), 11.
96. Hans-Ulrich Wehler, *Deutsche Gesellschaftsgeschichte*, vol. 1, 544.
97. Robert Clark, *Herder: His Life and Thought* (Berkeley: University of California Press, 1955), 35.
98. Wilhelm Schmidt-Biggemann, "Elemente von Herders Nationalkonzept," *Nationen und Kulturen: Zum 250. Geburtstag Johann Gottfried Herders*, edited by Regine Otto (Würzburg: Königshausen & Neumann, 1996), 27–34; 30.
99. Johann Gottfried Herder, *Werke in zehn Bände*, vol. 4, edited by Jürgen Brummack and Martin Bollacher (Berlin: Deutscher Klassiker Verlag, 1994), 40, emphasis added.
100. Hayden White, *Metahistory: The Historical Imagination in 19th-Century Europe* (Baltimore, MD: Johns Hopkins University Press, 2014), 70.
101. Andreas Wimmer, *Ethnic Boundary Making: Institutions, Power, Networks* (Oxford: Oxford University Press, 2013), 16.
102. Frederick Mechner Barnard, *J. G. Herder on Social and Political Culture* (Cambridge: Cambridge University Press, 1969), 7; Frederick Mechner Barnard, *Herder on Nationality, Humanity, and History* (Montréal: McGill-Queen's University Press, 2003), 50–51.
103. Heinrich Luden, *Studium der vaterländischen Geschichte*, 13.
104. Till Dembeck, "X oder U? Herders 'Interkulturalität,'" *Zwischen Provokation und Usurpation: Interkulturalität als (un-)vollendetes Projekt der Literatur- und Sprachwissenschaften*, edited by Dieter Heimböckel (Munich: Wilhelm Fink, 2010), 103–28; 114.
105. Jörg Echternkamp, *Der Aufstieg des deutschen Nationalismus (1770–1840)* (Frankfurt am Main: Campus, 1998), 231; Otto Johnston, *The Myth of a Nation: Literature and Politics in Prussia under Napoleon* (Rochester, NY: Camden House, 1989), 1–2.
106. Jacob and Wilhelm Grimm, *Briefe der Brüder Grimm und Paul Wigand*, 157.
107. Anselm Feuerbach, *Kleinen Schriften vermischten Inhalts* (Nuremberg: Theodor Otto, 1833), 6.
108. Arnold Heeren, *Vermischte historische Schriften*, vol. 2 (Göttingen: Johann Friedrich Römer, 1821), 10–32.
109. Heinrich Luden, *Studium der vaterländischen Geschichte*, 14.
110. Otto Johnston, *The Myth of a Nation*, 85.
111. Helmut Walser-Smith, *Germany, a Nation in Its Time: Before, During, and After Nationalism, 1500–2000* (New York: Liveright Publishing, 2020), 167.

112. Ernst Moritz Arndt, *Werke*, vol. 11, edited by August Leffson and Wilhelm Steffens (Berlin: Deutsches Verlagshaus Bong & Co, 1912), 70.
113. Jacob and Wilhelm Grimm, *Briefwechsel zwischen Jacob und Wilhelm Grimm*, 264.
114. Jacob and Wilhelm Grimm, *Briefwechsel zwischen Jacob und Wilhelm Grimm*, 308.
115. Johann Gottlieb Fichte, *Reden and die deutsche Nation*, edited by Alexander Aichele (Hamburg: Felix Meiner, 2008), 199.
116. Johann Gottlieb Fichte, *Reden and die deutsche Nation*, 204.
117. Johann Gottlieb Fichte, *Reden and die deutsche Nation*, 205.
118. Arash Abizadeh, "Was Fichte an Ethnic Nationalist? On Cultural Nationalism and Its Double," *History of Political Thought* 26.2 (2005): 334–59; 346.
119. Johann Gottlieb Fichte, *Reden and die deutsche Nation*, 145.
120. Jacob and Wilhelm Grimm, *Briefwechsel zwischen Jacob und Wilhelm Grimm*, 164.
121. Jacob and Wilhelm Grimm, *Briefe der Brüder Grimm an Savigny*, 73.
122. Carl Schmitt, *Theorie des Partisanen: Zwischenbemerkung zum Begriff des Politischen*, 8th ed. (Berlin: Duncker & Humblot, 2017), 49.
123. Dirk Baecker, *Wozu Kultur?* (Berlin: Kadmos, 2003), 68.
124. Friedrich Ludwig Jahn, *Werke*, vol. 1, edited by Carl Euler (Hof: Verlag von Rud. Lion, 1884), 164.
125. Friedrich Ludwig Jahn, *Werke*, vol. 1, 161.
126. Dieter Düding, *Organisierter gesellschaftlicher Nationalismus in Deutschland (1808–1847): Bedeutung und Funktion der Turner- und Sängervereine für die deutsche Nationalbewegung* (Munich: R. Oldenbourg Verlag, 1984).
127. Dieter Düding, *Organisierter gesellschaftlicher Nationalismus*, 41.
128. Karl Heinz Schäfer, *Ernst Moritz Arndt als politischer Publizist: Studien zur Publizistik, Pressepolitik und kollektivem Bewußstein im frühen 19. Jahrhundert* (Bonn: Ludwig Röhrschied Verlag, 1974), 230.
129. Ernst Weber, *Lyrik der Befreiungskriege*, 168.
130. Carl Schmitt, *Theorie des Partisanen*, 46.
131. John Gagliardo, *From Pariah to Patriot*, 205.
132. John Ferejohn and Frances McCall Rosenbluth, *Forged through Fire: War, Peace, and the Democratic Bargain* (New York: Liveright, 2017), 106.
133. Alfred Pundt, *Arndt and the Nationalist Awakening in Germany* (New York: Columbia University Press, 1935), 9–10.
134. Ute Frevert, "Citizen-Soldiers: General Conscription in the Nineteenth and Twentieth Centuries," *Enlightened War: German Theories and Cultures of Warfare from Frederick the Great to Clausewitz*, edited by Patricia Anne Simpson and Elisabeth Krimmer (Rochester, NY: Camden House, 2011), 219–37; 224.

135. John Ferejohn and Frances McCall Rosenbluth, *Forged through Fire*, 229–30.
136. Mark Hewitson, *The People's War*, 76.
137. Chris Thornhill, *The Sociology of Law*, 12–13.
138. Andreas Wimmer, *Nationalist Exclusion and Ethnic Conflict*, 57 and 74.
139. Ernst Moritz Arndt, *Ueber Volkshaß*, 13–14.
140. Ernst Moritz Arndt, *Ueber Volkshaß*, 3 and 10.
141. Johannes Lehmann, "Zorn, Hass, Entscheidung: Modelle der Feindschaft in den Hermannsschlachten von Klopstock zu Kleist," *Historische Anthropologie* 14.1 (2006): 11–29; 20.
142. Ernst Moritz Arndt, *Ueber Volkshaß*, 14.
143. Ernst Moritz Arndt, *Ueber Volkshaß*, 19.
144. Marc Redfield, *The Politics of Aesthetics: Nationalism, Gender, Romanticism* (Stanford, CA: Stanford University Press, 2003), 67.
145. Wilhelm Grimm, *Kleinere Schriften*, vol. 1, 536–57; Jacob Grimm, *Kleinere Schriften*, vol. 8, 397–415.
146. Jacob Grimm, *Kleinere Schriften*, vol. 1, 9; Steffen Martus, *Die Brüder Grimm*, 114.
147. Jacob Grimm, *Kleinere Schriften*, vol. 8, 398.
148. See for instance Wilhelm Grimm, *Kleinere Schriften*, vol. 1, 13, 19, 97, 108, 114, 552, 555.
149. Karin Raude notes that *eigenthümlich* appears more frequently in Jacob Grimm than the relatively sparingly used *Volksgeist*. See Karin Raude, "Jacob Grimm und der Volksgeist," *Romantik und Recht: Recht und Sprache, Rechtsfälle und Gerechtigkeit*, edited by Antje Arnold (Boston, MA: De Gruyter, 2018) 15–33; 18–19.
150. Wilhelm Grimm, *Kleinere Schriften*, vol. 3, edited by Gustav Hinrichs (Berlin: Ferdinand Dümmlers Verlagsbuchhandlung, 1883), 83.
151. Miroslav Hroch, *European Nations: Explaining Their Formation*, translated by Karolina Graham (London: Verso, 2015), 270–71.
152. Miroslav Hroch, *European Nations*, 270–71.
153. Arash Abizadeh, "The Demos and Its Kin," 867.
154. Ruth Michaelis-Jena, *The Brothers Grimm* (London: Routledge, 1970), 53–54.
155. Reinhold Steig, *Achim von Arnim*, 252.
156. Jennifer Schacker, *National Dreams: The Remaking of Fairy Tales in Nineteenth-Century England* (Philadelphia: University of Pennsylvania Press, 2003), 13–45; Doris Reimer, *Passion & Kalkül: der Verleger Georg Andreas Reimer (1776–1842)* (Berlin: Walter de Gruyter, 1999), 380.
157. Doris Reimer, *Passion & Kalkül*, 92.
158. Doris Reimer, *Passion & Kalkül*, 95 and 265.

159. Doris Reimer, *Passion & Kalkül*, 117 and 133.
160. Doris Reimer, *Passion & Kalkül*, 102.
161. Doris Reimer, *Passion & Kalkül*, 115; Wilhelm Grimm, *Kleinere Schriften*, vol. 1, 529–35.
162. Jörg Echternkamp, *Der Aufstieg des deutschen Nationalismus*, 345.
163. Doris Reimer, *Passion & Kalkül*, 364; Reinhold Steig, *Achim von Arnim*, 204.
164. Doris Reimer, *Passion & Kalkül*, 388.
165. Friedrich Ludwig Jahn, *Werke*, vol. 1, 381.
166. James Brophy, *Popular Culture and the Public Sphere in the Rhineland, 1800–1850*, 65.
167. Friedrich Ludwig Jahn, *Werke*, vol. 1, 387.
168. Ludwig Denecke, *Jacob Grimm und sein Bruder Wilhelm* (Stuttgart: J. B. Metzlersche Verlagsbuchhandlung, 1971), 64.
169. Jacob and Wilhelm Grimm, *Briefwechsel zwischen Jacob und Wilhelm Grimm*, 291.
170. Karl Heinz Schäfer, *Ernst Moritz Arndt*, 107.
171. Ernst Weber, *Lyrik der Befreiungskriege*, 165.
172. Karl Heinz Schäfer, *Ernst Moritz Arndt*, 196–99.
173. August Leffson, "Einleitung des Herausgebers," Ernst Moritz Arndt, *Werke*, vol. 3, edited by August Leffson and Wilhelm Steffens (Berlin: Deutsches Verlagshaus Bong & Co. 1912), 7–13; 10.
174. Ernst Moritz Arndt, *Werke*, vol. 3, edited by August Leffson and Wilhelm Steffens (Berlin: Deutsches Verlagshaus Bong & Co. 1912), 2.
175. Heide Crawford, "'Mit Märchen und mit Träumen / Erinn'rung zu mir schwebt!' Regional Identity and the Concept of 'Heimat' in Ernst Moritz Arndt's Märchen," *Ernst Moritz Arndt (1769–1860): Deutscher Nationalismus – Europa – Transatlantische Perspektiven*, edited by Walter Erhart and Arne Koch (Tübingen: Max Niemeyer Verlag, 2007), 137–45; 143.
176. Wilhelm Grimm, *Kleinere Schriften*, vol. 1, 326.
177. Wilhelm Grimm, *Kleinere Schriften*, vol. 1, 330.
178. Wilhelm Grimm, *Kleinere Schriften*, vol. 1, 332.
179. Hans-Jörg Uther, *Handbuch zu den "Kinder- und Hausmärchen" der Brüder Grimm: Entstehung, Wirkung, Interpretation* (Berlin: De Gruyter, 2008), 513–14.
180. Wilhelm Grimm, Kleinere Schriften, vol. 2, 40.
181. Jacob Grimm, *Kleinere Schriften*, vol. 1, 177; Jacob Grimm, *Kleinere Schriften*, vol. 8, 145.
182. Wilhelm Grimm, *Kleinere Schriften*, vol. 1, 326.
183. David Hopkin, "Folklore beyond Nationalism: Identity Politics and Scientific Cultures in a New Discipline," *Folklore and Nationalism during the Long Nineteenth Century*, edited by Timothy Bancroft and David Hopkin (Leiden: Brill, 2010), 371–401; 394.

184. Donald Sassoon, *The Culture of the Europeans*, 100.
185. Siegfried Neumann, "The Brothers Grimm as Collectors and Editors of German Folktales," *The Great Fairy Tale Tradition from Straparola and Basile to the Brothers Grimm*, edited by Jack Zipes (New York: Norton & Co, 2001), 969–80; 971–73; Maria Tatar, "Folklore and Cultural Identity," *A New History of German Literature*, edited by David Wellbery (Cambridge: Harvard University Press, 2004), 516–21; 517.
186. Tim Blanning, *The Pursuit of Glory*, 336.
187. Till Dembeck, "Lyrik kanonisieren: Herders Volksliedersammlung als Versuch einer Gattungskonstitution," *Rahmungen: Präsentationsformen und Kanoneffekte*, edited by Philip Arjouri, Ursula Kundert, and Carsten Rohde (Berlin: Erich Schmidt Verlag, 2017), 123–45.
188. Manfred Grätz, *Das Märchen in der deutschen Aufklärung: Von Feenmärchen zum Volksmärchen* (Stuttgart: J. B. Metzlertsche Verlagsbuchhandlung, 1988), 208–13.
189. Heinz Rölleke, "Grimms Märchen," 1153–54; Ethel Matala de Mazza, *Der verfasste Körper: Zum Projekt einer organischen Gemeinschaft in der politischen Romantik* (Freiburg: Rombach, 1999), 341–61.
190. Heinz Rölleke, "Grimms Märchen," 1155.
191. Wilhelm Grimm, *Kleinere Schriften*, vol. 1, 317–19.
192. Johann Karl August Musäus, *Volksmärchen der Deutschen*, vol. 1, edited by Paul Zaunert (Jena: Eugen Diederichs, 1912).
193. Johann Karl August Musäus, *Volksmärchen der Deutschen*, xxxi and xxxvi.
194. Hans-Jörg Uther, *Handbuch zu den "Kinder- und Hausmärchen,"* 494.
195. Albert Ludwig Grimm, *Kindermährchen* (Heidelberg: Mohr und Zimmer, 1809), 2–6.
196. Otmar [Johann Carl Christoph Nachtigall], *Volcks-Sagen* (Bremen: Friedrich Wilmans, 1800).
197. Otmar, *Volcks-Sagen*, 24.
198. Stefani Engelstein, "The Father in the Fatherland: Violent Ideology and Corporeal Paternity in Kleist," *Contemplating Violence: Critical Studies in Modern German Culture*, edited by Stefani Engelstein and Carl Niekerk (Amsterdam: Rodolpi, 2011), 49–66.
199. Jacob and Wilhelm Grimm, *Briefe der Brüder Grimm und Paul Wigand*, 191.

3 The Prince of Germany

1. Wilhelm Grimm, *Kleinere Schriften*, vol. 4, edited by Gustav Hinrichs (Gütersloh: C. Bertelsmann, 1887), 526, 537, and 542.
2. John-Evert Härd, *Das Nibelungenepos: Wertung und Wirkung von der Romantik bis zur Gegenwart*, translated by Christine Palm (Tübingen: Francke, 1996), 60.

3. Johannes Janota, *Eine Wissenschaft etabliert sich 1810–1870* (Tübingen: Max Niemeyer, 1980), 251.
4. August Wilhelm Schlegel, "Aus einer noch ungedruckten historischen Untersuchungen über das Lied der Nibelungen," *Deutsches Museum* 1.1 (1812): 9–36; Hinrich Seeba, "Nationalbücher: Zur Kanonisierung nationaler Bildungsmuster in der frühen Germanistik," *Wissenschaft und Nation: Studien zur Entstehungsgeschichte der deutschen Literaturwissenschaft*, edited by Jürgen Fohrmann and Wilhelm Voßkamp (Munich: Wilhelm Fink, 1991) 57–71; 57.
5. Alexander Beecroft, *An Ecology of World Literature: From Antiquity to the Present Day* (London: Verso, 2015), 229.
6. Pascal Casanova, "Combative Literatures," *New Left Review* 72 (2011): 123–34; 126.
7. Theodore Andersson, *A Preface to the Nibelungenlied* (Stanford, CA: Stanford University Press, 1987), 28.
8. Klaus von See, "Das Nibelungenlied – ein Nationalepos?" *Die Nibelungen: Sage – Epos – Mythos*, edited by Joachim Heinzle, Klaus Kleim, and Ute Obhof (Wiesbaden: Reichert, 2003), 309–43; 309.
9. Wilhelm Grimm, *Die Deutsche Heldensage*, 3rd ed., edited by Reinhold Steig (Gütersloh: C. Bertelsmann, 1889), 15–19.
10. Tom Shippey, "Introduction," *Beowulf: The Critical Heritage*, edited by Tom Shippey and Andreas Haarder (London: Routledge, 1998) 1–74; 6.
11. Wilhelm Grimm, *Kleinere Schriften*, vol. 1, 70.
12. Wilhelm Grimm, *Kleinere Schriften*, vol. 1, 67.
13. George Williamson, *The Longing for Myth in Germany*, 84.
14. Wilhelm Grimm, *Kleinere Schriften*, vol. 1, 67.
15. Schlegel, "Nibelungen," 9–36.
16. Wilhelm Grimm, *Kleinere Schriften*, vol. 1, 72.
17. Wilhelm Grimm, *Kleinere Schriften*, vol. 1, 72.
18. Klaus von See, "Das Nibelungenlied – ein Nationalepos?" 319.
19. Klaus Gille, "Germanistik and Nation in the 19th Century," *Nation Building and Writing Literary History*, edited by Menno Spiering (Amsterdam: Rodolpi, 1999) 27–55; 37.
20. Steffen Martus, *Die Brüder Grimm*, 134; Mark-Georg Dehrmann, *Studierte Dichter: Zum Spannungsverhältnis von Dichtung und philologisch-historischen Wissenschaften im 19. Jahrhundert* (Berlin: De Gruyter, 2015), 259.
21. Wilhelm Grimm, *Kleinere Schriften*, vol. 1, 108.
22. Wilhelm Grimm, *Kleinere Schriften*, vol. 1, 94.
23. Wilhelm Grimm, *Kleinere Schriften*, vol. 1, 93. See also *Kleinere Schriften*, vol. 2, 10.
24. Wilhelm Grimm, *Kleinere Schriften*, vol. 1, 98

25. Wilhelm Grimm, *Kleinere Schriften*, vol. 1, 98.
26. Wilhelm Grimm, *Kleinere Schriften*, vol. 1, 100.
27. Wilhelm Grimm, *Kleinere Schriften*, vol. 1, 101.
28. Mark-Georg Dehrmann, *Studierte Dichter*, 224–30.
29. Wilhelm Grimm, *Kleinere Schriften*, vol. 1, 101. See also Wilhelm Grimm, *Kleinere Schriften*, vol. 1, 173.
30. Slavica Ranković, "Who Is Speaking in Traditional Texts? On the Distributed Author of the Sagas of Icelanders and Serbian Epic Poetry," *New Literary History* 38.2 (2007): 293–307; 300.
31. Wilhelm Grimm, *Kleinere Schriften*, vol. 1, 101–2.
32. Wilhelm Grimm, *Kleinere Schriften*, vol. 1, 102.
33. Katie Trumpener, *Bardic Nationalism: The Romantic Novel and the British Empire* (Princeton, NJ: Princeton University Press, 1997).
34. Katie Trumpener, *Bardic Nationalism*, 4.
35. Wilhelm Grimm, *Kleinere Schriften*, vol. 1, 114.
36. Wilhelm Grimm, *Kleinere Schriften*, vol. 1, 114.
37. Sarah Pourciau, *The Writing of Spirit*, 124–25.
38. Reinhold Steig, *Achim von Arnim*, 118.
39. Wilhelm Grimm, *Kleinere Schriften*, vol. 2, 39.
40. George Boas, *Vox Populi: The History of an Idea* (Baltimore, MD: Johns Hopkins University Press, 1969) 131.
41. Mark-Georg Dehrmann, *Studierte Dichter*, 253.
42. Wilhelm Grimm, *Kleinere Schriften*, vol. 1, 108.
43. Wilhelm Grimm, *Kleinere Schriften*, vol. 1, 114.
44. Wilhelm Grimm, *Kleinere Schriften*, vol. 1, 108.
45. Wilhelm Grimm, *Kleinere Schriften*, vol. 1, 114; Jacob Grimm *Kleinere Schriften*, vol. 1, 400.
46. Jutta Strippel, "Zum Verhältnis von Deutscher Rechtsgeschichte und Deutscher Philologie," *Germanistik und die deutsche Nation 1806–1848*, edited by Jörg Jochen Müller (Stuttgart: Metzler, 2000) 111–66; 114–27.
47. Tamar Herzog, *A Short History of European Law: The Last Two and a Half Millennia* (Cambridge, MA: Harvard University Press, 2018), 207.
48. Jutta Strippel, "Deutscher Rechtsgeschichte," 130–35; Theodor Ziolkowski, *Clio the Romantic Muse: Historicizing the Faculties in Germany* (Ithaca, NY: Cornell University Press, 2004), 123–25.
49. Barbara Dölemeyer, "Die Beiträge der Brüder Grimm zur Rechtswissenschaft und Rechtsgeschichte," *Die Grimms: Kultur und Politik*, edited by Bernd Heidenreich and Ewald Grothe (Frankfurt: Frankfurter Societäts-Verlag), 163–88; 164–71.
50. Hermann Kantorowitz, "Volksgeist und historische Rechtsschule," *Historische Zeitschrift* 108.2 (1912): 295–325; 310.

51. Benjamin Lahusen, *Alles Recht geht vom Volksgeist aus: Friedrich Carl von Savigny und die moderne Rechtswissenschaft* (Berlin: Nicolai, 2013), 26–27.
52. Jacob Grimm, *Kleinere Schriften*, vol. 1, 117–18.
53. Wilhelm Grimm, *Kleinere Schriften*, vol. 1, 549–55.
54. Wilhelm Grimm, *Kleinere Schriften*, vol. 1, 550.
55. Wilhelm Grimm, *Kleinere Schriften*, vol. 1, 550.
56. Wilhelm Grimm, *Kleinere Schriften*, vol. 1, 555.
57. Friedrich Carl von Savigny, *Vom Beruf unsrer Zeit für Gesetzgebung und Rechtswissenschaft* (Freiburg: Akademische Verlagsbuchhandlung, 1892), 68.
58. Wilhelm Grimm, *Kleinere Schriften*, vol. 1, 551.
59. Wilhelm Grimm, *Kleinere Schriften*, vol. 1, 551.
60. Chris Thornhill, *German Political Philosophy: The Metaphysics of Law* (London: Routledge, 2007), 136.
61. Donald Kelly, "Historians and Lawyers," *The Cambridge History of Nineteenth-Century Political Thought*, edited by Gareth Stedman Jones and Gregory Claeys (Cambridge: Cambridge University Press, 2016) 147–70; 151.
62. Thomas Beebee, *Citation and Precedent: Conjunctions and Disjunctions of German Law and Literature* (New York: Continuum, 2012) 57–58; Friedrich Carl von Savigny, *Vom Beruf*, 26.
63. Chris Thornhill, *German Political Philosophy*, 135.
64. Friedrich Carl von Savigny, *Vom Beruf*, 68.
65. Erich Rothacker, "Savigny, Grimm, Ranke: Ein Beitrag zur Frage nach dem Zusammenhang der Historischen Schule," *Historische Zeitschrift* 128.3 (1923): 415–45; 423.
66. Chris Thornhill, *German Political Philosophy*, 183.
67. Thomas Beebee, *Citation and Precedent*, 50.
68. James Whitman, *The Legacy of Roman Law in the German Romantic Era*, (Princeton: Princeton University Press, 1990), 101.
69. James Whitman, *The Legacy of Roman Law*, 110.
70. Chris Thornhill, *German Political Philosophy*, 136.
71. Frederick Beiser, *The German Historicist Tradition*, 243.
72. James Whitman, *The Legacy of Roman Law*, 104.
73. Frederick Beiser, *The German Historicist Tradition*, 235.
74. Benjamin Lahusen, *Alles Recht geht vom Volksgeist aus*, 77.
75. Hans-Ulrich Wehler, *Deutsche Gesellschaftsgeschichte 1815–1848*, vol. 2, 317–18.
76. James Whitman, *The Legacy of Roman Law*, 198.
77. Jacob and Wilhelm Grimm, *Briefe der Brüder Grimm an Savigny*, 173.
78. Friedrich Carl von Savigny, *Vom Beruf*, 34.
79. Roland Feldmann, *Jacob Grimm und die Politik*, 151.
80. Frederick Beiser, *The German Historicist Tradition*, 223.
81. Jacob and Wilhelm Grimm, *Briefe der Brüder Grimm an Savigny*, 172.

82. Jacob and Wilhelm Grimm, *Briefe der Brüder Grimm an Savigny*, 183.
83. Jacob and Wilhelm Grimm, *Briefe der Brüder Grimm an Savigny*, 184
84. Jacob and Wilhelm Grimm, *Briefe der Brüder Grimm an Savigny*, 177.
85. Jacob and Wilhelm Grimm, *Briefe der Brüder Grimm an Savigny*, 174.
86. Jacob and Wilhelm Grimm, *Briefe der Brüder Grimm an Savigny*, 183.
87. Jacob and Wilhelm Grimm, *Briefe der Brüder Grimm an Savigny*, 188.
88. Sadhana Naithani, "A Wild Philology," *Marvels & Tales*, 28.1 (2014): 38–55; 42.
89. Gabriele Brandstetter and Gerhard Neumann, "Gaben: Märchen in der Romantik," *Romantik und Exil: Festschrift für Konrad Feilchenfeldt*, edited by Claudia Christophersen (Würzburg: Königshausen & Neumann, 2004) 17–37; 24.
90. Pascal Casanova, *The World Republic of Letters*, translated by M. B. DeBevoise (Cambridge: Harvard University Press, 2004), 79.
91. Wilhelm Grimm, *Kleinere Schriften*, vol. 1, 327.
92. Wilhelm Grimm, *Kleinere Schriften*, vol. 1, 320.
93. Wilhelm Grimm, *Kleinere Schriften*, vol. 1, 321.
94. Susan Stewart, *Crimes of Writing: Problems in the Containment of Representation* (Durham: Duke University Press, 1994), 105.
95. John Hutchinson, "Cultural Nationalism," *The Oxford Handbook of the History of Nationalism*, edited by John Breuilly (Oxford: Oxford University Press, 2013) 75–91; 80.
96. Wilhelm Grimm, *Kleinere Schriften*, vol. 1, 322.
97. Wilhelm Grimm, *Kleinere Schriften*, vol. 1, 326.
98. Wilhelm Grimm, *Kleinere Schriften*, vol. 1, 330.
99. Wilhelm Grimm, *Kleinere Schriften*, vol. 1, 330.
100. George Williamson, *The Longing for Myth in Germany*, 107.
101. Jacob Grimm, *Deutsche Mythologie*, vol. 1 (Gütersloh: C. Bertelsmann, 1835), xiii.
102. Elliott Schreiber, "Tainted Sources: The Subversion of the Grimms' Ideology of the Folktale in Heinrich Heine's Der Rabbi von Bacherach," *The German Quarterly* 78.1 (2005): 23–44; 26.
103. Pascal Casanova, "Combative Literatures," 126.
104. Wilhelm Grimm, *Kleinere Schriften*, vol. 1, 321.
105. Maria Tatar, "Folklore and Cultural Identity," 517.
106. Peter Fritzsche, *Stranded in the Present*, 151.
107. Wilhelm Grimm, *Kleinere Schriften*, vol. 1, 330.
108. Jay Bolter and Richard Grusin, "Remediation," *Configurations* 4.3 (1996): 311–358; 339, 346, and 350.
109. Jacob Grimm, *Kleinre Schriften*, vol. 8, 19.
110. Wilhelm Grimm, *Kleinere Schriften*, vol. 1, 320.

111. Jacob and Wilhelm Grimm, *The Annotated Brothers Grimm*, edited and translated by Maria Tatar (New York: Norton & Co., 2004) 435.
112. Wilhelm Grimm, *Kleinere Schriften*, vol. 1, 320.
113. *The Annotated Brothers Grimm*, 402.
114. Elliott Schreiber, "Tainted Sources," 25.
115. Marina Warner, *Once Upon a Time: A Short History of the Fairy Tale* (Oxford: Oxford University Press, 2014) 54.

4 Love of the Fatherland and Fatherly Love

1. Horst Grünert, "Vom heiligen Begriff der Freiheit: Jacob Grimm und die Revolution von 1848," *Brüder Grimm Gedenken* 19 (1987): 60–74; 60–62.
2. Steffen Martus, *Die Brüder Grimm*, 229–30.
3. Steffen Martus, *Die Brüder Grimm*, 239 and 255; Herfried Münkler, "Raub oder Rettung von Kulturgütern," *Merkur* 70, no. 802 (2016): 5–17; 16–17.
4. Steffen Martus, *Die Brüder Grimm*, 239.
5. Karl-Heinrich Rexroth, "Kassel 1805/6–1829," *200 Jahre Brüder Grimm*, edited by Hans-Bernd Harder and Ekkehard Kaufmann (Kassel: Weber & Weidemeyer, 1985), 23–79; 34.
6. Wilhelm Grimm, *Kleinere Schriften*, vol. 1, 556–57.
7. Steffen Martus, *Die Brüder Grimm*, 240–41.
8. Mark Jarrett, *The Congress of Vienna and Its Legacy* (London: I. B. Tauris, 2013), 152.
9. Jacob Grimm, *Kleinere Schriften*, vol. 8, 402.
10. Steffen Martus, *Die Brüder Grimm*, 244.
11. Eberhard Straub, *Der Wiener Kongress: Das Große Fest und die Neuordnung Europas* (Stuttgart: Klett-Cotta, 2014), 95–97.
12. Mark Jarrett, *The Congress of Vienna*, 209.
13. Ernst Rudolf Huber, *Deutsche Verfassungsgeschichte seit 1789*, vol. I (Stuttgart: W. Kohlhammer Verlag, 1957), 538–539; Wolfram Siemann, *Vom Staatenbund zum Nationalstaat*, 314–315.
14. Ernst Rudolf Huber, *Deutsche Verfassungsgeschichte seit 1789*, vol. I, 542.
15. Wolf Gruner, "The German Confederation: Cornerstone of the New European Security System," in *Securing Europe after Napoleon: 1815 and the New European Security Culture*, edited by Beatrice Graaf et al. (Cambridge: Cambridge University Press, 2019), 150–67; 160–61 and 164.
16. Steffen Martus, *Die Brüder Grimm*, 260, 264–65 and 271; Frederik Ohles, *Germany's Rude Awakening*.
17. Hans-Bernd Harder, "Die Brüder Grimm in ihrer amtlichen und politischen Tätigkeit: Einführung," 13–22; 16.
18. Steffen Martus, *Die Brüder Grimm*, 296, 288, 313.

19. Thomas Biskup, "The University of Göttingen and the Personal Union, 1737–1837," *The Hanoverian Dimension in British History, 1714–1837*, edited by Brendan Simms and Torsten Riotte (Cambridge: Cambridge University Press, 2007), 128–60.
20. David Barclay, *Frederick William IV*, 5.
21. Hans Boldt, *Deutsche Staatslehre im Vormärz* (Düsseldorf: Droste Verlag, 1975), 5; Ernst Rudolf Huber, *Deutsche Verfassungsgeschichte seit 1789*, vol. 3 (Stuttgart: W. Kohlhammer Verlag, 1963), 7; Ernst-Wolfgang Böckenförde, *Recht, Staat, Freiheit*, 244.
22. Jonathan Sperber, *The European Revolutions, 1848–1851* (Cambridge: Cambridge University Press, 1994), 66
23. Hans Boldt, *Deutsche Staatslehre*, 5–6.
24. Chris Thornhill, *The Sociology of Law*, 35.
25. Hans Boldt, *Deutsche Staatslehre*, 284; Chris Thornhill, *German Political Philosophy*, 159.
26. Hans Boldt, *Deutsche Staatslehre*, 56.
27. Hans Boldt, *Deutsche Staatslehre*, 60.
28. Hans Boldt, *Deutsche Staatslehre*, 6; Ernst-Wolfgang Böckenförde, *Recht, Staat, Freiheit*, 252–53.
29. Hans Boldt, *Deutsche Staatslehre*, 185.
30. Hans Boldt, *Deutsche Staatslehre*, 263; Hartwig Brandt, *Landständische Repräsentation im deutschen Vormärz: Politisches Denken im Einflußfeld des Monarchischen Prinzips* (Neuwied: Luchterhand, 1968), 169.
31. Ernst Rudolf Huber, *Deutsche Verfassungsgeschichte*, vol. 3, 3.
32. Hartwig Brandt, *Landständische Repräsentation*, 161.
33. James Sheehan, *German Liberalism*, 46.
34. Hartwig Schultz, "Dokumente zur Entlassung der Brüder Grimm," *Der Briefwechsel Bettine von Arnims mit den Brüdern Grimm*, edited by Hartwig Schultz (Frankfurt am Main: Insel, 1985), 329–66; 329.
35. Abigail Green, *Fatherlands*, 41.
36. Steffen Martus, *Die Brüder Grimm*, 382.
37. Quoted in Hartwig Schultz, "Dokumente zur Entlassung der Brüder Grimm," 331.
38. Otto Hintze, *Beamtentum und Bürokratie* (Göttingen: Vandenhoeck & Ruprecht, 1981), 21.
39. Abigail Green, *Fatherlands*, 72.
40. Steffen Martus, *Die Brüder Grimm*, 383; Wolfgang Bleek, *Vormärz*, 185–86.
41. Wilhelm Bleek, *Vormärz*, 186; Steffen Martus, *Die Brüder Grimm*, 390.
42. Steffen Martus, *Die Brüder Grimm*, 384.
43. Eric Hobsbawm, *The Age of Revolution*, 269 and 292.

44. Wilhelm Bleek, "Einleitung," *Protestation des Gewissens: Die Rechtfertigungsschriften des Göttinger Sieben*, edited by Bernhard Lauer (Kassel: Brüder Grimm-Gesellschaft, 2012), 9–38; 25.
45. Hartwig Schultz, "Einleitung," *Der Briefwechsel Bettine von Arnims mit den Brüdern Grimm*, edited by Hartwig Schultz (Frankfurt am Main: Insel, 1985), 5–20; 6–7.
46. Hartwig Schultz, "Einleitung," 11.
47. Jonathan Sperber, *The European Revolutions*, ix–x.
48. Jonathan Sperber, *The European Revolutions*, 110 and 121.
49. Hans-Ulrich Wehler, *Deutsche Gesellschaftsgeschichte*, vol. 2, 703.
50. Ernst Rudolf Huber, *Deutsche Verfassungsgeschichte seit 1789*, vol. 2 (Stuttgart: W. Kohlhammer Verlag, 1960), 593; Hans-Ulrich Wehler, *Deutsche Gesellschaftsgeschichte*, vol. 2, 737.
51. Wolfgang Hardtwig and Helmut Hinze, "Einleitung," *Deutsche Geschichte in Quellen und Darstellung*, edited by Wolfgang Hardtwig and Helmut Hinze (Stuttgart: Philipp Reclam, 2011), 5–34; 16.
52. Ernst Rudolf Huber, *Deutsche Verfassungsgeschichte seit 1789*, vol. 2, 592.
53. Chris Thornhill, *A Sociology of Constitutions: Constitutions and State Legitimacy in Historical-Sociological Perspective* (Cambridge University Press: Cambridge, 2011), 247.
54. Ernst Rudolf Huber, *Deutsche Verfassungsgeschichte seit 1789*, vol. 2, 607.
55. Steffen Martus, *Die Brüder Grimm*, 461; Helge Bech, "Jacob Grimm und die Frankfurter Nationalversammlung," 349.
56. James Sheehan, *German Liberalism*, 57.
57. Steffen Martus, *Die Brüder Grimm*, 461; Helge Bech, "Jacob Grimm und die Frankfurter Nationalversammlung," 353.
58. Jacob Grimm, *Kleinere Schriften*, vol. 8, 439–43.
59. Jacob Grimm, *Kleinere Schriften*, vol. 8, 440–41.
60. Monica Wienfort, *Monarchie in der bürgerlichen Gesellschaft*, 148; Andreas Wimmer, *Nationalist Exclusion*, 59.
61. Chris Thornhill, *A Sociology of Constitutions*, 213.
62. Steffen Martus, *Die Brüder Grimm*, 467; Helge Bech, "Jacob Grimm und die Frankfurter Nationalversammlung," 349 and 359.
63. Horst Grünert, "Vom heiligen Begriff der Freiheit," 67.
64. Hans-Ulrich Wehler, *Deutsche Gesellschaftsgeschichte*, vol. 2, 744.
65. Jacob and Wilhelm Grimm, *Briefwechsel zwischen Jacob und Wilhelm Grimm*, 765.
66. Jacob and Wilhelm Grimm, *Briefwechsel zwischen Jacob und Wilhelm Grimm*, 769; Horst Grünert, "Vom heiligen Begriff der Freiheit," 67.
67. Jacob and Wilhelm Grimm, *Briefwechsel zwischen Jacob und Wilhelm Grimm*, 769; Helge Bech, "Jacob Grimm und die Frankfurter Nationalversammlung," 359.

68. Anna Ross, *Beyond the Barricades: Government and State-Building in Post-Revolutionary Prussia, 1848–1858* (Oxford: Oxford University Press, 2019), 2.
69. Jonathan Sperber, *The European Revolutions*, 235.
70. Hans-Ulrich Wehler, *Deutsche Gesellschaftsgeschichte*, vol. 2, 722–23; Christopher Clark, *Iron Kingdom*, 483–84.
71. Jacob Grimm, *Kleinere Schriften*, vol. 8, 452.
72. Jacob and Wilhelm Grimm, *Briefwechsel zwischen Jacob und Wilhelm Grimm*, 399.
73. James Sheehan, *German Liberalism*, 19 and 47; Monica Wienfort, *Monarchie in der bürgerlichen Gesellschaft*, 185.
74. Jacob and Wilhelm Grimm, *Briefe der Brüder Grimm an Savigny*, 360.
75. Jacob and Wilhelm Grimm, *Briefe der Brüder Grimm an Savigny*, 299
76. Charles Ingrao, *The Hessian Mercenary State*, 32.
77. Steffen Martus, *Die Brüder Grimm*, 298.
78. Friedrich Kittler, "Das Subjekt als Beamter," *Die Frage nach dem Subjekt*, edited by Gérard Raulet, Manfred Frank, and Willem van Reijen (Frankfurt am Main: Suhrkamp, 1988), 401–20; 406–7.
79. Roland Feldmann, *Jacob Grimm und die Politik*, 122–23; Otto Hintze, *Beamtentum und Bürokratie*, 34.
80. Jacob Grimm, *Kleinere Schriften*, vol. 8, 424.
81. Jacob Grimm, *Kleinere Schriften*, vol. 8, 424; Otto Hintze, *Beamtentum und Bürokratie*, 21.
82. Hans-Ulrich Wehler, *Deutsche Gesellschaftsgeschichte*, vol. 2, 300.
83. Rainer Kolk, "Zur Professionalisierung und Disziplinentwicklung," 135.
84. Jacob and Wilhelm Grimm, *Briefwechsel zwischen Jacob und Wilhelm Grimm*, 745.
85. Arnulf Siebeneicker, "'Ich fühle mich eingenommen für alles Bestehende': Die Rechtfertigungsschrift Jacob Grimm über seine Entlassung," *Expedition Grimm*, edited by Thorsten Schmidt (Kassel: Sandstein Verlag, 2013), 113–21; 115.
86. Wilhelm Hansen, "Die Brüder Grimm in Berlin," 272.
87. Quoted in Helge Bech, "Jacob Grimm und die Frankfurter Nationalversammlung," 352.
88. Hans Boldt, *Deutsche Staatslehre*, 15–18; Otto Brunner, "Von Gottesgnadentum zum monarchischen Prinzip: Der Weg der Europäischen Monarchie seit dem hohen Mittelalter," *Das Königtum: Seine geistigen und rechtlichen Grundlagen* (Lindau: Jan Thorbecke Verlag, 1954), 279–305; 301.
89. Hartwig Brandt, *Landständische Repräsentation*, 45.
90. Ernst-Wolfgang Böckenförde, *Recht, Staat, Freiheit*, 252.
91. Jacob and Wilhelm Grimm, *Briefwechsel zwischen Jacob und Wilhelm Grimm*, 745.
92. Jacob Grimm, *Kleinere Schriften*, vol. 1, 2.

93. Jacob Grimm, *Kleinere Schriften*, vol. 1, 18.
94. Jacob Grimm, *Kleinere Schriften*, vol. 1, 18.
95. W. Günther Ganser, "Berlin 1841–1859/63," *200 Jahre Brüder Grimm*, edited by Hans-Bernd Harder and Ekkehard Kaufmann (Kassel: Weber & Weidemeyer, 1985), 106–52; 122.
96. Frederick Beiser, *The Romantic Imperative: The Concept of Early German Romanticism* (Cambridge, MA: Harvard University Press, 2003), 103.
97. Frederick Beiser, *The Romantic Imperative*, 104.
98. Frederick Beiser, *Hegel* (New York: Routledge, 2005), 113–14.
99. Roland Feldmann, *Jacob Grimm und die Politik*, 177.
100. Alexander Schmidt, *Vaterlandsliebe und Religionskonflikt: Politische Diskurse im alten Reich (1555–1648)* (Leiden: Brill, 2007), 418.
101. Frederick Beiser, *Schiller as Philosopher: A Re-Examination* (Oxford: Clarendon 2005), 164.
102. Jacob Grimm, *Über den altdeutschen Meistergesang* (Göttingen: Heinrich Dieterich, 1811), 9.
103. Walter Mack, *German Home Towns: Community, State, and the General Estate, 1648–1871* (Ithaca, NY: Cornell University Press, 1971), 258–59.
104. Jacob Grimm, *Über den altdeutschen Meistergesang*, 10.
105. Jacob Grimm, *Über den altdeutschen Meistergesang*, 10.
106. Jacob Grimm, *Über den altdeutschen Meistergesang*, 9.
107. Celia Applegate, *A Nation of Provincials: The German Idea of Heimat* (Berkeley: University of California Press, 1990), 8–11.
108. Steven Grosby, *Nationalism: A Very Short Introduction* (Oxford: Oxford University Press, 2005), 65.
109. Jacob Grimm, *Kleinere Schriften*, vol. 1, 164; Stefani Engelstein, *Sibling Action: The Genealogical Structure of Modernity* (New York: Columbia University Press, 2017), 162.
110. Ludwig Denecke, *Jacob Grimm und sein Bruder Wilhelm*, 54–55.
111. Simon May, *Love: A History* (New Haven, CT: Yale University Press, 2013), 9.
112. Jacob Grimm, *Kleinere Schriften*, vol. 1, 27.
113. Jacob Grimm, *Kleinere Schriften*, vol. 1, 27.
114. Jacob Grimm, *Kleinere Schriften*, vol. 1, 18.
115. Lutz Danneberg, "Altphilologie, Theologie und die Genealogie der Literaturwissenschaft," *Handbuch Literaturwissenschaft*, edited by Thomas Anz (Stuttgart: J. B. Metzler, 2007), 3–25; 4–14.
116. Vittorio Hösle, *Eine kurze Geschichte der deutschen Philosophie* (Munich: C. H. Beck, 2013), 105; Heinz Schlaffer, *Kleine Geschichte der deutschen Literatur*, 61.
117. Roland Feldmann, *Jacob Grimm und die Politik*, 122.

118. Eric Hobsbawm, *The Age of Revolution*, 269.
119. Roland Feldmann, *Jacob Grimm und die Politik*, 191.
120. Roland Feldmann, *Jacob Grimm und die Politik*, 191.
121. Ewald Grothe, "Die Brüder Grimm und der Liberalismus," 68.
122. Jacob and Wilhelm Grimm, *Briefe der Brüder Grimm an Savigny*, 363.
123. Jacob and Wilhelm Grimm, *Briefe der Brüder Grimm an Savigny*, 363.
124. Jacob and Wilhelm Grimm, *Briefe der Brüder Grimm an Savigny*, 358–59; Carl Schmitt, *Politische Romantik*, 6th ed. (Berlin: Duncker & Humblot, 1998).
125. Jacob and Wilhelm Grimm, *Briefe der Brüder Grimm an Savigny*, 360.
126. Jacob and Wilhelm Grimm, *Briefe der Brüder Grimm an Savigny*, 359.
127. Roland Feldmann, *Jacob Grimm und die Politik*, 59.
128. Jacob Grimm, *Kleinere Schriften*, vol. 1, 35.
129. Jacob Grimm, *Kleinere Schriften*, vol. 1, 29.
130. Jacob Grimm, *Kleinere Schriften*, vol. 1, 30.
131. Roland Feldmann, *Jacob Grimm und die Politik*, 60.
132. Jacob Grimm, *Kleinere Schriften*, vol. 1, 29.
133. Michael Freeden, "Is Nationalism a Distinct Ideology?" 751–52.
134. Michael Freeden, "Is Nationalism a Distinct Ideology?" 753.
135. Ewald Grothe, "Die Brüder Grimm und der Liberalismus," 81.
136. Jacob Grimm, *Kleinere Schriften*, vol. 8, 438–39.
137. Jürgen Fohrmann, *Das Projekt der deutschen Literaturgeschichte: Entstehung und Scheitern einer nationalen Poesiegeschichtsschreibung zwischen Humanismus und deutschem Kaiserreich* (Stuttgart: Metzler, 1989), 148.
138. Holly Case, "The 'Social Question,' 1820–1920," *Modern Intellectual History* 13.3 (2016): 747–75; 756.
139. Mike Rapport, *1848: Year of Revolution* (New York: Basic Books, 2008), 30–32.
140. Konstanze Bäumer and Hartwig Schultz, *Bettina von Arnim* (Stuttgart: J. B. Metzler, 1995), 94–105.
141. Steffen Martus, *Die Brüder Grimm*, 273–74.
142. Steffen Martus, *Die Brüder Grimm*, 272.
143. Jacob Grimm, *Kleinere Schriften*, vol. 8, 442.
144. Quoted in Roland Feldmann, *Jacob Grimm und die Politik*, 161.
145. Quoted in Ewald Grothe, "Die Brüder Grimm," 85.
146. Roland Feldmann, *Jacob Grimm und die Politik*, 69.
147. Ernst Rudolf Huber, *Deutsche Verfassungsgeschichte seit 1789*, vol. 2, 140–47.
148. Roland Feldmann, *Jacob Grimm und die Politik*, 66.
149. Wilhelm Grimm, *Kleinere Schriften*, vol. 1, 511–12.
150. Hartwig Brandt, *Landständische Repräsentation*, 168.

151. Jürgen Habermas, "Was ist ein Volk?" 27–28.
152. Jacob Grimm, *Kleinere Schriften*, vol. 8, 438.
153. Jacob Grimm, *Kleinere Schriften*, vol. 1, 29.
154. Quoted in Holger Ehrhardt, "Jacob Grimms politisches Auftreten vor seiner Wahl zur Frankfurter Nationalversammlung," *Jahrbuch der Brüder Grimm-Gesellschaft* 10 (2000): 145–51; 149.
155. F. M. Barnard, *Herder on Nationality, Humanity, and History*, 52.
156. Christopher Clark, *Iron Kingdom*, 436; David Barclay, *Frederick William IV*, 188; Wolfram Siemann, *Vom Staatenbund zum Nationalstaat*, 361.
157. John Edward Toews, *Becoming Historical*, 361.
158. Alan Patten, "The Most Natural State: Herder and Nationalism," *History of Political Thought* 31.4 (2010): 657–89; 680.
159. Alan Patten, "The Most Natural State," 680.
160. Otto Brunner, "Von Gottesgnadentum zum monarchischen Prinzip," 303.
161. Matthew Levinger, *Enlightened Nationalism: The Transformation of Prussian Political Culture 1806–1848* (Oxford: Oxford University Press, 2000), 108–10.
162. F. H. Hinsley, *Sovereignty* (Cambridge: Cambridge University Press, 1986), 1.
163. Albrecht Koschorke, *Der fiktive Staat*, 328; Arnulf Siebeneicker, "'Ich fühle mich eingenommen für alles Bestehende,'" 117.
164. Albrecht Koschorke, *Der fiktive Staat*, 349–50.
165. Ernst-Wolfgang Böckenförde, *Die deutsche verfassungsgeschichtliche Forschung im 19. Jahrhundert: Zeitgebundene Fragestellungen und Leitbilder* (Berlin: Duncker & Humblot, 1961), 94.
166. Jacob Grimm, *Kleinere Schriften*, vol. 1, 33.
167. Jacob Grimm, *Kleinere Schriften*, vol. 1, 33.
168. Jacob Grimm, *Kleinere Schriften*, vol. 1, 33.
169. Monica Wienfort, *Monarchie in der bürgerlichen Gesellschaft*, 177.
170. Ursula Püshel, *Bettina von Arnim – politisch: Erkundungen, Entdeckungen, Erkenntnisse* (Bielefeld: Aesthetis, 2005), 209.

5 The Mother Tongue at School

1. Thomas Paul Bonfiglio, *Mother Tongues and Nations: The Invention of the Native Speaker* (New York: De Gruyter, 2010), 185; Stefani Engelstein, *Sibling Action*, 131.
2. Friedrich Kittler, *Discourse Networks 1800/1900*, translated by Michael Metteer (Stanford, CA: Stanford University Press, 1987), 27–28.
3. Jacob Grimm, *Kleinere Schriften*, vol. 1, 278.
4. Jacob Grimm, *Kleinere Schriften*, vol. 1, 278
5. Jacob Grimm, *Kleinere Schriften*, vol. 8, 106.
6. Jacob Grimm, *Kleinere Schriften*, vol. 1, 411.

7. Heinz Schlaffer, *Die kurze Geschichte der deutschen Literatur*, 45.
8. Donald Sassoon, *The Culture of the Europeans*, 14.
9. Keith Darden and Harris Mylonas, "Threats to Territorial Integrity, National Mass Schooling, and Linguistic Commonality," *Comparative Political Studies*, 49.11 (2016): 1446–79.
10. *Verzeihniss der Abhandlungen der Königlich Preussischen Akademie der Wissenschaften von 1710–1870* (Berlin: F. Dümmler Verlags-Buchhandlung, 1871), 93–94; Hartmut Schmidt, "Bemerkungen zu Jacob Grimms Reden in der Berliner Akademie," *Zeitschrift für Phonetik, Sprachwissenschaft und Kommunikationsforschung* 38 (1985): 712–21.
11. Conrad Grau, *Die Preußische Akademie der Wissenschaften zu Berlin* (Heidelberg: Spektrum, 1993), 157–59.
12. Randall Collins, *The Sociology of Philosophies: A Global Theory of Intellectual Change* (Cambridge, MA: Harvard University Press, 1998), 640–41.
13. Jacob Grimm, *Kleinere Schriften*, vol. 1, 212.
14. Ludwig Denecke, "Über Schule Universität Academie," *Brüder Grimm Gedenken* 4 (1984): 1–12; 2–3.
15. Jacob Grimm, *Kleinere Schriften*, vol. 1, 237.
16. Charles McClelland, *State, Society, and University in Germany* (Cambridge: Cambridge University Press, 1980), 9.
17. Jacob Grimm, *Kleinere Schriften*, vol. 1, 244.
18. Jacob Grimm, *Kleinere Schriften*, vol. 1, 254.
19. Richard Gawthrop, "Literacy Drives in Preindustrial Germany," *National Literacy Campaigns: Historical and Comparative Perspectives*, edited by Robert Anrove and Harvey Graff (New York: Plenum, 1987), 29–48.
20. Robert Arnove and Harvey Graff, "Introduction," *National Literacy Campaigns: Historical and Comparative Perspectives*, edited by Robert Anrove and Harvey Graff (New York: Plenum, 1987), 1–28; 4.
21. Jacob Grimm, *Kleinere Schriften*, vol. 1, 222.
22. Jacob Grimm, *Kleinere Schriften*, vol. 1, 229.
23. Michael Mann, *The Rise of Classes and Nation-States, 1760–1914* (Cambridge: Cambridge University Press, 2002), 37–38.
24. Jacob Grimm, *Kleinere Schriften*, vol. 1, 229.
25. Jacob Grimm, *Deutsche Grammatik 1 (1870)*, xiii.
26. Jacob Grimm, *Kleinere Schriften*, vol. 1, 233.
27. Jacob and Wilhelm Grimm, *Briefe an Savigny*, 170.
28. Jacob und Wilhelm Grimm, *Briefe an Savigny*, 170.
29. Jacob Grimm, *Kleinere Schriften*, vol. 8, 30.
30. Karl Schleunes, *Schooling and Society: The Politics of Education in Prussia and Bavaria 1750–1900* (Oxford: Berg, 1989), 96–97.
31. Jacob Grimm, *Kleinere Schriften*, vol. 1, 229.

32. Karl Schleunes, *Schooling and Society*, 131.
33. Anthony La Vopa, *Prussian Schoolteachers: Profession and Office, 1763–1848* (Chapel Hill: University of North Carolina Press, 1980).
34. Jacob Grimm, *Kleinere Schriften*, vol. 1, 228.
35. Hans-Ulrich Wehler, *Deutsche Gesellschaftsgeschichte*, vol. 2, 735.
36. Heinrich Bosse, "Gelehrte und Gebildete – die Kinder des 1. Standes," *Das achtzehnte Jahrhundert* 32.1 (2008), 13–37; 14.
37. Hans-Ulrich Wehler, *Deutsche Gesellschaftsgeschichte 1700–1815* (Munich: C. H. Beck, 1987), 284–88.
38. Thomas Nipperdey, *Deutsche Geschichte 1800–1866: Bürgerwelt und starker Staat* (Munich: C. H. Beck, 1983), 451.
39. Jacob Grimm, *Kleinere Schriften*, vol. 1, 224.
40. Jacob Grimm, *Kleinere Schriften*, vol. 1, 221.
41. Jacob Grimm, *Kleinere Schriften*, vol. 1, 224.
42. Richard Gawthrop, "Literacy Drives," 41.
43. Darden and Mylonas, "National Mass Schooling," 1447.
44. Ernest Gellner, *Nations and Nationalism*, 34–37.
45. Alberto Alesina, Bryony Reich, and Alessandro Riboni, "Nation-Building, Nationalism and Wars," National Bureau of Economic Research, Working Paper 23435, 2017, www.nber.org/papers/w23435.pdf.
46. Herfried Münkler and Grit Straßenberger, *Politische Theorie und Ideengeschichte*, 75.
47. Jacob and Wilhelm Grimm, *Briefe an Savigny*, 73.
48. Johann Gottlieb Fichte, *Reden an die deutsche Nation*, 182.
49. Heinrich Bosse, *Bildungsrevolution 1770–1830*, edited by Nacim Ghanbari (Heidelberg: Winter, 2012), 59.
50. Karl Schleunes, *Schooling and Society*, 52.
51. Philippe Aghion, Torsten Persson, and Dorothee Rouzet, "Education and Military Rivalry," National Bureau of Economic Research, Working Paper 18049, 2012, www.nber.org/papers/w18049.
52. Jacob Grimm, *Kleinere Schriften*, vol. 1, 233.
53. Jacob Grimm, *Kleinere Schriften*, vol. 1, 229 and 222.
54. Friedrich Kittler, *Discourse Networks*, 37–38.
55. Barry McCrea, *Languages of the Night: Minor Languages and the Literary Imagination in Twentieth Century Ireland and Europe* (New Haven, CT: Yale University Press, 2015).
56. Roland Feldmann, *Jacob Grimm und die Politik*, 151.
57. James Scott, *Seeing Like a State: How Certain Schemes to Improve the Human Condition Have Failed* (New Haven, CT: Yale University Press, 1998), 72.
58. Jacob Grimm, *Kleinere Schriften*, vol. 1, 216.
59. Tuska Benes, *In Babel's Shadow*, 135.

60. Heinz Rölleke, *Die Märchen der Brüder Grimm*, 30.
61. Jacob Grimm, "Aufforderung an die gesammten Freunde deutscher Poesie und Geschichte erlassen," in Reinhold Steig, *Clemens Brentano und die Brüder Grimm* (Bern: Herbert Lang, 1969), 164–71; Heinz Rölleke, *Die Märchen der Brüder Grimm*, 63–69.
62. Reinhold Steig, *Clemens Brentano und die Brüder Grimm*, 165.
63. Jacob Grimm, *Kleinere Schriften*, vol. 1, 230.
64. Susan Stewart, *Crimes of Writing*, 105.
65. Boris Groys, *Logik der Sammlung: Am Ende des musealen Zeitalters* (Munich: Carl Hanser, 1997), 46–47.

6 The Names of the Barbarians

1. Jacob Grimm, *Kleinere Schriften*, vol. 8, 461.
2. Jacob Grimm, *Geschichte der deutschen Sprache*, vol. 1, 4.
3. Jacob Grimm, *Geschichte der deutschen Sprache*, vol. 1, 306.
4. Jacob Grimm, *Geschichte der deutschen Sprache*, vol. 2, *Werke*, vol. 16, edited by Maria Herrlich (Hildesheim: Olms-Weidmann, 1999), 718.
5. Walter Mack, *German Home Towns*, 251.
6. Anthony D. Smith, *The Ethnic Origins of Nations*, 214.
7. Mark Hewitson, *Nationalism in Germany, 1848–1866*, 17 and 25.
8. Jacob and Wilhelm Grimm, *Briefwechsel zwischen Jacob und Wilhelm Grimm*, 745.
9. Jacob Grimm, *Kleinere Schriften*, vol. 8, 461.
10. Jacob Grimm, *Geschichte der deutschen Sprache*, vol. 1, 4.
11. John Edward Toews, *Becoming Historical*, 364.
12. Jacob Grimm, *Geschichte der deutschen Sprache*, vol. 1, 6 and xiii.
13. Jacob and Wilhelm Grimm, *Briefwechsel zwischen Jacob und Wilhelm Grimm*, 764–66.
14. Jacob Grimm, *Geschichte der deutschen Sprache*, vol. 1, 4.
15. Jacob and Wilhelm Grimm, *Briefwechsel zwischen Jacob und Wilhelm Grimm*, 764.
16. Jacob and Wilhelm Grimm, *Briefwechsel zwischen Jacob und Wilhelm Grimm*, 766.
17. Brian Vick, *Defining Germany*, 31–32.
18. Adam Kuper, *The Reinvention of Primitive Society: Transformations of a Myth* (London: Routledge, 2005), 11.
19. Ludwig Denecke, *Jacob Grimm und sein Bruder Wilhelm*, 180.
20. Jacob Grimm, *Geschichte der deutschen Sprache*, vol. 1, x; Johann Kaspar Zeuss, *Die Deutschen und die Nachbarstämme* (Heidelberg: Carl Winters Universitätsbuchhandlung, 1925).

21. Jacob Grimm, *Geschichte der deutschen Sprache*, vol. 1, xi and 306.
22. Jacob Grimm, *Geschichte der deutschen Sprache*, vol. 1, xi.
23. Jacob Grimm, *Geschichte der deutschen Sprache*, vol. 1, xi.
24. Jacob Grimm, *Geschichte der deutschen Sprache*, vol. 1, xv–xvi.
25. Jacob Grimm, *Geschichte der deutschen Sprache*, vol. 1, v.
26. Jacob Grimm, *Geschichte der deutschen Sprache*, vol. 1, v.
27. Jacob Grimm, *Geschichte der deutschen Sprache*, vol. 1, v.
28. Eric Hobsbawm, *Nations and Nationalism since 1780: Programme, Myth, Reality* (Cambridge: Cambridge University Press, 1990), 31.
29. Jacob Grimm, *Geschichte der deutschen Sprache*, vol. 1, v.
30. Jacob Grimm, *Geschichte der deutschen Sprache*, vol. 1, v.
31. Helge Bech, "Jacob Grimm und die Frankfurter Nationalversammlung," 357.
32. Jacob Grimm, *Geschichte der deutschen Sprache*, vol. 1, iv.
33. Jacob Grimm, *Geschichte der deutschen Sprache*, vol. 1, iii.
34. Jacob Grimm, *Geschichte der deutschen Sprache*, vol. 1, iii.
35. Jacob Grimm, *Geschichte der deutschen Sprache*, vol. 1, v.
36. Jacob Grimm, *Geschichte der deutschen Sprache*, vol. 1, iii.
37. Jacob Grimm, *Geschichte der deutschen Sprache*, vol. 1, iv.
38. Jacob Grimm, *Geschichte der deutschen Sprache*, vol. 2, 435.
39. Peter Heather, *Empires and Barbarians: The Fall of Rome and the Birth of Europe* (Oxford: Oxford University Press, 2010), 11.
40. Christopher Clark, "Why Should We Think About the Revolutions of 1848 Now?" *London Review of Books* 41.5 (March 7, 2019): 12–16; 12.
41. Manfred Riedel, "Einleitung"; Friedrich Christoph Dahlmann, *Die Politik*, edited by Manfred Riedel (Frankfurt am Main: Suhrkamp 1968), 7–31.
42. Friedrich Christoph Dahlmann, *Die Politik, auf den Grund und das Maaß der gegebenen Zustände zurückgeführt*, vol. 1 (Göttingen: Verlag der Dieterischen Buchhandlung, 1835).
43. Manfred Riedel, "Einleitung," 12–19.
44. Walter Goffart, *Barbarian Tides: The Migration Age and the Late Roman Empire* (Philadelphia: University of Pennsylvania Press, 2006), 48.
45. Christoph Krebs, *A Most Dangerous Book: Tacitus's Germania from the Roman Empire to the Third Reich* (New York: Norton & Norton, 2012), 182–96.
46. Martin Thom, *Republics, Nations, and Tribes* (London: Verso, 1995), 259.
47. Martin Thom, *Republics, Nations, and Tribes*, 221 and 212.
48. Cornelius Tacitus, *The Agricola and the Germania*, translated by H. Mattingly and S. A. Handford (London: Penguin, 1970), 114.
49. J. G. A. Pocock, *Barbarism and Religion*, vol. 4 (Cambridge: Cambridge University Press, 2005), 12–13.
50. Cornelius Tacitus, *The Agricola and the Germania*, 108.

51. J. G. A. Pocock, *Barbarism and Religion*, vol. 4, 12–13.
52. Jacob Grimm, *Geschichte der deutschen Sprache*, vol. 1, 306.
53. Jacob Grimm, *Geschichte der deutschen Sprache*, vol. 1, 306.
54. John Edward Toews, *Becoming Historical*, 368.
55. Jacob Grimm, *Geschichte der deutschen Sprache*, vol. 1, 292.
56. Jacob Grimm, *Geschichte der deutschen Sprache*, vol. 1, 292.
57. Perry Anderson, *Lineages of Absolutism*, 109.
58. Cornelius Tacitus, *The Agricola and the Germania*, 110–13.
59. Ernst-Wolfgang Böckenförde, *Die deutsche verfassungsgeschichtliche Forschung*, 105 and 130.
60. Martin Thom, *Republics, Nations, and Tribes*, 1.
61. James Scott, *Against the Grain: A Deep History of the Earliest States* (New Haven, CT: Yale University Press, 2017), 221.
62. Chris Wickham, *The Inheritance of Rome: Illuminating the Dark Ages* (London: Penguin, 2009), 24; J. G. A. Pocock, *Barbarism and Religion*, vol. 6 (Cambridge: Cambridge University Press, 2015), 50.
63. Wolfram Herwig, "Origo Gentis: The Literature of Germanic Origins," *Early Germanic Literature and Culture*, edited by Brian Murdoch and Malcolm Read (Rochester, NY: Camden House, 2004), 39–54; 43.
64. Wolfram Herwig, "Origo Gentis," 39–40.
65. Richard Thomas, "The Germania as Literary Text," *The Cambridge Companion to Tacitus*, edited by A. J. Woodman (Cambridge: Cambridge University Press, 2010), 59–72; 59.
66. Patrick Geary, *The Myth of Nations: The Medieval Origins of Europe* (Princeton, NJ: Princeton University Press, 2002), 75.
67. Adrian Murdoch, "Germania Romana," *Early Germanic Literature and Culture*, edited by Brian Murdoch and Malcolm Read (Rochester, NY: Camden House, 2004), 55–71; 60.
68. Patrick Geary, *The Myth of Nations*, 77.
69. James Scott, *Against the Grain*, 223, 226, and 231.
70. Heinrich Luden, *Geschichte des teutschen Volkes*, vol. 1(Gotha: Justus Perthes, 1825), 460.
71. Heinrich Luden, *Geschichte des teutschen Volkes*, vol. 1, 461.
72. Heinrich Luden, *Geschichte des teutschen Volkes*, vol. 1, 459.
73. Walter Goffart, *Barbarian Tides*, 41.
74. Jacob Grimm, *Geschichte der deutschen Sprache*, vol. 1, 333.
75. Jacob Grimm, *Geschichte der deutschen Sprache*, vol. 1, 351.
76. Jacob Grimm, *Geschichte der deutschen Sprache*, vol. 1, 358–63.
77. Jacob Grimm, *Geschichte der deutschen Sprache*, vol. 1, 367.
78. Jacob Grimm, *Geschichte der deutschen Sprache*, vol. 1, 374.
79. Jacob Grimm, *Geschichte der deutschen Sprache*, vol. 1, 331.

80. Jacob Grimm, *Geschichte der deutschen Sprache*, vol. 2, 400–401.
81. Jacob Grimm, *Geschichte der deutschen Sprache*, vol. 2, 520.
82. Ulrich Wyss, *Wilde Philologie: Jacob Grimm und der Historismus* (Munich: C. H. Beck, 1979), 276.
83. Jacob Grimm, *Geschichte der deutschen Sprache*, vol. 1, 107.
84. Jacob Grimm, *Geschichte der deutschen Sprache*, vol. 1, 107.
85. Jacob Grimm, *Geschichte der deutschen Sprache*, vol. 1, 108.
86. Jacob Grimm, *Geschichte der deutschen Sprache*, vol. 1, 108.
87. Jacob Grimm, *Geschichte der deutschen Sprache*, vol. 2, 537.
88. Jacob Grimm, *Geschichte der deutschen Sprache*, vol. 2, 542.
89. Jacob Grimm, *Geschichte der deutschen Sprache*, vol. 2, 540.
90. Jacob Grimm, *Geschichte der deutschen Sprache*, vol. 1, 350.
91. Johann Kaspar Zeuss, *Die Deutschen und die Nachbarstämme*, 58.
92. Jacob Grimm, *Geschichte der deutschen Sprache*, vol. 2, 528.
93. Jacob Grimm, *Geschichte der deutschen Sprache*, vol. 2, 528.
94. Jacob Grimm, *Geschichte der deutschen Sprache*, vol. 2, 531.
95. Jacob Grimm, *Geschichte der deutschen Sprache*, vol. 2, 531.
96. Cornelius Tacitus, *The Agricola and the Germania*, 141.
97. Jacob Grimm, *Kleinere Schriften*, vol. 8, 27.
98. Jacob Grimm, *Kleinere Schriften*, vol. 7, 566.
99. Matthias Buschmeier, "Medien der Nation: Hoffmann von Fallerslebens *Das Lied der Deutschen* als demokratische Gesangsübung," *Zwischen Gattungsdisziplin und Gesamtkunstwerk: Literarische Medialität 1815–1848*, edited by Stefan Keppler-Tasaki and Wolf Gerhard Schmidt (Berlin: De Gruyter, 2015) 465–89.
100. Hoffmann von Fallersleben, *Mein Leben*, vol. 3 (Eschborn bei Frankfurt am Main: Dietmar Klotz, 1996), 47–48.
101. Jacob Grimm, *Geschichte der deutschen Sprache*, vol. 2, 563.
102. Jacob Grimm, *Geschichte der deutschen Sprache*, vol. 2, 563.
103. Jacob Grimm, *Kleinere Schriften*, vol. 1, 259.
104. William Jones, *Discourses Delivered before the Asiatic Society and Miscellaneous Papers on the Religion, Poetry, Literature Etc., of the Nations of India* (London: Charles S. Arnold, 1824), 28–29; Aamir Mufti, *Forget English! Orientalisms and World Literature* (Cambridge, MA: Harvard University Press, 2018), 67–72; M. H. Abrams, *The Mirror and the Lamp: Romantic Theory and the Critical Tradition* (Oxford: Oxford University Press, 1953), 87.
105. Jacob Grimm, *Kleinere Schriften*, vol. 1, 259.
106. Aamir Mufti, *Forget English!* 74; Devin Griffiths, "The Comparative Method and the History of the Modern Humanities," *History of the Humanities* 2.2 (2017): 473–505; 478.

Conclusion

1. Andreas Wimmer, *Nationalist Exclusion and Ethnic Conflict*, 52.
2. Eric Hobsbawm, *Nations and Nationalism since 1780*, 117.
3. Wilhelm Grimm, *Kleinere Schriften*, vol. 2, 493. See Werner Plumpe, "Eigentum – Eigentümlichkeit. Über den Zusammenhang ästhetischer und juristischer Begriffe im 18. Jahrhundert," *Archiv für Begriffsgeschichte* 23.2 (1979): 175–96.
4. Ernest Gellner, *Nations and Nationalism*, 120.
5. On the fate of Icelandic, see Jacob Grimm, *Deutsche Grammatik 1 (1840), Werke*, vol 9.2, edited by Elisabeth Feldbusch and Ludwig Erich Schmitt (Hildesheim: Olms-Weidmann, 1995), 421.

Bibliography

Abizadeh, Arash. "Was Fichte an Ethnic Nationalist? On Cultural Nationalism and Its Double." *History of Political Thought* 26.2 (2005): 334–59.

——— "On the Demos and Its Kin: Nationalism, Democracy, and the Boundary Problem." *American Political Science Review* 106.4 (2012): 867–82.

Abrams, Meyer Howard. *The Mirror and the Lamp: Romantic Theory and the Critical Tradition*. Oxford: Oxford University Press, 1953.

Adelman, Jeremy. "Empires, Nations, and Revolutions." *Journal of the History of Ideas* 79.1 (January 2018): 73–88.

Aghion, Philippe, Torsten Persson, and Dorothee Rouzet. "Education and Military Rivalry." National Bureau of Economic Research, Working Paper 18049, 2012, www.nber.org/papers/w18049.

Alesina, Alberto, Bryony Reich, and Alessandro Riboni, "Nation-Building, Nationalism, and Wars," National Bureau of Economic Research, Working Paper 23435, 2017, www.nber.org/papers/w23435.pdf.

Anderson, Benedict. *Imagined Communities: Reflections on the Origin and Spread of Nationalism*. London: Verso, 1991.

Anderson, Perry. *Passages from Antiquity to Feudalism*. London: Verso, 1974.

——— *Lineages of the Absolutist State*. London: Verso, 1974.

Andersson, Theodore. *A Preface to the Nibelungenlied*. Stanford, CA: Stanford University Press, 1987.

Ansel, Michael. *Prutz, Hettner und Haym: Hegelianische Literaturgeschichtsschreibung zwischen spekulativer Kunstdeutung und philologischer Quellenkritik*. Tübingen: Max Niemeyer Verlag, 2003.

Applegate, Celia. *A Nation of Provincials: The German Idea of Heimat*. Berkeley: University of California Press, 1990.

Arendt, Hannah. *On Revolution*. London: Penguin, 2006.

Arndt, Ernst Moritz. *Ueber Volkshaß und ueber den Gebrauch einer fremden Sprache*. Leipzig 1813.

——— *Werke*, vol. 11, edited by August Leffson and Wilhelm Steffens. Berlin: Deutsches Verlagshaus Bong & Co, 1912.

Arnove, Robert, and Harvey Graff. "Introduction." *National Literacy Campaigns: Historical and Comparative Perspectives*, edited by Robert Anrove and Harvey Graff. New York: Plenum, 1987. 1–28.

Atwood, Rodney. *The Hessians: Mercenaries from Hessen-Kassel in the American Revolution*. Cambridge: Cambridge University Press, 1980.
Baecker, Dirk. *Wozu Kultur?* Berlin: Kadmos, 2003.
Balibar, Étienne. "The Nation Form: History and Ideology." *Becoming National: A Reader*, edited by Geoff Eley and Ronald Suny. Oxford: Oxford University Press, 1996. 132–49.
Barclay, David. *Frederick William IV and the Prussian Monarchy 1840–1861*. Oxford: Clarendon, 1995.
Barnard, Frederick M. *J. G. Herder on Social and Political Culture*. Cambridge: Cambridge University Press, 1969.
Herder on Nationality, Humanity, and History. Montréal: McGill-Queen's University Press, 2003.
Bäumer, Konstanze, and Hartwig Schultz, *Bettina von Arnim*. Stuttgart: J. B. Metzler, 1995.
Bech, Helge. "Jacob Grimm und die Frankfurter Nationalversammlung." *Euphorion* 61.3 (1967): 349–60.
Beebee, Thomas. *Citation and Precedent: Conjunctions and Disjunctions of German Law and Literature*. New York: Continuum, 2012.
Beecroft, Alexander. *An Ecology of World Literature: From Antiquity to the Present Day*. London: Verso, 2015.
Beiser, Frederick. *The Romantic Imperative: The Concept of Early German Romanticism*. Cambridge, MA: Harvard University Press, 2003.
Hegel. New York: Routledge, 2005.
Schiller as Philosopher: A Re-Examination. Oxford: Clarendon 2005.
The German Historicist Tradition. Oxford: Oxford University Press, 2011.
Benes, Tuska. *In Babel's Shadow: Language, Philology, and the Nation in Nineteenth-Century Germany*. Detroit, MI: Wayne State University Press, 2008.
Benner, Erika. "Nationalism: Intellectual Origins." *The Oxford Handbook of the History of Nationalism*, edited by John Breuilly. Oxford: Oxford University Press, 2013. 36–52.
Berdahl, Robert. *The Politics of the Prussian Nobility: The Development of a Conservative Ideology 1770–1848*. Princeton, NJ: Princeton University Press, 1988.
Berding, Helmut. *Napoleonische Herrschaft und Gesellschaftspolitik im Königreich Westfalen: 1807–1813*. Göttingen: Vandenhoeck & Ruprecht, 1973.
"Das Königreich Westphalen als napoleonischer Modell- und Satellitenstaat (1807–1813)." *Modell und Wirklichkeit: Politik, Kultur und Gesellschaft im Großherzogtum Berg und im Königreich Westphalen 1806–1813*, edited by Gerd Dethlefs et al. Paderborn: Ferdinand Schönigh, 2008. 15–29.
Berlin, Isaiah. *The Crooked Timber of Humanity*. Princeton, NJ: Princeton University Press, 2013.
Bernstein, Susan. "Journalism and German Identity: Communiques from Heine, Wagner, and Adorno." *New German Critique* 66 (1995): 65–93.
Biskup, Thomas. "The University of Göttingen and the Personal Union, 1737–1837." *The Hanoverian Dimension in British History, 1714–1837*, edited by

Brendan Simms and Torsten Riotte. Cambridge: Cambridge University Press, 2007. 128–60.
Black, Jeremy. *European Warfare 1660/1815*. New Haven, CT: Yale University Press, 1994.
Blackbourn, David. *History of Germany 1780–1918: The Long Nineteenth Century*. Oxford: Blackwell 2003.
Blanning, Tim. *The Pursuit of Glory: The Five Revolutions That Made Modern Europe 1648–1815*. London: Penguin, 2007.
Bleek, Wilhelm. "Einleitung." *Protestation des Gewissens: Die Rechtfertigungsschriften des Göttinger Sieben*, edited by Bernhard Lauer. Kassel: Brüder Grimm-Gesellschaft, 2012. 9–38.
Vormärz: Deutschlands Aufbruch in die Moderne: Szenen aus der deutschen Geschichte 1815–1848. Munich: C. H. Beck, 2019.
Bleek, Wilhelm, and Daniela Lülfing. "'Meinem edelen und mannhaften Freunde Jakob Grimm, dem Bruder Wilhelms, in Dank + Liebe gewidmet.' Das Fragment einer politischen Biographie Friedrich Christoph Dahlmanns." *Jahrbuch der Brüder Grimm-Gesellschaft* 3 (1993): 11–28.
Blumenberg, Hans. "Wirklichkeitsbegriff und Staatstheorie." *Schweizer Monatshefte: Zeitschrift für Politik, Wirtschaft und Kultur* 48.2 (1968): 121–46.
Boas, George. *Vox Populi: The History of an Idea*. Baltimore, MD: Johns Hopkins University Press, 1969.
Boldt, Hans. *Deutsche Staatslehre im Vormärz*. Düsseldorf: Droste Verlag, 1975.
Bolter, Jay, and Richard Grusin. "Remediation." *Configurations* 4.3 (1996): 311–58.
Bonfiglio, Thomas Paul. *Mother Tongues and Nations: The Invention of the Native Speaker*. New York: De Gruyter, 2010.
Bosse, Heinrich. "Gelehrte und Gebildete – die Kinder des 1. Standes." *Das achtzehnte Jahrhundert* 32.1 (2008), 13–37.
Bildungsrevolution 1770–1830, edited by Nacim Ghanbari. Heidelberg: Winter, 2012.
Böckenförde, Ernst-Wolfgang. *Die deutsche verfassungsgeschichtliche Forschung im 19. Jahrhundert: Zeitgebundene Fragestellungen und Leitbilder*. Berlin: Duncker & Humblot, 1961.
Recht, Staat, Freiheit: Studien zur Rechtsphilosophie, Staatstheorie und Verfassungsgeschichte. Frankfurt am Main: Suhrkamp, 1991.
Brandstetter, Gabriele, and Gerhard Neumann. "Gaben: Märchen in der Romantik." *Romantik und Exil: Festschrift für Konrad Feilchenfeldt*, edited by Claudia Christophersen. Würzburg: Königshausen & Neumann, 2004. 17–37.
Brandt, Harm-Hinrich. "The Revolution of 1848 and the Problem of Central European Nationalities." *Nation-Building in Central Europe*, edited by Hagen Schulze. Leamington Spa: Berg, 1987. 107–34.
Brandt, Hartwig. *Landständische Repräsentation im deutschen Vormärz: Politisches Denken im Einflußfeld des Monarchischen Prinzips*. Neuwied: Luchterhand, 1968.
"Einleitung." *Restauration und Frühliberalismus 1814–1840*, edited by Hartwig Brandt. Darmstadt: Wissenschaftliche Buchgesellschaft, 1979. 1–84.

"Die 'Germanisten' des Vormärz zwischen politischer Theorie und praktischer Politik." *Zur Geschichte und Problematik der Nationalphilologien in Europa: 150 Jahre Erste Germanistenversammlung von 1846*, edited by Frank Fürbeth. Tübingen: Max Niemeyer, 1999. 77–84.

Breuer, Stefan. *Der Staat: Entstehung, Typen, Organisationsstadien*. Hamburg: Rowohlt, 1998.

Breuilly, John. "On the Principle of Nationality." *The Cambridge History of the Nineteenth-Century Political Thought*, edited by Gareth Stedman Jones and Gregory Claeys. Cambridge: Cambridge University Press, 2016. 77–109.

Brophy, James. *Popular Culture and the Public Sphere in the Rhineland, 1800–1850*. Cambridge: Cambridge University Press, 2007.

"Which Political Nation? Soft Borders and Popular Nationhood in the Rhineland, 1800–1850." *Nationhood from Below: Europe in the Long Nineteenth Century*, edited by Maarten van Ginderachter and Marnix Beyen. Houndmills, UK: Palgrave Macmillan, 2012. 162–89.

Brunner, Otto. "Von Gottesgnadentum zum monarchischen Prinzip: Der Weg der Europäischen Monarchie seit dem hohen Mittelalter." *Das Königtum: Seine geistigen und rechtlichen Grundlagen*. Lindau: Jan Thorbecke Verlag, 1954. 279–305.

Buschmeier, Matthias. "Medien der Nation: Hoffmann von Fallerslebens *Das Lied der Deutschen* als demokratische Gesangsübung." *Zwischen Gattungsdisziplin und Gesamtkunstwerk: Literarische Medialität 1815–1848*, edited by Stefan Keppler-Tasaki and Wolf Gerhard Schmidt. Berlin: De Gruyter, 2015. 465–89.

Bußmann, Walter. *Zwischen Preußen und Deutschland: Friedrich Wilhelm IV. Eine Biographie*. Berlin: Goldmann, 1990.

Canovan, Margaret. *The People*. Cambridge: Polity, 2005.

Carr, William. *Schleswig-Holstein, 1815–1848: A Study in National Conflict*. Manchester, UK: Manchester University Press, 1963.

Casanova, Pascal. *The World Republic of Letters*, translated by M. B. DeBevoise. Cambridge, MA: Harvard University Press, 2004.

"Combative Literatures," *New Left Review* 72 (2011): 123–34.

Case, Holly. "The 'Social Question,' 1820–1920." *Modern Intellectual History* 13.3 (2016): 747–75.

Cheneval, Francis. *Demokratietheorien*. Hamburg: Junius, 2015.

Clark, Christopher. *Iron Kingdom: The Rise and Downfall of Prussia, 1600–1947*. Cambridge, MA: Harvard University Press, 2006.

"Why Should We Think About the Revolutions of 1848 Now?" *London Review of Books* 41.5 (March 7, 2019): 12–16.

Clark, Robert. *Herder: His Life and Thought*. Berkeley: University of California Press, 1955.

Coetsem, Frans von. "Grimm's Law: A Reappraisal of Grimm's Formulation from a Present-Day Perspective." *The Grimm Brothers and the Germanic Past*, edited by Elmer Antonsen. Amsterdam: John Benjamins Publishing Company, 1990. 43–59.

Collins, Randall. *The Sociology of Philosophies: A Global Theory of Intellectual Change*. Cambridge, MA: Harvard University Press, 1998.

Connelly, John. *From Peoples to Nations: A History of Eastern Europe*. Princeton, NJ: Princeton University Press, 2020.

Crawford, Heide. "'Mit Märchen und mit Träumen / Erinn'rung zu mir schwebt!' Regional Identity and the Concept of 'Heimat' in Ernst Moritz Arndt's Märchen." *Ernst Moritz Arndt (1769–1860): Deutscher Nationalismus – Europa – Transatlantische Perspektiven*, edited by Walter Erhart and Arne Koch. Tübingen: Max Niemeyer Verlag, 2007. 137–45.

Dahlmann, Friedrich Christoph. *Die Politik, auf den Grund und das Maaß der gegebenen Zustände zurückgeführt*, vol. 1. Göttingen: Verlag der Dieterischen Buchhandlung, 1835.

Danneberg, Lutz. "Altphilologie, Theologie und die Genealogie der Literaturwissenschaft." *Handbuch Literaturwissenschaft*, vol. 3, edited by Thomas Anz. Stuttgart: J. B. Metzler, 2007. 3–25.

Darden, Keith, and Harris Mylonas. "Threats to Territorial Integrity, National Mass Schooling, and Linguistic Commonality." *Comparative Political Studies*. 49.11 (2016): 1446–79.

Dehrmann, Mark-Georg. *Studierte Dichter: Zum Spannungsverhältnis von Dichtung und philologisch-historischen Wissenschaften im 19. Jahrhundert*. Berlin: De Gruyter, 2015.

Dembeck, Till. "X oder U? Herders 'Interkulturalität.'" *Zwischen Provokation und Usurpation: Interkulturalität als (un-)vollendetes Projekt der Literatur- und Sprachwissenschaften*, edited by Dieter Heimböckel. Munich: Wilhelm Fink, 2010. 103–28.

"Lyrik kanonisieren: Herders Volksliedersammlung als Versuch einer Gattungskonstitution." *Rahmungen: Präsentationsformen und Kanoneffekte*, edited by Philip Arjouri, Ursula Kundert, and Carsten Rohde. Berlin: Erich Schmidt Verlag, 2017.

Denecke, Ludwig. *Jacob Grimm und sein Bruder Wilhelm*. Stuttgart: J. B. Metzlersche Verlagsbuchhandlung, 1971.

"Über Schule Universität Academie." *Brüder Grimm Gedenken* 4 (1984): 1–12.

Dölemeyer, Barbara. "Die Beiträge der Brüder Grimm zur Rechtswissenschaft und Rechtsgeschichte." *Die Grimms: Kultur und Politik*, edited by Bernd Heidenreich and Ewald Grothe. Frankfurt: Frankfurter Societäts-Verlag. 163–88.

Düding, Dieter. *Organisierter gesellschaftlicher Nationalismus in Deutschland (1808–1847): Bedeutung und Funktion der Turner- und Sängervereine für die deutsche Nationalbewegung*. Munich: R. Oldenbourg Verlag, 1984.

Echternkamp, Jörg. *Der Aufstieg des deutschen Nationalismus (1770–1840)*. Frankfurt am Main: Campus, 1998.

Eiden-Offe, Patrick. "Dichter, Fürst und Kamarilla: Heinrich Heine berät Friedrich Wilhelm IV. Notiz zum Wintermärchen." *Rat geben: Zu Theorie und Analyse des Beratungshandelns*, edited by Michael Niehaus and Wim Peeters. Bielefeld: Transcript, 2014. 275–300.

Engelstein, Stefani. "The Father in the Fatherland: Violent Ideology and Corporeal Paternity in Kleist." *Contemplating Violence: Critical Studies in Modern German Culture*, edited by Stefani Engelstein and Carl Niekerk. Amsterdam: Rodolpi, 2011. 49–66.
  Sibling Action: The Genealogical Structure of Modernity. New York: Columbia University Press, 2017.
Ehrhardt, Holger. "Jacob Grimms politisches Auftreten vor seiner Wahl zur Frankfurter Nationalversammlung." *Jahrbuch der Brüder Grimm-Gesellschaft* 10 (2000): 145–51.
Eßbach, Wolfgang. *Die Junghegelianer: Soziologie einer Intellektuellengruppe*. Munich: Wilhelm Fink, 1988.
Evans, Richard. *The Pursuit of Power: Europe 1815–1914*. London: Penguin, 2016.
Fallersleben, Hoffmann von. *Mein Leben*, vol. 3. Eschborn bei Frankfurt am Main: Dietmar Klotz, 1996.
Feldmann, Roland. *Jacob Grimm und die Politik*. Kassel: Bärenreiter Verlag, 1970.
Felsch, Philipp. "Antiakademismus." *Zeitschrift für Ideengeschichte* 11.3 (2017): 113–20.
Ferejohn, John, and Frances McCall Rosenbluth. *Forged through Fire: War, Peace, and the Democratic Bargain*. New York: Liveright, 2017.
Feuerbach, Paul Johann Anselm von. *Kleinen Schriften vermischten Inhalts*. Nuremberg: Theodor Otto, 1833.
Fichte, Johann Gottlieb. *Reden and die deutsche Nation*, edited by Alexander Aichele. Hamburg: Felix Meiner, 2008.
Fohrmann, Jürgen. *Das Projekt der deutschen Literaturgeschichte: Entstehung und Scheitern einer nationalen Poesiegeschichtsschreibung zwischen Humanismus und deutschem Kaiserreich*. Stuttgart: Metzler, 1989.
  "Grußwort anlässlich des Gedenkbandes zum 150. Todestag von Friedrich Christoph Dahlmann." *Friedrich Christoph Dahlmann: ein politischer Professor im 19. Jahrhundert*, edited by Thomas Becker, Wilhelm Bleek, and Tilman Mayer. Göttingen: Vandenhoeck & Ruprecht, 2012. 9–10.
Foucault, Michel. *The Order of Things: An Archaeology of the Human Sciences*. New York: Random House, 1970.
  The Government of Self and Others: Lectures at the Collège de France 1982–1983, translated by Graham Burchell. New York: Palgrave Macmillan, 2008.
Freeden, Michael. "Is Nationalism a Distinct Ideology?" *Political Studies* 75 (1998): 748–65.
Frevert, Ute. "Citizen-Soldiers: General Conscription in the Nineteenth and Twentieth Centuries." *Enlightened War: German Theories and Cultures of Warfare from Frederick the Great to Clausewitz*, edited by Patricia Anne Simpson and Elisabeth Krimmer. Rochester, NY: Camden House, 2011. 219–37.
Friemel, Berthold. "Jacob Grimms unpreußische Ansichten über Polen und Sachsen." *Brüder Grimm Gedenken* 10 (1993): 68–81.
Fritzsche, Peter. *Stranded in the Present: Modern Time and the Melancholy of History*. Cambridge, MA: Harvard University Press, 2004.

Gagliardo, John. *Enlightened Despotism.* New York: Thomas Y. Crowell, 1967.
From Pariah to Patriot: The Changing Image of the German Peasant 1770–1840. Lexington: University Press of Kentucky, 1969.
Ganser, W. Günther. "Berlin 1841–1859/63." *200 Jahre Brüder Grimm*, edited by Hans-Bernd Harder and Ekkehard Kaufmann. Kassel: Weber & Weidemeyer, 1985. 106–52.
Gawthrop, Richard. "Literacy Drives in Preindustrial Germany." *National Literacy Campaigns: Historical and Comparative Perspectives*, edited by Robert Anrove and Harvey Graff. New York: Plenum, 1987. 29–48.
Geary, Patrick. *The Myth of Nations: The Medieval Origins of Europe.* Princeton, NJ: Princeton University Press, 2002.
Gellner, Ernest. *Nations and Nationalism.* Oxford: Blackwell, 1983.
Gille, Klaus. "Germanistik and Nation in the 19th Century." *Nation Building and Writing Literary History*, edited by Menno Spiering. Amsterdam: Rodolpi, 1999. 27–55.
Goffart, Walter. *Barbarian Tides: The Migration Age and the Late Roman Empire.* Philadelphia: University of Pennsylvania Press, 2006.
Gosewinkel, Dieter. "Staatsbürgerschaft–ein Relikt europäischer Rechstkultur." *Merkur* 70.810 (2016): 18–30.
Grau, Conrad. *Die Preußische Akademie der Wissenschaften zu Berlin.* Heidelberg: Spektrum, 1993.
Grätz, Manfred. *Das Märchen in der deutschen Aufklärung: Von Feenmärchen zum Volksmärchen.* Stuttgart: J. B. Metzlertsche Verlagsbuchhandlung, 1988.
Green, Abigail. *Fatherlands: State-Building and Nationhood in Nineteenth-Century Germany.* Cambridge: Cambridge University Press, 2001.
Griffiths, Devin. "The Comparative Method and the History of the Modern Humanities." *History of the Humanities* 2.2 (2017): 473–505.
Grimm, Albert Ludwig. *Kindermährchen.* Heidelberg: Mohr und Zimmer, 1809.
Grimm, Jacob. *Über den altdeutschen Meistergesang.* Göttingen: Heinrich Dieterich, 1811.
Deutsche Mythologie, vol. 1. Gütersloh: C. Bertelsmann, 1835.
Kleinere Schriften, vol. 1, edited by Karl Müllenhoff. Berlin: Ferdinand Dümmlers Verlagsbuchhandlung, 1864.
Kleinere Schriften, vol. 4, edited by Karl Müllenhoff. Berlin: Ferdinand Dümmlers Verlagsbuchhandlung, 1869.
Kleinere Schriften, vol. 7, edited by Eduard Ippel. Berlin: Ferdinand Dümmlers Verlagsbuchhandlung, 1884.
Kleinere Schriften, vol. 8, edited by Eduard Ippel. Gütersloh: C. Bertelsmann, 1890.
Deutsche Grammatik 1 (1840), Werke, vol 9.2, edited by Elisabeth Feldbusch and Ludwig Erich Schmitt. Hildesheim: Olms-Weidmann, 1995.
Deutsche Grammatik 1 (1870), Werke, 10.1, edited by Elisabeth Feldbusch and Ludwig Erich Schmitt. Hildesheim: Olms-Weidmann, 1989.
Geschichte der deutschen Sprache, vol. 1, *Werke*, vol. 15, edited by Maria Herrlich. Hildesheim: Olms-Weidmann, 1999.

Geschichte der deutschen Sprache, vol. 2, *Werke*, vol. 16, edited by Maria Herrlich. Hildesheim: Olms-Weidmann, 1999.
Jacob and Wilhelm Grimm, *Briefwechsel zwischen Jacob und Wilhelm Grimm, Dahlmann und Gervinus*, vol. 2, edited by Eduard Ippel. Berlin: Ferdinand Dümmlers Verlagsbuchhandlung, 1886.
Briefe der Brüder Grimm und Paul Wigand, edited by E. Stengel. Marburg: N. G. Elwert, 1910.
Briefe der Brüder Grimm an Savigny aus dem Savignyschen Nachlaß, edited by Wilhelm Schoof and Ingeborg Schnack. Berlin: Erich Schmidt Verlag, 1953.
Briefwechsel zwischen Jacob und Wilhelm Grimm, Briefwechsel Kritische Ausgabe 1.1, edited by Heinz Rölleke. Stuttgart: S. Hirzel Verlag, 2001.
The Annotated Brothers Grimm, edited and translated by Maria Tatar. New York: Norton & Co., 2004.
Wilhelm Grimm, *Die Deutsche Heldensage*, 3rd ed., edited by Reinhold Steig. Gütersloh: C. Bertelsmann, 1889.
Kleinere Schriften, vol. 1, edited by Gustav Hinrichs. Berlin: Ferdinand Dümmlers Verlagsbuchhandlung, 1881.
Kleinere Schriften, vol. 2, edited by Gustav Hinrichs. Berlin: Ferdinand Dümmlers Verlagsbuchhandlung, 1882.
Kleinere Schriften, vol. 3, edited by Gustav Hinrichs. Berlin: Ferdinand Dümmlers Verlagsbuchhandlung, 1883.
Kleinere Schriften, vol. 4, edited by Gustav Hinrichs. Gütersloh: C. Bertelsmann, 1887.
Grosby, Steven. *Nationalism: A Very Short Introduction*. Oxford: Oxford University Press, 2005.
Grosse, Rudolf. "Volk und Nation bei Grimm und seinen Nachfolgern," *Zeitschrift für Phonetik, Sprachwissenschaft und Kommunikationsforschung* 38.5 (1985): 481–88.
Grothe, Ewald. "Die Brüder Grimm und der Liberalismus." *Jahrbuch zur Liberalismus-Forschung* 15 (2003): 65–89.
Groys, Boris. *Logik der Sammlung: Am Ende des musealen Zeitalters*. Munich: Carl Hanser, 1997.
Gruner, Wolf. "The German Confederation: Cornerstone of the New European Security System." *Securing Europe after Napoleon: 1815 and the New European Security Culture*, edited by Beatrice Graaf et al. Cambridge: Cambridge University Press, 2019. 150–67.
Grünert, Horst. "Vom heiligen Begriff der Freiheit: Jacob Grimm und die Revolution von 1848." *Brüder Grimm Gedenken* 19 (1987): 60–74.
Haase, Donald. "Feminist Fairy-Tale Scholarship." *Fairy Tales and Feminism: New Approaches*, edited by Donald Haase. Detroit: Wayne State University Press, 2004. 1–36.
Habermas, Jürgen. *Eine Art Schadensabwicklung: Kleine Politische Schriften*, vol. 6. Frankfurt am Main: Suhrkamp, 1987.
"Was ist ein Volk? Bemerkungen zum politischen Selbstverständnis der Geisteswissenschaften im Vormärz, am Beispiel der Frankfurter

Germanistenversammlung von 1846." *Zur Geschichte und Problematik der Nationalphilologien in Europa. 150 Jahre Erste Germanistenversammlung von 1846*, edited by Frank Fürbeth. Tübingen: Max Niemeyer, 1999. 23–39.
Hagemann, Karen. *Revisiting Prussia's Wars Against Napoleon: History, Culture and Memory*. Cambridge: Cambridge University Press, 2015.
Hansen, Wilhelm. "Die Brüder Grimm in Berlin." *Brüder Grimm Gedenken*, edited by Ludwig Denecke and Ina-Maria Greverus. Marburg: N. G. Elwert, 1963. 227–307.
Härd, John-Evert. *Das Nibelungenepos: Wertung und Wirkung von der Romantik bis zur Gegenwart*, translated by Christine Palm. Tübingen: Francke, 1996.
Hardtwig, Wolfgang, and Helmut Hinze. "Einleitung." *Deutsche Geschichte in Quellen und Darstellung*, edited by Wolfgang Hardtwig and Helmut Hinze. Stuttgart: Philipp Reclam, 2011. 5–34.
Haß-Zumkehr, Ulrike. "Das Deutsche Wörterbuch von Jacob und Wilhelm Grimm als Nationaldenkmal." *Nation und Sprache: Die Diskussion ihres Verhältnisses in Geschichte und Gegenwart*, edited by Andreas Gardt. Berlin: De Gruyter, 2000. 229–246
Haugen, Einar. "Dialect, Language, Nation." *American Anthropologist* 68.4 (1966): 922–35.
Heather, Peter. *Empires and Barbarians: The Fall of Rome and the Birth of Europe*. Oxford: Oxford University Press, 2010.
Heeren, Arnold. *Vermischte historische Schriften*, vol. 2. Göttingen: Johann Friedrich Römer, 1821.
Heine, Heinrich. *Historisch-kritische Gesamtausgabe der Werke*, vol. 9, edited by Manfred Windfuhr. Hamburg: Hoffmann und Campe 1987.
Herder, Johann Gottfried, *Werke in zehn Bände*, vol. 4, edited by Jürgen Brummack and Martin Bollacher. Berlin: Deutscher Klassiker Verlag, 1994.
Herwig, Wolfram. "Origo Gentis: The Literature of Germanic Origins." *Early Germanic Literature and Culture*, edited by Brian Murdoch and Malcolm Read. Rochester, NY: Camden House, 2004. 39–54.
Herzog, Tamar. *A Short History of European Law: The Last Two and a Half Millennia*. Cambridge, MA: Harvard University Press, 2018.
Hewitson, Mark. *Nationalism in Germany, 1846–1866: Revolutionary Nation*. Basingstoke: Palgrave Macmillan, 2010.
The People's Wars: Histories of Violence in the German Lands 1820–1888. Oxford: Oxford University Press, 2017.
Hinsley, Francis H. *Sovereignty*. Cambridge: Cambridge University Press, 1986.
Hintze, Otto. *Beamtentum und Bürokratie*. Göttingen: Vandenhoeck & Ruprecht, 1981.
Hobsbawm, Eric. *The Age of Revolution: 1789–1848*. New York: Vintage, 1962.
Nations and Nationalism since 1780: Programme, Myth, Reality. Cambridge: Cambridge University Press, 1990.
Hont, István. "The Permanent Crisis of a Divided Mankind: 'Contemporary Crisis of the Nation State' in Historical Perspective." *Political Studies* 42.1 (1994): 166–231.

Hopkin, David. "Folklore beyond Nationalism: Identity Politics and Scientific Cultures in a New Discipline." *Folklore and Nationalism during the Long Nineteenth Century*, edited by Timothy Bancroft and David Hopkin. Leiden: Brill, 2010. 371–401.
  Voices of the People in Nineteenth-Century France. Cambridge: Cambridge University Press, 2012.
Hösle, Vittorio. *Eine kurze Geschichte der deutschen Philosophie*. Munich: C. H. Beck, 2013.
Hroch, Miroslav. *European Nations: Explaining Their Formation*, translated by Karolina Graham. London: Verso, 2015.
Huber, Ernst Rudolf. *Deutsche Verfassungsgeschichte seit 1789*, vol. 1. Stuttgart: W. Kohlhammer Verlag, 1957.
  Deutsche Verfassungsgeschichte seit 1789, vol. 2. Stuttgart: W. Kohlhammer Verlag, 1960.
  Deutsche Verfassungsgeschichte seit 1789, vol. 3. Stuttgart: W. Kohlhammer Verlag, 1963.
Huizinga, Johan. *Men and Ideas: History, the Middle Ages, the Renaissance*, translated by James S. Holmes and Hans van Marle. New York: Meridian Books, 1959.
Hunger, Ulrich. "Gründung oder Prozess: Die Entwicklung der wissenschaftlichen Germanistik, ein Werk Jacob Grimms?" *Jahrbuch der Brüder Grimm-Gesellschaft* 5 (1995): 153–76.
Hurka, Thomas. "The Justification of National Partiality." *The Morality of Nationalism*, edited by Jeff McMahan and Robert McKim. Oxford: Oxford University Press 1997. 139–57.
Hutchinson, John. "Cultural Nationalism." *The Oxford Handbook of the History of Nationalism*, edited by John Breuilly. Oxford: Oxford University Press, 2013. 75–91.
Iggers, George. *The German Conception of History: The National Tradition of Historical Thought from Herder to the Present*. Middletown, CT: Wesleyan University Press, 1988.
Ingrao, Charles. *The Hessian Mercenary State: Ideas, Institutions, and Reform under Frederick II, 1760–1785*. Cambridge: Cambridge University Press, 1987.
Jahn, Friedrich Ludwig. *Werke*, vol. 1, edited by Carl Euler. Hof: Verlag von Rud. Lion, 1884.
Janota, Johannes. *Eine Wissenschaft etabliert sich 1810–1870*. Tübingen: Max Niemeyer, 1980.
Jarrett, Mark. *The Congress of Vienna and Its Legacy*. London: I. B. Tauris, 2013.
Johnston, Otto. *The Myth of a Nation: Literature and Politics in Prussia under Napoleon*. Rochester, NY: Camden House, 1989.
Jones, William. *Discourses Delivered before the Asiatic Society and Miscellaneous Papers on the Religion, Poetry, Literature Etc., of the Nations of India*. London: Charles S. Arnold, 1824.
Jurasinski, Stefan. *Ancient Privileges: Beowulf, Law, and the Making of Germanic Antiquity*. Morgantown: West Virginia University Press, 2006.

Kelly, Donald. "Historians and Lawyers." *The Cambridge History of Nineteenth-Century Political Thought*, edited by Gareth Stedman Jones and Gregory Claeys. Cambridge: Cambridge University Press, 2016. 147–70.
Kelly, Duncan. "Popular Sovereignty as State Theory." *Popular Sovereignty in Historical Perspective*, edited by Richard Bourke and Quentin Skinner. Cambridge: Cambridge University Press, 2016. 270–96.
Kalyvas, Andreas. "Constituent Power." *Political Concepts: A Critical Lexicon*, edited by J. M. Bernstein, Adi Ophir, and Ann Laura Stoler (New York: Fordham University Press, 2017), 87–110.
Kantorowitz, Hermann. "Volksgeist und historische Rechtsschule." *Historische Zeitschrift* 108.2 (1912): 295–325.
Kedourie, Elie. *Nationalism*. New York: Frederick A. Praeger, 1960.
Kittler, Friedrich. *Discourse Networks 1800/1900*, translated by Michael Metteer. Stanford, CA: Stanford University Press, 1987.
"Das Subjekt als Beamter." *Die Frage nach dem Subjekt*, edited by Gérard Raulet, Manfred Frank, and Willem van Reijen. Frankfurt am Main: Suhrkamp, 1988. 401–20.
Kolk, Rainer. "Zur Professionalisierung und Disziplinentwicklung in der Germanistik." *Wissenschaft und Nation: Studien zur Entstehungsgeschichte der deutschen Literaturwissenschaft*, edited by Jürgen Fohrmann and Wilhelm Voßkamp. Munich: Wilhelm Fink, 1991. 127–40.
Koschorke, Albrecht, Susanne Lüdemann, Thomas Frank, and Ethel Matala de Mazza. *Der fiktive Staat: Konstruktionen des politischen Körpers in der Geschichte Europas*. Frankfurt am Main: Fischer Taschenbuch Verlag, 2007.
Koselleck, Reinhart. *Vergangene Zukunft: Zur Semantik geschichtlicher Zeiten*. Frankfurt am Main: Suhrkamp, 1989.
Kramer, Lloyd. *Nationalism: Political Cultures in Europe and America*. New York: Twayne, 1998.
Krebs, Christoph. *A Most Dangerous Book: Tacitus's Germania from the Roman Empire to the Third Reich*. New York: Norton & Norton, 2012.
Kuper, Adam. *The Reinvention of Primitive Society: Transformations of a Myth*. London: Routledge, 2005.
Lahusen, Benjamin. *Alles Recht geht vom Volksgeist aus: Friedrich Carl von Savigny und die moderne Rechtwissenschaft*. Berlin: Nicolai, 2013.
Lamar, Glenn. *Jérôme Bonaparte: The War Years, 1800–1815*. Westport: Greenwood Press, 2000.
La Vopa, Anthony. *Prussian Schoolteachers: Profession and Office, 1763–1848*. Chapel Hill: University of North Carolina Press, 1980.
Lämmert, Eberhard. "Zurück zu den Anfängen? Die kulturwissenschaftliche Weite der Germanistik von 1846." *Zur Geschichte und Problematik der Nationalphilologien in Europa. 150 Jahre Erste Germanistenversammlung von 1846*, edited by Frank Fürbeth. Tübingen: Max Niemeyer, 1999. 7–22.
Leerssen, Joep. *National Thought in Europe: A Cultural History*. Amsterdam: Amsterdam University Press, 2018.

Leffson, August. "Einleitung des Herausgebers." Ernst Moritz Arndt, *Werke*, vol. 3, edited by August Leffson and Wilhelm Steffens. Berlin: Deutsches Verlagshaus Bong & Co. 1912. 7–13.
Lehmann, Johannes. "Zorn, Hass, Entscheidung: Modelle der Feindschaft in den Hermannsschlachten von Klopstock zu Kleist." *Historische Anthropologie* 14.1 (2006): 11–29.
Levinger, Matthew. *Enlightened Nationalism: The Transformation of Prussian Political Culture 1806–1848.* Oxford: Oxford University Press, 2000.
Levy, Jacob. *The Multiculturalism of Fear.* Oxford: Oxford University Press, 2000.
Losch, Philipp. *Geschichte des Kurfürstentums Hessen 1803 bis 1866.* Marburg: N. G. Elwert, 1922.
Luden, Heinrich. *Einige Worte über das Studium der vaterländischen Geschichte.* Jena: Akademische Buchhandlung, 1810.
Macho, Thomas. "Was tun?" *Think Tanks: Die Beratung der Gesellschaft*, edited by Thomas Brandstetter, Claus Pias, and Sebastian Vehlken. Zürich: Diaphanes, 2010. 59–85.
Mack, Walter. *German Home Towns: Community, State, and the General Estate, 1648–1871.* Ithaca, NY: Cornell University Press, 1971.
Mandelbaum, Moran. "The Fantasy of Congruency: The Abbé Sieyès and the Nation-State Problematique Revisited." *Philosophy and Social Criticism* 42.3 (2016): 246–66.
Mann, Michael. *The Rise of Classes and Nation-States, 1760–1914.* Cambridge: Cambridge University Press, 2002.
Margalit, Avishai. "The Moral Psychology of Nationalism." *The Morality of Nationalism*, edited by Jeff McMahan and Robert McKim. Oxford: Oxford University Press, 1997. 74–87.
Martus, Steffen. *Die Brüder Grimm: Eine Biographie.* Berlin: Rowohlt, 2009.
 "Moderne Traditionalisten: Die Brüder Grimm und ihre Zeit." *Expedition Grimm*, edited by Thorsten Smidt. Kassel: Sandstein Verlag, 2013. 17–27.
Matala de Mazza, Ethel. *Der verfasste Körper: Zum Projekt einer organischen Gemeinschaft in der politischen Romantik.* Freiburg: Rombach, 1999.
May, Simon. *Love: A History.* New Haven, CT: Yale University Press, 2013.
McClelland, Charles. *State, Society, and University in Germany, 1700–1914.* Cambridge: Cambridge University Press, 1980.
 "Die deutschen Hochschullehrer als Elite 1815–1850." *Deutsche Hochschullehrer als Elite*, edited by Klaus Schwabe. Boppard am Rhein: Harald Boldt Verlag, 1988. 27–53.
McCrea, Barry. *Languages of the Night: Minor Languages and the Literary Imagination in Twentieth Century Ireland and Europe.* New Haven, CT: Yale University Press, 2015.
Mewes, Uwe. "Das Fach deutsche Sprache und Literatur an den deutschen Universitäten im Jahr 1846." *Zur Geschichte und Problematik der Nationalphilologien in Europa: 150 Jahre Erste Germanistenversammlung von 1846*, edited by Frank Fürbeth. Tübingen: Max Niemeyer, 1999. 85–103.

Michaelis-Jena, Ruth. *The Brothers Grimm*. London: Routledge, 1970.
Mikaberidze, Alexander. *The Napoleonic Wars: A Global History*. Oxford: Oxford University Press, 2020.
Miller, David. "The Ethical Significance of Nationality." *Ethics* 98.4 (1988): 647–62.
Minogue, Kenneth. *Nationalism*. London: Batsford, 1967.
Moore, Margaret. *A Political Theory of Territory*. Oxford: Oxford University Press, 2015.
Morgan, Edmund. *Inventing the People*. New York: Norton & Co., 1988.
Möckl, Karl. "Hof und Hofgesellschaft in den deutschen Staaten im 19. und beginnenden 20. Jahrhundert: Einleitende Betrachtungen." *Hof und Hofgesellschaft in den deutschen Staaten im 19. und beginnenden 20. Jahrhundert*, edited by Karl Möckl. Berlin: De Gruyter, 1990. 7–15.
Mufti, Aamir. *Forget English! Orientalisms and World Literature*. Cambridge, MA: Harvard University Press, 2018.
Muhlack, Ulrich. "Der 'politische Professor' im Deutschland des 19. Jahrhunderts." *Materialität des Geistes: Zur Sache Kultur – im Diskurs mit Ulrich Oevermann*, edited by Roland Burkholz, Christel Gärtner, and Ferdinand Zehentreiter. Weilersvist: Velbrück Wissenschaft, 2001. 185–204.
Münkler, Herfried. "Raub oder Rettung von Kulturgütern." *Merkur* 70.802 (2016): 5–17.
Münkler, Herfried, and Grit Straßenberger. *Politische Theorie und Ideengeschichte: Eine Einführung*. Munich: C. H. Beck, 2016.
Murdoch, Adrian. "Germania Romana." *Early Germanic Literature and Culture*, edited by Brian Murdoch and Malcolm Read. Rochester, NY: Camden House, 2004. 55–71.
Musäus, Johann Karl August. *Volksmärchen der Deutschen*, vol. 1, edited by Paul Zaunert. Jena: Eugen Diederichs, 1912.
Nairn, Tom. *The Break-Up of Britain*. London: NLB, 1977.
Naithani, Sadhana. "A Wild Philology." *Marvels & Tales*, 28.1 (2014): 38–55.
Netzer, Katinka. *Wissenschaft aus nationaler Sehnsucht: Verhandlungen der Germanisten 1846–1847*. Heidelberg: Winter, 2006.
Neumann, Siegfried. "The Brothers Grimm as Collectors and Editors of German Folktales." *The Great Fairy Tale Tradition from Straparola and Basile to the Brothers Grimm*, edited by Jack Zipes. New York: Norton & Co, 2001. 969–80.
Nielsen, Hans Frede. "Jacob Grimm and the 'German' Dialects." *The Grimm Brothers and the Germanic Past*, edited by Elmer Antonsen. Amsterdam: John Benjamins Publishing Company, 1990. 25–42.
Nipperdey, Thomas. *Deutsche Geschichte 1800–1866: Bürgerwelt und starker Staat*. Munich: C. H. Beck, 1983.
Ochoa Espejo, Paulina. "Populism and the Idea of the People." *Oxford Handbook of Populism*, edited by Cristobal Rovira Kaltwasser et al. Oxford: Oxford University Press, 2017. 607–28.

Ohles, Frederik. *Germany's Rude Awakening: Censorship in the Land of the Brothers Grimm*. Kent, OH: The Kent State University Press, 1992.
Osterhammel, Jürgen. *Die Verwandlung der Welt: Eine Geschichte des 19. Jahrhunderts*. Munich: C. H. Beck, 2009.
Otmar (Johann Karl Christoph Nachtigal). *Volcks-Sagen*. Bremen: Friedrich Wilmans, 1800.
Patten, Alan. "The Most Natural State: Herder and Nationalism." *History of Political Thought* 31.4 (2010): 657–89.
Paye, Claudie. *"Der französischen Sprache mächtig": Kommunikation im Spannungsfeld von Sprachen und Kulturen in Königreich Westphalen 1807–1813*. Munich: Oldenburger Wissenschaftsverlag, 2013.
Payk, Marcus M. "Dahlmann, der Konflikt um Schleswig-Holstein und die 'Konstitutionalisierung der Nation' in Deutschland 1815–1850." *Friedrich Christoph Dahlmann: ein politischer Professor im 19. Jahrhundert*, edited by Thomas Becker, Wilhelm Bleek, and Tilman Mayer. Göttingen: Vandenhoeck & Ruprecht, 2012. 105–17.
Pedersen, Holger. *The Discovery of Language: Linguistic Science in the Nineteenth Century*, translated by John Webster Spargo. Bloomington: Indiana University Press, 1931.
Pedlow, Gregory. *The Survival of the Hessian Nobility 1770–1870*. Princeton, NJ: Princeton University Press, 1988.
Planert, Ute. "Resistance to Napoleonic Reform in the Grand Duchy of Berg, the Kingdom of Westphalia and the South German States." *The Napoleonic Empire and the New European Political Culture*, edited by Agustin Guimera and Peter Hicks. Basingstoke: Palgrave Macmillan, 2012. 148–59.
Plato. *Republic*, translated by Benjamin Jowett. New York: Barnes & Noble, 2004.
Plumpe, Werner. "Eigentum – Eigentümlichkeit. Über den Zusammenhang ästhetischer und juristischer Begriffe im 18. Jahrhundert." *Archiv für Begriffsgeschichte* 23.2 (1979): 175–96.
Pocock, John Greville Agard. *The Machiavellian Moment*. Princeton, NJ: Princeton University Press, 1975.
Barbarism and Religion, vol. 4. Cambridge: Cambridge University Press, 2005
Barbarism and Religion, vol. 6. Cambridge: Cambridge University Press, 2015.
Pourciau, Sarah. *The Writing of Spirit: Soul, System, and the Roots of Language Science*. New York: Fordham University Press, 2017.
Puhvel, Jan. *Comparative Mythology*. Baltimore, MD: Johns Hopkins University Press, 1987.
Pundt, Alfred. *Arndt and the Nationalist Awakening in Germany*. New York: Columbia University Press, 1935.
Püshel, Ursula. *Bettina von Arnim – politisch: Erkundungen, Entdeckungen, Erkenntnisse*. Bielefeld: Aesthetis, 2005.
Rankovíc, Slavica. "Who Is Speaking in Traditional Texts? On the Distributed Author of the Sagas of Icelanders and Serbian Epic Poetry." *New Literary History* 38.2 (2007): 293–307.
Rapport, Mike. *1848: Year of Revolution*. New York: Basic Books, 2008.

Raude, Karin. "Jacob Grimm und der Volksgeist." *Romantik und Recht: Recht und Sprache, Rechtsfälle und Gerechtigkeit*, edited by Antje Arnold. Boston: De Gruyter, 2018. 15–33.

Rautenberg, Ursula. *Das "Volksbuch vom armen Heinrich": Studien zur Rezeption Hartmanns von Aue im 19. Jahrhundert und zur Wirkungsgeschichte der Übersetzung Wilhelm Grimms*. Berlin: Erich Schmidt, 1985.

Redfield, Marc. *The Politics of Aesthetics: Nationalism, Gender, Romanticism*. Stanford, CA: Stanford University Press, 2003.

Reimer, Doris. *Passion & Kalkül: der Verleger Georg Andreas Reimer (1776–1842)*. Berlin: Walter de Gruyter, 1999.

Rexroth, Karl-Heinrich. "Kassel 1805/6–1829." *200 Jahre Brüder Grimm*, edited by Hans-Bernd Harder and Ekkehard Kaufmann. Kassel: Weber & Weidemeyer, 1985. 23–79.

Riedel, Manfred. "Einleitung." Friedrich Christoph Dahlmann, *Die Politik*, edited by Manfred Riedel. Frankfurt am Main: Suhrkamp 1968. 7–31.

Robertson, Priscilla. *Revolutions of 1848: A Social History*. New York: Harper & Row, 1960.

Rodrik, Dany. "Who Needs the Nation-State." *Economic Geography* 89.1 (2012): 1–19.

Rölleke, Heinz. "Grimms Märchen." *Kinder- und Hausmärchen gesammelt durch die Brüder Grimm (1837)*, edited by Heinz Rölleke. Frankfurt am Main: Deutscher Klassiker Verlag, 1985. 1151–1177.

Die Märchen der Brüder Grimm. Munich: Artemis, 1985.

Rosanvallon, Pierre. *Democracy Past and Future: Selected Essays*, edited by Samuel Moyn. New York: Columbia University Press 2007.

Ross, Anna. *Beyond the Barricades: Government and State-Building in Post-Revolutionary Prussia, 1848–1858*. Oxford: Oxford University Press, 2019.

Rothacker, Erich. "Savigny, Grimm, Ranke: Ein Beitrag zur Frage nach dem Zusammenhang der Historischen Schule." *Historische Zeitschrift* 128.3 (1923): 415–45.

Rowe, Michael. *From Reich to State: The Rhineland in the Revolutionary Age, 1780–1830*. Cambridge: Cambridge University Press, 2003.

Sassoon, Donald. *The Culture of the Europeans: From 1800 to the Present*. London: Harper Press, 2006.

Savigny, Friedrich Carl von. *Vom Beruf unsrer Zeit für Gesetzgebung und Rechtswissenschaft*. Freiburg: Akademische Verlagsbuchhandlung, 1892.

Schacker, Jennifer. *National Dreams: The Remaking of Fairy Tales in Nineteenth-Century England*. Philadelphia: University of Pennsylvania Press, 2003.

Schäfer, Karl Heinz. *Ernst Moritz Arndt als politischer Publizist: Studien zur Publizistik, Pressepolitik und kollektivem Bewußtsein im frühen 19. Jahrhundert*. Bonn: Ludwig Röhrschied Verlag, 1974.

Schieder, Theodor. "Partikularismus und Nationalbewußtsein im Denken des deutschen Vormärz." *Staat und Gesellschaft im deutschen Vormärz*, edited by Werner Conze. Stuttgart: Ernst Klett Verlag, 1962.

Schlaffer, Heinz. *Die kurze Geschichte der deutschen Literatur*. Cologne: Anaconda, 2013.

Schlegel, August Wilhelm. "Aus einer noch ungedruckten historischen Untersuchungen über das Lied der Nibelungen." *Deutsches Museum* 1.1 (1812): 9–36.
Schleunes, Karl. *Schooling and Society: The Politics of Education in Prussia and Bavaria 1750–1900.* Oxford: Berg, 1989.
Schmidt, Alexander. *Vaterlandsliebe und Religionskonflikt: Politische Diskurse im alten Reich (1555–1648).* Leiden: Brill, 2007.
Schmidt, Hartmut. "Bemerkungen zu Jacob Grimms Reden in der Berliner Akademie." *Zeitschrift für Phonetik, Sprachwissenschaft und Kommunikationsforschung* 38 (1985): 712–21.
Schmidt-Biggemann, Wilhelm. "Elemente von Herders Nationalkonzept." *Nationen und Kulturen: Zum 250. Geburtstag Johann Gottfried Herders*, edited by Regine Otto. Würzburg: Königshausen & Neumann, 1996. 27–34.
Schmitt, Carl. *Politische Romantik.* Berlin: Duncker & Humblot, 1998.
Theorie des Partisanen: Zwischenbemerkung zum Begriff des Politischen. Berlin: Duncker & Humblot, 2017.
Schofield, Malcolm. *Saving the City: Philosopher-Kings and Other Classical Paradigms.* London: Routledge, 1999.
Schöndorf, Kurt Erich. "Noch einmal: Jacob Grimms Theorie von der Besiedlung Jütlands in der germanischen Frühzeit oder von den Grenzen der Germanistik." *Spurensuche in Sprach- und Geschichtslandschaften: Festschrift für Ernst Erich Metzner*, edited by Andrea Hohmeyer et al. Münster: LIT, 2003. 37–51.
Schreiber, Elliott. "Tainted Sources: The Subversion of the Grimms' Ideology of the Folktale in Heinrich Heine's Der Rabbi von Bacherach." *The German Quarterly* 78.1 (2005): 23–44.
Schultz, Hartwig. "Einleitung," *Der Briefwechsel Bettine von Arnims mit den Brüdern Grimm*, edited by Hartwig Schultz. Frankfurt am Main: Insel, 1985. 5–20.
"Dokumente zur Entlassung der Brüder Grimm." *Der Briefwechsel Bettine von Arnims mit den Brüdern Grimm*, edited by Hartwig Schultz. Frankfurt am Main: Insel, 1985. 329–66.
Schulze, Hagen. *States, Nations and Nationalism*, translated by William E. Yuill. Oxford: Blackwell, 1996.
Scott, James. *Seeing Like a State: How Certain Schemes to Improve the Human Condition Have Failed.* New Haven, CT: Yale University Press, 1998.
Against the Grain: A Deep History of the Earliest States. New Haven, CT: Yale University Press, 2017.
See, Klaus von. *Die Göttinger Sieben: Kritik einer Legende.* Heidelberg: C. Winter, 1997.
"Das Nibelungenlied – ein Nationalepos?" *Die Nibelungen: Sage – Epos – Mythos*, edited by Joachim Heinzle, Klaus Kleim, and Ute Obhof. Wiesbaden: Reichert, 2003. 309–43.
Seeba, Hinrich. "Nationalbücher: Zur Kanonisierung nationaler Bildungsmuster in der frühen Germanistik." *Wissenschaft und Nation: Studien zur*

Entstehungsgeschichte der deutschen Literaturwissenschaft, edited by Jürgen Fohrmann and Wilhelm Voßkamp. Munich: Wilhelm Fink, 1991. 57–71.

Seier, Hellmut. "Der unbewältigte Konflikt: Kurhessen und sein Ende 1803–1866." *Die Geschichte Hessens*, edited by Uwe Schultz. Stuttgart: Konrad Theiss, 1983. 160–70.

Seton-Watson, Hugh. *Nations and States: An Enquiry into the Origins of Nations and the Politics of Nationalism*. Boulder, CO: Westview Press, 1977.

Sheehan, James. *German Liberalism in the Nineteenth Century*. Chicago: University of Chicago Press, 1978.

Shippey, Tom. "Introduction." *Beowulf: The Critical Heritage*, edited by Tom Shippey and Andreas Haarder. London: Routledge, 1998. 1–74.

Siebeneicker, Arnulf. "'Ich fühle mich eingenommen für alles Bestehende': Die Rechtfertigungsschrift Jacob Grimm über seine Entlassung." *Expedition Grimm*, edited by Thorsten Schmidt. Kassel: Sandstein Verlag, 2013. 113–21.

Siemann, Wolfram. *Vom Staatenbund zum Nationalstaat: Deutschland 1806–1871*. Munich: C. H. Beck, 1995.

Smith, Anthony D. *The Ethnic Origins of Nations*. Oxford: Blackwell, 1986.

Snyder, Louis. *The Roots of German Nationalism*. Bloomington: Indiana University Press, 1996.

Speitkamp, Winfried. "Das Kurfürstentum Hessen und sein Ende 1866." *1866: Vom Deutschen Bund zum Deutschen Reich*, edited by Bernd Heidenreich and Evelyn Brockhoff. Oldenburg: De Gruyter, 2017. 69–85.

Sperber, Jonathan. *The European Revolutions, 1848–1851*. Cambridge: Cambridge University Press, 1994.

Steig, Reinhold. *Achim von Arnim und die ihm nahe standen*, vol. 3. Stuttgart and Berlin: J. G. Cotta'schen Buchhandlung, 1904.

Clemens Brentano und die Brüder Grimm. Bern: Herbert Lang, 1969.

Stewart, Susan. *Crimes of Writing: Problems in the Containment of Representation*. Durham, NC: Duke University Press, 1994.

Stilz, Anna. "Nations, States, and Territory." *Ethics* 121.3 (2011): 572–601.

Storost, Jürgen. "Jacob Grimm und die Schleswig-Holstein-Frage: Zu den Kontroversen von 1850." *Brüder Grimm Gedenken* 8 (1988): 64–80.

Straub, Eberhard. *Der Wiener Kongress: Das Große Fest und die Neuordnung Europas*. Stuttgart: Klett-Cotta, 2014.

Strauss, Leo. "Plato." *History of Political Philosophy*, edited by Leo Strauss and Joseph Cropsey. Chicago: Rand McNally & Company, 1963. 7–63.

Strippel, Jutta. "Zum Verhältnis von Deutscher Rechtsgeschichte und Deutscher Philologie." *Germanistik und die deutsche Nation 1806–1848*, edited by Jörg Jochen Müller. Stuttgart: Metzler, 2000. 111–66.

Tacitus, Cornelius. *The Agricola and the Germania*, translated by H. Mattingly and S. A. Handford. London: Penguin, 1970.

Tatar, Maria. *The Hard Facts of the Grimms' Fairy Tales*. Princeton, NJ: Princeton University Press, 2003.

"Folklore and Cultural Identity." *A New History of German Literature*, edited by David Wellbery. Cambridge, MA: Harvard University Press, 2004. 516–21.

Thom, Martin. *Republics, Nations, and Tribes*. London: Verso, 1995.

Thomas, Richard. "The Germania as Literary Text." *The Cambridge Companion to Tacitus*, edited by A. J. Woodman. Cambridge: Cambridge University Press, 2010. 59–72.

Thornhill, Chris. *German Political Philosophy: The Metaphysics of Law*. London: Routledge, 2007.

A Sociology of Constitutions: Constitutions and State Legitimacy in Historical-Sociological Perspective. Cambridge: Cambridge University Press. 2011.

The Sociology of Law and the Global Transformation of Democracy. Cambridge: Cambridge University Press, 2018.

Tilly, Charles. "Reflections on the History of European State-Making." *The Formation of National States in Western Europe*, edited by Charles Tilly. Princeton, NJ: Princeton University Press, 1975. 3–83.

Todorov, Nicola. "The Napoleonic Administrative System in the Kingdom of Westphalia." *The Napoleonic Empire and the New European Political Culture*, edited by Agustin Guimera and Peter Hicks. Basingstoke: Palgrave Macmillan, 2012. 173–85.

Toews, John Edward. *Becoming Historical: Cultural Reformation and Public Memory in Early Nineteenth-Century Berlin*. Cambridge: Cambridge University Press, 2004.

Trabant, Jürgen. *Europäisches Sprachdenken von Platon bis Wittgenstein*. Munich: C. H. Beck, 2003.

Treitschke, Heinrich von. *History of Germany in the Nineteenth Century*, translated by Eden Paul and Cedar Paul. Chicago: University of Chicago, 1975.

Trumpener, Katie. *Bardic Nationalism: The Romantic Novel and the British Empire*. Princeton, NJ: Princeton University Press, 1997.

Tuck, Richard. *The Sleeping Sovereign: The Invention of Modern Democracy*. Cambridge: Cambridge University Press, 2016.

Turner, James. *Philology: The Forgotten Origins of the Modern Humanities*. Princeton, NJ: Princeton University Press, 2014.

Uther, Hans-Jörg. *Handbuch zu den "Kinder- und Hausmärchen" der Brüder Grimm: Entstehung, Wirkung, Interpretation*. Berlin: De Gruyter, 2008.

Valjavec, Fritz. *Die Entstehung der Politischen Strömungen in Deutschland 1770–1815*. Munich: R. Oldenbourg, 1951.

Verhandlungen der Germanisten zu Frankfurt am Main am 24., 25., und 26. September 1846. Frankfurt am Main: J. D. Sauerländer's Verlag, 1847.

Verzeihniss der Abhandlungen der Königlich Preussischen Akademie der Wissenschaften von 1710–1870. Berlin: F. Dümmler Verlags-Buchhandlung, 1871.

Vick, Brian. *Defining Germany: The 1848 Frankfurt Parliamentarians and National Identity*. Cambridge, MA: Harvard University Press, 2002.

Walser-Smith, Helmut. *Germany, a Nation in Its Time: Before, During, and After Nationalism, 1500–2000*. New York: Liveright Publishing, 2020.

Warner, Marina. *Once Upon a Time: A Short History of the Fairy Tale*. Oxford: Oxford University Press, 2014.
Weber, Ernst. *Lyrik der Befreiungskriege (1812–1815): Gesellschaftliche Meinungs- und Willensbildung durch Literatur*. Stuttgart: J. B. Metzlersche Verlagsbuchhandlung, 1991.
Weber der Jüngere, Veit. *Kriegslieder der Deutschen*. Kassel: Germanien, 1813.
Wehler, Hans-Ulrich. *Deutsche Gesellschaftsgeschichte 1700–1815*, vol. 1. Munich: C. H. Beck, 2008.
Deutsche Gesellschaftsgeschichte 1815–1848/49, vol. 2. Munich: C. H. Beck, 2008.
Wende, Peter. "Der 'politische Professor.'" *Historisierung und gesellschaftlicher Wandel in Deutschland im 19. Jahrhundert*, edited by Ulrich Muhlack. Berlin: Akademie Verlag, 2003.
White, Hayden. *Metahistory: The Historical Imagination in 19th-Century Europe*. Baltimore, MD: Johns Hopkins University Press, 2014.
Whitman, James. *The Legacy of Roman Law in the German Romantic Era*. Princeton, NJ: Princeton University Press, 1990.
Wienfort, Monica. *Monarchie in der bürgerlichen Gesellschaft: Deutschland und England*. Göttingen: Vandenhoeck & Ruprecht, 1993.
Wickham, Chris. *The Inheritance of Rome: Illuminating the Dark Ages*. London: Penguin, 2009.
Williamson, George. *The Longing for Myth in Germany: Religion and Aesthetic Culture from Romanticism to Nietzsche*. Chicago: Chicago University Press, 2004.
Wilson, Peter. *The Heart of Europe: A History of the Holy Roman Empire*. Cambridge, MA: Harvard University Press, 2016.
Wimmer, Andreas. *Nationalist Exclusion and Ethnic Conflict: Shadows of Modernity*. Cambridge: Cambridge University Press, 2002.
Waves of War: Nationalism, State Formation, and Ethnic Exclusion in the Modern World. Cambridge: Cambridge University Press, 2013.
Ethnic Boundary Making: Institutions, Power, Networks. Oxford: Oxford University Press, 2013.
Wolfe, Larry. *Inventing Eastern Europe: The Map of Civilization on the Mind of the Enlightenment*. Stanford, CA: Stanford University Press, 1994.
Wollstein, Günter. *Das Großdeutschland der Paulskirche: Nationale Ziele der bürgerlichen Revolution 1848/49*. Düsseldorf: Droste Verlag 1977.
Wulf, Andrea. *The Invention of Nature: Alexander von Humboldt's New World*. New York: Vintage Books, 2015.
Wyss, Ulrich. *Wilde Philologie: Jacob Grimm und der Historismus*. Munich: C. H. Beck, 1979.
Yack, Bernard. "Popular Sovereignty and Nationalism." *Political Theory* 29.4 (2001): 517–36.
Zeuss, Johann Kaspar. *Die Deutschen und die Nachbarstämme*. Heidelberg: Carl Winters Universitätsbuchhandlung, 1925.
Ziolkowski, Theodore. *German Romanticism and Its Institutions*. Princeton, NJ: Princeton University Press, 1990.

    Clio the Romantic Muse: Historicizing the Faculties in Germany. Ithaca, NY: Cornell University Press, 2004.
Zipes, Jack. *Fairy Tales and the Art of Subversion: The Classical Genre for Children and the Process of Civilization.* New York: Wildman Press, 1983.
    The Brothers Grimm: From Enchanted Forests to the Modern World. New York: Palgrave Macmillan, 2002.

Index

absolutism, 35–36, 47–48, 117, 133
academies, 145
affinity, cultural, 182
Albrecht, Wilhelm Eduard, 139
Alsace, 30
Anderson, Benedict, 10, 11, 41
Anglo-Saxons (tribe), 163, 165
anthropology, 63, 68
aristocracy, 43, 44, 70
  proposed elimination of ranks of, 121–22, 135
Aristotle, 168
armies, 51
  conscription, 70
  education as preparation for, 152–54
  Hessian, 52–53
Arndt, Ernst Moritz, 67, 70–71, 72, 75, 76–77, 78, 133
  Catechism for German Soldiers, 75
  On Folk Hatred, 71
  folktales, collection of, 77
  Frankfurt Parliament, representative in, 121
  Frederick William IV and, 120
  and monarchy, 138
  on particularity (*Eigenthümlichkeit*), 73
  "What Is the Germans' Fatherland? [Was ist des deutschen Vaterlands?]", 70, 77
Arnim, Achim von, 61, 75, 76, 91, 131, 156
  Des Knaben Wunderhorn, 81, 106
Arnim, Elisabeth (Bettina) von, 61, 81, 120, 135
Arnim, Johannes Freumund von, 61
Austria, 4, 120
authenticity, 80, 103
  of folk tales, 18
  national, 92–93
  of national literature, 91
authority
  epistemic, 48
  legal, 96
  philological, 3–4, 5–6
  professorial, 98–101

royal, 116
  see also monarchy; rule.
authorship, distributed, 90
autocracy, 53

Baecker, Dirk, 68
Barnard, F. M., 137
Battle of Leipzig (1813), 51, 61
Bavaria, 4
Bavarians (tribe), 174
Beowulf (epic poem), 87–88
Berlin, 21, 95, 120, 145
  Prussian Academy of the Sciences, 120, 145
bilingualism, 42
Bismarck, Otto von, 46
Blackbourn, David, 6
Boas, George, 91
Boldt, Hans, 118
Bonaparte, Jérôme, 12, 33, 40, 54, 55
  J Grimm's criticism of, 57, 131
  return to France, 51
Bonaparte, Napoleon, 40, 54–55, 65, 115
boundaries
  between collector and collected, 107, 109–10
  defensible, 35
  folk hatred, secured through, 71
  German, 134, 136–37
  legitimization, 38
  linguistic, 163
  national, 4, 27, 29–31
  of the people (*Volk*), 35
  philologically defined, 31–32, 49
  spatial, 35
  state, 35
Brandt, Hartwig, 118
Brentano, Clemens, 156
  Des Knaben Wunderhorn, 81, 106
Breuilly, John, 9
brotherhood, 129
Burgundians (tribe), 163, 164, 165

247

Burke, Edmund, 168
Burschenschaften (fraternities), 136

Catharina of Württemberg (Queen of Westphalia), 57
Catherine the Great of Russia, 47
censorship, 48, 117, 135
character
  national, 88
  of nationalism, 9–11
  see also identity.
Charlemagne, 28
Chatten (tribe), 172
chauvinism, ethnic, 34
Christian VIII (King of Denmark), 1, 44
Christianity, 24, 25, 159
closeness *see* intimacy.
collection, 11, 106–8, 183
  and collector, 107, 109–10
  of folk tales, 77
  of folklore, 156–57
collectivity
  of community, 169–70
  cultural, 20, 86–87, 90, 183
community
  collective origin of, 169–70
  cultural artefacts, developed by, 86–87, 90, 91–92
  and identity, 11
  legal norms, developed by, 96
  love, formed by, 126, 127, 128–29, 130–31
  names and naming of, 173–74
  nation as, 37, 38, 154
  people (*Volk*) as, 35, 37
  rights of, 68
  territorialization of, 38
  vs. state, 128–29
conformity, social, 151–52
Congress of Vienna (1814–15), 4, 30, 34, 116–17
Constant, Benjamin, 133
constitution
  abrogation of, 119
  national, 70
  utility of, 139–40
  viability of, 167
constitutional monarchy, 34, 117–20, 126, 138–40
constitutionalism, 133, 135
Creutzer, Carl Friedrich, 89
cultural extinction, fears of, 66–68, 163–64
cultural particularity (*Eigenthümlichkeit*), 40–41, 64–68
  defense of, 71, 185
  folktales, evidence of, 73–74
  of Grimms' *Tales*, 78–80
  in legal norms, 96, 97

cultural recycling, 157
culture
  ancient, importance of, 73
  arming of, 68, 69
  collective, 20, 86–87, 90, 183
  construction of, 62
  differences in, 57
  diversity of, 19–20
  encounters between, 172, 174–76
  foreign influence on, 89, 93
  German, 24–25, 28
  and identity, 152
  loss of, through formal education, 144
  and nation, 16, 23, 37, 38–39
  nationalist dependence on, 18
  Nordic/Scandanavian, 87, 89, 175–76
  ownership of, 87–88
  philogists, redeemed by, 18–19
  preservation of, 104–7, 108–12
  resurrection of, 111
  sophistication of, 92–93
  temporal age of, 87
  transmission of, 19–20, 88–91, 104, 106, 184
  uniformity of, 155–56
vernacularization, 103

Dahlmann, Friedrich Christoph, 43–45, 46, 47, 84, 119, 120, 133
Die Politik, 167–68
Danish language, 26–27, 42, 44
Daub, Karl, 89
democracy, 37, 69, 135
denationalization, cultural, 89, 93
Denmark, 122
  Copenhagen, 43
  First Schleswig War, 45–46
  and Schleswig-Holstein, 1, 22–23, 29, 42–43, 44, 45–46
despotism, enlightened, 15, 47–48
Deutscher Bund (German Confederation), 4, 34, 43, 116
Deutsches Museum (journal), 87
dialects, 13, 31
  interconnectedness of, 162
  loss of, 154–56
  preservation of, 158
  recording of, 156, 157
diglossia, 42
diversity, 184
  cultural, 19–20, 57, 71, 155
  human, 65
  linguistic, 12, 41–42, 154–56
  loss of, 19–20
  unity in, 162

domestic spaces, 104, 105
domesticity, 61

Eddas (poems), 175–76
education, 19–20, 145–51
  academies, 145
  German nation, relation to, 145
  institutions of, 145–46
  language learning
    familial, 146, 147
    scholastic, 147–48
  mass, 143–44
    and dialect loss, 154–56
    and state loyalty, 151–54
  maternal, 143
  as military preparation, 152–54
  nation-building through, 144
  schools, 19–20, 145–50
  teachers, 147–50
    and preservation of folk culture, 156–57
    soldiers, compared to, 153–54
    wet-nurses, compared to, 150–51
  universities, 145,
empire, 41, 170–71
  British, 179
  critique of, 162
  Holy Roman, 29, 40, 52, 65
  see also imperialism.
enemies, collective, 70, 71
English language, 31,
Enlightenment, 47, 63, 127
Ernst August (King of Hanover, Duke of Cumberland), 21, 34, 43, 119–20
ethnicity, 5, 41
  and chauvinism, 34
extinction, cultural, fears of, 66–68, 163–64

fairy tales *see* folktales.
Fallersleben, August Heinrich Hoffmann von, 177
familiarity, 96, 97
family, 129, 146, 147
fatherland, 20, 141
  definitions of, 129–30
  love of, 126–27, 128–30
  see also identity, national.
federalism, 116
Feuerbach, Paul Johann Anselm von, 66
Fichte, Johann Gottlieb, 9, 67–68, 71, 72, 133, 152–53, 154
folk culture, 184
folk hatred, 70, 71, 76–77
folk song, 81
  and epic poetry, 89, 90
folklore, 156–57

folktales, 6, 7, 15–16, 19
  authenticity of, 18
  cultural particularity of (*Eigenthümlichkeit*), 78–80, 83, 84
  cultural prestige of, 101–2
  cultural tradition in, 61
  epic poetry, preserved by, 104–5
  French, 80
  literary status of, 103–4
  mythology, preserved by, 105
  and national identity, 58
  and nationalism, 61–63, 78–84
  natural, vs. artful, 102–3
  pedagogic value of, 82
  preservation of, 108–12
  provenance, 62
  Sleeping Beauty (*Dornröschen*), 105, 110
Fontane, Theodor, 137
foreignness, influence of, 89, 93, 137, 153
France
  folktales from, 80
  rule in Germany, 12, 33, 34, 40, 65
  resistance to, 65–68, 70–71
Frankfurt am Main, 22, 28–29, 34, 122
Frankfurt Parliament (*Frankfurter Nationalversammlung*), 34, 46, 120–22
  professors in, 46–47
Frankish language, 30
Franks (tribe), 163, 164, 165, 172
fraternities (*Burschenschaften*), 136
fraternity, 129
Frederick the Great (Frederick II, King of Prussia), 15
Frederick VII (King of Denmark), 45, 122
Frederick William III (King of Prussia), 153
Frederick William IV (King of Prussia), 49, 135, 137, 161
  appoints Grimms to Prussian Academy, 120, 125
  Grimm's letter to, 1–2, 21, 50
  and Heine, 48
Freeden, Michael, 134
freedom, 59, 97, 165, 168
  national, 30
  of scholarship, 59
  popular, 8, 118, 126, 169
French language, 104
French Revolution, 33, 35–36, 40, 117
Friedrich II (Landgrave of Hesse-Kassel), 52
Frisians (tribe), 174
Fritzsche, Peter, 106

Geary, Patrick, 170
Gellner, Ernest, 9, 152, 184

George III (King of Great Britain and
    Hanover), 117
German Confederation (Deutscher Bund), 4, 34,
    43, 116
German language, 18
  vs. Danish, 26–27
  education in, 153
  as mother tongue, 143–44
  sound shifts, 6, 26, 27, 168–69
  standardized, 154–56
  and "undeutsch" [un-German], 27–28
  usage in Schleswig-Holstein, 42,
    43, 44
Germanic language, 24
  ancient, 25
  distinctiveness, 26–27
Germanic tribes, 159, 161–62, 168–76
  historical evidence for, 170–72
  historiography of, 175–76
  losses of, 163, 164
  migrations of, 165–66, 168
  names of, 171, 172–76
  political organization of, 169
  Roman governance, resistance to, 168,
    170
  and sound shifts, 168–69
Germanisten-Versammlung (Germanist
    assembly)
  Frankfurt 1846:, 22–23, 33, 43–45, 46, 177
    J Grimm as chair of, 24
    J Grimm's address to, 25, 28–29, 30–32
  Lübeck 1847:, 127
Germanness
  definitions of, 27–29
  lack of, 46, 57
  of literature, 91
  loss of, 165
Germany
  Bavaria, 4
  Denmark, war with, 122
  Deutscher Bund (German Confederation), 4,
    34, 43, 116
  boundaries of, 29–31
  First Schleswig War, 45–46
  Frankfurt am Main, 22, 28–29, 34, 122
  French occupation of, 12
  Göttingen, 21, 34, 56, 117, 118–20
  Hanover, 4, 43, 118–20
  Kingdom of Westphalia, 12, 40, 51, 54–56,
    57
  Marburg, 53
  as nation-state, 53
  political structure of, 4, 120
  principalities of, 38, 162
  school system in, 148, 150

Württemberg, 4
see also Austria; Frankfurt Parliament; Hesse/
    Hesse-Kassel; Holstein; Kassel; Prussia;
    Schleswig.
Gervinus, Georg Gottfried, 119, 160
Goethe, Johann Wolfgang von, 87
Goffart, Walter, 171
Gönner, Nikolaus Thaddäus von, 94, 96–98
Gothic language, 30
Goths (tribe), 170
Göttingen, 21, 34, 56, 117, 118–20
Göttingen Seven protest, 119–20, 132
government see rule.
gradualism, 31, 96, 99, 133
grammar, 26, 27
Grimm, Albert Ludwig, *Children's Tales*
    [*Kindermärchen*], 82
Grimm, Jacob
  biography, 33–34
  childhood, 53
  death, 46, 181
  education, 53
  in Napoleonic wars, 51–52, 54–56
  social status, 183
  career, 6–8, 10–11, 86, 114–26, 156–57, 181–82
    censor, 117, 135
    chair of Germanisten-Versammlung
        (German Assembly), 23, 24, 25, 28–29,
        30–32
    as civil servant, 33
    Congress of Vienna, delegation secretary,
        33, 56, 116–17
    Frankfurt Parliament, representative in, 34,
        45, 46, 120–22
    and Frederick William IV of Prussia, 1–2,
        21, 50
    Hessian allied mission, secretary to, 115
    under Jérôme Bonaparte, 12, 55
    librarian, 117
    monarchs, service to, 123–26
    professorship at Göttingen, 56, 117
    professorship at Prussian Academy, 120, 145
    professorship, loss of, 34
    Wilhelm I of Hesse, support for, 51–52
  cultural and political views, 3–6, 17–18, 19,
    34–35
    ambivalent, 132–34
    empire, critique of, 132
    Germanness, definitions of, 27–29
    Göttingen Seven protest, 119–20, 132, 139
    on Jérôme Bonaparte, 57
    liberalism, perceived, 132
    on mass education, 145–49, 153–56, 157–58
    modern, 14
    on monarchy, 125–26

Index

on mother tongue, 143–44
on Napoleonic occupation, 55
nationalist, 14, 16–17, 40–41, 64, 130–31
noble rank, elimination of, 121–22
organicist, 136
on particularity (*Eigenthümlichkeit*), 12–13, 73
people (*Volk*), definition of, 23
philologically based, 114–15
reticence, 32, 45, 134–35
Romanticist, 128
on Schleswig-Holstein, 45
on school teachers, 150–51, 153–54
fellow writers, commentary on
Arndt, Ernst Moritz, 67
Fichte, Johann Gottlieb, 68
Jahn, Friedrich Ludwig, 69
Kleist, Henrich von, 84
Luden, Heinrich, 66
Savigny, Friedrich Carl von, 95, 99–100
Grimm, Jacob: works
German Grammar [*Deutsche Grammatik*], 6, 24, 26, 147
German Legal Antiquities [*Deutsche Rechtsalterthümer*], 24
German Mythology [*Deutsche Mythologie*], 24, 105
The History of the German Language [*Geschichte der deutschen Sprache*], 26, 159–80
arcane quality of, 173
collective German origin in, 169–70
cultural loss, fears of, 163–64
on the *Eddas*, 175–76
on Germanic tribe names, 172–76
on Germanic tribes, 168–76
imperial philology in, 178–80
imperial sources for, 170
and linguistic national boundaries, 162–63
methodology of, 161–62
national identity, basis for, 163–65
nationalism in, 162–63
political nature of, 7
political philosophy of, 166–68
on tribal migration, 165–66
writing of, 143
"School University Academy" ["Schule Universität Academie"] (lecture), 145–51
Über den altdeutschen Meistergesang, 128–29
Grimm, Jacob and Wilhelm: joint works
Children's and Household Tales [*Kinder- und Hausmärchen*], 6, 7, 15–16, 18, 58, 60–63, 101–7
editing of, 80, 83
editorial role in, 102–3

English versions, 75
German particularity of, 78–79
nationalism of, 61–63, 74–76, 77, 78–81
prefaces, 60, 61, 78–79, 101–4, 108–10
publication history, 75–76
Der Arme Heinrich, 51–52, 56, 58–59, 60, 77, 83
Deutsche Sagen [*German Legends*], 107–8
Deutsches Wörterbuch [*German Dictionary*], 6, 145
Grimm, Wilhelm
biography, 4
childhood, 53
education, 53
health, 55
in Napoleonic wars, 51–52, 54–56
social status, 183
career, 6–8, 115, 124
in Berlin, 120
and Frederick William IV of Prussia, 21
librarian at Göttingen, 56
librarian at Kassel, 56
Wilhelm I of Hesse, support for, 51–52
cultural and political views, 18–19, 77, 86–98
Göttingen Seven protest, 119
on Jahn, Friedrich Ludwig, 69, 76
liberalism, perceived, 132
on monarchy, 125
on Napoleonic occupation, 55
on national poetry [*Nationalpoesie*], 86–92
nationalist, 64, 70, 72
on natural vs. artful poetry [*Naturpoesie* vs. *Kunstpoesie*], 93–94
on the *Nibelungenlied*, 87–90
on particularity (*Eigenthümlichkeit*), 73
on Savigny, 95, 99–101
Grimm, Wilhelm: works
on folk tales, 61
folktales, editing of, 7
"On Legislation and Jurisprudence in Our Time [Über Gesetzgebung und Rechtswissenschaft in unserer Zeit]", 94–98, 99
political impact of, 10–11
and *Prussian Correspondent* (journal), 75
see also Grimm, Jacob and Wilhelm.
Grimm's Law, 6
Groys, Boris, 157

Hagen, Friedrich Carl von der, 88
Haller, Karl Ludwig von, 133
Hanover, 4, 43, 118–20
hatred, folk, 70, 71, 76–77
Heeren, Arnold, 66,
Hegel, Georg Wilhelm Friedrich, 40, 99, 127
Heimat (homeland), 53

Heine, Heinrich, 7, 15, 48
  Germany: A Winter's Tale, 49
Herder, Johann Gottfried, 9, 64–65
  and folk culture, 81
Herrmann (Arminius, Germanic chieftain), 84
Herwig, Wolfram, 170
Hesse/Hesse-Kassel, 4, 52–53
  diplomatic missions of, 115–16
  Electorate, restored to, 34
  as Landgraviate, 52–53
  potential tribal origins of, 172
  see also Kassel.
history
  cultural, 85–86
  linguistics, based on, 161–62
  national identity, supported by, 163–65
  and poetry, 89, 90
  political use of, 47
Holstein, 1, 22–23, 29–30, 42–46, 122
Holy Roman Empire, 29, 40, 52, 65
home *see* domesticity; domestic spaces.
homeland (*Heimat*), 53
Homer, 88
homogeneity, 16, 42, 164, 165, 184
Hopkin, David, 7
Hroch, Miroslav, 74
Huber, Ernst Rudolf, 118
Huizinga, Johan, 53
humanity, plural, 65, 68
Humboldt, Alexander von, 21
Hutchinson, John, 103

identity
  communal, 11
  cultural, 152
  national, 134, 157, 183
    and folk tales, 58
    history, supported by, 163–65
    language, defined by, 142–44
  and social status, 121–22
imperialism, 12, 13, 14, 138
  decline of, 39–40
  French, 65
  German, 28, 29
  Napoleonic, 54–55
  nationalist arguments against, 166
  and philology, 20, 161, 178–80
  resistance to, 65–68
independence, political (*Selbstständigkeit*), 65–66
individualization, 93
inequalities, 135
intellectuals, 48–49
intimacy
  cultural, 96, 176–78
  between monarch and people, 57, 58

Jahn, Friedrich Ludwig, 68–69, 72, 75, 76, 78, 138
Jones, William, 179
Jordanes (historian), 170, 173
journalism, political, 15
Julius Caesar, 170
jurists, 98–99

Karadžić, Vuk, 10, 143
Kassel, 4, 18, 51,
  under Jérôme Bonaparte, 33, 40, 55
kings
  advisors to, 47
  dynastic, 38
  Grimms' engagement with, 7–8
  and nationality, 2
  philologist, 2–4, 8, 11–12, 17–18, 21, 34, 47
  philosopher, 2–3, 12
  prerogatives of, 5
  see also monarchy; rule.
kinship, 129
Kleist, Heinrich von, 44, 84
  The Battle of Herrmann [*Die Herrmannsschlacht*], 84
knowledge
  empirical, 3
  metaphysical, 3
  and political legitimacy, 50
  rule, separation from, 32

language
  bilingualism, 42
  dialects, 13, 31
    interconnectedness of, 162
    loss of, 154–56
    preservation of, 158
    recording of, 156, 157
  distinctiveness, 18
  grammar, 26, 27
  learning
    familial, 146, 147
    scholastic, 147–48
  mother tongue, 19–20, 42, 142–44, 146, 154
    vs. language of school, 147–48, 151
  national boundaries, defined by, 27, 162–63
  national identity, defined by, 142–44
  people (*Volk*), defined by, 25
  plasticity of, 30–31
  plurality of, 12
  of rulers, 57, 58
  spelling, 21
  unity of, 147
languages
  Danish, 26–27, 42, 44
  English, 31,
  Frankish, 30

French, 104
German, 18
　vs. Danish, 26–27
　education in, 153
　as mother tongue, 143–44
　sound shifts, 6, 26, 27, 168–69
　standardized, 154–56
　and "undeutsch" [un-German], 27–28
　usage, in Schleswig-Holstein, 42, 43, 44
Germanic, 24
　ancient, 25
　distinctiveness, 26–27
Gothic, 30
Latin, 149–50
loss of, 67, 165, 166
Middle High German, 88
Latin language, 149–50
law
　authority of, 96
　communal development of, 96
　cultural particularity (*Eigenthümlichkeit*) in, 96, 97
　French rule, introduced by, 40
　Germanic tradition of, 24
　legitimate, 97
　monarchy, bound by, 97
　rationalist models of, 96, 97
　reform of, 94–98
　scholarship of, 98–99
learning *see* education; scholarship.
legitimacy
　legal, 97
　mass education, disrupted by, 144
　of rule, 14, 69–70
　　through love, 131
　　via philology, 8, 13, 34, 57, 58, 85–86
　　popular, 34, 58
　　through shared culture/ethnicity, 5
Leipzig, 51
liberalism, 44, 132, 136
liberty *see* freedom.
linguistics
　comparative, 12
　Grimm's Law, 6
　of names, 172–73
literacy, 153
　education for, 146–47
　universal, 144
literature
　alien occupation, diminished by, 67
　collective, 20, 86–87
　drama, 84
　Eddas, 175–76
　German
　　historical depth of, 103
　　recuperation of, 104–5
　　reputation of, 105
　individualized production of, 92–93
　nationalist, 62–63, 75–84
　patriotic, 59–60
　poetry, 59–60
　　cultural evolution of, 92–94
　　epic, 86, 87–90, 104–5
　　national [*Nationalpoesie*], 86–92
　　natural vs. artful [Naturpoesie vs Kunstpoesie], 93–94, 102–3, 113
　　see also folktales.
locality, 13–14
Lombards, 163, 165, 174
love, 126–31
　community formed by, 127, 128–29
　of fatherland, 126–27, 128–30
　of monarch for nation, 126, 131, 140–41
　nation as community of, 126, 130–31
Luden, Heinrich, 65, 66, 171
Luther, Martin, 44

Marburg, 53
Marcomanni (tribe), 172
Marx, Karl, 15, 161
mass communication, 15
Maximilian I (Holy Roman Emperor), 29
Metternich, Klemens von, 116, 120
Middle High German language, 88
Migration Period (*Völkerwanderung*), 89
militarization, 51, 52–53, 70
　and education, 152–54
　of nationalism, 70
modernization, 88, 94, 106, 185
　Napoleonic, 13, 40, 55, 63
monarchy, 8, 182
　abolition of, 139
　constitutional, 34, 117–20, 126, 138–40
　divinely ordained, 36
　law, bound by, 97
　limited, 169
　loyalty to, 59
　nation, love of, 126, 131, 140–41
　and nationality, 5
　people, relationship with, 57, 58, 132–33, 138, 139
　rule of, 34
　service to, 123–26
　succession, 43
　succession, female, 1, 43, 119
　support for, 138
　see also kings.
Montesquieu, Robert de, 168
mothers/motherhood, 142–43, 144, 150–51
Müller, Adam, 133

Murdoch, Adrian, 170
Musäus, J. K. A., *Folk Tales of the Germans* [*Volksmärchen der Deutschen*], 81
mythology, 105
  indigenous German, 24
  Norse, 175

Nachtigall, Johann Carl Christoph (Otmar), *Folk Tales* [*Volcks-Sagen*], 82–83
names and naming, 171
Napoleon Bonaparte, 40, 51, 54–55, 65, 115
Napoleonic wars, 18, 40, 51–52, 54–56, 58–60
  Battle of Leipzig (1813), 51, 61
nation/nationhood, 185
  as community, 154
  boundaries of, 4, 27, 29–31
  construction of, 154
  cultural congruence of, 66
  cultural identity of, 23, 37
  vs. culture, 16
  folktales, as proof of, 18, 105
  and grammar, 26, 27
  language, defined by, 142–44
  vs. locality, 13–14
  and love, 126, 130–31
  loyalty to, 151–54
  organic quality of, 68
  philological definition of, 18, 26, 27, 38–39, 112–13
  and popular sovereignty, 39
  prior evidence of, 73–74, 91–92
  as protection against imperial rule, 14
  scholarship, produced through, 50
  territorial definition of, 17–18
  unit of rule, ideal, 65, 137, 181
  see also state/statehood.
nationalism, 9–17, 63–72, 184–85
  bardic, 91
  character of, 9–11
  cultural diversity, impact on, 155
  and cultural particularity (*Eigenthümlichkeit*), 11–14, 65–68
  culture, defense of, 68–69
  development of, 63–64
  and fears of cultural extinction, 66–68
  and folk hatred, 70, 71
  ideological thinness of, 134
  imperialism, arguments against, 166
  liberal, 44
  linguistic, 166
  literary culture, dependence on, 18
  literature of, 62–63, 75–84
  militarized, 70
  occupation, response to, 40–41
  paradoxes of, 14–15
  philological, 10–11, 136–37
  and political legitimacy, 69–70
  propaganda of, 76–77
  religious qualities of, 10
  scholarship, validated by, 49–50, 73–75
  in universities, 145
nationality, 139
  character of, 88
  language, defined by, 1
  and monarchy, 5
  preservation of, 69
  un-Germanness, 27–29, 46, 57
  see also identity, national.
newspapers, 15, 136
Nibelungenlied (epic poem), 86, 87–90, 92, 105
nobility, 43, 44, 70
  proposed elimination of ranks of, 121–22, 135
nominalism, cultural, 13
Nordic culture, 87, 89
  Eddas, 175–76
nostalgia, 61

ontology, social, 64, 68
organicism, political, 136
Otmar (Johann Carl Christoph Nachtigall), *Folk Tales* [*Volcks-Sagen*], 82–83

paganism, 24, 105, 175
Paris, 115,
parliament *see* Frankfurt Parliament.
particularity, 11–14, 16, 40–41, 185
  cultural (*Eigenthümlichkeit*), 40–41, 64–68
  defense of, 71
  folktales, evidence of, 73–74
  of Grimms' *Tales*, 78–80
  in legal norms, 96, 97
  protection of, 185
  and foreign rule, 56
  historical, 167
  national, 183
patriotism, 126–27, 128–30, 153
  poetry, expressed in, 59–60
Paul, Jean, 76, 143
peasantry, 70
people (*Volk*)
  as demos, 36
  as fundamental political unit, 34
  boundaries of, 35, 36
  definition of, 6, 23, 35
  cultural-lingusitic, 25–26, 37, 38–39
  unstable, 31
  and folk culture, 80–83, 84
  homogeneity, assumed, 42
  legal norms, source of, 96
  as national community, 37

organic formation of, 69
power of, 33
ruler, intimacy with, 57, 58
see also folk culture; folklore; folktales.
philologist king, concept of, 2–4, 8, 11–12, 17–18, 21, 34, 47
philologists
  as cultural guardians, 93–94, 99–101
  as imperial figures, 161
  vs. intellectuals, 48–49
  vs. philosophers, 47–48
  political role of, 85–86
  as redeemers, 18–19, 109–13
  vs. royal advisors, 47
philology, 3
  as labour of love, 126, 127
  authority through, 3–4, 5–6
  cultural closeness, value of, 176–78
  cultural mediation through, 102–3, 106–7, 111–12
  external viewpoint, value of, 178
  imperial nature of, 20, 161, 178–80
  limits of, 176
  mass education as opportunity for, 156–58
  national boundaries, defined by, 27, 31–32
  and nationalism, 10–11
  nationalist, 136–37
  nationhood, facilitation of, 112–13
  people (*Volk*), definition of, 25–26, 38–39
  political power of, 32–33, 47–50
  political value of, 8, 27, 28, 35, 39, 85–86, 183
  sacralized, 130
philosopher king, concept of, 2–3, 12
philosophies, political
  democracy, 37, 69, 135
  liberalism, 44, 132, 136
  republicanism, 136
  see also nationalism.
philosophy, 47–48
place
  domestic, 104, 105
  homeland (*Heimat*), 53
  locality, 13–14
  see also fatherland; nation; territory.
Plato, 2–3
pluralism, 16, 64–65
plurality *see* diversity.
poetry
  cultural evolution of, 92–94
  epic, 86, 87–90, 104–5
  national [*Nationalpoesie*], 86–92
  natural vs. artful [*Naturpoesie* vs. *Kunstpoesie*], 93–94, 102–3, 113
  war, 59–60
Poland, 30

political philosophies/concepts
  democracy, 37, 69, 135
  liberalism, 44, 132, 136
  republicanism, 136
  see also nationalism.
political units
  nation as ideal, 65, 137, 181
  people as, 34
  tribes as, 169
  see also empire; rule; sovereignty.
Pourciau, Sarah, 28
prejudice, 34
preservation
  of culture, 104–7, 108–12
  of dialects, 158
  of folk culture, 156–57
  of nationality, 69
press, 15, 136
principalities, 38, 162
propaganda, 76–77
Prussia, 4, 30
  Berlin, 21, 95, 120, 145
  Denmark, truce with, 46, 122
  state education in, 148, 153
  territories, loss of, 153
  Treaty of Tilsit (Franco-Prussian, 1807), 153
Prussian Academy of the Sciences (Berlin), 120, 145
Prussian Correspondent, The (journal), 75
Ptolemy, Claudius, 170
purity, 31

Ranković, Slavica, 90
rationalism/reason, 127, 128
  universal, 97
Reimer, Georg Andreas, 60, 75–76
religion
  Christianity, 24, 25, 159
  indigenous German, 24
  paganism, 105, 175
republicanism, 136
reticence, political, 32, 45, 134–35
revolutions
  of 1848, 120–21, 135
  French, 33, 35–36, 40, 117
Reyscher, August Ludwig, 45, 50
Rheinischer Merkur (journal), 30, 72, 94
Rhoxolani (tribe), 172, 173
rights, 68, 134
Romanticism, 127–28
rule
  absolutism, 35–36, 47–48, 117, 133
  authority of, 3–4, 5–6
  autocracy, 53
  democracy, 37, 69, 135

rule (cont.)
  despotism, 97–98
  enlightened despotism, 15, 47–48
  French model of, 54–55
  imperial, 12, 13, 14, 138
    decline of, 39–40
    French, 65
    German, 28, 29
    nationalist arguments against, 166
    resistance to, 65–68
  and knowledge, separation of, 32
  and law, development of, 96, 97
  legitimate, 14, 69–70
    via philology, 8, 13, 34, 57, 58, 85–86
    popular, 34, 58
    through shared culture/ethnicity, 5
  limits of, 135
  philological challenges to, 32–33
  see also kings; monarchy; sovereignty.

Sassoon, Donald, 143
Savigny, Friedrich Carl von, 94–95
  Grimms, influence on, 18, 24, 99–101, 112
  on historical basis of law, 98–99
  on legitimacy, 97
Scandanavian culture, 87, 89, 175–76
Schiller, Friedrich, 59
Schlegel, August Wilhelm, 40, 87, 88
Schlegel, Friedrich, 87, 127
Schleiermacher, Friedrich, 66, 75
Schleswig, 1, 22–23, 29–30, 42–46, 122
scholarship
  cultural mediation through, 102–3, 111–12
  historical culture, founded on, 85–86
  legal, 98–99
  nationalism validated by, 73–75
school teachers, 147–50
  and preservation of folk culture, 156–57
  soldiers, compared to, 153–54
  wet-nurses, compared to, 150–51
schools, 19–20, 145–50
Scott, James, 155, 170, 171,
Sheehan, James, 118
Sigambern (tribe), 172
sovereignty, 35
  popular, 34, 36–37, 41, 69, 138
    and determination, 35
    and monarchy, 118
    and nationhood, 39
    and territory, 38
  royal, 69
  and rule, 139
  state, 139
space
  boundaries of, 35
  domestic, 104, 105
  see also place.
standardization, 185
state/statehood, 35–36, 38, 67
  boundaries, 35
  centralized, 41
  vs. communities, 128–29
  loyalty to, 151–54
  schooling, mandated, 145–50
  sovereignty of, 139
  and tribes, 171
  see also nation/nationhood.
status, social, 70, 148–50
  see also nobility.
Stein, Baron vom, Heinrich Friedrich Karl, 66, 67
Stewart, Susan, 103
stories see folktales.
storytelling, 79, 102, 105, 106, 184
  decline of, 106
Strabo, 173
Studien (edited volume series), 89
Sturluson, Snorri, 175

Tacitus, Cornelius, *Germania*, 168, 169, 170, 175
Tatar, Maria, 106
teachers, 147–50
  and preservation of folk culture, 156–57
  soldiers, compared to, 153–54
  wet-nurses, compared to, 150–51
territory
  ethnic/linguistic diversity in, 41–42
  ethnic/linguistic divisions of, 42
  ownership of, 35, 38
  people's relationship to, 38
Thibaut, Anton Friedrich Justus, 98
Thomas, Richard, 170
Thorkelín, Grímur Jónsson, 87
Tieck, Ludwig, 76
Treaty of Tilsit (Franco-Prussian, 1807), 153
tribes see Germanic tribes.

unification, 33, 70, 159–60, 163, 181
  and loss of cultural diversity, 19–20
uniformity, 13, 155–56, 164, 165
units of political rule
  nation as ideal, 65, 137, 181
  people as, 34
  tribes as, 169
  see also empire; rule; sovereignty.
unity, 16
  in diversity, 162
  of German people, 28
  of language, 147

Index

universalism
  of reason, 97
  resistance to, 12, 40, 41
universities, 145,

Vandals (tribe), 172
variety *see* diversity.
Victoria (Queen of the United Kingdom), 119
Vienna, 120
Visigoths (tribe), 165
Volk see people.
Völkerwanderung (Migration Period), 89
Voltaire (François-Marie Arouet), 15
vom Stein, Baron, Heinrich Friedrich Karl, 66, 67
Vormärz era, 117–18, 139

Waitz, Georg, 169
Warner, Marina, 109
wars
  cultural representation of, 59–60, 87
  First Schleswig War, 45–46
  Napoleonic, 18, 40, 51–52, 54–56, 58–60
    Battle of Leipzig (1813), 51, 61
    nationalism, arising from, 70
    Treaty of Tilsit (Franco-Prussian, 1807), 153
Weber der Jüngere, Veit *see* Wigand, Paul.
Westphalia, Kingdom of, 12, 40, 51, 54–56, 57
wet-nurses, teachers as, 150–51
Wigand, Paul (Veit Weber der Jüngere), 59–60, 62, 70, 78, 133, 136
  War Poems of the Germans [*Kriegslieder der Deutschen*], 59–60
Wilhelm I (Elector of Hesse), 51, 54, 55, 56–57
Wilhelm II (Elector of Hesse), 117
Wilhelmina Caroline of Denmark (Electress of Hesse), 60
William IV (King of the United Kingdom and Hanover), 119
Wolf, Friedrich August, 90
Württemberg, 4
Wyss, Ulrich, 173

Zeuss, Johann Kaspar, 161, 174

For EU product safety concerns, contact us at Calle de José Abascal, 56–1°, 28003 Madrid, Spain or eugpsr@cambridge.org.

www.ingramcontent.com/pod-product-compliance
Lightning Source LLC
LaVergne TN
LVHW020343260326
834688LV00045B/1503